Innovation in
American Government

ALAN A. ALTSHULER
ROBERT D. BEHN
Editors

Innovation in American Government

Challenges, Opportunities, and Dilemmas

BROOKINGS INSTITUTION PRESS
Washington, D.C.

ABOUT BROOKINGS

The Brookings Institution is a private nonprofit organization devoted to research, education, and publication on important issues of domestic and foreign policy. Its principal purpose is to bring knowledge to bear on current and emerging policy problems. The Institution maintains a position of neutrality on issues of public policy. Interpretations or conclusions in publications of the Brookings Institution Press should be understood to be solely those of the authors.

Copyright © 1997 by

THE BROOKINGS INSTITUTION
1775 Massachusetts Ave., N.W., Washington, D.C. 20036

Library of Congress Cataloging-in-Publication data

Innovation in American government : challenges, opportunities, and
  dilemmas / Alan A. Altshuler and Robert D. Behn, editors.
    p. cm.
  Includes bibliographical references and index.
  ISBN 0-8157-0358-9 (cloth : alk. paper).—ISBN 0-8157-0357-0
(pbk. : alk. paper)
    1. Political planning—United States. 2. Administrative agencies—
United States—Management. 3. Organizational change—United
States. I. Altshuler, Alan A. II. Behn, Robert D.
JK468.P64155 1997
352.3—dc21   97-21096
                                                           CIP

9 8 7 6 5 4 3 2 1

The paper used in this publication meets the minimum requirements of the American National Standard for Information Sciences— Permanence of Paper for Printed Library Materials, ANSI Z39.48-1984.

Typeset in Times Roman

Composition by Linda Humphrey
Arlington, Virginia

Printed by R. R. Donnelley & Sons Co.
Harrisonburg, Virginia

Contents

Part Three: INNOVATION AND THE MEDIA

Part Four: INNOVATION IN POLICY FIELDS

Part Five: IMPLEMENTING INNOVATION

Preface

A DECADE AGO, the Ford Foundation launched its now famous Awards Program for Innovations in State and Local Government, currently called Innovations in American Government (because the federal government is also included). This program has several purposes. It seeks to recognize innovative leaders in government—people who have made distinguished contributions through their successful efforts to create new strategies for tackling important public problems—and thus to encourage others to do the same. It highlights that excellence exists in the public (as well as the private) sector by publicizing the accomplishments of the award winners. Through this publicity, it seeks to improve the effectiveness of public agencies elsewhere by helping them to adopt (and adapt) the ideas developed and implemented by the winners. Finally, the Ford Foundation seeks to enrich our knowledge of how to govern ourselves well and to enhance the performance of public agencies.

As part of this latter purpose, the Kennedy School of Government at Harvard University has drawn on the experiences and lessons of the winners and finalists in the Awards Program to develop a variety of teaching cases targeted on the pre-professional and mid-career training of public servants. These curriculum-development and pedagogical activities are also meant to influence broader audiences of public officials, civic leaders, and professional commentators on public affairs.

The Ford Foundation has supported research on public sector innovation at the Kennedy School, the Terry Sanford Institute of Public Policy at Duke University, and elsewhere. One objective of the work is to deepen our understanding of the innovation process and clarify the place of innovation within a more general conception of excellence in American government (especially excellence in public management). This book is one part of the overall research effort.

The research presented in this volume comes from many sources. Originally the Kennedy School sponsored some chapters; the Sanford Institute, others. Some of the authors gathered data from a subset of the winners and finalists of the Awards Program. Others wrote directly of the experiences of these recognized innovators. Some authors collected data from innovators and innovations not represented in the awards competition. Some scholars sought to understand innovation in particular policy areas; others examined the task of innovating in government from a more global perspective. Some scholars tested specific propositions; others explained well-recognized phenomena. Still, the primary focus of the authors, and thus of this book, is on the process of innovation rather than on specific public policy results.

As the scholars examined innovation in American government, they uncovered challenges, opportunities, and dilemmas. The two of us debated and then chose a framework for organizing their work, though other frameworks could have proved equally useful. For, as the first chapter explicitly reveals—as does even a casual reading of the other chapters—these scholars often examined similar questions, analyzing them from different perspectives. Indeed, this volume describes a variety of challenges confronting those who seek to innovate, suggests a number of opportunities to do so, and examines a host of dilemmas that confront any effort to be innovative in American government.

All three activities—awards, teaching, and research—seek to describe, analyze, and communicate our knowledge about innovation in the public sector. Two normative components are also significant.

First, this emphasis on innovation in American government conveys the idea that excellence in public service means ingenious, creative problem solving as well as honesty, efficiency, and accountability. Indeed, this focus on innovation suggests that true distinction in public service now includes these new norms. In evaluating the performance of elected officials and appointed managers, honesty, efficiency, and accountability are assumed; to be recognized for truly distinguished service the new virtues of ingenuity and creativity that truly improve performance must be added.

Second, the emphasis on innovation seeks to alter the balance between bad and good news about American government. For many reasons, journalists selectively emphasize—and the public focuses on—the bad news: scandals, mistakes, obvious inefficiencies, and petty, personal conflicts. Still, choosing to "right" this "imbalance" is a normative decision. Many Americans (and most journalists) would deny that any imbalance exists to be righted. Nevertheless, journalists are often attracted to the novelty of public sector innovation as well as to the more conventional stories about governmental failure. Thus, although mere honesty and efficiency are obviously not newsworthy, a discussion of innovations offers the public an opportunity to hear some good news about American government.

Journalists are not the only ones who emphasize the inadequacies of government. Social scientists and policy researchers also seize on issues that exude conflict, scandal, and failure, partly because policy issues with these characteristics make for intriguing, suspenseful stories and partly because investigations, court records, and media exposés provide piles of data and unusual access to inside information. And, of course, scholars can more easily seem wise when they try to explain (that is, second guess) an obvious failure than when they try to interpret a success that others can easily discount as trivial.

Unfortunately, such an emphasis (or bias) has consequences. For years, journalism, scholarship, and education on public policy has contained an inadvertent, subliminal message: public managers rarely succeed. They are sort of dumb, and they regularly get themselves and their agencies into big trouble. The effect of this message may be to deter many people from entering public service and to reenforce, for those who are still willing to do so, all the other incentives to avoid the large, obvious risks (and the too subtle rewards) of being innovative.

Our response—the response from the Ford Foundation, Harvard University, and Duke University—has not been to create "good news" journalism, scholarship, or education. Rather, we consciously seek a better balance. After all, if we are to improve the quality of American government, we need lessons not only from failures but also from successes. The research in this book offers one opportunity to learn about the successes and failures—and about the challenges, opportunities, and dilemmas—of innovation in American government.

Finally, we are grateful to Nancy Davidson at the Brookings Institution for her editorial advice. Colleen McGuiness edited the manuscript, Ellen Garshick proofread it, and Mary Mortensen prepared the index.

Alan A. Altshuler
Robert D. Behn

Part One

WHY INNOVATE?

CHAPTER ONE

The Dilemmas of Innovation in American Government

Robert D. Behn

WHY INNOVATE? Why should American government innovate? Because business does it. Because government's standard operating procedures are proving inadequate. Because government needs to improve performance. Because all organizations need innovation.

Why innovate? Why should American government innovate? Because business does it. In the United States it has become fashionable to worship the techniques of business management and seek to implement them in government. And American business believes in innovation. As Alan A. Altshuler writes in chapter 2, "Business leaders and analysts have become preoccupied with innovation." "In business firms," notes Marc D. Zegans in chapter 5, "innovation is increasingly seen as the key to competitive success." Thus "not surprisingly," observe Altshuler and Zegans in chapter 3, "as concern about innovation swept the world of business in the eighties, it began to filter into thought about governmental performance." If business does it, it has to be good—good for government, too.

Why innovate? Why should American government innovate? Because government's standard operating procedures are proving inadequate. In the opening sentence of chapter 7, Olivia Golden sets forth the case for innovation: "Managers in state and local human services agencies are trying to solve problems for which routine government practice is failing; thus they cannot do without innovation." In chapter 4, Laurence

3

E. Lynn, Jr., echoes this "sense of urgency" for "inducing innovation" in government: "Society needs effective government, and public bureaucracies have proved disappointing for so long that change is essential." Similarly, Altshuler and Zegans write that "a widespread sense exists that public agencies utilize resources inefficiently, that they are stuck in outmoded routines, that they are insensitive to citizen concerns, and that they are run more for the benefit of employees than clients."

Why innovate? Why should American government innovate? Because government needs to improve performance. And innovation is about performance, the continuous task of improving government performance. If American government is to improve its performance—the performance not only of its human services agencies, but also of its environmental agencies, police and fire departments, school systems, and military divisions—it needs innovation. Thus Altshuler writes of "the never-ending task of mission-drive innovation." And Zegans worries about the "innovation gap"—"a growing gap between the public's desire for quality service and the capacity of government agencies to meet it"—which "innovations in technology and service delivery can reduce." Innovation provides a means to close government's performance gap.

Why innovate? Why should American government innovate? Because all organizations need innovation. Altshuler and Zegans emphasize that "the most successful enterprises are generally marked by a capacity for continuous, high-quality innovation." They conclude, "The case for innovation . . . is no less urgent in the public than the private sector." Government needs to improve, and, as in business, innovation provides the opportunity to make these improvements.

The Fear of Innovation

The belief that American government needs more innovation to improve performance is less a fact than a judgment. And this judgment is not universally shared. Altshuler and Zegans write, "Limited appreciation is evident of the value of innovation across the spectrum of government activity." Some people do not want to improve government's performance; they simply want government to go away. They value innovation, but only if it can make government less expensive and, even better, smaller.

Moreover, Lynn offers "a warning: Innovations can be bad as well as good." And even if innovation is not necessarily evil, it might be nothing more than policy chic. For example, the managers with whom Zegans talked worried that innovation was just another "trendy" management fad that would soon disappear like planning program budgeting (PPB), management by objectives (MBO), or zero-based budgeting (ZBB). More significantly, they voiced "concern that the recent vogue for innovation was creating perverse incentives."

Relying on innovation as the cure for what ails government may be a risky strategy. "Improving governmental performance through innovation may not be so straightforward," observes Lynn. "A distressingly high 'ephemerality rate' appears among innovations and innovators, and a randomness exists to long-term success." In chapter 11, Richard F. Elmore suggests that, although "education is awash in innovation," those innovations have achieved little progress in advancing the performance of schools, students, or graduates. He challenges the conventional wisdom about the value of innovation throughout government: "The management and policy literature on innovation suggests that if the world were populated by clever people with good ideas and ingenious implementation strategies and who operated in organizations that promote innovation, public enterprises would steadily improve in their efficiency and effectiveness." Similarly, Zegans has noted that "scholars interested in the topic of innovation tend to exhibit a strong pro-innovation bias."[1] Thus Elmore challenges the "prevailing conceptions of the value of innovation in improving public services" and urges scholars to question and test it.

From political history, American citizens have learned to be wary of innovation. We tolerate—and expect—our elected political leaders to be innovative. And voters reward innovative politicians.[2] But, as Altshuler and Zegans emphasize, "top-down innovation alone" cannot guarantee that any institution—private or public—will "achieve excellence." All institutions need not only top-down innovation but also innovation from within. Yet, Altshuler and Zegans continue, "American society is ambivalent" about innovations launched by civil servants. The U.S. democratic system gives policymaking responsibility to elected officials (and their direct politically appointed subordinates). Then civil servants are to faithfully implement these policies.

1. Zegans (1990, p. 1).
2. Polsby (1984).

The general notion that innovation is one of the basic tasks of all public employees has much less appeal. Zegans believes that "innovation is an intrinsic part of the public manager's job." But the rest of the American public may not be so sure. Each citizen has his or her own reason to fear innovation.[3] As Altshuler and Zegans observe: "Conservatives fear bureaucratic aggrandizement. Liberals fear agency capture by special interests and civil liberties abuses. Minorities fear discrimination. Good government groups fear corruption." Few, they continue, easily accept the idea "that civil servants as well as elected officials have legitimate roles to play as public innovators."

Although top-level officials recognize the political value of their own policy innovations, they, too, fear innovations launched from within public agencies. Lynn describes this behavior:

> If you are an elected official, or an appointee of one, how much system-challenging experimentation that ends in failure are you eager to defend and protect because good government requires that creative people be given latitude and funds for trial and error? Everyone will claim credit for the successful innovation after the fact, but who will defend, against political opposition and lawsuits and negative evaluation findings and hostile media coverage, the several failures that are necessary to achieve a single success?

While citizens may fear innovative civil servants only in the abstract, political leaders can see them as a direct, personal threat to their careers. As Altshuler asks: "Why should elected officials, who have the most to lose when innovations fail, take the risk of encouraging civil servants to devise them?"

Private sector leaders worship innovation, business magazines and journals feature articles about the benefits of innovation, and bookstores carry numerous books with the word "innovation" in the title. Tom Peters, the author of numerous management books, may have captured the private sector's perspective when he admonished business executives to "Get Innovative or Get Dead."[4] Despite the nation's appreciation of the benefits of America's private sector—of America's innovative private sector—the electorate still worries that innovation may not be such a great idea in government. "While business leaders are focusing today on

---

3. "The fear of innovation" is known in business as well as government. See Schön (1966).
4. Peters (1990–91).

innovation as a key to competitive success," note Altshuler and Zegans, "government policymakers are preoccupied with damage control."

Thus the opportunity to innovate is hindered by the Trust Dilemma: Innovation may be necessary for establishing public faith in the ability of government agencies to perform. But before the public grants government agencies a license to be truly innovative, it needs to be convinced that these same agencies have the ability to perform.

Defining Innovation

To put a different spin on Cole Porter, what is this thing called innovation? More specifically, what do citizens, managers, and scholars mean by innovation in American government? If we think innovation is (more or less) a good thing, if we think it can improve the performance of government, then we ought to be able to define it. So, what exactly is this funny—and good—thing called innovation?

Altshuler and Zegans offer a concise definition: Innovation is "novelty in action." The innovation is something new, but it is more than a new idea; it is a new idea that has been put into practice. Golden notes that, for the purposes of the Ford Foundation and John F. Kennedy School of Government Awards Program for Innovation in State and Local Goverment, "the implicit definition of an innovation is an innovative operating program, not an innovative idea." In chapter 12, Mark H. Moore, Malcolm Sparrow, and William Spelman report that "a simple definition works well: An innovation is any reasonably significant change in the way an organization operates, is administered, or defines its basic mission."

But how novel must the "novelty" be to qualify as an innovation? How "significant" must the "change" be to count? A "novelty" need hardly be consequential. The word "novelty" seems to imply that the change need not be all that meaningful. A "novelty" used to be something purchased at the 5-and-10-cent store.

Lynn, however, will have none of this quibbling. To him:

Innovation must not be simply another name for change, or for improvement, or even for doing something new lest almost anything qualify as innovation. Innovation is properly defined as an original, disruptive, and fundamental transformation of an organization's core tasks. Innovation changes deep structures and changes them permanently.

Lynn wants to ensure that innovation is not "defined too promiscuously"—that the concept does not "lose credibility." He wants a definition that characterizes innovation as "relatively rare and rightly so."

But the definition offered by Altshuler and Zegans—"novelty in action"—is not as trivial as those three words might imply. Novelty counts as an innovation, they write, only if it renders "the whole notably different from what has gone before." Similarly, Moore, Sparrow, and Spelman note:

> Not all organizational changes qualify as innovations. Some are simply too small, obvious, or idiosyncratic to warrant much analytic attention. Those changes worth recognizing as innovations should be globally (or at least locally) new to the organization; be large enough, general enough, and durable enough to appreciably affect the operations or character of the organization; or be consciously designed or adapted as a response to a perceived problem by some level of the organization.

The scholars writing in this volume may not all insist that a change be disruptive to be innovative. But they do not count a change as an innovation unless it is somehow significant.

Usually this means that the change has a significant impact on performance. For example, Moore, Sparrow, and Spelman report that many public managers who head police departments "would also insist that an innovation worth analyzing should improve the performance of an organization"—thus excluding efforts that failed. And, they continue, if the purpose is "to explore how innovations improve organizational performance, the criterion of success must be included in the operational definition."

The public managers surveyed by Zegans also offered a narrow definition of innovation, but one that contrasted sharply with Lynn's. Although these managers believed that innovation was "an important part of their work," they viewed managerial innovation as strictly about means. Any innovation that concerned ends was the "exclusive responsibility" of those elected to public office:

> Civil servants, they believed, should be authorized to implement ideas that advanced established policies without making major claims on new resources, but new ideas altering basic purposes or requiring significant new resources should be implemented only with prior legislative approval.

Moreover, continues Zegans, these public managers concluded that "employees throughout the organization seek to innovate as part of normal practice without subverting routine." To Lynn, in contrast, innovation ought to subvert the routine. To Zegans's public managers, innovation is part of the everyday search for ways to improve performance; to Lynn, it is and should be "relatively rare."

How scholars (and others) define innovation has one more dimension: To what use will they put the definition? As Moore, Sparrow, and Spelman observe, how scholars define innovation depends upon their analytic purpose. What questions do they seek to answer? By specifying these questions, they may be forced to decide what kind of changes—disruptive ones or ones that do not subvert routines—should be captured in their analytical net. For example, Moore, Sparrow, and Spelman argue that "to study the process of innovation—in particular, to analyze how organizations distinguish successful from unsuccessful innovations—failures as well as successes must be examined." In that case, a scholar would not want to make improved performance an essential component of his or her definition.

This debate over the definition of "innovation" is not mere semantics. It reflects values—what citizens, managers, and scholars think is important. After all, everyone likes innovation because it is the opposite of bureaucratization—because it is good. Thus the debate is about where to draw the line between a change that creates a truly significant benefit and one that is acceptable but not that consequential. Just how innovative does an innovation have to be? Does it have to be a big deal? Or is it fair to call a small but clever improvement an innovation?

Note that choosing from among such adjectives as "original," "radical," "risky," and "disruptive" does not solve the definitional problem. These words, too, are open to subjective interpretation. Lynn argues that the Family Learning Center in Leslie, Michigan, which provided high school education to pregnant teen-agers and teen-age mothers, was not an innovation by his criteria. Yet this initiative was sufficiently radical for that rural community in the 1970s to get the director's mailbox bombed—twice.

Innovation can be original, radical, risky, disruptive, and dangerous.

The Dilemmas of Innovation

Any public executive who seeks to innovate immediately confronts a variety of quandaries. What kind of organizational arrangement begets the most innovation? How can the constraints imposed by the United States' federal system of government be overcome? How much analysis should precede implementation? How much experimentation and modification will be required to get it right? Do small innovations encourage or thwart more significant ones? How can proven innovations be best disseminated and replicated? How can innovation be rewarded? How should innovation be rewarded? Who has to authorize an innovation? Is innovation within public agencies compatible with the concept of democratic accountability? The task of innovation in American government is not straightforward. Those who seek to innovate face a number of specific dilemmas, which means that they can never be solved.

For example, innovation is often driven by the need to change: Something is significantly out of kilter and needs to be fixed. This need to change may be publicly dramatized by a series of short-term crises, each of which must be dealt with quickly and effectively. If the would-be innovator fails to respond effectively to such crises, he or she will have no chance to innovate. If the would-be innovator does not handle the crises at least adequately, someone else may soon be leading the agency; or its responsibilities may be privatized, and the organization, itself, abolished. Effective, short-run fire fighting is often a prerequisite for innovation.

But fire fighting—even brilliant fire fighting—should never be confused with innovation. Innovation is a long-term process, not a quick fix. How does the leadership team of a public agency both cope adequately with the immediate crises and simultaneously build the foundation for long-term innovation? How should the precious resource of leadership's time be allocated between short-run fire fighting and long-run innovating? This is a real dilemma. No universally right answer exists. Even the most successful innovators can squeeze only 168 hours out of their week.

In chapter 16, Ellen Schall concludes that a public manager simply has to do both. As an innovator, she writes, you have to "develop a long-term strategy while you manage the short-term crises." The trap is, she warns, that "the demands of the immediate crises can easily drive out any long-term thinking or planning." Thus, to succeed, the public manager needs to "develop the capacity to build a long-term strategic agenda while simultaneously managing the short-term crises." If you wait until you have resolved all the short-term crises, Schall argues, you will never have a significant impact. At the same time, if you fail to cope with these short-term crises, no one will give you a chance to innovate.

At the New York City Department of Juvenile Justice (DJJ), Schall's leadership team "created a mechanism to force ourselves to focus on the future." To avoid the fire-fighting trap, it created a strategy group, with regular monthly meetings and specific assignments. DJJ's leadership used such action-forcing activities to compel itself to behave as if it were innovative—in Schall's words, "to act revitalized before we were." Yet the formal systems of teams, meetings, and assignments could only help organize DJJ to be innovative; to cope effectively with this dilemma required mental not mechanistic changes. "Like much else asked of leaders who aspire to be innovative, this required a great leap of faith," writes Schall. "We had to hold the future as real as we struggled to overcome the difficulties of the present." Yet this Fire-Fighting Dilemma is only one of many that confront innovators in government.

Accountability Dilemmas

Who is responsible for innovating? Who can authorize an attempt at innovation? Who should authorize it? How can innovative individuals and teams be held accountable? How should they be held accountable? To whom? The process of innovation raises some important issues of political accountability. For most of the twentieth century, Americans have worried that their civil servants will undertake policy initiatives without proper authorization by elected officials. But innovation requires initiative and thus creates some fundamental dilemmas of political accountability.

Altshuler writes, "Those who favor adoption of the innovative paradigm in government have their work cut out for them." For the traditional "paradigm of accountability," he notes, relies upon the direct reporting of civil servants to elected officials. Consequently, Altshuler argues, those who emphasize government performance "have to make the case that encouraging mid-level and front-line civil servants to be innovative can yield important value for the public without significant loss of accountability." And to do this requires a "reexamination of the concept of accountability itself." Altshuler says "innovative thinking is needed about accountability no less than about programmatic efficiency."

Authorization Dilemma

Americans want their public managers to be innovative and, at the same time, accountable to the traditional norms of their democracy. They want managers who are creative and also responsive to their elected overseers in the executive and legislative branches. American citizens are extremely wary of bureaucratic initiative that has not been previously authorized by these elected officials. "In government," writes Lynn, "a fundamental conflict arises between, on one hand, innovation, which requires autonomy, decentralization, risk taking, and unprogrammed tasks, and, on the other hand, accountability, which requires predictability, standardization, replicability, and stability."

More than a century ago, as a young scholar, Woodrow Wilson set down the basic distinction between politics and administration, which, he wrote, "is now, happily, too obvious to need further discussion." The process of government ought to be sequential: The questions of politics—that is, policy—are to be first decided by the elected officials. Then the task of administration is to be taken up by the civil servants in a "businesslike" manner.[5]

Unfortunately, as Altshuler observes, "laws tend to be vague, to be silent on many pertinent issues, to promise more than can be produced with the resources provided, and often to conflict with one another." This "fallacy of legislative clarity," as I have called it, undermines both the validity and the utility of the Wilsonian distinction.[6] Civil servants have to make policy decisions. They have no choice. Elected officials do not—cannot—establish policy in such a way that the civil servants need only figure out the technical, administrative details.

Thus, today, no one believes in the outdated Wilsonian distinction. Just ask people. They will quickly deny the validity of the idea. But do not watch how they behave. For if you do, you will discover that the Wilsonian dichotomy still lives. It meshes neatly with the American distrust of government—particularly the distrust of the permanent government of "bureaucrats." Legislators, elected executives, appointed executives, the public, and career public managers expect that the job of civil servants—from front-line workers to bureau chiefs—is to administer faithfully the policy decisions of elected officials.

Are career public managers confused? Not at all. Just ask them. Zegans did. And, he reports, they quickly denied the existence of the dilemma. They are innovative, but they do not make policy. They are innovative only about the means of carrying out existing policies. And if a question arises, they check with their superiors. They clearly under-

5. Wilson (1887).
6. Behn (1987, p. 57).

stand exactly what kind of initiatives have to be checked exactly how far up the bureaucratic and political hierarchy. Zegans reports that, although these managers "did cite a few aspects of the control system that could be improved, they argued that the existing rules governing bureaucratic action were not a significant impediment to innovative initiative." There is no conflict at all. Civil servants, it would appear, resolve the Authorization Dilemma by denying its existence.

Public managers—regardless of whether they accept it intellectually or believe it personally—must figure out how to cope with the Wilsonian dichotomy between politics and administration, with the Authorization Dilemma. Many of the bureaucratic routines of government are designed expressly to take the politics out of administration. And for every effort to reinvent government by eliminating these constraints, outright scandals and more subtle distrust cause elected officials to replace them with new rigidities.

Zegans observes that "rule-obsessed organizations turn the timid into cowards and the bold into outlaws." Governments that are true to the spirit and letter of the Wilsonian dichotomy convert their most intrepid public managers into "outlaws."

In chapter 13, Thomas N. Gilmore and James Krantz note a similar phenomenon. "The current climate of contempt for bureaucrats" encourages would-be innovators to ignore the formal structures of government—to operate outside the law. Furthermore, this "denigration of the line organization" directly and symbolically undercuts any effort to develop the operational capacity and innovativeness of existing agencies. Conclude Gilmore and Krantz: "Such contempt for the formal machinery and the corollary love of the back channel can lead only to stagnation and disinvestment in changing basic governmental processes and to periodic abuse and scandal on the part of the so-called innovators."

Some revel in their outlaw status. Some flaunt it until a Wilsonian sheriff threatens to hang them in the public square (or expose them on television), at which point they escape across the border into the private sector. Others stay and fight and eventually are strung up as an example for all to see. Still others, as Zegans's managers report, are intimidated by the administratively correct police.

Citizens want civil servants to be neither outlaws nor cowards. They simply want innovative public officials who develop and implement new ways to solve society's problems. And that creates the Authorization Dilemma.

Like Zegans's managers, Schall and her colleagues at DJJ were "as careful as we knew how to keep our various overseers and involved publics informed." Nevertheless, Schall writes, you have to create your own opportunities, and thus "we just moved ahead." When Schall was sworn in as DJJ commissioner, Mayor Edward I. Koch gave her only a two-sentence mandate: "Don't let them out. Do as much for them as you can."[7] Schall drew her authorization from this vague mandate from the mayor, DJJ's enabling statutes, frequent reports to political superiors, and her personal commitment to the overall purpose of the agency.

Clearly, this is one way for public managers to balance the competing demands of the Authorization Dilemma: Obtain whatever vague direction you can from your political superiors. Operate within the framework of your authorizing legislation. And keep your superiors informed about what you are doing—and particularly about your successes.

Altshuler offers another approach: citizen participation. Citing the "general acceptance that modern government is too complex for democracy to function adequately through the mechanisms of voting and bureaucratic oversight by elected officials alone," he suggests that "groups of citizens with significant interests or values at stake should routinely be consulted as bureaucratic decisions take shape." Such citizen participation, notes Altshuler, is a mechanism both to encourage "better, more innovative government" and to "legitimize the exercise of discretion in response to citizen views."

Using citizen participation as a mechanism for obtaining authorization is part of Altshuler's effort to rethink the accountability paradigm. He asks the question: "What is most important for the public to control, and how can it best do so?" And, he suggests, "thinking of civil servants as merely accountable to elected chief executives and legislators is insufficient." To create a new concept of accountability that "incorporates both the values of responsiveness and high performance," he looks to innovators who "do not merely consult and seek formal authorization where required," but who are also "deft and energetic in recruiting external support." "By influencing the political context within which their elected overseers act," Altshuler continues, these innovators "blur the directional lines of political accountability."

Does this resolve the Authorization Dilemma? Is it acceptable, as Altshuler writes, for "nonelected civil servants" to "function as politicians,

7. Varley (1987, p. 4).

finding support and building dominant coalitions where they may"? Civil servants have always built coalitions—whether to support a new, innovative program or to protect an old, stagnant one. But that does not convert such entrepreneurship into a basis for political accountability. As Altshuler notes, the fundamental question remains: "Can civil servants who establish strong, direct constituency relationships be held adequately accountable to their hierarchal superiors and to the body politic?"

Successful innovators can develop a number of strategies to file down the sharp horns of this dilemma. But the authorization problem will not go away.

Failure Dilemma

Altshuler and Zegans summarize the results of the recent literature on business management: "Successful companies imbue their employees with a broad sense of purpose and then give them wide day-to-day latitude" with which they can take some risks. "Those who risk, though, often fail," they continue. "So an essential feature of the innovative company is high tolerance for well-conceived failure." The dirty little secret is that innovation requires failure. The corollary is that unless an organization tolerates—and supports—failure, it is unlikely to get much innovation.

Yet, asks Lynn, who in the public sector is going to support failure? Most elected officials and political appointees run from failure as fast as possible. Who will be accountable for failure? Who will be willing to support the general concept of innovation, if this requires simultaneously supporting some future (undefinable but guaranteed) failure? Political leaders seek to avoid this Failure Dilemma by attempting to get the benefits of innovation without paying the costs of the inevitable failures. Like all true dilemmas, there is no way out. To get the benefits of innovation, politicians—or managers or citizens—will have to accept the costs of failures. And because even the smallest mistake in the public sector can be magnified into a major embarrassment or even a sensational scandal, leaders in government have a much lower tolerance for failure than those in business. Is this why business appears to be more innovative than government?

Customer Dilemma

The innovation in governmental staff agencies, described by Michael Barzelay and Babak J. Armajani in chapter 6, introduces another

Accountability Dilemma. Staff agencies, such as the offices of budget, personnel, procurement, and support services, have "customers"—internal customers in the line agencies. But to whom should these staff agencies be accountable? To their old "customers" (and traditional overseers): the elected officials? Or to their new "customers": the line agencies? As Barzelay and Armajani write: "A fundamental strategic choice is whether the principal customers of particular staff-agency employees are overseers or line agencies."

Conceivably, the answer might be both. A fundamental principle of American government is that everyone who works in government should be accountable to elected officials. At the same time, staff agencies ought to help the line agencies do their job. Given that the purpose of innovation is to improve governmental performance, the staff agencies ought to have some responsibility to help the line agencies do precisely that. The line agencies, not the staff units, produce the services that government provides. Thus, Barzelay and Armajani write, "If line-agency managers believe that, to achieve their mandate, they need to use more data processing services, staff agencies should not stand in the way."

This, however, is a contemporary idea—an innovation. Traditionally, the staff agencies were responsible not for helping the line agencies but for controlling them. That was their implicit, and often explicit, mandate. Now, however, these staff units may not be exclusively in the control business. They may also be in the service business. And this creates what Barzelay and Armajani call "the service-control tension."

To resolve this Customer Dilemma, and "to increase the number of innovation-inducing organizations in government," Lynn would, among other things, restrict the ability of staff agencies to control the behavior of line agencies. "Deregulate public administration," he writes. "There is a breakthrough concept!" Lynn would "simplify statutes to give greater discretion and autonomy to agency managers and field workers with regard to budgetary reprogramming and personnel actions."

Another way to resolve this dilemma, argue Barzelay and Armajani, is to determine the primary function of the staff unit. If the staff agency is in the business of control, its "customers" should be its political overseers, such as the governor and the members of relevant legislative committees. If the staff agency performs a service, its customers should be the managers of the agencies to whom it provides the service.

But what if a staff agency has both service and control functions? One answer is to split the organization in two, giving responsibilities for service to one unit and the task of control to another. Yet even this structural solution may not eliminate the dilemma. "In a few instances," write Barzelay and Armajani, "staff-agency employees should regard both line-agency managers and overseers as their customers." For example, they argue that the procurement and personnel units have both sets of customers; their activities "need to reflect line agencies' mandate-driven needs, as well as the public's interests in central control."

Perhaps the Customer Dilemma is not a dilemma at all. Perhaps it is possible to decide whether the customers of the staff agency are the line agencies who are responsible for performance or the political overseers who are responsible for control. When this is not possible, however, the dilemma remains. In that situation, the political overseers will have to resolve it by "balancing" the staff unit's accountability for both improved, line-agency performance and centralized, political control.

Paradigm Dilemmas

Even the most innovative mind is constrained. All human thinking is shaped by a cognitive architecture that helps people imagine particular possibilities, attracting them to some, limiting their appreciation of others, and forcing them to scorn many. Furthermore, each person has accumulated a lifetime of experiences that preclude him or her from even conceiving of other prospects; the individual never even gets to the state of toying with them.

Such mental paradigms seriously constrain how innovatively people can think about the role and activities of government. All of us—from citizens to managers to elected officials—have convictions about what is right and proper, and what is wrong or inappropriate. We all have faith that our existing activities are having some impact and an understanding of the linkages that create that impact. We all have expectations that some people and organizations can do some things but not others. We all accept many things in political and organizational life as simply givens. And the collection of such beliefs about a public agency creates a mental paradigm within which all our innovative thinking occurs.

For example, Altshuler argues that any emphasis on government performance, and thus on government innovation, requires a rethinking of the paradigm of accountability—a "reexamination of the concept of accountability itself." But, because the traditional accountability paradigm is so familiar—so commonplace—people hardly recognize how constraining it is.

The leaders, staff, overseers, and stakeholders of any public agency have a (usually implicit) mental paradigm that characterizes the nature of the organization and its activities. (Sometimes they all share the same paradigm; sometimes their collection of key beliefs differ significantly or even conflict.) This paradigm defines the agency's mission, clarifies what it does (and what it does not do), and establishes how it measures progress and success. Significant and useful innovations can be developed within this standard model. But sometimes the demand for innovation requires a complete rethinking of the organization's paradigm. This creates not only a challenge but also a dilemma: How can people think outside their own (implicit) mental framework?

Routinization Dilemma

Much of the work of government is routinized. To rationalize the traditional concept of accountability to elected officials with the vagueness of their laws, government employs what Altshuler calls "rule-based routinization." For example, to achieve the "three basic virtues" that Zegans examines—honesty, fairness, and efficiency—government creates rules. Front-line workers in the welfare department cannot make individual judgments about who should be eligible for welfare benefits and how much they should receive. Office managers in a tax agency cannot make localized decisions about what the region's refund policy will be. District engineers cannot make personal decisions about which counties deserve to have their highways repaired. To ensure the consistent implementation of its policies, government needs rules and routinization.

But citizens hold government to more values than just consistency. Citizens also care about performance. Moreover, Altshuler observes, routinization "conflicts" with two important ideals: "sympathetic responsiveness to the needs of specific people in particular situations," and "adaptation to changing circumstances." And these ideals require innovation.

For more than a century, as Zegans argues, American citizens have emphasized the three virtues of honesty, fairness, and efficiency. Now, however, citizens have added three new values: flexibility, ingenuity, and adaptivity. The conflict between these two sets of virtues creates the Dilemma of Routinization. How can public agencies perform their necessarily routine tasks honestly, fairly, and efficiently, and at the same time be flexible, ingenious, and adaptive enough to develop innovative ways to perform these tasks even more honestly, fairly, and efficiently? The need to emphasize consistency contradicts—and can easily undermine—any effort to encourage innovation. It presents a conflict in paradigms. Those who place a higher value on honesty, fairness, and efficiency will work and think within the routinization paradigm. Those who think flexibility, ingenuity, and adaptivity are more important (because they can produce better performance and better results) will function within the innovative paradigm.

The Routinization Dilemma is a true dilemma. Public agencies cannot be simultaneously honest and ingenious, fair and flexible, efficient and adaptive. A public agency that is adaptive risks being inefficient until all the kinks are worked out of the innovative adaptation. A public agency that is flexible invites people to complain that a flexible interpretation of the rules or statutes is unfair to them. A public agency that creates the opportunity for its employees to be a little ingenious also creates the possibility that they will be a little too clever and thus, perhaps, a little less honest. The mental paradigm that any agency's leaders employ determines whether they emphasize the routine or the innovative.

Scale Dilemma

How significant does a change have to be to count as an "innovation"? Different authors establish different standards, some setting the bar very high, others willing to place it lower. But more than a semantic debate is involved. The level of significance reflects a concern for the amount of progress needed—for how much government ought to improve performance. Do small changes warrant attention and praise? Or should only major improvements deserve to be lauded as true "innovations"?

This might not be such a big issue, except that some scholars conclude that small innovations can preclude larger ones. By adopting a modest innovation, Moore, Sparrow, and Spelman argue, an organization may hinder its ability to adopt a more strategic one. Innovative technologies, programs, or administrative systems that mesh perfectly with a policy area's existing strategy "may not only fail to move the field forward. They may more solidly anchor" the organization in the past, becoming "a drag on the future development of policing" (which is these authors' major concern). Although police agencies are innovating, write Moore, Sparrow, and Spelman, the field's "basic strategy remains unchanged: Police respond to incidents, which they then examine to see whether a law has been broken and whether an arrest is appropriate." For this incident-response strategy, the principal measure of success has been the response time (the time the police take to arrive at the scene of the incident).

Unfortunately, continue Moore, Sparrow, and Spelman, this focus on response times, combined with the technological innovations of a "communication system linking citizens to police officers through telephones, centralized dispatching, and two-way radios," prevents real innovation. Police spend most of their time responding to incidents because, having made a major investment in this communication equipment, they are locked into the incident-response strategy, which the public easily understands and implicitly accepts without challenge. As a result, write Moore, Sparrow, and Spelman, "the police find themselves now struggling to meet a very specific, well-defined, easily measured, and politically visible objective: to keep response times low. The pressure exerted by this system has made it difficult to explore any alternative uses of police resources."

For education, Elmore makes a similar argument: Teachers and schools create lots of innovation in "instructional practice." But it is mostly within a framework for teaching that was established a century ago: "the age-grade structure for organizing instruction, tracking and ability grouping within age groups, the comprehensive secondary school with its diverse and sprawling curriculum, and teacher-centered instruction." These concepts create the mental paradigm within which innovation in teaching inevitably occurs. "No shortage of good ideas exists about how to improve school organization and instruction," Elmore writes, but such "innovations seldom change such commonplace practices as teacher-centered instruction, textbook-driven content, and compartmentalized knowledge."

Consequently, although "education is awash in innovation," such innovations do not have "much sustained effect on the enterprise as a whole." Elmore calls this "the paradox of innovation in education": Continual innovation seems to have little impact on the knowledge and analytical skills of students. He cites three reasons for this paradox: "instructional practice is intractable and inherently complex," "the political structure of public education creates powerful forces for stability," and "the innovations themselves are poorly designed and implemented." Elmore argues that designing innovations for policy systems that possess complex core technologies—"practices that require a high level of knowledge and judgment"—is difficult unless the innovator can also change, in fundamental ways, those core technologies. And that inevitably means changing the mental paradigm of those who practice those technologies.

The first two reasons behind Elmore's "paradox of innovation" also apply to policing: The practice of policing is "intractable and inherently complex," and its political structure "creates powerful forces for stability." The complex core technologies that Elmore finds in education also exist in policing: Teachers and police officers—those who do the work and deliver the services—require a high level of knowledge about their business and exercise considerable judgment.

Furthermore, observes Deborah A. Stone in chapter 10, these characteristics of the policy systems of policing and education apply to health. In particular, she argues that many innovations in health policy "perpetuate the institutions, rules, and practices of the current system." Significantly, she continues, innovations to increase access to health care or to reduce its costs develop within "the current paradigm of health insurance." "By supporting and extending" this paradigm, Stone goes on, these innovations "intensify the very practices that create high costs and low access in the first place."

How innovative must an innovation be to count as an innovation? Here Lynn's suggestion that innovation should be disruptive may be helpful—not from a definitional perspective but from a paradigmatic one. If innovators accept that innovation ought to be disruptive, and if they accept that innovation is required, then they may be less willing to accept as "innovative thinking" changes that reflect only modifications within the existing paradigm. Recognizing that innovation needs to be disruptive may help would-be innovators to challenge the existing paradigm.

Analytical Dilemma

How much analysis should go into designing an innovation? This question appears not to be complicated. The answer is a lot. What is the dilemma? A public agency should certainly not launch an innovation without much serious, analytical thought.

Golden found, however, from her examination of a number of successful innovations in human services, that in the "start-up phase, the role of analysis—at least in its more specialized forms—seems limited."

The innovators whom Golden studied "did not achieve their innovations through extended planning and development of an initial policy idea. Instead, the innovation developed through action, over time, so that the idea at the time of the [Ford Foundation] award often bore little resemblance to the idea at the beginning of the program. These managers acted quickly, so that they could start gaining operational experience as soon as possible." Successful innovators, Golden concludes, "grope along."[8] To Golden, "the central lesson of the innovation-by-groping-along story is that the manager should not at this stage pay much attention to comprehensive policy analyses or elaborate contingency plans."

Despite the best of planning, there will be flaws and failures; and when this happens, Schall concludes, innovators must "face mistakes and fix them." At DJJ, Schall wanted "to learn from our early efforts." She argues that, "by working to get it right first, the manager can see gaps in the original design and thinking" and fix them. Schall and her staff "moved ahead as we figured out where we wanted to go and how we might get there."

So there is a dilemma after all. How much analysis should go into an innovation? And when? Can analysis support the innovative process of groping along? If so, how? Can innovators identify a useful balance between analysis and groping? As Golden asks: "How can someone be advised on how to walk this difficult line, achieving the right balance of analysis and action?" This conflict between analysis and action creates the Analytical Dilemma.

Golden concludes that the proper "balance between analysis and action is in part a matter of timing." Analysis is less useful when launching an innovation than in guiding the later process of groping along. Once the innovation is in operation, Golden writes, "the manager is trying to quickly learn from experience and is greedy for information—information that is reliable, relevant to the real problem, highly detailed, reasonably comprehensive, and available quickly." Consequently, analysis is now extremely valuable. As innovators grope along, they need information—and analysis of that information. Golden calls this "the excellent manager's bias toward information, rich information that conveys as much experience as possible." Analysis can help the innovators grope along intelligently.

---

8. For a discussion of the concept of "management by groping along," see Behn (1988); and Behn (1991, chapter 7).

So maybe there is no dilemma. Maybe no trade-off exists between analysis and groping along—at least once the innovation has been launched. At the beginning of the innovation process, however, the dilemma remains. How much can the innovator learn from prior analysis? And how much can the innovator learn only from an analysis of the data that can only be obtained from the active experimentation of groping along? The Analytical Dilemma is not created by the trade-off between analysis and groping along. This trade-off is a myth. The analysis depends upon the information collected by groping. And the groping needs to be guided by the feedback from this analysis.

Instead, the Analytical Dilemma arises, as Golden suggests, from the question of timing. How much analysis should be conducted before the innovation is launched versus how much analysis should be devoted to the groping? Like other resources, the innovator's "analytical budget" is constrained. And clearly not all of it should be used up before the innovation—and the groping—begin.

Structural Dilemmas

How a public manager, an elected official, or a citizen thinks about innovation—how any individual analyzes a problem and the prospects for making an improvement—is constrained by his or her mental framework. But that mental framework is shaped by the nature of the organization within which that innovation must be conceived, fostered, authorized, implemented, and sustained. Public organizations—the entire political system—have unique and important characteristics that cannot be ignored by would-be innovators.

Organizational-Diversity Dilemma

Three decades ago, James Q. Wilson, the James Collins Professor of Management at the University of California at Los Angeles, suggested that the character of an organization affected its propensity to conceive, propose, and adopt innovations. Specifically, Wilson focused on the "diversity" of the organization, by which he meant "the complexity of the task structure and the incentive system." He argued that "the greater the diversity of the organization, the greater probability that members will conceive of major innovations[,] . . . the greater the probability that major innovations will be proposed[, and] . . . the smaller the proportion of major innovation proposals that will be adopted."[9] More recently, Wilson wrote: "An agency that wants its managers and operators to suggest new ways of doing their tasks will be open, collegial, and supportive; an agency that wishes to implement an innovation over the opposition of some of its members often needs to concentrate power in the hands of the boss sufficient to permit him or her to ignore (or even dismiss) opponents."[10] For example, Elmore notes that the highly decentralized nature of the American educational system means that it is "awash" in curricular innovations. But that same decentralization also means that those innovations are rarely adopted systemwide or even in a small subset of that entire system.

So if public managers want to create more innovation, what should they do? Create a diverse, decentralized organization hoping that this organization will generate enough proposals to overwhelm the blockages to adoption? Or should they create a uniform, centralized organization accepting that it will conceive and propose few innovations but counting on most of those being implemented? "There appears," Lynn emphasizes, "to be no good way around this dilemma."

Nevertheless, organizational leaders try to find one. Those who are dissatisfied with the ideas being generated through normal channels create what Gilmore and Krantz call "ad hoc processes," such as task forces explicitly charged with conceiving and proposing innovative ideas. But this increased diversity does not help with implementation; it hinders it. Precisely because such parallel processes are outside the regular structure, that organization is extremely resistant to implementing the outsiders' innovations. After all, observe Gilmore and Krantz, "the creation of a special group is an implied attack on the existing structure's inability to deal effectively with the issue."

Is it possible to get around this dilemma? Gilmore and Krantz propose a transitional perspective: creating parallel processes specifically for the purpose of "enabling some new relationships to come into being that will allow the dismantling of the supports and transitions to ongoing structure and processes." Such parallel processes—which Gilmore and Krantz call "scaffolding"—would be created, but only temporarily, around the existing organization, directed to create solutions to some specific problems,

9. Wilson (1966, pp. 198–202).
10. Wilson (1989, p. 230).

and charged with bracing and bolstering the existing organization (and adapting its new ideas to it) until the permanent structure could bear the full load itself.

Baltimore County's Citizen Oriented Police Enforcement (COPE) Program, observe Moore, Sparrow, and Spelman, was originally "a separate unit, small and vulnerable." This parallel process permitted COPE to grow. Now, they write, "COPE has reached the stage where further development requires disseminating the techniques into the general operations of the department and the dissolution of the special unit." But did the original, special unit function well as scaffolding? Will the permanent department be able to bear the full load? Moore, Sparrow, and Spelman ask the same question: "Is the COPE 'culture' now strong enough to stand on its own without the protection of a special structure and powerful enough to dominate the traditional patrol culture?" Or will the department reject it as some kind of alien virus? "The answer," continue these scholars, "will determine whether COPE remains an important program in the repertoire of police operations or becomes an important wedge in transforming the overall strategy of policing."

Gilmore and Krantz do recognize the many "drawbacks and dangers" of employing a parallel process, for it "frequently runs into trouble during the institutionalization phase of an innovation." The danger is that the organization will see itself divided into two groups: the creative elite and the routine rabble. Gilmore and Krantz believe that such efforts to bypass the regular organization can result in "the long-term demoralization" of those working in that organization "as they feel written-off and disempowered." Consequently, they argue, "the relationships between a parallel process and the existing organization need careful management." The job of the parallel unit needs to be clear (and narrow) and bounded in time. When its task is completed, it should be disbanded and the ongoing responsibilities folded back into the regular organization. Everyone should know that the scaffolding is scaffolding and will soon be torn down.

Federalism Dilemma

We Americans are proud of our highly decentralized, highly diversified federal system of government. We celebrate our fifty states as U.S. Supreme Court Justice Louis Brandeis's "laboratories of democracy." The idea is simple: Different jurisdictions experiment with different innovations; then other jurisdictions learn about and adopt the best. Have we thus managed to get around the Organizational-Diversity Dilemma?

Elmore's analysis of innovation in education suggests not. Yes, Americans benefit from the diversity and decentralization that generates an abundance of innovations. The states—as well as the school systems, schools, and classrooms—are laboratories of education, constantly experimenting with different managerial and pedagogical strategies. But when it comes to adoption, Elmore argues, all this diversity and decentralization is a hindrance. American educators cannot seem to learn what the best laboratories are producing or how to institutionalize them nationwide (let alone statewide, citywide, or even schoolwide).

Stone argues that the American federal system hurts health policy, too, but in a different way. Education is overwhelmingly supported by state and local taxes. The national government does impose some conditions on the use of its money—primarily to promote equity—but it makes little effort to create any national education policy. Not so in health. Here, the national government puts up big bucks and imposes significant restrictions on how these funds can be used. Consequently, state-level innovation usually requires a change in federal laws and regulations—or, at a minimum, that federal regulators grant a waiver to their rules so that the state can experiment with its innovation.

This need for federal approval certainly can inhibit innovation by groping along. A state agency would find it difficult to solicit and obtain a waiver every time it wanted to modify its strategy and grope in a slightly different direction. And the waiver system would make it difficult for different parts of an agency to simultaneously grope in several different directions.

Golden's analysis would seem to support Stone's conclusion. Most of the innovations Golden examined followed the groping-along instead of the policy-planning model. The biggest exception was the Medicaid Demonstration Project in Santa Barbara County, California, which needed, among other things, a federal waiver. Consequently, the county undertook detailed planning. If innovation happens more by groping along than through policy planning, and if, as Golden suggests, "networks of intergovernmental regulation" require "more extended advance planning," then more innovation may occur in programs not hampered by such intergovernmental entanglements.

The Organizational-Diversity Dilemma applies not only to a business firm or a government agency but also to the entire American system of governance. The United States has decentralized education, creating substantial experimentation but little adoption. The nation has also centralized health policy, severely limiting experimentation. Nevertheless, the United States is occasionally able to authoritatively adopt an innovative policy nationwide. Thus the Federalism Dilemma is simply a special case of the Organizational-Diversity Dilemma.

Replication Dilemmas

The benefits that we Americans hope will accrue from innovation include more than the improved performance of the innovating organization. Citizens and leaders also want any innovation to help improve performance in other, similar agencies. Americans want every innovation to be disseminated and replicated throughout American government. Fostering innovation in general is more appealing if the fundamental concepts of each individual innovation can be transferred across the country.

Nevertheless, once an innovation proves "successful," the dissemination of that innovation is not automatic. As Lee S. Friedman writes in chapter 15, "The effectiveness of a diffused innovation cannot be assumed." For the tasks of dissemination and replication raise another set of questions: When should the innovation be disseminated? What strategies of dissemination are most effective? What does the replicating organization have to do to repeat the success of the original? Can it merely copy the original innovation? If not, what must it change? And what is to be replicated? What are the essential components of the innovation—the ones that produced the success? What exactly is the original innovation anyway? How, exactly, can the success of a public-sector innovation be replicated elsewhere?

Unfortunately, note Altshuler and Zegans, even "programs that seem fairly simple may be difficult to transfer within a single culture." As an illustration, they cite One Church, One Child, one of the most famous winners of the Ford Foundation Innovations Award. When the Illinois Department of Child and Family Services (DCFS) found a backlog of hard-to-adopt African-American children, it built a partnership with the state's black churches, created new mechanisms for outreach into African-American communities, and eliminated the backlog. Thus, report Altshuler and Zegans, the federal government and foundations provided grants to help DCFS disseminate this "enormously successful" program.

As a result:

> Several states now have implemented variants of the program with
> success, but efforts in others have foundered. Suitable champions
> were lacking; key actors could not overcome differences in view-
> point about how the program should be administered; top manage-
> ment turnover set progress at key moments back to square one.

Conclude Altshuler and Zegans: "Replication of any but the simplest
technical innovations is rarely mechanical."

Adaptation Dilemma

To examine replication, Paul Berman and Beryl Nelson studied fifteen
elementary schools in California, each of which had "well-implemented
and competently delivered examples" of one of five different models for
educating students with limited English proficiency (LEP). These fifteen
examples of "exemplary programs" offer some evidence, write Berman
and Nelson in chapter 14, to support "an important hypothesis about the
replication of innovation: no adaptation, no success." Successful replicators, they found, "did not seek pure fidelity to the original model."
Instead, "exemplary schools started with a basic model and adapted it to
create a program-in-practice that reflected local sociopolitical circumstances." Moreover, Berman and Nelson continue, "had they not adapted
the models, these schools probably would have failed to develop effective programs."

The adaptation necessary to design the initial replication is "only the
beginning of an extended and continuous process." Thus, write Berman
and Nelson, "during implementation, exemplary programs evolved to
meet changing conditions; they were shaped, crafted, revised, and
renewed." Adaptation cannot stop with full implementation, for the
process of replication is "an iterative one with each decision creating
new issues, new requirements, and new practices." Five years after a
school selected a model, Berman and Nelson found that "the program-in-
practice often deviated remarkably from its progenitor." All of which
sounds like "replication by groping along."

The idea of replication as faithful copying is silly—and harmful.
Instead, public managers—innovators, disseminators, and replicators—
need to adopt the concept of replication by adaptation. The necessity of
adaptation, write Berman and Nelson, "has important implications for both

organizations promoting replications and those seeking to adopt successful models." Specifically, it raises the Adaptation Dilemma: How much
adaptation is essential? What kind of adaptation is required? Even for the
replication of one, specific innovation, no perfect answer to these questions exists. Different replicators will have to adopt different adaptations.

Replicators have to be open to adaptation. So do disseminators. Those
who advocate replication of successful innovations ought not to insist
that the replicators be slavishly faithful to the original. Instead, they
should tolerate—and encourage—adaptations.

Organizational-Adaptation Dilemma

Replication requires two kinds of adaptation. Not only must the
details of the innovation be adapted to the needs of the replicating organization, but the organization must also adapt itself to the core features
of the innovation. And this task may prove much more difficult. The
challenge of adapting the innovation to the organization is strictly analytical. Which details of the original innovation do the replicators need to
change to make it work in their political and organizational environment?
In contrast, the task of adapting the organization to the innovation raises
basic questions about long-held practices and beliefs. The managers,
staff, and stakeholders of the replicating organization have little personal
stake in the details of the original innovation. So they may be willing to
modify the innovation to fit their needs. Will they, however, be as willing
to modify themselves to fit the needs of the innovation?

A public agency is more likely to replicate an innovation if its existing routines and culture mesh well with the practices and norms that
make the innovation work. For example, writes Friedman, "some evidence" suggests that a pretrial-release program supervised by a probation
department is more likely to adopt the call-in requirement than one
reporting to a judge, a judicial council, or an administrative officer of the
court. This seems reasonable, he continues, for probation departments
have call-in requirements as one of their standard operating procedures.

Similarly, Moore, Sparrow, and Spelman found that police departments "preferred innovations that had a favorable impact on officer
morale, fitted comfortably within the existing culture of the police, and
survived. They were less inclined toward innovations that faced opposition." That is, police agencies are less interested in replicating innovations that require them to adapt. They favor innovations that mesh well

with the existing organizational structure, operating procedures, and culture.[11] Thus the probability of replication may depend less on the ability of the innovation to improve the replicating agency's performance than on how well it meshes with that organization's structure, culture, and routines.

Berman and Nelson found that schools that successfully implemented any of the five LEP models did so through faculty collaboration that changed the nature of instructional practice within those schools. Some schools adopted team teaching; others created a preschool LEP program modeled after the one being used in the elementary grades. And these organizational adaptations to the needs of the model had an impact. The success of the replication of an LEP model appeared to depend less on how the model was adapted than on how the organization adapted.

Organization adaptation is required, argue Berman and Nelson, because all meaningful innovations require organizational change, and so do all meaningful replications. Berman and Nelson write that "would-be replicators have stumbled in the past by not taking into account all of the sources for success in the originating site. In their attempts to export their model, many have ignored precisely the impact of those contextual and organizational elements that contribute to the model's effectiveness."

This requirement for organizational adaptation creates another sub-dilemma: The organizations most in need of innovation are usually least capable of making the necessary organizational adaptations. "The purpose of replicating successful models," write Berman and Nelson, "is often to assist organizations, be they countries or schools, that are in need of change." Yet "needy, low-capacity organizations are, ironically, least able to implement models that might help them get better." They conclude that "a prerequisite of effective replication is often the enhancement of the capacity of the potential replicators."

Berman and Nelson observe that the replication of an innovation fails when the replicators ignore "the organizational context" and, for example, "try to implement a program that runs parallel to the standard activities in the organization." Instead of adapting the organization to the replication, they simply bypass the organization by creating a new, and competing, one. As Gilmore and Krantz explain, however, this can create tensions between the two structures. And their concept of "scaffolding"

---

11. Not all of the experts on policing consulted by Moore, Sparrow, and Spelman agreed with this view. Some "sounded a different note. Important innovations were the risky ones. Instead of fitting neatly within the organization's culture, these innovations challenged it."

may be helpful not only for an innovating organization but also for a replicating agency.

Dissemination Dilemma

Replication does not just happen. Between the original innovation and its replication, some dissemination is required. The originators of the innovation or some other organization can take on this task. Or some other medium—newspapers and popular magazines, policy journals and specialized newsletters, or informal, professional associations and networks—can spread the word. But, if, as Golden suggests, the innovators are groping along, the innovation is continually changing. So when is it appropriate to begin dissemination?

Stone worries that dissemination happens too quickly. "States are so hungry for solutions," she finds, "that they begin imitating a promising innovation before it has gotten off the drawing boards in its home state." And this could create a controversy that kills the original innovation before it has a chance to prove itself. Dissemination, writes Stone, "brings national exposure to a fledgling state innovation, rendering it an object of national political conflict before it is off the ground."

Quick dissemination and early efforts at replication could generate a wider set of variations on the original idea—and more experimentation, more groping along, and more learning. Unfortunately, writes Stone, "state-level public managers are more inclined to copy another state than to grope along finding their own solution." Dissemination can happen when an innovator in a state or local agency explains it to a national institution (such as a federal agency, professional association, or foundation), which in turn tells other state and local agencies. If this is done too soon, Stone argues, "states may copy an innovation before its shortcomings have been revealed or evaluated."

The federal agency might not merely pass the innovative idea along to state and local governments. It could also write that innovation into its own rules and regulations. "Once a federal agency or national foundation latches onto a particular idea," writes Stone, it can offer "states money to test it." As a result, she continues, "further innovation at the state-level may be short-circuited as states scurry to acquire the new money attached to the federally favored innovation."

"Diffusion of innovations is generally considered to be a good thing," continues Stone, "but it is worth questioning whether rapid diffusion can sometimes be a hindrance to innovation." This is the Dissemination Dilemma. If you disseminate an innovation too quickly, you may hurt instead of help both the original innovation and the diversity of potential replications. If you wait too long, however, benefits to the replicating jurisdictions may be needlessly lost.

Definitional Dilemma

The speed of the diffusion that Stone observes in health policy may not be at the core of the problem. Perhaps the mechanisms of dissemination and the proclivities of the replicators are the source of the trouble. If would-be replicators, as Stone writes, "are more inclined to copy" each other "than to grope along," the suggestion that an innovation can be copied may produce disastrous results. For any hint that replicators can follow someone else's instruction manual will preclude precisely the kind of adaptation—both of the innovation and by the replicating organization—that Berman and Nelson find so necessary. Regulations—even guidelines—for replicators may be a catastrophe.

This raises the Definitional Dilemma: What exactly is the innovation? What should be disseminated? How can the essence of the innovation be disseminated in such a way as to provide guidance to would-be replicators without suggesting that all they need do is faithfully follow the recipe from this latest innovator's cookbook? How can the innovation be disseminated so as to encourage replicators to adapt the innovation to their needs—and to adapt themselves to the needs of its essence? How can the innovation be disseminated so as to encourage the replicators to grope along?

Unfortunately, the replicators may be uncertain about what, exactly, caused the innovation to be successful. Observe Berman and Nelson: "Knowing that a model produces desirable outcomes in one location is not the same as knowing what makes the model work." Note that all of the successful replications of the five LEP programs that they studied instituted team teaching or a preschool program as part of their own adaptation. Maybe the specifics of these five models were not the key to success. Maybe the real essence of these innovations was team teaching or preschool programs.

Friedman also emphasizes the importance of defining the core of the original innovation. As he notes: "The details matter." But which ones? Which specific features of a multifaceted innovation account for the improved results? The answer is often not obvious and warrants some analysis. Thus dissemination and replication involve two tasks: (1) identifying the true core of the innovation, and (2) figuring out how to adapt its other features to best fit the needs of the new environment.

To resolve the Definitional Dilemma, Friedman offers "the economic tool of production analysis." This involves examining a set of different incarnations of the same innovation, identifying the different components that are (or are not) present in these incarnations, and employing the tools of statistics to relate key indicators of success to those components. Unfortunately, as Friedman points out, no individual state or local agency has the resources or incentive to conduct this analysis. Consequently, he advocates that some kind of national, research and development organization undertake such work.

Motivation Dilemmas

Finally, who will innovate? What motivates innovators? Noting the "numerous factors" that discourage innovation, Altshuler observes that, nevertheless, "numerous civil servants do think ingeniously about how to accomplish their missions more effectively or at lower cost." And then he asks the key question. "What motivates them?" If citizens and elected officials really desire more innovation, they need to understand the psychology of innovators. What makes them tick? What must who do to encourage more innovation? Do legislators and elected executives need to invent ways to reward it? Or should they concentrate on eliminating the existing practices that punish it? Can they create incentives that will encourage innovators and innovations?

Media Dilemma

The most obvious motivation problem is created by journalists who rarely reward successful innovators but who are happy to punish unsuccessful attempts at innovation (or even successful ones). W. Lance Bennett, in chapter 8, and Robert M. Entman, in chapter 9, analyze how journalistic organizations function and explain why they tend to ignore successful innovations but cover unsuccessful ones. To Bennett, the key is the mismatch between the bureaucratic routines of news organizations and the process of policy innovation; to Entman, it is the "production biases" that result from the "constraints imposed by the nature of the news industry and its competitive markets." Yet the consequence is the same. Bennett reports a "sheer lack of fit between news-gathering routines and innovative policy processes." Entman observed that "the values and biases that shape policy reporting" can "establish disincentives and barriers to innovative leadership." For public sector innovators, the result is rarely a happy one.

For people in government, these bureaucratic routines, values, and biases of journalism mean that innovation can be hazardous. "Whereas business managers search avidly for new ideas, public managers take refuge in the familiar. They are threatened not by program weaknesses per se, but by political and media criticism, and they are most likely to attract such criticism if they stand out." And while the downside looms large, there appears to be very little upside. As Altshuler writes: "When potential gains are hard to envision, any risk looms large. A central dilemma for those who believe that more bureaucratic innovation would be desirable is that few government innovations, or managerial ideas of any type, have much voter or media appeal."

Is it possible to redesign innovations, the innovation process, or how government presents innovations to the media? Both Bennett and Entman answer yes. Entman suggests that innovators need to match their innovations with the biases of journalism; that is, journalists will cover an innovation if it is simple, personal, and symbolic. Bennett counsels innovators "to satisfy the bureaucratic requirements of news production." The irony here is that, for innovators to get their efforts into the news, they have to mesh their innovative activities with journalism's bureaucratic routines.

Reward Dilemma

Do rewards motivate innovators? What possible extrinsic rewards could governments employ to encourage more innovation? Governments might increase the budget of the innovators' agency. Governments might offer innovators a salary increase or some kind of bonus. Governments might promote innovators. But would such rewards encourage more innovation?

For example, to improve the financial rewards for innovation, Lynn recommends that governments allow public agencies "to create an innovation fund from savings they achieve through frugality and increases in efficiency and to spend this fund without having to account to any legislative body." But are elected officials willing to offer this flexibility reward? And if so, will it motivate significantly more innovation?

Unfortunately, instead of increasing the budget of an innovative agency, governments often cut the budget of one that somehow manages to improve efficiency. The macro budgetary logic is obvious: In an era of fiscal constraints, the efficiency gains from one agency are best used to fund the most pressing needs (which are apt to be in other areas). But the micro motivational consequences are equally as obvious: If improvements lead to budgetary punishment (instead of budgetary rewards), agencies will either hide any savings they generate or avoid making them.

Nevertheless, Friedman is hopeful. He suggests that, although innovation itself may not be rewarded directly, an aura of competence—to which an innovation or two can contribute—may, over the long run, generate budgetary benefits. Effectiveness and performance, competence and innovation may be connected to budgets, but only subtly and indirectly.

What about personal rewards to the individuals who invented and perfected the innovation? These, too, are rare. As government shrinks—particularly in the ranks of its middle managers—fewer positions are available into which innovators can be promoted. And besides, the civil service paradigm places a greater emphasis on equity than on excellence. Clever leaders can always figure out ways to reward—and thus motivate—innovation, but this requires a commitment of time and resources. Even if a jurisdiction has a system of bonuses for distinguished performance, to win such a bonus for a subordinate, a manager must jump through numerous bureaucratic hoops, and for a prize that is monetarily trivial.

But the size of the bonus may be less important than its symbolism. What counts for most innovators are the intrinsic rewards: the sense of self-accomplishment and recognition from peers. That is the conclusion of a number of authors in this volume: Altshuler and Zegans; Friedman; Moore, Sparrow, and Spelman; Schall; and Zegans. If this is true, rewarding—and thus motivating—innovation may not be as difficult as it appears. If the reward in the bonus is not so much the money as the recognition, then managers can simply ignore the money and focus on the recognition.

Elected-Official Dilemma

Motivating civil servants to innovate is one challenge. Motivating elected officials to encourage such innovation is another. Altshuler asks:

"Why should elected officials, who have the most to lose when innova-tions fail, take the risk of encouraging civil servants to devise them?" Any effort to encourage innovation must, he argues, "be consistent with the incentive systems guiding elected officials, and particularly elected chief executives." He wants to know: "How have some elected officials turned support for innovation into a political plus, and what general propositions, if any, can be derived from their experiences?"

Altshuler answers this question by cataloging a collection of "meta-innovations"—citizen participation, customer focus, consumer choice, privatization, public-private competition, and performance benchmark-ing—which political leaders do support. These are "umbrella strategies," he emphasizes, not "particular efforts to address highly specific prob-lems." Each addresses a problem "of intense public concern." And these six meta-innovations are "value-neutral"; they "promise greater effec-tiveness" in achieving a wide variety of policy purposes. Finally, although these innovations do involve the "broad delegation of authority to originate innovative ideas," they also preserve "final authority to authorize adoption in the hands of elected officials."

But innovators also need to learn how to reward their political over-seers—to share the credit widely enough. When innovators struggle to make a new idea work over the indifference or hostility of political supe-riors, they have little desire to share any of the credit. Doing so would appear to be misleading. Nevertheless, it is helpful. A political leader who shares the initial praise for an innovation will be less likely to turn on it later. Public managers who learn how to make their organization's innovations mesh with journalism's news-gathering routines can use this skill to create public prestige for those who created the innovation. But such broad attention may be wasted on many civil servants. Elected offi-cials are the ones who value positive coverage in the media.

Elected officials need to appreciate that if they expect civil servants to improve performance through innovation, they have to recognize the contributions of those whose innovative efforts improved performance. Civil servants need to appreciate that if they expect elected officials to support their risky attempts at innovation, they have to recognize the con-tributions of those who may have done no more than leave them alone to experiment with their innovative ideas.

Resolving these Motivational Dilemmas may be the biggest challenge to innovation in American government.

References

Behn, Robert D. 1987. "A Curmudgeon's View of Public Administration: Routine Tasks, Performance, and Innovation." *State and Local Government Review,* vol. 19, no. 2 (Spring): 47, 54–61.

_____. 1988. "Management by Groping Along." *Journal of Policy Analysis and Management,* vol. 7, no. 4 (Fall): 643–63.

_____. 1991. *Leadership Counts: Lessons for Public Managers from the Massachusetts Welfare, Training, and Employment Program.* Harvard University Press.

Peters, Tom. 1990–91. "Get Innovative or Get Dead." Parts 1 and 2. *California Management Review,* vol. 33, no. 1 (Fall): 9–26; vol. 33, no. 2 (Winter): 9–23.

Polsby, Nelson W. 1984. *Political Innovation in America: The Politics of Policy Initiation.* Yale University Press.

Schön, Donald A. 1966. "The Fear of Innovation." *International Science and Technology* 14 (November): 70–78.

Varley, Pamela. 1987. *Ellen Schall and the Department of Juvenile Justice.* Case C16–87–793.0. Harvard University, John F. Kennedy School of Government.

Wilson, James Q. 1966. "Innovation in Organizations: Notes toward a Theory." In *Approaches to Organizational Design,* edited by James D. Thompson, 193–218. University of Pittsburgh Press.

_____. 1989. *Bureaucracy: What Government Agencies Do and Why They Do It.* Basic Books.

Wilson, Woodrow. 1887. "The Study of Administration." *Political Science Quarterly,* vol. 2 (June): 197–222.

Zegans, Marc. 1990. "Strategy, Innovation, and Inertia: Unbundling Some Old Assumptions." Paper prepared for the Annual Research Conference of the Association for Public Policy and Management, San Francisco.

CHAPTER TWO

Bureaucratic Innovation, Democratic Accountability, and Political Incentives

Alan A. Altshuler

AXIOMATIC IN MOST SECTORS of business is that what counts as excellent today will be inadequate tomorrow. In recent decades, the pace of product and service innovation has sharply accelerated, and the scope of competition has dramatically broadened. Once-local markets have become national. Once-national markets have become global. And product life cycles have shortened. The period during which the producer of even the most successful new product can anticipate high profit margins because of limited competition is much shorter than in earlier generations. As close substitute products appear, patents expire, and direct competitors multiply, business survival itself typically depends on maintaining a constant flow of new products, while finding ways to produce the older ones more cheaply.[1]

So business leaders and analysts have become preoccupied with innovation. They have recognized increasingly, moreover, that it cannot simply be a top management responsibility. The most fundamental task of management is to mold innovative organizations; that is, enterprises structured and inspired at all levels to innovate.[2] If top managers succeed in establishing this foundation of innovativeness, they must still provide direction and screen potential innovations. In the absence of a strong

1. Stone (1976, chapter 4); Smith and Reinertsen (1991, pp. 1–13); and Utterback (1994, chapters 4, 9, and 10).
2. Peters and Waterman (1982, chapters 7–8); and Kanter (1983, chapters 5–7 and 12).

foundation, however, it scarcely matters how good they are in charting courses and screening proposals.

Is Innovation a Legitimate Function of Public Management?

In the public sector, innovation has never achieved comparable status as a criterion of organizational excellence. Three reasons stand out. First, while government agencies face urgent problems, passionate claimants, and muckraking journalists, they experience little direct competition. Second, the political arena is characterized by high conflict; no analog of profitability exists as a consensual criterion for appraising public sector innovations. Third, people in government fear nothing more than newsworthy failure. Old programs are commonly much less effective or efficient than they might be, but their familiarity insulates them from much media attention. And even when they do attract attention, responsible officials can plausibly defend themselves by noting that they have simply been following standard practice. However, when new initiatives fail—and inevitably a large proportion do—they become highly newsworthy, with a focus on who is to blame. In such cases, the "standard practice" defense is unavailable.

Even among those who deem innovation no less important in the public sector than the private, a deep ambivalence typically exists about the idea of encouraging civil servants at all levels to seek better means of pursuing public purposes. Innovation requires discretion, and the dominant tradition of U.S. administrative reform has been to stamp out bureaucratic discretion.[3] The roots of this tradition lie in the country's constitutional heritage, which assigns the highest priority to keeping government power in check and firmly rooted in popular sovereignty.

Within the framework of this heritage, the two primary sources of legitimacy for public action are preexisting law and (for those who would enact new law) electoral victory. Permanent bureaucracies, which never stand for election but exercise enormous authority, should be closely supervised by elected officials and held accountable for strict adherence to precisely drafted laws. Bureaucratic discretion is not only contrary to the ideal of a government of laws but also an open invitation to abuse of citizen rights, corruption, favoritism, racial and ethnic discrimination, and sloth.[4]

3. Barzelay (1992, pp. 3–5, 117–33).
4. For an excellent critique of this tradition, see Barzelay (1992, pp. 3–8). A modern, highly influential call for its reinvigoration is found in Lowi (1979, especially chapter 13).

A commonplace of modern scholarship is that this sharp dichotomy between lawmaking and law execution—or, as more commonly phrased, between policymaking and administration—cannot be sustained in practice because every situation has elements of uniqueness. So preexisting guidelines cannot cover all contingencies, and discretion is endemic.[5] To admit this, however, is not necessarily to forswear the aim of *minimizing* discretion. And the validity of this aim continues to be taken for granted in most American political debate, media commentary, and popular discussion.

How can bureaucratic discretion be minimized in practice? The most obvious method is personal supervision by elected supervisors, but they have limited expertise and numerous other priorities. A second method is judicial oversight, with opportunities built into the law for class action suits as well as for actions by individual parties suffering substantial harm. But this is expensive, time-consuming, and rigid, and it can overwhelm the judicial system.[6]

These methods tend to be backups, consequently, for rule-based routinization. Laws tend to be vague, to be silent on many pertinent issues, to promise more than can be produced with the resources provided, and often to conflict with one another. But they can be fleshed out with regulations, and the regulations can be made so numerous and detailed as eventually to cover most contingencies.

Routinization minimizes discretion but conflicts with two other ideals: (1) sympathetic responsiveness to the needs of specific people in particular situations, and (2) adaptation to changing circumstances. In conflicting with the first ideal, routinization alienates civil servants from their clients, whom they are instructed to treat as examples of categories rather than as the unique beings with special problems that they think they are. In conflicting with the second ideal, it reinforces the stereotype that public bureaucracies are rigid and resistant to learning when measured against strong private organizations.

While often acknowledging these problems, defenders of routinization insist that it remains the best available strategy in an imperfect world. Society can scarcely have civil servants adjusting the criteria for welfare eligibility case by case or determining what procedures to employ in arraigning criminal suspects. As its critics note, moreover,

---

5. Rourke (1984, pp. 35–44); Lipsky (1979, pp. 18–53); and Edwards (1980, pp. 17–39).
6. Kagan (1991, pp. 375–79).

routinization is never complete. Some room is invariably left for civil servants to address the particulars of individual situations. Finally, routinization is not always in conflict with the themes of responsiveness and adaptation. Computer-assisted public information programs, for example, are routinizing in the sense that they excel in providing consistent responses to any given query, but they are also good at tailoring their responses to the particular questions posed by any inquirer, and they represent a creative use of new technology. Similarly, automated street signals can be programmed in accord with precise rules to respond to moment-by-moment traffic conditions.

What do the advocates of routinization think should be done when egregious instances of governmental failure and inefficiency are exposed or as evidence accumulates that citizens are losing confidence in their government? Their answers are generally clear: Promulgate more rules. Add more layers of oversight and audit. Tighten enforcement all along the line.

So those who favor adoption of the innovative paradigm in government have their work cut out for them. First, they have to make the case that encouraging mid-level and front-line civil servants to be innovative can yield important value for the public without significant loss of accountability. Second, they must address the problem of political incentives. Why should elected officials, who have the most to lose when innovations fail, take the risk of encouraging civil servants to devise them? To be credible, finally, they need to offer some effective tactics. How have some elected officials turned support for innovation into a political plus, and what general propositions, if any, can be derived from their experiences?

Three Arguments for Bureaucratic Innovation

Those who champion the ideal of the innovative public agency, encouraging its employees at all levels to approach their tasks creatively, typically offer several arguments: First, bureaucratic innovation is about means, not ends. Second, it is essential to the accomplishment of assigned missions and to the recovery of public confidence in government. Third, it is—or, in cases where it is not now, can be made—subject to adequate control by elected officials.

MEANS, NOT ENDS. According to the first argument, no conflict exists. Civil servants should exercise their judgment and ingenuity, but only within tightly defined limits. A particular attraction as well as limitation of this argument is that it poses no objection to the aim of minimizing bureaucratic discretion.

One might expect senior civil servants to find this formulation unduly confining. The group described by Marc D. Zegans in chapter 5, however, embraced it. These nine career state and local government managers all "saw innovation as an important part of their work." They also agreed that employees throughout their organizations sought to innovate "as part of normal practice." Zegans's managers were emphatic, though, that the innovations they had in mind, while important, were purely about means. That is, they were fully consistent with existing missions, resources, and routines. Innovations requiring the relaxation of any of these constraints were, these managers insisted, exclusively the responsibility of elected officials.

In short, for this group, the traditional distinction between making policy and executing it was more than just alive and well. It was essentially unchallenged. How was this possible? I hypothesize that the idea of a sharp dichotomy between policy and administration serves as a useful shield against criticism for civil servants, leading many to internalize it as an ideal and to speak of it (even in semiprivate, confidential settings) as fully operative.[7] The question is whether this mindset leaves adequate scope for bureaucratic innovation.

NECESSITY. What does the public want? The answer seems to be both accountable and high-performance government. Neither alone is sufficient. It wants the police, for example, not only to function with discipline, courtesy, and meticulous respect for the law but also to reduce crime and disorder. It wants the schools not only to implement myriad state and local educational policies, to give unruly students all the benefits of due process, and to respect the sensitivities of all the subcultures represented in their student bodies, but also to enable every student to feel valued and safe, and to turn out literate, law-abiding, highly employable graduates. And it wants these aims to be achieved along with tax cuts if possible.

In addition, public expectations of service quality are rising, largely because of implicit competition from the private sector. When members of the public visit the motor vehicle department, they expect the same kind of

7. The term "many" is deliberately vague. Zegans's sample was small and nonrandom, so his findings are only suggestive. The unanimity of his sample, though, suggests that the patterns he identified may be widespread.

service they get at McDonald's: quick, efficient, and courteous. When they call the Internal Revenue Service, they expect to be treated as they would be when calling L. L. Bean or American Express. They may even expect such services to be available seven days a week, twenty-four hours a day. Numerous public managers understand this and have moved with considerable success to respond.[8] For example, the Social Security Administration achieved a public relations coup in 1995 when DALBAR, Inc., ranked its 800-number better than that of any major business corporation.

In this context, a new vision of public management has been emerging. As Michael Barzelay and Babak J. Armajani write in chapter 6, this new vision holds the performance of line agencies to be a prime value. In contrast, the old vision either subordinated this value to others—such as fiscal accountability, impersonal administration, and economy—or it simply ignored performance.[9]

A central premise of this new vision is that high-performance government is not feasible unless civil servants have wide latitude to innovate. Government bureaucracies commonly function in conditions of acute overload; that is, with resources in no way commensurate with their assigned tasks. These tasks are themselves commonly so numerous and ill-defined that action can only be taken by selecting from a vast menu of possibilities.[10] The police cannot hope, for example, to address more than a minuscule fraction of violations, and they cannot look to the law for guidance as to which should be their priorities. Nor can they look, generally, to their political masters, who are themselves severely overloaded and whose general inclination is to concentrate on other matters. Meanwhile, new problems, public expectations, technologies, and best-practice standards are constantly bursting on the scene.

So the only hope for effective, adaptive government is for public employees at all levels to become engaged in the never-ending task of mission-driven innovation. It follows that a central aim of public management should be to encourage such innovation, not merely to tolerate the few examples that emerge even when government is organized to prevent them.

ACCOUNTABILITY. While the public would like greater value for its dollars and votes, it also seems—with constant prompts from cam-

8. Fountain and others (1994); Osborne and Gaebler (1992, chapter 6); and Levin and Sanger (1994, chapters 3–5).
9. Barzelay (1992, chapter 8).
10. Lipsky (1979, pp. 14–15, 18–23).

paigning politicians and the media—more suspicious of government than ever before and no less disposed toward the traditional strategy of bureaucratic reform: more rules, more tightly enforced.[11]

The central challenge facing advocates of the performance paradigm, therefore, is to demonstrate its compatibility with the paradigm of accountability. Insofar as this challenge can be overcome, it must involve some reexamination of the concept of accountability itself. What is most important for the public to control, and how can it best do so? Stated another way, innovative thinking is needed about accountability no less than about programmatic efficiency.

One approach is to focus on the distinction between acts of invention and acts of adoption in the process of innovation. One can envision civil servants as authorized to propose innovations, and perhaps to implement small trials of their effectiveness, but also as required to consult widely and to obtain the approval of elected overseers before proceeding with implementation on any substantial scale. Given the disinclination, however, of most elected officials to identify with administrative innovations until the political benefits of doing so clearly outweigh the risks, it is too much to expect that political approvals will often be forthcoming in timely fashion. So, the question arises: When, and following what types of consultation, should their usual inaction be considered sufficient?

In chapter 16, Ellen Schall writes about her experience as commissioner of New York City's Department of Juvenile Justice (DJJ). She was a political appointee with a broad view of her managerial responsibility to innovate, extending to significant redefinition of her agency's mission. But DJJ was a small agency, in which elected officials had little interest. From her boss, Mayor Edward I. Koch, she had only a two-sentence directive: "Don't let them out. Do as much for them as you can."[12] She could expect nothing more. There were enabling statutes, but they were little more specific. So she recalls:

> We did not wait to be asked to invent. We moved ahead and took risks. No one suggested that we find ways to work effectively

11. The Harris Poll since 1966 has tracked an "alienation index" reflecting the proportion of respondents in a national sample agreeing with each of five statements to the effect that those with power, influence, and money are indifferent to ordinary people. One example: "The people running the country don't really care what happens to you." The index is calculated from the mean proportion of those agreeing with each of the five statements. It has risen from 27 in 1966 to 67 in 1995; see Taylor (1996). On public distrust of bureaucracy specifically, see Kaufman (1981).

12. Varley (1987, p. 4).

with the families of children in our custody. It was our conclusion based on our work with clients, and we authorized ourselves to move ahead.

She and her associates were, she emphasizes, "as careful as we knew how to keep our various overseers and involved publics informed." But they had little guidance as to who they should inform about what, or how they should react if they received mixed responses to their messages—or, more commonly, none at all.

Were they adequately accountable? The argument in the affirmative is that they could easily have been curbed. The mayor, city council, and state overseers were not paying attention, but they would have pointed their spotlight quickly enough at DJJ if significant constituencies had become agitated or if negative media reports had appeared. And their authority was never in question. Bearing the potential for stop orders (and her own removal) constantly in mind, Schall and her colleagues took great care to avert them. Within this implicit set of constraints, however, they exercised all the ingenuity at their disposal.

Writing more generally about winners of the Ford Foundation and John F. Kennedy School of Government Awards Program for Innovations in State and Local Government, Alan A. Altshuler and Marc D. Zegans observe in chapter 3 that successful innovators routinely exhibit the following behaviors:

— "They are close to their clients and can count on a preponderance of positive messages to political authorities from them."

— "They cast their nets widely in search of support, and they are ingenious in linking their efforts to sources of funding and institutional capacity that have not previously been applied toward the missions with which they are concerned."

— "They are skilled at building and sustaining networks that embrace the various centers of authorizing and implementation capacity that are essential to success. One aspect of such network building is the recruitment of champions who can bring specific groups and institutions into the fold."

These innovators, in short, do not merely consult and seek formal authorization where required. They are also deft and energetic in recruiting external support. By influencing the political context within which their elected overseers act, they blur the directional lines of political accountability.

Advocates of the traditional reform paradigm find such cases highly troubling. Advocates of a new paradigm see in them, however, evidence of the need for a fresh understanding of the concept of accountability. They maintain that thinking of civil servants as merely accountable to elected chief executives and legislatures is insufficient. Because elected officials are themselves accountable to the public, yet lack the time, expertise, and inclination to provide much administrative guidance, direct bureaucratic-public relationships are reasonably thought of as elements in an overall network of accountability. This vision of accountability incorporates the values of both responsiveness and high performance. It also suggests that, by a curious paradox, less detailed control of bureaucratic action by government superiors is likely to yield better control by the measures of public satisfaction and effectiveness in carrying out policy mandates.

These are beguiling ideas. They implicitly suggest that nonelected civil servants should function as politicians, finding support and building dominant coalitions where they may. Is this a near-complete abandonment of the traditional idea that civil servants should be "neutral instruments" of the policy process?[13] Can civil servants who establish strong, direct constituency relationships be held adequately accountable to their hierarchical superiors and to the body politic?

How Does Business Do It?

Corporate executives—and students of their practice—have been preoccupied for some time with the question of how to optimize performance without loss of accountability. The goals are different in the private sector, and authority is far more concentrated. But one thing is clear: No management strategy is likely to attract many business adherents unless it keeps employees sharply focused on enterprise objectives, as specified at the top, and unless it yields highly competitive performance. If it fails either test—accountability or performance—any other virtues it may have are irrelevant.

As it happens, considerable agreement has emerged in the business world that a serious tension exists between micromanagement and high performance, and about how it should be addressed. The solution, in a

---

13. Kaufman (1956); Heclo (1975); and Moore (1995).

phrase popularized by Thomas J. Peters and William H. Waterman, is "simultaneous loose-tight" organization. The successful companies profiled in their worldwide best seller *In Search of Excellence* were, they wrote, "fanatic centralists around the few core values they hold dear," but they "allow (indeed, insist on) autonomy, entrepreneurship, and innovation from the rank and file."[14]

Among the preconditions for effective loose-tight organization, the most important is trust. Senior officials must trust that those below, if given wide discretion, will exercise it reliably in the service of organizational values, will discern the level of approvals required for each proposed departure from routine, and will secure these approvals before proceeding to implementation. Subordinate employees must trust that their superiors will appraise their work wisely and fairly—recognizing the challenges they face, providing generous rewards (psychological if not tangible) for those who succeed, and calmly encouraging those responsible for well-conceived failures to try again.

Among these elements of mutual trust, the last may be most important of all. The innovative organization is one whose members are a constant source of ingenious ideas, providing management with a rich reservoir from which to select. Yet those who try new things fail more often than they succeed, and the bolder the innovation the greater the risk. So a central management challenge is to provide a favorable balance of incentives for trying, even as most initiatives are eventually rejected. As Altshuler and Zegans put it, "an essential feature of the innovative company is high tolerance for well-conceived failure as well as powerful rewards for success."[15]

Why It Is Harder in Government

Mutual confidence is no more automatic in the corporate than the public world. Where it exists, though, it tends to be a product of high personnel and core-value stability, reinforced by a constant flow of communications, periodic training programs, and other socialization activities.[16]

---

14. Peters and Waterman (1982, pp. 15–16, 318–25); and Kanter (1983, pp. 275–77, 294–96, 358–63).

15. See also Peters and Waterman (1982, p. 285).

16. Selznick (1984, pp. 112–19); and Peters and Waterman (1982, pp. 91–106, 262–91, 318–25).

Such consistency and reinforcement over time are far easier to achieve in the private sector than in the public. Authority to shape an overall management strategy is highly concentrated in the typical corporation. Leadership continuity tends to be high. Democratic ideology is not a factor. Core values are rarely in dispute. And the external evaluators who have to be taken seriously (such as Wall Street analysts) generally focus in a professional manner on standard measures of performance.

In government, by contrast, authority is highly fragmented, top management turnover is rapid, and value conflict is endemic. Looked at whole, moreover, governments tend to be such grab bags of activities, often in conflict (for example, tobacco subsidies and antismoking campaigns), that it is extremely difficult to specify which values are "core."

In most government agencies, furthermore, employee socialization is haphazard.[17] Elected officials and the media commonly view training activities as frills. Senior managers, most of whom are elected or politically appointed, tend to concentrate on politics and policy far more than management. And even those who do focus on management routinely move on too soon to leave firm legacies.[18] One consequence is that socialization is done predominantly by the educational institutions that employees attend before appointment and by peers. Another is that the best socialized are often deeply imbued with values that run counter to those espoused by top management.[19]

Above all, however, the problem is that most elected chief executives perceive bureaucratic innovation as very risky. Challengers, legislators, and the media concentrate almost exclusively on failure. Failure is news. It generates controversy, particularly about who was responsible, and can be portrayed as scandalous. So it provides ready publicity for politicians on the attack. And it meshes well with the norms and predispositions of journalists. (See the analyses by W. Lance Bennett in chapter 8 and Robert M. Entman in chapter 9.) Success typically generates little controversy, so the media do not consider it newsworthy. What coverage does occur is generally a product of proactive efforts to obtain publicity

17. The exceptions are certain federal career services, most notably the uniformed services. See Janowitz (1960, chapter 7); and Kaufman (1960, chapter 6).

18. Heclo (1977, pp. 100–12).

19. Mosher (1982, pp. 133–42); Lipsky (1979, pp. 16–25, 185–88); Rubinstein (1973, chapters 2, 9, and 10); and Skolnick (1975, chapters 3, 11, and 12).

and takes the form of one-day stories on back pages (or their electronic equivalents).

Why Does Anyone Innovate?

Numerous factors, in short, militate against bureaucratic innovation in the public sector: the traditional ideology of American public administration, the competitive pressures facing elected overseers, and the character of media coverage. Yet numerous civil servants do think ingeniously about how to accomplish their missions more effectively or at lower cost. And they generate significant amounts of valuable innovation. What motivates them?

Hard evidence is lacking, so what is left are speculation and impressions. In chapter 4, Laurence E. Lynn, Jr., speculates, for example, that some civil servants innovate to enhance their power or prestige (but he has little to say about why they should consider innovation a promising path to these objectives). In chapter 15, Lee S. Friedman suggests that perhaps for the best public managers innovation is just one among many things they do well, and their many effective activities (including innovation) may "persuade funders that the agency is in good hands and thereby increase the chances for securing better [personal] rewards." He adds, however, that "funders do not know the true effectiveness of the agency, let alone what explains it," so the relationship between effectiveness and rewards is at best "indirect." And he does not suggest any motivation whatever for government employees below the senior management level to innovate.

Most of the authors in this volume who comment on motivation, though, judge that government employees who innovate are most commonly driven by mission-associated challenges and internalized professional norms. For example, in chapter 3, Altshuler and Zegans found that winners of the Ford Foundation Innovations award are "spurred mainly by professionalism and commitment to mission" and that innovation appears to be "central to their job satisfaction and self-esteem." Zegans writes separately in chapter 5 that the public managers he studied "described their principal motivation to innovate as putting useful ideas into action. They also cited funding crises, technical changes, and burgeoning demands for public services. . . . But they did not . . . [mention] a personal need for creative expression or public credit."

Innovation and the Structure of Incentives for
Elected Officials

It is not difficult to imagine ways of redesigning public organizations to encourage innovation. Demonstrations that new management approaches can yield improved performance are unlikely by themselves, however, to ensure widespread adoption. Better agency performance is not enough. Any new management strategy must also be consistent with the incentive systems guiding elected officials, and particularly elected chief executives. Yet it is precisely these incentive systems—rooted in the structure of electoral and media competition, and in American political culture—that have produced the historic thrust toward greater and greater rule-based consistency and accountability. So one's first instinct may be to say: Aha, Catch–22!

Elected officials face multiple incentives, however, not all of which point toward routinization. Even as they have the strongest claims to legitimacy as innovators, they have the strongest incentives to associate themselves with fresh ideas. With the rise of primaries as the path to electoral nomination, and with the decline of political parties, individual candidates are on their own in the electoral arena. They desperately need distinguishing symbols to attract media coverage, interest group support, and name recognition. Furthermore, the voters expect candidates to demonstrate their energy and capacity by championing new ideas.[20] Those who ignore this expectation are likely to find themselves largely ignored or—if they are too prominent for that (such as presidential candidates Michael S. Dukakis in 1988, George Bush in 1992, and Robert J. Dole in 1996)—widely disparaged on this count.

But there is a great difference between championing an innovative policy idea and encouraging career civil servants to behave innovatively. A campaigning politician who advocates a new idea has to worry only about the impact of his or her own rhetoric. An elected official who encourages civil servants to innovate has to worry about the behavior of large numbers of people, most of them strangers.[21]

As debated in the political arena, moreover, new ideas tend to be extremely general. Even years later, long after the typical advocate has moved on, determining whether any specific idea was adopted and

---

20. See Polsby (1984, pp. 161–65); and Wilson (1992, pp. 436–37, 442–45, 617–18).
21. Heclo (1977, chapters 2 and 5).

received a fair test is often difficult. If program weaknesses are too obvious to deny, they can usually be attributed to legislative and funding compromises or to bureaucratic ineptitude. Did the War on Poverty yield only modest benefits because it was misconceived or because it was inadequately funded? Did medicaid costs explode because the original advocates erred or because Congress caved in to health care providers in enacting key provisions of the law? Controversy rages on these issues, even after several decades.

Bureaucratic innovations, meanwhile, usually occur in the realm of action, where the focus is on particulars instead of general ideas, where embarrassing failures can become apparent quickly, and where the evidence can be very difficult to explain away.

As a result, elected officials have strong incentives to pitch their advocacy—even of innovation—at a fairly high level of generality, positioning themselves not only to take credit for implementation successes but also to join the critics when failures come to light. Even such general advocacy entails a modicum of risk that blame will attach if things go wrong. But that need not be fatal. Politics is a game of risk. The serious question is how potential benefits and risks stack up.[22]

Meta-Innovation: A Strategy for Overcoming the Political Incentive Problem?

When potential gains are hard to envision, any risk looms large. A central dilemma for those who believe that more bureaucratic innovation would be desirable is that few government innovations, or managerial ideas of any type, have much voter or media appeal. But there have been exceptions historically. And there are some today. Such ideas typically share three characteristics: They address problems of intense public concern. They are broadly strategic, with a focus on institutional design, and thus are applicable to a wide range of circumstances. And they are value-neutral, in the sense that they promise greater effectiveness in pursuing diverse policy objectives.

---

22. This is not to deny that politicians act on their values as well as interests and that they differ in their risk aversion. Nor is it to deny that they frequently support proposals with narrow constituencies. It is to emphasize, however, that with rare exceptions the politicians who win elections are acutely sensitive to, and adept in calculating, their electoral interests. So they are not likely with great frequency to take risks that seem out of proportion to likely electoral benefits.

The classic example is civil service. A central instrument of Progressive reform in the late nineteenth and early twentieth centuries, it attracted broad political support as a weapon against corrupt machine politics. Politicians who supported it reinforced their "good government" images. Its advocates plausibly claimed that it was applicable in any program context and regardless of the substantive policy choices made by any jurisdiction.

The leading contemporary examples aim at different alleged ills and propose different methods. They may be viewed as antidotes to overdoses of Progressive reform that have accumulated over the decades. Whereas Progressive reform focused on the ills of corruption and patronage, contemporary reform tends to focus on those of inefficiency, ineffectiveness, and nonresponsiveness. Whereas the Progressives viewed accountability strictly in terms of process control, contemporary reformers argue for at least a comparable emphasis on outcome evaluation.

In the contemporary reform vision, public dissatisfaction with government is attributable to the belief that government costs too much per unit of benefit delivered (inefficiency), that many of its activities fail to generate much benefit at all (ineffectiveness), and that it seems unable to customize the application of general policy to specific cases, taking into account the needs and preferences of those most directly affected (nonresponsiveness). What is required, in this view, is to broaden the conception of accountable government—placing far greater emphasis on the outcome criteria of efficiency, effectiveness, and public satisfaction, far less on the input criteria of process consistency, rule adherence, and detailed hierarchical control.

These priorities are reflected in six approaches to managerial reform that have attracted interest in some political quarters in recent years: citizen participation, customer focus, consumer choice, privatization, public-private competition, and performance benchmarking. For want of a better term, I label these "meta-innovations." Each is an umbrella concept whose advocates view it as conducive to better, more innovative government in a wide variety of circumstances. Citizen participation, customer focus, and consumer choice focus on the theme of responsiveness to those members of the public most directly affected by specific government actions. Privatization, public-private competition, and performance benchmarking emphasize efficiency and effectiveness.

Citizen Participation

Traditionally a core theme of American politics, citizen participation emerged as a major component of administrative reform in the 1960s, when it became a rallying cry for protesters of all persuasions. The idea quickly gained general acceptance that modern government is too complex for democracy to function adequately through the mechanisms of voting and bureaucratic oversight by elected officials alone. By way of supplement, in this view, groups of citizens with significant interests or values at stake should routinely be consulted as bureaucratic decisions take shape. Citizens should be welcomed as participants, for example, in the drafting of regulations and plans, the design of capital projects, the management of schools, and the review of private development proposals. They should be entitled to judicial relief, moreover, if they can demonstrate that government agencies are acting contrary to law or failing to act as mandated by law.[23]

These arguments run directly counter to the idea that bureaucratic discretion can be eliminated. In its stead, they suggest that each unit should experience the direct heat of public opinion, at least as expressed by the citizens most interested in its activities. Citizen participation provisions neither supersede legal requirements, nor do they alter formal channels of bureaucratic accountability. But they provide new opportunities for citizens to become informed, to express their views, and, where dissatisfied, to seek redress. As such, they not only direct the attention of civil servants outward, to the citizens most affected by their actions, but they also legitimize the exercise of discretion in response to citizen views.

Since at least the 1960s, numerous politicians have found it attractive to champion citizen participation in bureaucratic decisionmaking. They have often backtracked when such participation has produced outcomes infuriating to previously dominant interests,[24] but in general they have found that they can have their cake and eat it too, endorsing participations while remaining free to dissociate themselves from any specific citizen demands they find personally distasteful or politically disadvantageous.

23. Berry, Portney, and Thomsen (1989, pp. 208–22); Altshuler and Gómez-Ibáñez (1993, pp. 20–22, 146); Langton (1978, chapter 1); and Rosenbaum (1978).
24. Moynihan (1970).

Customer Focus

As a theme of reform, citizen participation addresses primarily the making of decisions likely to affect substantial groups of people. It is far less concerned with the handling of individual cases. In this sense, it is about citizens as voters more than as service recipients.

By contrast, the customer concept is borrowed from the world of business, where individual customers both provide the revenue from which all else flows and are entitled to the services they finance. In public life, most revenues are obtained by taxation and allocated by legislative decision. So the idea that public clients are "customers" is more normative than economic. It is a powerful construct, however, for directing the attention of civil servants outward, to the ostensible beneficiaries of their work, instead of merely upward, to overseers, and to the rule books. And it lends itself to monitoring by consumer surveys even if not by measures of revenue flow.[25]

In practice, the customer concept has serious ambiguities in the public context. Given the separation of payment from receipt of service in government, for example, how should the claims to "customer" status of those who pay and those who benefit be balanced? Government actions, moreover, are often justified as benefiting multiple beneficiaries, whose interests are far from identical. Schools, for example, are charged to serve students with widely different needs, but they are also expected to reflect community values (which may be hotly disputed) and to serve broader societal objectives such as economic competitiveness and civic order. Finally, government does a great deal more than provide services. It also enforces obligations and punishes violators. Are the direct recipients of tax bills, regulatory orders, and prison sentences "customers" of the administering agencies? In certain ways they are, but the fact remains that these agencies are more in the business of coercing than serving their most direct clients.[26]

The customer concept has proven a valuable instrument of performance-oriented management in a wider array of circumstances than one

25. Revenue measures are available for agencies that levy fees for their services. Even in these cases, however, they are generally of limited utility because the services are provided on a monopoly basis and the prices are determined politically. For a useful, but too celebratory, discussion of the potential of the customer concept in public contexts, see Osborne and Gaebler (1992, chapter 6).

26. Sparrow (1994, pp. 107–12); and Behn (1994).

might initially anticipate. Michael J. Barzelay and Babak J. Armajani report in chapter 6, for example, on uses of the customer concept to structure interagency relationships within government itself. Nor is their discussion purely hypothetical. It is based on the experience of Minnesota under Governor Rudy Perpich in the 1980s.

Barzelay and Armajani focus on the work of overhead staff agencies—bureaus of management and budget, for example, of audit and control, of personnel, of procurement, and of technical services such as telecommunications, computation, and printing. These units deal directly with other public agencies, not members of the public at large. In doing so, they perform a mix of control and service functions. As controllers, they work clearly and unambiguously for their superiors. As service providers, their mission is to assist line agencies. The latter is where they have frequently failed in the past. They have often come to be perceived as impediments to effective procurement or personnel recruitment, for example, because they have concentrated single-mindedly on their control functions to the exclusion of their service functions. Barzelay and Armajani label this problem "the service-control tension."

Line agencies are certainly not ultimate customers. But it can be extraordinarily useful, Barzelay and Armajani maintain, if service-providing overhead units think of them as proximate customers. A government seeking to capitalize on this insight must begin by disentangling the control and service functions. As Barzelay and Armajani put it: "A fundamental strategic choice is whether the principal customers of particular staff-agency employees are overseers or line agencies."

Where possible, they argue, control and service functions should be separated structurally as well as conceptually, so that employees have clear guidance on how to conceive their roles. The clearest test of whether a function belongs in the service category is whether agencies would pay for it voluntarily. A pure service agency in this view—for example, one providing computer or printing services—should be able to support itself entirely from agency fees, even in the face of private competition. Where it cannot, something is wrong, and the appropriate answer may be full reliance on private providers.

Clear choices are not always feasible or advisable, however. Barzelay and Armajani note that procurement and personnel stand out as areas in which a dual customer orientation, toward both overseers and line agencies, is most appropriate. They caution, however, that "overseers should hold the managers of such activities accountable for meeting the needs of line-agency customers" as well as for achieving central control objectives. In the absence of special attention to this balancing problem, they observe, control missions will tend to undercut service orientations.

The need to balance the conflicting demands of different claimants for recognition as customers does not negate the value of the concept. Rather, its surprising heuristic value in thinking about management problems requiring such balance illustrates its broad potential for contributing to improved government performance.

Consumer Choice

For the customer to be king, service providers must face competition. That is private sector wisdom, and an increasing number of people favor applying it in the public sector as well. Government officials have traditionally been highly resistant to the idea of letting citizens choose among competing service providers, arguing that competition in the public sector, even if not in the private, is inherently wasteful. But they are increasingly on the defensive.

There are two ways of thinking about consumer choice in government, both of which have enormous power to focus the attention of civil servants on pleasing service recipients and, thereby, to stimulate innovation. One is to provide eligible service recipients with vouchers and authorize them to purchase services from either public or private service providers. The other is to authorize recipient choice among multiple government providers.

Medicare, medicaid, federal aid for students in higher education, the food stamp program, certain housing programs, and numerous social service programs have been administered on a voucher or voucher-equivalent basis for decades. Competition within the public sector itself is less common, but since the late 1980s it has become a major theme of educational reform.

The most important source of impetus for raising the prominence of choice on the public agenda has been parent dissatisfaction with "assigned" public schools. Public debate has focused most sharply on voucher proposals, but the idea of authorizing parents to expend public money on private school tuition has thus far proven so explosive that only a single, small publicly funded "experiment" has gone forward.

(Several other small trials of the voucher concept have been implemented with private funding.[27])

Since the mid-1980s, however, choice programs without the private school option have been adopted in numerous jurisdictions. Most commonly, local school boards have enabled parents to select any public school within their jurisdiction—subject to racial balance constraints where applicable and to rationing by lottery when particular schools are oversubscribed. Several states have authorized limited cross-district choice programs as well. By 1993, the most recent year for which comprehensive data are available, 11 percent of American children in grades three through twelve were attending "chosen" public schools, more than were attending private schools.[28] More recently, the charter school movement has taken off. While entirely public in their funding, charter schools are typically independent of local control, exempt from some though not all state regulations, and authorized to recruit students anywhere within their state. As of March 1996, twenty-one states had enacted charter school laws—all since 1991, and nearly half within the previous twelve months—and more than two hundred such schools were in operation.[29]

Privatization

At first glance, privatization seems out of place here because it is often proposed as a way of shrinking rather than improving government. When politicians debate privatization in real-life situations, however, the idea is generally more limited. The purpose is to shift operational responsibility to private contractors or franchisees, while retaining government control over policy through contract specifications and regulatory oversight. A government that contracts out the provision of a social service, for example, may shrink by the measures of employment and detailed management control, but not by the measures of responsibility for policy guidance, financing, and outcomes. For members of the public, advocates of privatization argue, the effect will be better or cheaper service, not less service.[30]

27. Paul E. Peterson, "Vouching for a Religious Education," *Wall Street Journal,* December 28, 1995, p. A6; and Peterson and Noyes (1996).

28. By comparison, 80 percent attended "assigned" public schools and 9 percent attended private schools. See National Center for Education Statistics (1995).

29. U.S. Department of Education (1996); and Hassel (1996).

30. Savas (1987, chapter 4); and Osborne and Gaebler (1992, chapter 1).

The implicit threat of privatization is now a factor in virtually all debates about government performance, because it has become clear that, technically, few limits exist on the potential for private operation. Most health care is already provided by private vendors. The nation's military arsenal is produced and, in many cases, maintained by private contractors.[31] States have contracted for the management of prisons and social services.[32] And localities have been identified contracting for more than one hundred functions, including such unlikely candidates as fire fighting.[33]

Even where full privatization is not an option, the idea of reliance on private vendors to accommodate growth in the demand for services is often taken seriously. Is civil adjudication too expensive and time-consuming? Many believe that the answer is to encourage more litigants to rely on the growing industry of private dispute resolution. Are states short of funds to expand highway capacity? Several have already granted franchises to private companies for the construction and operation of toll facilities (and federal aid in partial support of such projects has been authorized since 1991).[34] The list could be expanded almost indefinitely.

Public-Private Competition

Where privatization is among the feasible options, explicit public-private competition may be a strategy to invigorate as well as shrink the public service. Public employees can rarely hope to prevail in such competitions, however, simply by working harder. They need to exercise their ingenuity, to come up with ways to revamp their operations—in short, to innovate (by local if not national standards).

Mayor Stephen Goldsmith, the Republican mayor of Indianapolis, was elected originally on a platform of privatization. Early in his first term, though, he became persuaded that, wherever privatization was an option, public employees should be enabled to compete. As he moved

31. Donahue (1989, chapter 6).
32. Savas (1987, part III); and Smith and Lipsky (1993).
33. John D. Donahue writes: "As of mid-1987, there were some twenty-eight thousand recorded instances of public services being provided by private firms under contract to local governments. Virtually every function of local government has been delegated to the private sector at some time, in some city." Quoted from Donahue (1989, p. 135).
34. Gómez-Ibáñez and Meyer (1995, p. 253).

toward implementation of public-private competition, he soon realized that the city's cost accounting system was a severe impediment to intelligent decisionmaking about which services to put out to competition, to the development of good contract specifications, and to the fair comparison of public and private proposals. A quick canvass revealed that no other public jurisdiction had an adequate system, either. So Goldsmith enlisted the assistance of a leading national accounting firm to develop more useful cost and service measures. And soon he was putting services—more than sixty of them through 1995—out to bid.

Over time this effort, which came to be known as the Competition and Costing initiative, appears to have yielded dramatic savings for the city, and it enabled Goldsmith to cut the city labor force by fully one-third during his first four-year term. It also became a centerpiece of Goldsmith's local image as an effective mayor, and it brought him favorable publicity nationally. One reason for this is, remarkably, that the initiative gained broad employee acceptance. Local employees prevailed in most of the competitions; those who won were delighted at this demonstration of their entrepreneurial capacity; and those who lost (excluding some managers) were offered retraining and transfers to other city jobs. When this initiative received a Ford Foundation Innovations award in 1994, the mayor's office and the city's largest labor union were joint applicants.[35]

Performance Benchmarking

Traditionally governments have been managed and evaluated in terms of resource inputs (for example, dollars expended), easily measurable outputs (for example, number of drug arrests), and compliance with process rules (for example, on contracting). But little, if any, attention has focused on outcomes. How well are children learning? Are crime rates as low as they ought to be? Are the streets and parks sufficiently clean and well maintained?

The reasons for this omission are no great mystery. Establishing a clear connection between government actions and societal outcomes is typically very hard. Schools may improve but students learn less. Eco-

---

35. Other jurisdictions are also pursuing versions of this approach. I have focused on Indianapolis because it was early and remains an exemplar. For a more detailed account of the Indianapolis experience, see Husock (1995); and Peirce (1995). For a discussion of some others, see Osborne and Gaebler (1992, chapter 3).

nomic development programs may become more ingenious but unemployment rates increase. In addition, many outcomes emerge gradually. When will the time be ripe to evaluate the outcomes of current investments in preschool education or in the amelioration of global warming? And others can never be proven. Did the Reagan administration military buildup, for example, hasten the end of the cold war? How much more time, if any, would Americans need to accomplish their travel objectives if the interstate highway system had never been built? Finally, outcomes include the unintended as well as intended, so efforts to appraise them can often intensify controversy. Do environmental programs merely improve public health and amenity, or do they also divert economic activity to other countries? Do welfare programs merely alleviate hardship, or do they also generate dependency and family breakup?

Despite these obstacles, numerous efforts have been made over the years to bring outcome evaluation into the mainstream of government. And some have even enjoyed a brief vogue—for example, planning program budgeting (PPB). But each has quickly lost its luster. The analytic burden of supporting every expenditure category with a serious evaluation is insupportable, and agencies in charge of their own evaluations almost invariably arrive at positive findings. These methods have been cast as "inside" management tools, moreover, and they have lacked any significant external constituency. So it has been easy, as their limitations have become apparent and their original political advocates have moved on, to discard rather than refine them. Some evaluation activity has remained, but it has generally focused on small, social program initiatives and had virtually no impact on overall government priorities.

To alter this state of affairs may be impossible, except by concentrating the analytic effort on a limited number of outcome objectives about which public constituencies care intensely. The contemporary initiative that builds most squarely on this insight is Oregon Benchmarks.[36]

Oregon Benchmarks emerged from a strategic planning process initiated in the late 1980s by Governor Neil Goldschmidt. The resulting plan, prepared with input from seventeen citizen advisory panels and published in May 1989, recommended that the state develop and focus sharply on measurable indicators of progress toward its strategic objec-

---

36. The following account is based primarily on an unpublished 1994 report by Robert D. Behn, prepared for the Ford Foundation and John F. Kennedy School of Government Program on Innovations in State and Local Government, and attachments thereto. Oregon Benchmarks did win an Innovations award that year.

tives. Governor Goldschmidt promptly created a new agency, the Oregon Progress Board, to implement this recommendation. Following extensive further public consultation, the Progress Board proposed 158 indicators to the Oregon Legislature, with benchmark targets for 1995, 2000, and 2010. For example, the Oregon teen pregnancy rate (per thousand females aged ten through seventeen) had been 24.7 in 1980 and 19.5 in 1990. The benchmark proposals were 9.8 in 1995, 8.0 in 2000, and 8.0 in 2010. The legislature adopted these proposals in 1991 and two subsequent revisions (with 279 and 259 benchmarks, respectively) in 1993 and 1995.

With the growing number of benchmarks, the need for prioritization was increasingly apparent. In its December 1992 report, the Progress Board delineated "core" and "urgent" benchmarks from the rest. The former were intended to provide "fundamental, enduring measures of Oregon's vitality and health," while the latter were meant to highlight critical short-term objectives. For example, the core group included benchmarks dealing with crime rates and manufacturing export performance. The urgent group included targets for the educational achievement levels of Oregon schoolchildren and compliance with federal air quality standards. In 1996 Oregon had twenty-three core and twenty urgent benchmarks.[37]

When Barbara Roberts assumed the governorship in 1991, she adopted the benchmarks system and organized her budget preparation process around it. Soon legislative committees as well began pressing state agency representatives to demonstrate that their activities were cost-effective in achieving key benchmarks. Local governments, industry associations, foundations, and churches began using the approach, too, often adopting particular state benchmarks as priorities for their own civic action. None of this would have been possible in the absence of an aggressive outreach effort to engage organizations and citizens in the state's own benchmark deliberations.[38]

The process of establishing benchmark targets, in short, has been essentially political; that is, more about the articulation of societal aspi-

37. These had been recommended to the legislation in Oregon Progress Board (1994).
38. One consequence of this emphasis on constituency relations has been the establishment of some unrealistic targets. The teen pregnancy rate, for example, which was 24.7 in 1980 and 19.5 in 1990, has a benchmark target of 8.0 for the year 2000. Unless the benchmark-setting process evolves over time to distinguish more consistently between aspirations and serious targets, this tendency may well diminish the potential of the benchmarks to serve as action-forcing stimuli and focal points of policy debate.

rations and the nurturance of constituency support than about analyzing existing programs. In this, it differs greatly from PPB and other "inside" management strategies (for example, zero-based budgeting and management by objectives) with the proclaimed objective of focusing attention on outcomes.

Once key elected officials and constituency groups became committed to benchmark-focused management, technical challenges did come to the fore. State agencies, accustomed to justifying their activities in terms of input and output trends (for example, costs are not rising very fast; the number of police on the street has increased by 5 percent over the past year), are now pressed to explain how they plan to realize target outcomes.

To meet this challenge, and thereby to compete effectively for resources, they must rethink their operations and the indicators on which they have traditionally relied. The first challenge may spur them to innovate. The second may spur them to devise output measures that are not only suitable for day-to-day management use—because they are easily and quickly measurable, and because they are indisputably functions of agency activity—but that are also demonstrably related to priority outcome indicators.

Among its numerous offshoots, the benchmark process became the basis in 1994 for a federal-state demonstration project known as the Oregon Option. The purpose of this effort is to refocus federally aided service delivery in the field of human investment—consolidating funding categories, suspending numerous rules and paperwork requirements, and concentrating instead on holding the state accountable for achieving target outcomes. Though still at a very early stage, the Oregon Option is being closely watched nationally as an important test of the potential of outcome-oriented management.[39]

The Prospects for Bureaucratic Innovation

In sum, American policy elites and the general public are deeply ambivalent about the desirability of bureaucratic innovation in the public sector. Innovation suggests discretion, and discretion has long been perceived as the antithesis of democratic accountability. However, broad

39. Governor Roberts chose not to seek reelection in 1994, but Oregon Benchmarks continues to thrive under her successor, John Kitzhaber. It is generally agreed to have matured beyond the point of being identified with any single administration.

agreement exists on the need to improve government performance. It is hard to imagine how that can be achieved without both encouraging public servants at all levels to take responsibility for performance and giving them some leeway to pursue it. In turn, it is difficult to imagine how incentives can be altered to encourage such innovation unless elected officials first become convinced that it is compatible with their own political interests.

Business, where the concern with keeping employees focused on institutional objectives is certainly no less than in government, has found a solution to this set of quandaries. It is simultaneous loose-tight organization, which combines strong central guidance on core values with broad employee discretion in pursuing them. At its best, this strategy enables top managers to unleash the talents of their subordinates, confident that they will be judged in the end on the basis of overall performance instead of particular failures.

Numerous obstacles arise to applying this strategy in the public sector, but two in particular stand out. First, evaluation systems in the public sector, driven by media and electoral competition, are far more haphazard than in business and much less forgiving of isolated failures. Second, elected officials typically know and trust their subordinates far less than do senior executives and board members in private corporations.

Candidates for elective office, including incumbents, do have strong incentives to associate themselves with fresh ideas. The ideas most likely to further their careers, however, share three characteristics. They enjoy or seem likely to attract constituency support. They unite voters—or at least those voters to whom a candidate hopes to appeal. And they are sufficiently general to insulate elected officials if implementation attracts intense criticism.

Thus the innovations with greatest appeal to elected officials are typically meta-innovations—umbrella strategies rather than particular efforts to address highly specific problems. Meta-innovations can tap effectively into popular themes of American culture (for example, that ordinary consumers benefit when providers have to compete) and promise to address macro problems that people believe are urgent (for example, excessive government costs). If they envision broad delegation of authority to originate innovative ideas, while preserving final authority to authorize adoption in the hands of elected officials, they can minimize conflict with the traditional, discretion-phobic ideology of American public administration. And if cast (as they tend to be) in highly general terms, they can leave elected officials with ample freedom to join the attackers whenever specific implementation errors occur.

The six meta-innovations highlighted above may or may not prove to be harbingers of a shift in the fundamental paradigm of American public management toward performance and innovation. If such a transformation does occur in the coming decades, however, it is most likely to arrive via meta-innovations of this type—those that attract support because their themes are mainstream, that are sufficiently general to provide politicians with a modicum of comfort, that are essentially neutral with respect to programmatic purposes, and that encourage innovation in ways that arguably enhance democratic accountability.

References

Altshuler, Alan A., and José A. Gómez-Ibáñez. 1993. *Regulation for Revenue: The Political Economy of Land Use Exactions.* Brookings.

Barzelay, Michael. 1992. *Breaking Through Bureaucracy: A New Vision for Managing in Government.* University of California Press.

Behn, Robert D. 1994. "The Massachusetts Department of Revenue." Teaching Case. Duke University, Governors Center.

Berry, Jeffrey M., Kent E. Portney, and Ken Thomson. 1989. "Empowering and Involving Citizens." In *Handbook of Public Administration,* 1st ed., edited by James L. Perry, 208–22. Jossey-Bass.

Donahue, John D. 1989. *The Privatization Decision: Public Ends, Private Means.* Basic Books.

Edwards, George C. 1980. *Implementing Public Policy.* Congressional Quarterly Press.

Fountain, Jane, and others. 1994. *Customer Service Excellence: Using Information Technologies to Improve Service Delivery in Government.* Harvard University, John F. Kennedy School of Government, Strategic Computing and Telecommunications Program.

Gómez-Ibáñez, José A., and John R. Meyer. 1995. "Private Toll Roads in the United States: Recent Experiences and Prospects." In *Transport and Urban Development,* edited by David Banister. London: Chapman and Hall.

Hassel, Bryan. 1996. "Autonomy and Constraint in Charter School Programs." Working Paper. Harvard University, John F. Kennedy School of Government.

Heclo, Hugh. 1975. "OMB and the Presidency: The Problem of 'Neutral Competence.' " *Public Interest,* no. 38 (Winter): 80–98.

_____. 1977. *A Government of Strangers: Executive Politics in Washington.* Brookings.

Husock, Howard. 1995. "Organizing Competition in Indianapolis: Mayor Stephen Goldsmith and the Quest for Lower Costs." Case Program, parts A, B, and C. Harvard University, John F. Kennedy School of Government.

Janowitz, Morris. 1960. *The Professional Soldier: A Social and Political Portrait.* Free Press.

Kagan, Robert A. 1991. "Adversarial Legalism and American Government." *Journal of Policy Analysis and Management,* vol. 10, no. 3 (Summer): 369–406.

Kanter, Rosabeth Moss. 1983. *The Change Masters: Innovations for Productivity in the American Corporation.* Simon and Schuster.

Kaufman, Herbert. 1956. "Emerging Conflicts in the Doctrines of Public Administration." *American Political Science Review,* vol. 50, no. 4 (December): 1057–73.

_____. 1960. *The Forest Ranger: A Study in Administrative Behavior.* Johns Hopkins Press.

_____. 1981. "Fear of Bureaucracy: A Raging Pandemic." *Public Administration Review,* vol. 41, no. 1 (January/February): 1–9.

Langton, Stuart, ed. 1978. *Citizen Participation in America: Essays on the State of the Art.* Lexington, Mass.: Lexington Books.

Levin, Martin A., and Mary Bryna Sanger. 1994. *Making Government Work: How Entrepreneurial Executives Turn Ideas into Real Results,* 1st ed. Jossey-Bass.

Lipsky, Michael E. 1979. *Street-Level Bureaucracy: Dilemmas of the Individual in Public Service.* New York: Russell Sage Foundation.

Lowi, Theodore J. 1979. *The End of Liberalism: The Second Republic of the United States.* W. W. Norton.

Moore, Mark Harrison. 1995. *Creating Public Value: Strategic Management in Government.* Harvard University Press.

Mosher, Frederick C. 1982. *Democracy and the Public Service,* 2d ed. New York: Oxford University Press.

Moynihan, Daniel P. 1970. *Maximum Feasible Misunderstanding.* Free Press.

National Center for Education Statistics. 1995. *Use of School Choice.* Publication NCES 95-742R (June). U.S. Department of Education.

Oregon Progress Board. 1994. *Oregon Benchmarks: Report to the 1995 Legislature.* Salem, Ore.: Oregon Progress Board.

Osborne, David E., and Ted Gaebler. 1992. *Reinventing Government: How the Entrepreneurial Spirit Is Transforming the Public Sector.* Reading, Mass.: Addison-Wesley.

Peirce, Neal R. 1995. "Here's an Alternative to Privatizing." *National Journal,* no. 47 (November 25): 2939.

Peters, Thomas J., and Robert H. Waterman. 1982. *In Search of Excellence: Lessons from America's Best-Run Companies,* 1st ed. Harper and Row.

Peterson, Paul E., and Chad Noyes. 1996. "Under Extreme Duress, School Choice." Occasional Paper 96-1. Harvard University, Program in Education Policy and Governance.

Polsby, Nelson W. 1984. *Political Innovation in America: The Politics of Policy Initiation.* Yale University Press.

Rosenbaum, Walter A. 1978. "Public Involvement as Reform and Ritual: The Development of Federal Participation Programs." In *Citizen Participation in America,* edited by Stuart Langton, chapter 7. Lexington, Mass.: Lexington Books.

Rourke, Francis E. 1984. *Bureaucracy, Politics, and Public Policy,* 3d ed. Little Brown.

Rubinstein, Jonathan. 1973. *City Police.* Farrar, Straus, and Giroux.

Savas, Emanuel S. 1987. *Privatization: The Key to Better Government.* Chatham, N.J.: Chatham House.

Selznick, Philip. 1984. *Leadership in Administration: A Sociological Interpretation.* University of California Press.

Skolnick, Jerome H. 1975. *Justice without Trial: Law Enforcement in Democratic Society,* 1st ed. John Wiley and Sons.

Smith, Preston G., and Donald G. Reinertsen. 1991. *Developing Products in Half the Time.* Van Nostrand Reinhold.

Smith, Steven Rathgeb, and Michael Lipsky. 1993. *Nonprofits for Hire: The Welfare State in the Age of Contracting.* Harvard University Press.

Sparrow, Malcolm K. 1994. *Imposing Duties: Government's Changing Approach to Compliance.* Westport, Conn.: Praeger.

Stone, Merlin. 1976. *Product Planning: An Integrated Approach.* Wiley.

Taylor, Humphrey. 1996. *Americans More Alienated Than at Any Time in Last Thirty Years.* Louis Harris and Associates.

U.S. Department of Education. 1996. "A Look at Charter Schools." Background Paper for Satellite Town Meeting (March 19).

Utterback, James M. 1994. *Mastering the Dynamics of Innovation: How Companies Can Seize Opportunities in the Face of Technological Change.* Harvard Business School Press.

Varley, Pamela. 1987. *Ellen Schall and the Department of Juvenile Justice* Case C16-87-793.0. Harvard University, John F. Kennedy School of Government.

Wilson, James Q. 1992. *American Government: Institutions and Policies,* 5th ed. Lexington, Mass.: D. C. Heath.

CHAPTER THREE

Innovation and Public Management:
Notes from the State House and City Hall

Alan A. Altshuler and Marc D. Zegans

THE MOST SUCCESSFUL ENTERPRISES are generally marked by a capacity for continuous, high-quality innovation. This idea has taken firm hold in the world of business. Managing so as to nurture innovation has come to be perceived as perhaps the single greatest challenge of business leadership.

In the public sector, by contrast, innovation tends to be viewed with considerable ambivalence. Widespread support exists for programs of scientific and technical research, intended to undergird the nation's competitiveness and to overcome dread diseases. But limited appreciation is evident of the value of innovation across the spectrum of government activity. Nor is there easy acceptance of the view that civil servants as well as elected officials have legitimate roles to play as public innovators.

The case for innovation, however, is no less urgent in the public than the private sector. Although voters, since the late seventies, have been highly resistant to new taxes, their service demands have continued to

This chapter was originally published as Altshuler, Alan, and Marc D. Zegans. 1990. "Innovation and Creativity: Comparisons between Public Management and Private Enterprise." *Cities,* vol. 7, no. 1 (February): 16–24. Used with permission from Elsevier Science Ltd., The Boulevard, Langford Lane, Kidlington OX5 1GB, UK.

We are deeply indebted to several colleagues and students on whose ideas and comments we have drawn in framing this paper, including Michael Barzelay, Olivia Golden, Steven Jenkins, Steven Miller, Mark Moore, and Michael O'Hare at the John F. Kennedy School of Government, and Babak Armajani, deputy commissioner of revenue for the state of Minnesota.

escalate. Thus pressure intensifies to accomplish more with less. The problems they want solved—from the decline of the family to the crack epidemic to global ozone depletion—are ever more complicated and continuously, often rapidly, evolving. Citizens are also demanding more personalized service. They feel aggrieved if bureaucrats treat their problems mechanically, by the book, instead of with sensitivity to their unique concerns.

So, to be deemed effective, governments in the modern era must be highly adaptive—to changing demands, problem configurations, and possibilities. Like physicians, moreover, they must find ways to deal with the particular needs of individual clients even as they seek principles of equity applicable to all clients.

The following discussion emerges from our involvement in the Program on Innovations in American Government, an ongoing joint venture of the Ford Foundation and Harvard University's John F. Kennedy School of Government. The program objectives are to identify valuable innovations at all levels of American government, to publicize them as sources of inspiration for other prospective innovators, and to develop curricular materials that may prove useful in training public officials to approach missions creatively. It includes both an annual competition and a program of research. Each of the ten annual winners in the competition receives a cash grant of $100,000 from the Ford Foundation, to be used for purposes of program enhancement or dissemination. The intellectual agenda of the Innovation program has two main components: to pursue greater understanding of the dynamics of innovation in American government, and to clarify thought about the place of innovation in the context of American public values.

Learning from Business (or Not)

Reflecting the dominance of private enterprise values in American society, American ideas about public management have generally been drawn from the world of business.[1] During the heyday of family enterprise, with its patterns of nepotism and personal favoritism, the spoils system ruled supreme. With the rise of corporate capitalism, formal budget, accounting, and personnel systems came into vogue, along with

1. Miller (1989).

such ideas as professional city management. When scientific management and assembly line production dominated thought about business administration, the politics-administration dichotomy dominated thought about governmental management. In each case, the idea was that action throughout large organizations should be in accord with strict rules, specified in detail by those at the top.

Not surprisingly, as concern about innovation swept the world of business in the eighties, it began to filter into thought about governmental performance. But the migration of management ideas from business to the public sector is by no means invariant. The answers to four questions affect its timing and character in specific circumstances.

First, how satisfied are citizens with current levels of government performance? By their votes and their opinion-poll responses, American citizens have in recent years conveyed a strong sense of dissatisfaction. A widespread sense exists that public agencies utilize resources inefficiently, that they are stuck in outmoded routines, that they are insensitive to citizen concerns, and that they are run more for the benefit of employees than clients. The result, other things being equal, should be high receptivity to new management ideas.

Second, how compatible is the proposed reform with prevailing managerial incentives? The answer to this question is far less favorable to innovation as a theme of public management reform. Business innovation is driven mainly by competition. The stick is fear of business failure; the carrot, wealth. Investors and boards of directors track market share and financial results continuously. Managerial rewards, both positive and negative, are tied closely to indicators of bottom-line performance. Great care is taken to match authority with responsibility, to recruit and nurture talent, and to ensure that those who venture and succeed are handsomely rewarded. Bureaucratic resistance to change is common, but it often crumbles in the face of declining market share and profit margins.

Most competition in the public sphere, by contrast, is electoral. This does inspire many politicians to welcome new ideas. If they are not so novel as to invite media ridicule, and if they respond to important constituency demands, fresh ideas can be a significant political resource. Public agencies, meanwhile, are typically monopolists within their specified jurisdictions, with management systems that provide few stimuli for innovation. Their "bottom lines" are difficult or impossible to measure. Little attention is paid to recruiting and nurturing talent. Managerial rewards for success are, with rare exceptions, purely psychic. Penalties, though, can be severe. Legislative overseers and the media tend to focus on examples of egregious behavior, however isolated, and invariably arrive at the same lesson: New control mechanisms should be adopted. So the cumulative pattern of "good government" reform has been to restrict bureaucratic discretion ever more tightly.[2] The message to managers is that their highest priority should be to minimize the risk of embarrassing incidents, rather than to optimize overall performance.

Third, how compatible is the proposed reform with fundamental public attitudes? Again, the answer with respect to innovation as a theme of public management reform is "not very." Two basic obstacles are evident: public ambivalence about whether government managers have any business aspiring to innovate, and public resistance to the kind of decentralized, free-wheeling administration that seems most conducive to innovation in the private sector.

Conventional wisdom in business holds that innovation tends to bubble up from the ranks. Top management can establish a favorable context. It has critical roles to play as well in screening new ideas, nurturing those that seem promising through their development stages, and where appropriate bringing them to market. But the early phases of innovation tend to involve tinkering and experimentation by employees in the ranks. Useful product innovations are most likely to be initiated by employees in close touch with customers, who typically have both unmet needs and gripes about existing products. Useful ideas about improving production processes are most likely to come from those who spend their days producing.

The key lesson that has emerged in the private sector is that successful companies imbue their employees with a broad sense of purpose and then give them wide day-to-day latitude. Such companies also convey the message to employees that standing pat is not a viable strategy. The competition is constantly coming up with better or cheaper products. Thus it is essential to be venturesome. Nothing risked, nothing gained. Those who risk, though, often fail. So an essential feature of the innovative company is high tolerance for well-conceived failure, combined with powerful rewards for success.[3]

A central premise of this administrative strategy is that employees allowed broad discretion generally concentrate on pursuing company

2. Barzelay and Armajani (1990); and Moore (1988).
3. Kanter (1988, pp. 179–83).

objectives, and do so more effectively than if tightly controlled from above. This premise is foreign to traditional American ways of thinking about public administration. In practice, close observers of the governmental process understand that discretion is everywhere. The police cannot give equal priority to every type of crime. Teachers must tailor their interactions with each student. Driving test examiners must judge who passes. To say that some discretion is inevitable, though, is far from saying that it is desirable. The predominant American view has been that public administrators should not be entrusted with any more discretion than absolutely necessary. Fear of abuse far outweighs any faith in the potential benefits of unleashing bureaucratic ingenuity.

Fourth, how compatible is the proposed reform with the interests of powerful constituencies? Here again the answer tends to be negative. Specific innovations often attract favorable balances of constituency support, but the general theme inspires suspicion across the political spectrum. Conservatives fear bureaucratic aggrandizement. Liberals fear agency capture by special interests and civil liberties abuses. Minorities fear discrimination. Good government groups fear corruption.

The upshot is that, while business leaders are focusing today on innovation as a key to competitive success, government policymakers are preoccupied with damage control. Whereas business leaders delegate more and more broadly, public leaders impose new procedural safeguards, layers of oversight, and provisions for judicial review. Whereas business managers search avidly for new ideas, public managers take refuge in the familiar. They are threatened not by program weaknesses per se, but by political and media criticism, and they are most likely to attract such criticism if they stand out.

What is remarkable in this context is that so many public employees do strive to innovate. We cannot begin to quantify their number or proportion. The Innovations awards competitions have just scratched the surface. Examples cannot demonstrate frequency. They can indicate, however, that a phenomenon is reasonably common. Our experience in the Innovations program suggests, at very least, that the ideal of creative accomplishment is widespread in American public service. Substantial numbers of public employees take for granted that they are paid to exercise initiative, not merely to carry out established routines. This is central to their job satisfaction and self-esteem. The more venturesome among them seem motivated by their clients, their missions, and their personal (including professional) values far more than by organizational incentives. Within the framework of prevailing legal constraints, they feel driven to find better ways of carrying out their assigned missions— whether to improve the parenting skills of low-income mothers, to provide safe shelter for homeless adults, or to arrange for environmentally sound waste disposal. Do they often end up seeking expanded mandates and resource allocations? Yes, but they succeed only when constituencies mobilize in support and elective authorities concur.

Terms of Discourse

Making headway in thinking about public sector innovation is difficult without defining a few key terms.

An innovation consists of at least two elements: a fresh idea, and its expression in a practical course of action. The idea may be an invention (if it is a product of creativity) or a discovery (if it has been found in nature or in some wider human environment). The innovator, who may or may not have generated the idea, contributes the effective linkage of the fresh idea to a practical problem or objective. Thus we find it useful to think of innovation as novelty in action.

Innovative programs typically consist of a mix of novel and familiar components, with the latter more numerous. The element of novelty may be a service concept, a technology, a way of putting the components together, or some combination of these. When the novel element, whether invented or discovered, is sufficiently important as to render the whole notably different from what has gone before, we speak of an innovation. The degree to which it is innovative must be appraised on the basis of the character of the whole rather than any mechanical accounting (if such were possible) of the parts.

Specific innovations are typically discussed as though each had a fixed form. In practice, however, most innovations are constantly evolving, and any description must be understood as a snapshot. Like children, they tend to evolve most rapidly when youngest and to evolve in different ways at different times. Regarding industrial innovation, William J. Abernathy and James M. Utterback note that phases of product innovation tend to be followed, as a dominant product design stabilizes, by stages of (cost-reducing) process innovation.[4] One can observe analo-

4. Abernathy and Utterback (1978).

gous patterns in the public sector, with the caveat that production processes resist standardization far more than those in manufacturing. When diffusion occurs, it generally involves considerable adaptation in each jurisdiction to fit local conditions. Thus diffusion should be understood in terms of core ideas, with wide variation upon the overall program pattern.

Our interest in appraisal stemmed initially from our need for Innovations award selection criteria. We became increasingly aware, however, that as scholars, too, we needed a systematic approach to appraisal—as a basis for categorizing innovations and as a means of sifting through the multitudes of candidates for study.

Quantification is usually impossible in this arena, so our primary aim in defining criteria has been conceptual clarity. We have also found that raters could not keep large numbers of criteria in mind. As a result, we now concentrate on just four: novelty, quality, significance, and replicability.

NOVELTY. How great a leap of creativity was required to generate this new program or process? At one extreme, did it entail great ingenuity, perhaps even a kind of genius? At the other, did it represent pedestrian tinkering at the margins of previous practice?

QUALITY. How clear and profound are the net benefits for those affected, regardless of how many or few they are? The issue here is value within the domain of impact, as opposed to magnitude of impact.

In estimating benefits, the focus is primarily on value for clients, as opposed to, for example, providers, politicians, and interest group representatives. This approach was developed primarily with an eye toward human service programs and fits them most comfortably. Even in human service programs, however, room often exists for controversy about how to define clientele. Does it consist of active clients only or also of potential clients within the target population? How broad is the target population? Should it be conceived more broadly? In practice, many public innovations entail reaching out to new clients.

As one moves beyond the human service arena, client identification becomes even more complex. Some programs have diffuse clienteles, most of whom never come into direct contact with the agency (such as the beneficiaries of environmental regulation and criminal incarceration). Some that do have discrete clienteles are valued as much for their indirect benefits as those that accrue to users directly (for example, public education). In evaluating such programs, value judgments may have to be imputed to clients who are largely indifferent or who, like the unborn and murder victims, cannot speak for themselves. How to determine the value of such programs remains debatable. The quality criterion as here defined does not resolve this conundrum, but it highlights the need for evaluators to treat it explicitly.

SIGNIFICANCE. What is the magnitude of impact? Again the emphasis here is on the client perspective insofar as possible. Subelements include numbers of beneficiaries, geographic scope, and the range of services affected.

REPLICABILITY. The focus here is on effects beyond the immediate jurisdiction and current time. Some innovations, as observed in their setting of origin, have the potential to inspire widespread emulation. Others are so profoundly adapted to unique local circumstances that it is hard to imagine what might be transferable.

This criterion is most useful when one can already see evidence of diffusion beyond the site or program of origin. Forecasting, however, tends to be perilous. It was commonly believed not long ago that, while Japanese management practices were highly effective in their home setting, they were unlikely to prove applicable in Western settings. As Japanese companies have built plants in the West, however, it has become clear that many of their practices—for example, reductions in status symbolism between managers and production workers, quality circles, just-in-time production, long-run ties with suppliers, and enhanced job security for employees—have very broad applicability.

However, replication is often surprisingly difficult within a single culture. Consider the case of One Church, One Child, a 1986 Innovations award winner. This program, enormously successful in its home state, was initiated by the Illinois Department of Child and Family Services (DCFS). Utilizing black churches as allies and instruments of community outreach, the program aggressively recruits families to adopt hard-to-place African American children. Following publicity about its early success, officials in numerous other states expressed interest in reproducing the program. DCFS received federal and Ford Foundation grants to help it market the program nationally and provide technical assistance to counterpart agencies. Interest ran so high that DCFS could, for a time, not keep up with the requests for technical assistance. Several states now have implemented variants of the program with success, but efforts in others have foundered. Suitable champions were lacking; key actors could not overcome differences in viewpoint about how the program should be administered; top management turnover set progress at key moments back to square one.[5]

In short, replication of any but the simplest technical innovation is rarely mechanical. Emulators are required to innovate as well, though less profoundly in most cases than those from whom they take their inspiration.

Sources and Strategies of State and Local Innovation

Our research thus far is highly exploratory, but some clear impressions have begun to emerge. We view them as hypotheses, not definitive findings, but we share a few of them here as indicative of our general approach and in a spirit of continuing inquiry.

Where do the ideas providing the original spark for innovation originate? Overwhelmingly, the award-winning programs in the Innovations program competitions have been based upon discovery rather than invention. The discoveries, moreover, have generally been unsystematic, typically involving one person or a small group drawing upon past experiences or informal communications with colleagues in other settings. Following initial conception, the ideas have generally been tried out quickly in practice and have subsequently evolved via trial and error, not formal experimentation or analysis.[6] Given that state and local governments almost never invest in research and development, this pattern was perhaps to be expected. We have been a bit surprised, though, by the meager role of systematic policy analysis at any stage of the process.

Practitioners may draw two lessons from these observations. First, one does not have to be an Edison to innovate successfully. One simply has to be on the lookout for promising ideas, perceptive about how they might be utilized in one's own program context, and skilled at making the connections. Second, environmental scanning is a powerful source of innovative capacity.

What is novel about the most notable state and local innovations? The Innovations program award winners have been as likely to involve a reconception of mission and clientele as to involve a new service concept or technology. The prime initiators have typically combined some

5. Jenkins (1989).
6. Golden (1990).

recently acquired idea with a long-standing perception of need. The perception of need, almost invariably, has been deeply rooted in practice and frustration.

The initiators are extremely varied. The public servants among them are more likely to be working at the level of direct client contact than to be senior managers. Senior managers who spark innovation are likely to be recent recruits, often from outside of government. Some initiators are private citizens, who actively seek out public sector allies and then, at times, enter public service to participate in carrying out their innovations. Some innovations, finally, are sparked by efforts to achieve public-private partnerships and go forward as fully joint efforts.

A few illustrations follow. The Family Learning Center of Leslie, Michigan, a 1986 Innovations award winner, provides a continuum of educational and social services for teen-aged mothers. The innovator was a local private citizen who brought her idea to the school board. When it was reluctant to provide space or funding, she identified state funding and space in a local church. She entered public service to run the program. Gradually she identified additional client needs and found resources to achieve substantial increases in the number of clients served and the range of services provided. She also achieved program acceptance over time as an integral part of the local school system.

The Kentucky Parent and Child Project, a 1987 award winner, emerged primarily as a result of car-pool conversations between two professional employees of the state education department. It involves educational programs under the same roof for low-income mothers and their young children, with significant attention paid to enhancing the quality of parent-child interaction. This program, with the championship of a powerful legislative ally, is now rapidly expanding across Kentucky and into other states.

The Minnesota Strive Toward Excellence in Performance (STEP) Program, a 1986 award winner, was sparked by a new, politically appointed top manager with the active support of an incoming governor. It originated in the state Department of Administration and is process-oriented. That is, it is concerned with the quality and efficiency of service delivery instead of with generating new programs. Its essence is the involvement of employees throughout the ranks in rethinking service delivery strategies, a shift in the balance of organizational incentives toward innovation, and high-visibility recognition for those who participate in launching successful innovations.

The Integration Assistance Program in east suburban Cleveland, a 1988 Innovations award winner, evolved over a period of years via the collaboration of private homeowners and realtors, local elected officials, and a senior manager hired from outside the community. Eventually one of the citizen activists entered public service himself as director of the implementing agency. The One Church, One Child program is another prime example of an innovation that evolved through intensive public-private collaboration—in this case, between state officials responsible for services to children and a group of African American clergymen.

How do successful innovators surmount the massive obstacles to public sector innovation? Specific strategies vary widely, but the most salient fall into several broad categories.

First, they proceed incrementally. Numerous cases exist of creative adaptation, but few, if any, great leaps forward are recorded in the files of the Innovations program.

Second, they act to alleviate problems that are widely recognized as urgent, and they are adept at explaining the connection.

Third, they are close to their clients and can count on a preponderance of positive messages to political authorities from them.

Fourth, they cast their nets widely in search of support, and they are ingenious in linking their efforts to sources of funding and institutional capacity that have not previously been applied toward the missions with which they are concerned.

Fifth, they are skilled at building and sustaining networks that embrace the various centers of authorizing and implementation capacity that are essential to success. One aspect of such network building is the recruitment of champions who can bring specific groups and institutions into the fold. Success in this endeavor generally requires considerable openness to the views of coalition partners and a willingness to share credit widely.

Sixth, successful innovators are open to feedback. They recognize innovation as a process of continuous learning and adaptation.

Finally, they are tenacious, passionately committed, and optimistic. More often than not they experience major setbacks along the way to success and long periods without recognition or apparent progress. They (and others whose support they need) are typically sustained during these periods by their profound sense of mission and of conviction that right will triumph in the end.

Creativity and Accountability

Few modern institutions can achieve excellence on the basis of top-down innovation alone. American society is ambivalent, however, about public employee creativity. While electoral incentives drive many politicians to champion fresh ideas, managerial incentives tend to discourage initiative in the ranks.

Numerous public servants, at all levels, innovate nonetheless. Spurred mainly by professionalism and commitment to mission, often in the face of negative incentives, they account for much that is praiseworthy in American government. Their ability to view problems afresh, to spot relevant ideas in domains outside their own, and to adapt them for application in new contexts constitutes a vital resource. The challenge for academics and practitioners alike is to identify means of unleashing such creativity in ways compatible with essential norms of democratic accountability.

References

Abernathy, William J., and James M. Utterback. 1978. "Patterns of Industrial Innovation." *Technology Review,* vol. 80 (June/July): 41–47.

Barzelay, Michael, and Babak J. Armajani. 1990. "Managing State Government Operations: Changing Visions of Staff Agencies." *Journal of Policy Analysis and Management,* vol. 9, no. 3 (Summer): 307–38.

Golden, Olivia. 1990. "Innovation in Public Sector Human Services Programs: The Implications of Innovation by 'Groping Along.'" *Journal of Policy Analysis and Management,* vol. 9, no. 2 (Spring): 219–48.

Kanter, Rosabeth Moss. 1988. "When a Thousand Flowers Bloom: Structural, Collective, and Social Conditions for Innovation in Organization." *Research in Organizational Behavior,* vol. 10: 169–211.

Jenkins, Steven. 1989. "Dissemination of Innovations: Lessons from the Experience of One Church, One Child." Innovations Program Working Paper. Harvard University, John F. Kennedy School of Government.

Miller, Steven E. 1989. "The Emergence of the Public Sector as the Focus of Value-Creating Partnerships: Roots of a New Vision." Innovations Program Working Paper. Harvard University, John F. Kennedy School of Government.

Moore, Mark H. 1988. "Small Scale Statesmen: A Normative Conception of the Role and Functions of Public Management in Contemporary American Government." Paper prepared for the Third International Colloquium of the Journal *Politique et Management Publique*.

Part Two

INNOVATION AND ORGANIZATION

CHAPTER FOUR

Innovation and the Public Interest
Insights from the Private Sector

Laurence E. Lynn, Jr.

INDUCING INNOVATION in public bureaucracies is a cause pursued with a sense of urgency. Society needs effective government, and public bureaucracies have proved disappointing for so long that change is essential. The cause, moreover, is bipartisan. Both liberals and conservatives favor innovative government, though their reasons differ. Conservatives expect the gains from innovation to be converted into tax reductions and less government. Liberals expect the gains to be converted into increases in the availability and quality of public services.

What can those concerned with creating innovation-inducing organizations in government learn from organizations that must survive in the marketplace? Innovation has been a concern of business leaders, consultants, and scholars for nearly four decades. Are there lessons from their experiences, reflections, and research that might help designers of public bureaucracies?

To most, innovative bureaucracies are agencies with an ongoing commitment to state-of-the-art performance in all phases of operation. From the executive level to the street level, personnel in such agencies are constantly searching for innovative ideas to improve performance, trying them out, and learning from their experience. They lead the organizational equivalent of "the examined life." They do not fear change, uncertainty, tight budgets, or ambiguous and conflicting mandates. Adversity is opportunity. The real danger is inertia.

Anything that moves a public agency closer to this ideal state might seem to warrant encouragement. At the least, society should publicize and reward exemplary agencies, offices, programs, and specific creative acts; celebrate transformational leaders and public employees who appear to be effective change agents; carefully document successes and disseminate the findings to other would-be innovators; and create a general climate that encourages innovators to thrive and multiply and innovations to diffuse throughout the governmental system. At the federal, state, and local level, public agencies are so far from the ideal state that promoting innovation in government for its own sake seems appropriate.

Improving governmental performance through innovation may not be so straightforward, however. A distressingly high "ephemerality rate" appears among innovations and innovators, and a randomness exists to long-term success. Evidence is available that organizational structures that encourage innovation proposals discourage their adoption. Political contexts differ widely in their receptivity to innovation—purposeful action can be so controversial that some public officials can be regarded as having "impossible jobs."[1] Thus change may be both risky and costly, and the way these risks and costs are distributed among political actors may induce a watering-down or distortion of proposed innovations that, in the end, discredits them.

Achieving Corporate Breakthroughs

In a 1986 study entitled *Breakthroughs!*, two senior consultants at Arthur D. Little, Inc., identified a dozen breakthroughs achieved by corporations worldwide.[2] Their book describes the processes whereby these breakthroughs—for example, Post-it Note Pads, Sony's Walkman, the microwave oven, Federal Express service, polypropylene—occurred. The lessons they derived from their case studies are, at least at first glance, surprising.

We have found no company that succeeded in developing an "environment for creativity" [and] . . . no "corporate culture" that is more felicitous to breakthroughs than any other culture. . . . New,

1. Hargrove and Glidewell (1990).
2. Nayak and Ketteringham (1986, p. 344).

extraordinary ideas can emerge from any environment. . . . Break-throughs are not organizational creations, although afterward they are eagerly claimed by organizations. . . . [They] are children not of the milieu, but of the mind.[3]

The authors reach another surprising conclusion. The popular notion that breakthroughs are a response to signals from the market is a myth. The source of each breakthrough concept is "a problem—an itch that its possessor cannot easily scratch."[4] Moreover, "always, the solution to the problem has little in common with the established order of things. . . . The definition of a breakthrough person is that he does not take the Establishment seriously."[5]

This characterization of the breakthrough process has important, if somewhat disturbing, implications for management. "The message seems to be that in many cases the best thing that can happen to a new idea is that management doesn't notice it until it is too late for management to kill it."[6] If anything distinguishes "breakthrough managers," the authors say, it is the measure of trust they convey to their people.[7] "Management actions that have fostered breakthroughs fall more accurately in the realm of 'responsiveness' rather than under the heading of 'management'. . . . There are both moments when traditional management can be terribly destructive and moments when responsive people in traditional management roles can save the concept from destroying itself."[8]

These kinds of insights do not imply the kind of smothering love that many foundations, management teachers, consultants, and journalists want to lavish on innovators. These authors are not endorsing Total Quality Management or "managing for innovation" or creating prizes for innovators. What is the difference, then, between what these authors see as the truth of innovation and the beliefs that motivate much recent interest in the subject?

The authors of *Breakthroughs!* themselves distinguish between breakthroughs and innovations. "Innovation," they say, "is the art of doing the same thing you are doing now but doing it better," applying new ideas to the fulfillment of and the concept of existing missions or mandates. A

3. Nayak and Ketteringham (1986, pp. 343, 344).
4. Nayak and Ketteringham (1986, p. 347).
5. Nayak and Ketteringham (1986, p. 348).
6. Nayak and Ketteringham (1986, p. 357).
7. Nayak and Ketteringham (1986, p. 358).
8. Nayak and Ketteringham (1986, pp. 345, 346).

breakthrough is "beyond innovation," an act of doing something so different that it cannot be compared with any existing practice or perception; that is, an invention, as that term is used in innovation research.[9]

By distinguishing breakthroughs from innovations, the authors mean to caution that truly transforming organizational change is, in a crucial respect, necessarily individual and intellectual and is, therefore, as unprogrammable in an instrumental sense as pathbreaking achievements in the arts or sciences.

Innovation and Markets

Two types of literature are concerned with innovation in business organizations. The first, didactic literature, is concerned primarily with prescription and is often a personal and subjective distillation from practical experience and observation. It has a message. The second employs the empirical methods of social science to explain the phenomenon of innovation in complex organizations. Prescriptions, if any, follow directly from systematically assembled evidence, not from intuitive leaps based on impressionistic, anecdotal material.

JUST DO IT. "Innovators," says Warren Bennis, "like all creative people, see things differently, think in fresh and original ways. They have useful contacts in other areas, other institutions; they are seldom seen as good organization men or women and often viewed as mischievous troublemakers."[10] So far, the ideas echo *Breakthroughs!* He goes on to say, however, that "the true leader not only is him- or herself an innovator but makes every effort to locate and use other innovators in the organization."[11] In an attempt to overcome the natural conservatism of any social system, "he or she creates a climate in which conventional wisdom can be questioned and challenged and one in which errors are embraced rather than shunned in favor of safe, low-risk goals."[12]

Innovation is a way of life in excellent companies, according to Thomas J. Peters and Robert H. Waterman in *In Search of Excellence*. Moreover, "most of their real innovation comes from the market."[13] The

9. Nayak and Ketteringham (1986, p. 344).
10. Bennis (1989, p. 29).
11. Bennis (1989, pp. 29–30).
12. Bennis (1989, p. 30).
13. Peters and Waterman (1982, p. 193).

authors quote an extensive study of innovation in the chemical and scientific instrument industries as concluding: "Successful innovators innovate in response to market needs, involve potential users in the development of the innovation, and understand user needs better."[14] They reject the notion that users, at least "lead users" who are near to the state of the art, want more of the same instead of true innovation. Innovation, they argue, results from being intensely close to your best customers.

"Outstanding competitors . . . understand that consistent innovation is the key to a company's survival," says Andrall E. Pearson. "Being innovative some of the time, in one or two areas, just won't work. . . . Competitive companies constantly look for ways to change every aspect of their businesses. Then, when they've found them, they make sure that they translate those changes into advantages customers will appreciate and act on."[15] He goes on to describe five steps "you can take to make your company more innovative:

—"Create a corporate environment that puts constant pressure on everyone to beat your specific competitors at innovation.

—"Structure your organization so that you promote innovation instead of thwarting it.

—"Develop a realistic strategic focus to channel your innovative efforts.

—"Know where to look for good ideas and how to use your business system to leverage them once they're found.

—"Throw the book at good ideas once you've developed them fully."[16]

Do you want innovation? Pearson is asking. Then lavish attention on it and make it happen.

Is it beginning to sound as if one's approach to innovation will depend on who one's management guru is? Perhaps social science will help.

THINK BEFORE LEAPING. The systematic study of innovation in the firm originated in a concern that business exploited scientific discoveries that were occurring at an accelerating rate during and after World War II. Such studies were also associated with the growing popularity of human relations approaches to organizations and with the advent of behaviorism in the social sciences.

It was quickly recognized that innovation meant change and that

14. Peters and Waterman (1982, p. 197).
15. Pearson (1988, p. 104).
16. Pearson (1988, p. 110).

change is a social process. For example, Philip Selznick observed in 1957 that "a company's decision to add a new product may be routine if the new is but an extension of the old. It is a critical decision, however, when it calls for a re-examination of the firm's mission and role. . . . The latter choice will inevitably affect the outlook of management, the structure and control of the company, and the balance of forces in the industry."[17]

A lengthy chapter of James G. March and Herbert A. Simon's *Organizations* is devoted to "Planning and Innovation in Organizations." "The rate of innovation is likely to increase," they argue, "when changes in the environment make the existing organizational procedures unsatisfactory" although "some innovation will result from accidental encounters with opportunities."[18] "The innovative process is not itself programmed," although it can be encouraged by "additional programmed stimuli" such as setting internal goals that require change and offering recognition and reward for changes.[19]

Carrying these ideas further, Tom Burns and G. M. Stalker observed, on the basis of their research into innovation in electronics firms in Great Britain, that "all novelty involves some degree of risk" and thus the potential for harm as well as gain. "The risks attendant upon change may have to be weighed against other risks arising from maintaining the same state of affairs."[20] To ensure some risk taking, they argue:

> What is essential is that nothing should inhibit individuals from applying to others for information and advice, or for additional effort. This in turn depends on the ability to suppress differences of status and of technical prestige on occasions of working interaction, and on the absence of barriers to communication founded on functional preserves, privilege, or personal reserve.[21]

The tendency must be resisted to program managerial decisions.

In the mid-1960s, James Q. Wilson and Harvey M. Sapolsky identified an important dilemma. Beginning with the conception of an organization as an economy of incentives that convenes around a set of tasks, Wilson was interested in explaining important innovations, which he defined as a "fundamental change in a 'significant' number of tasks."[22] He argued

17. Selznick (1984, p. 136).
18. March and Simon (1958, p. 183).
19. March and Simon (1958, p. 184).
20. Burns and Stalker (1961, p. 21).
21. Burns and Stalker (1961, p. 252).
22. Wilson (1966, p. 196).

that the factors that increase the probability that organizational participants will devise and present innovation proposals, namely diversity of
incentive and task structures (present, for example, when agency professionals have outside reference groups and unprogrammed tasks), are precisely those factors that decrease the probability that the organization
will adopt the proposals because a central authority that can and will
compel dissidents to fall in line is absent.

Sapolsky attempted to test this important proposition with data from a
group of department stores. He found that:

> Diversity in department store reward structures, specifically the
> increased professionalization of the retail controllers, led to the
> conceptualization of several important innovations. Diversity in
> department store task structures, or the autonomy of the control
> division in accounting matters, facilitated the presentation of inno-
> vational proposals. Yet diversity in department store structural
> arrangements, the decentralization of decision-making authority,
> and the existence of a large number of equally situated subunits
> frustrated attempts to implement these proposals.[23]

There appears, he concluded, to be no good way around this dilemma.

In their overview of a set of papers on organizational innovation in
the *Journal of Business,* Selwyn W. Becker and Thomas L. Whisler
argue that innovation is distinct from invention and "is fundamentally
a co-operative group action." To distinguish innovation from change or
adaptation, they suggest that innovation be defined as "the first or early
use of an idea by one of a set of organizations with similar goals." [24]
Among the meritorious ideas concerning innovation, they believe, are
the notion that "any proposal which would alter the organization itself
is more radical or difficult to accomplish than a proposal that does not
do so"; the distinction between "controllable" and "uncontrollable"
factors predisposing an organization toward innovation; and the argument, originating in the work of Wilson and Sapolsky, that diversity of
task and incentive structure stimulates innovation proposals but inhibits
their adoption—that is, diversity in subcultures stimulates proposals
and centralized authority leads to their acceptance.[25] The only thread of
agreement among diverse contributors, they argue, is that innovation is

---

23. Sapolsky (1967, p. 509).
24. Becker and Whisler (1967, p. 463).
25. Becker and Whisler (1967, p. 464).

a four-stage process involving stimulus, conception, proposal, and adoption.[26]

Roger D. Schroeder and his associates focused on the processes by which innovation ideas evolve and both shape and are shaped by the organization. Dissatisfied with various multistage models of innovation processes, they studied seven different organizational innovations, all but one in the private sector. They concluded that "innovation is stimulated by shocks"—such things as "new leadership, product failure, a budget crisis, and an impending loss of market share"—"either internal or external to the organization."[27] They identified a subtle, interactive innovation process that may lead to different outcomes: "The entire organization fundamentally changes direction as a result of the innovation, . . . the innovation can be . . . blended into the old organization, or . . . the old and new can coexist in parallel progression with linkages between the old and the new."[28]

One of the most comprehensive discussions of innovation in the corporate sector is that of Rosabeth Moss Kanter. In *The Change Masters: Innovations for Productivity in the American Corporation,* she identifies innovation as "the process of bringing any new, problem-solving idea into use. . . . It can involve creative use as well as original invention. Application and implementation are central to this definition; it involves the capacity to change or adapt."[29] Though a few quotations cannot do justice to the rich texture of Kanter's discussion of innovation, they can convey a sense of her argument.

"Innovating companies provide the freedom to act, which arouses the desire to act."[30] Managers who would stimulate innovation will not hide the organization's problems from its employees; they will share them. They will create broad job charters, overlapping turfs, ambiguous assignments, and substantial local autonomy and independence of higher levels of authority.[31] She cautions, however, that "hope of obtaining conventional rewards seems to play very little role in stimulating innovativeness."[32] An innovating company, Kanter argues, "begins to substitute a

---

26. Becker and Whisler (1967).
27. Schroeder and others (1989, p. 132).
28. Schroeder and others (1989, p. 132).
29. Kanter (1983, pp. 20–21).
30. Kanter (1983, p. 142).
31. Kanter (1983, p. 143).
32. Kanter (1983, p. 152).

control system based on debate among peers for one based on top-down authority" and the manipulation of financial inducements.[33]

But, Kanter notes, the Wilson and Sapolsky dilemma has not been banished. "Innovation . . . requires that the innovators get enough power to mobilize people and resources to get something *non-routine* done."[34] This is not a matter of exercising hierarchical authority. Innovation is not accomplished by command. It requires participation and coalitions to support its full implementation and will probably require the exercise of considerable political skill: bargaining, negotiating, collaborating, and so on.

Kanter places great emphasis on the "intellectual problem of understanding exactly why something works. . . . Behind every institutionalized practice is a theory about why things work as they do; the success and efficiency of the organization's use of the practice depend on the strength of that theory."[35] Otherwise, she says, innovation is no more than a "roast pig," referring to the discovery of roast pig: A house burned down in a village that cooked no food, and a roasted pig was discovered inside and found to smell and taste delicious, resulting in a rash of house fires and tasty meals.

"If innovation is a priority," says Gareth Morgan, "then flexible, dynamic, project-oriented matrix or organic forms of organization will be superior to the mechanistic-bureaucratic" form.[36] He cautions that "the deep structure of forces . . . sustain the status quo" and that

> many aspects of social and organizational culture and structure serve conscious and unconscious purposes that are invisible to the human eye. This means that they can be changed only if the underlying concerns and preoccupations are modified in some way. . . . People may build a dependency on some aspect of culture or social life that leads them to resist innovations that would undermine this dependency.[37]

Social science research concerned with identifying factors associated with high rates of innovation in complex organizations has produced few convergent or robust findings. Much of the work is descriptive rather than analytical, and little testing is done of specific propositions derived

33. Kanter (1983, p. 179).
34. Kanter (1983, p. 213).
35. Kanter (1983, pp. 301, 303).
36. Morgan (1986, p. 73).
37. Morgan (1986, p. 230).

from theory. Common sense suggests, for example, that inducing fundamental change in an organization is different from inducing change that
leaves existing modes of operation and distributions of influence relatively intact and that only the former qualify as innovations. Inducing
changes involving high-resource requirements is more problematic than
inducing low-cost change; budgetary constraints may stimulate innovation but bias its character and purposes. Unfortunately, theory is too
weak to permit the significance of these types of distinctions to be
explored in empirical work. Social science, then, sheds light but does not
reveal the shining path.

Innovation and Politics

In the late 1960s, Lawrence B. Mohr studied the determinants of innovation in ninety-three local departments of public health.[38] He defined
innovation as "the successful introduction into an applied situation of
means or ends that are new to that situation."[39] His empirical findings,
unfortunately, are neither robust nor particularly suggestive. Bigger organizations are more innovative than smaller ones, he concludes, though it
is not clear why. Moreover, "a great deal of innovation in organizations,
especially large or successful ones, [results from] the quest for prestige"
instead of a concern for effectiveness or profit.[40]

In the early 1970s, citing the Wilson and Sapolsky dilemma, Jerald
Hage and Robert Dewar studied innovation in sixteen health and welfare
organizations that provided rehabilitation services in a large midwestern
city.[41] Their objective was to determine the relative influence of "elite
values" (those of an inner circle of decisionmakers), leader values (those
of the executive director personally), member (employee) values, and
organizational structure (complexity, decentralization, formalization) on
the adoption of innovations. Innovation, they found, was most strongly
associated with the values of the inner circle. This influence was abetted
by a diversity of professional perspectives within the agency but not by
decentralization of authority per se.

38. Mohr (1969).
39. Mohr (1969, p. 112).
40. Mohr (1969, p. 126).
41. Hage and Dewar (1973).

Simply moving towards a more democratic power structure does have a small influence on innovation, presumably by allowing circulation of new ideas from various staff members, and perhaps by less blockage of innovative ideas. However, if the leader and the elite favor change, this is much more influential in innovation than decentralizing the power structure . . . The inclusion of more and more people into the decision-making process may tend to reduce possibilities for change, perhaps because of a greater likelihood for people to have different priorities.[42]

In the late 1980s, Olivia Golden examined innovation processes in seventeen human services programs cited by the 1986 Ford Foundation and John F. Kennedy School of Government Awards Program for Innovations in State and Local Government.[43] The criteria for designation as an innovation included creativity or inventiveness, adoption and implementation, program effectiveness, long-term and indirect impacts, and potential usefulness and adaptability to other jurisdictions.[44] Her purpose was to "distinguish between two models for successful innovation: a policy planning model and Behn's model of 'groping along.' "[45] She found that innovations by award recipients were not instrumental, top-down applications of well-formed ideas. They were, instead, a result of the ongoing, unprogrammed experience of learning from action directed at solving a problem. The raw material of innovation is not analysis and creativity in the abstract, but feedback from active change processes.[46]

In his book *Bureaucracy,* James Q. Wilson presents an updated version of his ideas on innovation. Organizations, he argues, are biased in favor of existing task definitions, and that is as it should be. Standard operating procedures are the purpose of organization, especially when constituencies demand explanations for particular case decisions. They will readily adopt new ideas that do not alter existing arrangements and resist all others. He defines innovation as "not any new program or technology, but only those that involve the performance of new tasks or a sig-

---

42. Hage and Dewar (1973, p. 285).
43. Golden (1990).
44. Golden (1990, p. 246).
45. Golden (1990, p. 219); and Behn (1988).
46. Critical evaluation of such studies is beyond the scope of this paper. The value of this conclusion is questionable, however. For example, whether her findings are meant to challenge the Hage and Dewar conclusions is not clear. Also, evaluating the degree of selection bias in the findings is impossible, despite her claim that it is not great.

nificant alteration in the way in which existing tasks are performed. . . .
Real innovations are those that alter core tasks; most changes add to or
alter peripheral tasks," and they are easily reversed.[47]

As for promoting innovation, Wilson says, "almost every important
study of bureaucratic innovation points to the great importance of executives in explaining change."[48] That innovations depend on "the chance
appearance of a change-oriented personality" explains the relatively
weak state of innovation theory; it is hard to create a theory to account
for unexplained variance. It is also the occasion for a warning: Innovations can be bad as well as good. "Government executives are particularly prone to adopt one kind of often ill-advised change—those that
appear to enhance their own power."[49] Also, "when government executives are the source of change, they are likely to overestimate its benefits
and underestimate its costs."[50] A corollary is that outsiders are more
likely to seek changes than those promoted from within, but their motivation may be as much short-term political prestige and advancement as
long-term improvement in organizational capacity and performance.

Finally, restating his earlier paradox, Wilson argues that "an agency
that wants its managers and operators to suggest new ways of doing their
tasks will be open, collegial, and supportive; an agency that wishes to
implement an innovation over the opposition of some of its members
often needs to concentrate power in the hands of the boss sufficient to
permit him or her to ignore (or even dismiss) opponents."[51] The most
notable innovations will be those that overturn entrenched routines.
"Innovation requires an exercise of judgment, personal skill, and misdi-
rection, qualities that are rare among government executives. And so
innovation is rare."[52]

The promotional efforts of the Ford Foundation and a similar effort by
the Fiscal Austerity and Urban Innovation Project based at the University
of Chicago, as well as the popularity of books such as David E. Osborne
and Ted Gaebler's *Reinventing Government,* are the current manifesta-
tions of interest in innovation.

In the view of Fred Jordan, innovations are ways "of doing things fun-

47. Wilson (1989, pp. 222, 225).
48. Wilson (1989, p. 227).
49. Wilson (1989, p. 228).
50. Wilson (1989, p. 229).
51. Wilson (1989, p. 230).
52. Wilson (1989, p. 232).

damentally different from that which went before, . . . better ways of addressing tough social problems. . . . [The] goal is a climate in government in which innovation can flourish."[53] Based on experience with identifying award recipients, Jordan concludes that "innovators have typically applied a new idea to a problem that has long been recognized but has proven difficult to solve."[54] Innovators were not "loose cannons," however. "Far from it. They were team players trying to improve their agencies' performance, and they were accountable to their bosses, to their elected officials, and to the voters. Even more important, they demonstrated that the kind of accountability that holds the worker responsible yet permits him or her the leeway needed to get results is far preferable to red-tape accountability."[55]

It is virtually impossible to determine the extent to which such assured conclusions—breakthroughs in the public sector, unlike the private sector, originate with organization-minded team players—are a product of selection bias and subtle definitional manipulation, but suspicion is warranted.

The Fiscal Austerity and Urban Innovation Project was conceived to gather data on how more than sixty U.S. cities have been adapting to fiscal austerity. Those Illinois cities demonstrating particular innovativeness have received urban innovation awards and recognition among peers. Participants in the project have developed a number of research themes:

— "Local officials listen more seriously to other local officials showing them how something works than they do to academicians, consultants, or federal officials. But as local officials seldom publicize their innovations, an outside data-collection effort can bring significant innovations to more general attention."[56]

— "The best work to date is unclear concerning how to make [innovative] programs more palatable."[57]

— "The most popular strategies seem to be the least threatening to established bureaucratic interests and offer tangible benefits to some staff. User fees are a case in point: Their adoption avoids cutbacks, necessitates no changes in agency procedures, and may increase autonomy of the agency adopting the fee."[58]

53. Jordan (1990, pp. 6, 9).
54. Jordan (1990, p. 15).
55. Jordan (1990, p. 119).
56. Clark (1988, p. 97).
57. Clark (1988, p. 97).
58. Appleton and Clark (1989, p. 59).

In *Reinventing Government,* Osborne and Gaebler make a number of observations concerning innovation in government, many of them insights from their reflections on private sector experience. In the private sector, they say, innovation is tied to survival.[59] Competition rewards innovation, they say; monopoly stifles it.[60] Customer-driven systems stimulate more innovation; "when providers . . . get their funds from their customers rather than from a legislature, they . . . have far greater incentives to *invest* in innovation."[61] They note the difficulty of raising innovation capital in government. Furthermore, "decentralized institutions are far more innovative than centralized ones," a conclusion that draws primarily on the Ford Foundation and Kennedy School award experience.[62] "To empower employees to act on their ideas, policy makers must decentralize the locus of decision-making."[63]

Informing the Drive for Innovation

The current approach to promoting innovations in government confuses and trivializes an important issue and diverts attention from questions that must be addressed if governmental performance is to be measurably improved.

—If the concept of innovation is to contribute clarity to efforts to improve governmental performance, it must suggest distinctions, criteria for evaluation. Innovation must not be simply another name for change, or for improvement, or even for doing something new lest almost anything qualify as innovation. Innovation is properly defined as an original, disruptive, and fundamental transformation of an organization's core tasks. Innovation changes deep structures and changes them permanently.

—Innovation necessarily involves all of the difficulties associated with arranging cooperative collective action: conflict, defection, asymmetric information, and assessment and assignment of risks. A change unaccompanied by conflict and controversy is a change that is likely to have left the status quo untransformed and those in power more powerful still, and therefore is not an innovation.

59. Osborne and Gaebler (1992, p. 345).
60. Osborne and Gaebler (1992, p. 83).
61. Osborne and Gaebler (1992, p. 182).
62. Osborne and Gaebler (1992, p. 252).
63. Osborne and Gaebler (1992, p. 275).

—Innovation is fueled by creativity, and creativity is difficult to program. Creativity is individual, a product of passion and intellect, and the natural inclination of iconoclasts who thrive on taking risks and challenging the status quo. Committees organized to represent affected interests and to produce innovations through teamwork are extremely unlikely to be creative or the wellsprings of innovation, though they will congratulate themselves on having been just that.

—Organizational structures matter. An innovative organization is flexible to the point of being a bit chaotic. Turf is up for grabs. The ambitious, clever entrepreneur thrives. The intellectual tone is active, contentious, and exciting. Young turks challenge "the bureaucrats." Contempt is evident for seniority, expertise, and hierarchy. It is not who is right, but what is right, that counts.

—At the same time, innovation requires a locus of authority or leadership, an individual or team at the top that exploits shocks, responds to new ideas, and has the power to call the shots and the judgment to know when to do so and the arrogance to believe in it. Leaders of innovation-inducing organizations are likely to be, by nature, change agents, possibly charismatic but at least secure enough to tolerate and enjoy argument, passion, risks, and action. They take enormous satisfaction in making something happen and in watching the timid squirm.

—Innovation is a permanent change, an accomplished transformation of the status quo at the core. Today's innovation, once it becomes the status quo, may be preempted by tomorrow's innovation, but it will not simply disappear in a new budget season or with a change in political leadership. A change that disappears following an executive or political transition was not an innovation; core tasks and organizational routines were not permanently altered.

—Innovation is an ongoing process, not a one-time event. Innovation is a characteristic of organizations, not a description of specific acts. Even the most resolutely entrenched organization will occasionally do something novel. Novel events do not constitute innovation; token novelty is often a sign that innovation at the core is being fought off. The relatively short half-life of bureaucratic changes touted as innovations may well be because the changes were grafted-on novelties that did not take; they were not innovations in the first place.

—Labeling particular actions as innovations is much less important than understanding change in public organizations, how and why it comes about, and the character of changes that might be called innovations because they are transforming and fundamental. The public sector needs its own Rosabeth Moss Kanter and its own *Change Masters.*

Viewed this way, innovation is relatively rare and rightly so. If the concept of innovation is defined too promiscuously or is watered down— if it is infected by the criteria of political correctness, if is weighed down by too many other agendas (citizen participation, quality improvement, empowerment, decentralization), and if it becomes a device to reward promise, good ideas, and good things that have not been done before instead of actual, documentable organizational transformations—it will lose its power as a device to stimulate nontrivial improvements in government performance. The concept will lose credibility because it has no meaning.

If, moreover, invention—the demonstration of a new idea on a small scale without disrupting the status quo—is seen as equivalent in importance to innovation as defined here, then the difficult task of "scaling up" small successes to the level of systemwide transformation will never be accorded the attention and recognition it deserves. Innovations will have no more specific gravity than the moons of Saturn.

An example of an innovation by the above criteria is Robert S. McNamara's introduction into the Department of Defense of a new approach to planning military forces and budgets in 1961. Examples of qualified successes are (1) the consolidation in the state of Florida of a large number of human services programs in the newly created Department of Health and Rehabilitative Services and the reorganization of line supervision of service delivery within the new department, and (2) the adoption of a case-management approach to the management of juveniles in the custody of New York City's Department of Juvenile Justice. An example of a failed innovation was Gordon Chase's attempt to reform the delivery of health services to New York City's prison population. Each of these innovations sought the transformation of core activity, replacing existing approaches to basic tasks with new approaches, and they were successful to the extent that the status quo of an operating agency was irrevocably changed.

Attempts to bring about change or achieve something new that are not innovations by the above criteria include two of Chase's successes as a public manager—creating a lead-based paint screening program and a methadone maintenance program; the creation of the Family Learning Center in a rural school district in Michigan cited by Olivia Golden; and the Striving Toward Excellence in Performance or STEP program created by Minnesota Governor Rudy Perpich and documented by Michael Barzelay.[64] Though each effort was useful and either created something new or brought recognition to formerly unrecognized activities, none involved the fundamental transformation of an organizational status quo.

Promoting Innovation in Government

Promoting innovation in government will always be harder than promoting innovation in the for-profit sector, because government is different. In the for-profit sector, innovation is a means, and only one of many means, to an end: market share, profitability, and growth. It necessarily involves maintaining and increasing customer satisfaction, because customers are the source of revenue. Government agencies secure their revenues from the overhead agencies of the executive branch and ultimately from legislators. Survival and prosperity depend only tenuously and indirectly, if at all, on "customer satisfaction" as ordinarily conceived. Agency survival depends far more on "interest group satisfaction," and, as is well known, interest groups only imperfectly represent "customers." The problem with government, conservatives will argue, is that it has been satisfying too many alleged customers and not enough citizens.

In government, moreover, a fundamental conflict arises between, on the one hand, innovation, which requires autonomy, decentralization, risk taking, and unprogrammed tasks, and, on the other hand, accountability, which requires predictability, standardization, replicability, and stability. It is tempting to try and escape this dilemma by arguing that innovation requires a new form of accountability, measurable by performance and not by activity. This is not a viable escape. In the contentious, pluralist U.S. system, performance measures will proliferate so that every interest can have its own, conflicts over validity or appropriateness will arise, conceptual problems will prove intractable, and supporting data will be expensive to collect and subject to controversy. No progress will be made.

Is this too pessimistic or cynical? If you are an elected official, or an appointee of one, how much system-challenging experimentation that ends in failure are you eager to defend and protect because good government requires that creative people be given latitude and funds for trial and

64. Golden (1990); and Barzelay (1992).

error?[65] Everyone will claim credit for the successful innovation after the fact, but who will defend, against political opposition and lawsuits and negative evaluation findings and hostile media coverage, the several failures that are necessary to achieve a single success? Who will, having lost or compromised, let the winners decide on the performance measures?

For those who, courageously, answer, "I'll defend creativity, share the risks, defer to the winners," the question becomes: What, if anything, can be done to increase the number of innovation-inducing organizations in government at federal, state, and local levels? Four kinds of changes—political innovations—are essential.

(1) Deregulate public administration. Deregulate the regulators? There is a breakthrough concept! Increase the authority of elected executives to reorganize and reallocate resources.[66] Simplify statutes to give greater discretion and autonomy to agency managers and field workers with regard to budgetary reprogramming and personnel actions. As a preliminary step, a conference of representatives—past and present—of the Office of Management and Budget, the General Accounting Office, the two government operations committees of Congress, the Congressional Budget Office, and the National Academy of Public Administration might be convened under foundation sponsorship to define a deregulation agenda and identify strategies and their consequences. Similar conferences at state and municipal levels could be held.

(2) Evalute candidates for public executive appointments in terms of their managerial abilities. A coalition of current and former elected officials, appointed officials, and experienced scholars might be created to investigate and then advocate reforms in the philosophy and practice of appointments to executive positions in government. Among the strategies considered should be a restructuring of government at all levels so that the appointed heads of departments serve fixed, renewable terms that do not coincide with the term of the elected chief executive and who are answerable to a board of directors that includes experts and citizens, insiders and outsiders, and that establishes and enforces criteria for effective performance.

(3) Restructure the public budgeting process. Strong professional support exists for establishing consistent capital budgeting principles for

---

65. Lynn (1992).

66. This strategy has been advocated by, among others, Bardach and Kagan (1982); Gormley (1989); and Kelman (1990).

every level of government. Public agencies might be allowed to create an innovation fund from savings they achieve through frugality and increases in efficiency and to spend this fund without having to account to any legislative body.[67]

(4) Take the influence of private money out of elections. Giving citizens direct access to candidates and inducing candidates to talk to them without fear of reprisal from political action committees (PACs) and wealthy elites would bring greater pressure to perform in the public interest to bear on public officials. Empowered citizens are the customers for innovative government.

These proposals are controversial, likely to encounter resistance, risky, disruptive, a radical departure from the status quo, and of uncertain benefit. All innovations are.

67. Osborne and Gaebler (1992) make a similar proposal.

References

Appleton, Lynn M., and Terry Nichols Clark. 1989. "Coping in American Cities: Fiscal Austerity and Urban Innovations in the 1980s." In *Urban Innovation and Autonomy: Political Implications of Policy Change,* edited by Susan E. Clarke, 31–68. Newbury Park, Calif.: Sage Publications.

Bardach, Eugene, and Robert A. Kagan. 1982. *Going by the Book: The Problem of Regulatory Unreasonableness.* Temple University Press.

Barzelay, Michael. 1992. *Breaking through Bureaucracy: A New Vision for Managing in Government.* University of California Press.

Becker, Selwyn W., and Thomas L. Whisler. 1967. "The Innovative Organization: A Selective View of Current Theory and Research." *Journal of Business,* vol. 40, no. 4 (October): 463.

Behn, Robert D. 1988. "Management by Groping Along." *Journal of Policy Analysis and Management,* vol. 7, no. 4 (Fall): 643–63.

Bennis, Warren G. 1989. *Why Leaders Can't Lead: The Unconscious Conspiracy Continues.* Jossey-Bass.

Burns, Tom, and G. M. Stalker. 1961. *The Management of Innovation.* London: Tavistock.

Clark, Terry Nichols. 1988. "The Fiscal Austerity and Urban Innovation Project." *PS/Political Science and Politics,* vol. 21, no. 1 (Winter): 97.

Golden, Olivia. 1990. "Innovation in Public Sector Human Services Programs: The Implications of Innovation by 'Groping Along.' " *Journal of Policy Analysis and Management,* vol. 9, no. 2 (Spring): 219–48.

Gormley, William T., Jr. 1989. *Taming the Bureaucracy: Muscles, Prayers, and Other Strategies.* Princeton University Press.

Hage, Jerald, and Robert Dewar. 1973. "Elite Values versus Organizational Structure in Predicting Innovation." *Administrative Science Quarterly,* vol. 18, no. 3 (September): 279–90.

Hargrove, Erwin C., and John C. Glidewell, eds. 1990. *Impossible Jobs in Public Management.* University Press of Kansas.

Jordan, Fred. 1990. *Innovating America: Innovations in State and Local Government: An Awards Program of the Ford Foundation and the John F. Kennedy School of Government, Harvard University.* New York: Ford Foundation.

Kanter, Rosabeth Moss. 1983. *The Change Masters: Innovations for Productivity in the American Corporation.* Simon and Schuster.

Kelman, Steven. 1990. *Procurement and Public Management: The Fear of Discretion and the Quality of Government Performance.* Washington, D.C.: AEI Press.

Lynn, Laurence E., Jr., 1992. "Dividing the Job: The Intergovernmental Dimension." *Public Manager,* vol. 21, no. 3 (Fall): 7–10.

March, James G., and Herbert A. Simon. 1958. *Organizations.* Wiley.

Mohr, Lawrence B. 1969. "Determinants of Innovation in Organizations." *American Political Science Review,* vol. 63, no. 1 (March): 111–26.

Morgan, Gareth. 1986. *Images of Organization.* Beverly Hills, Calif.: Sage Publications.

Nayak, P. Ranganath, and John M. Ketteringham. 1986. *Breakthroughs!* New York: Rawson Associates.

Osborne, David E., and Ted Gaebler. 1992. *Reinventing Government: How the Entrepreneurial Spirit Is Transforming the Public Sector.* Reading, Mass.: Addison-Wesley.

Pearson, Andrall E. 1988. "Tough-Minded Ways to Get Innovative." *Harvard Business Review,* vol. 66, no. 3 (May/June). Reprinted in John M. Ivancevich and Michael T. Matteson. 1990. *Organizational Behavior and Management,* 2d ed., 104–10. Homewood, Ill.: BPI/Irwin.

Peters, Thomas J., and Robert H. Waterman. 1982. *In Search of Excellence: Lessons from America's Best-Run Companies,* 1st ed. Harper and Row.

Sapolsky, Harvey M. 1967. "Organizational Structure and Innovation." *Journal of Business,* vol. 40, no. 4 (October): 497–510.

Schroeder, Roger D., and others. 1989. "The Development of Innovation Ideas." In *Research on the Management of Innovation: The Minnesota Studies,* edited by Andrew H. Van de Ven, Harold L. Angles, and Marshall Scott Poole, 107–34. Harper and Row.

Selznick, Philip. 1984. *Leadership in Administration: A Sociological Interpretation.* University of California Press.

Simon, Herbert A. 1967. "The Changing Theory and Changing Practice of Public Administration." In *Contemporary Political Science: Toward Empirical Theory,* edited by Ithiel de Sola Pool. McGraw-Hill.

Wilson, James Q. 1966. "Innovation in Organizations: Notes toward a Theory." In *Approaches to Organizational Design,* edited by James D. Thompson, 193–218. University of Pittsburgh Press.

_____. 1989. *Bureaucracy: What Government Agencies Do and Why They Do It.* Basic Books.

CHAPTER FIVE

The Dilemma of the Modern Public Manager:
Satisfying the Virtues of Scientific and Innovative Management

Marc D. Zegans

IN BUSINESS FIRMS, innovation is increasingly seen as the key to competitive success. For the better part of a decade, leading American companies have been changing their cultures and gearing themselves for adaptability, invention, and constant learning.[1] Many observers of government wonder whether public agencies should pursue innovation with equal vigor and, if so, whether lessons from the private sector apply. But what do public managers think? Do they believe that innovation is as important to the success of their agencies as do managers of private firms? By what means, if any, do they think innovation should be pursued? And what limits would they put on the exercise of creative initiative by public employees?

These questions were put to nine senior state and local managers in two focus groups. These managers were in substantial agreement about what innovation means, the role it plays in public agencies, the role they think it should play, and how it best should be managed. Most important,

An earlier version of this chapter was published as Zegans, Marc D. 1992. "Innovation in the Well-Functioning Public Agency." *Public Productivity Review,* vol. 16, no. 2 (Winter): 141–56.

I would like to express my thanks to Alan Altshuler, Michael Barzelay, Jennifer Lawrence, David Luberoff, Mark Moore, Andrew Stone, Leonard Zegans, and two anonymous referees for their helpful comments on early drafts, and to Marcia Ellison for research assistance.

1. This trend was first brought to popular attention by Kantor (1983). For a more recent, lively account, see Dumaine (1991).

they accept the traditional distinction between policy and administration first put forward by Woodrow Wilson; yet they reject, with equal conviction, the idea (embodied in the public administration model that flowed from this policy administration distinction) that administrative discretion should be suppressed.[2] Put differently, they challenge the claim—embedded in the rules governing their agencies—that administrative work is best performed in a steeply hierarchical, highly segmented, rule-driven bureaucracy.[3]

Their challenge to strict hierarchy and rules is rooted in three beliefs:

— First, that policy should be concerned with broad direction setting, not with the codification of particular objectives and work methods;

— Second, that public managers should have discretion to interpret policy, if they can make a solid case for their actions; and

— Third, that such discretion should be extended, in varying degrees, to civil servants at all levels of a public organization.

The consistency of these managers' views suggests that widely shared professional norms may be important in shaping their attitudes about innovation in public agencies.

Why Should We Think Hard about Group Attitudes?

In recent years, the public sector has witnessed a growing gap between the public's desire for quality service and the capacity of public agencies to meet it. In addition to burgeoning service demands, this gap can be attributed to increasing environmental complexity and public resistance to new taxes. Innovations in technology and service delivery can reduce this gap, but traditional constraints on employee discretion combined with strong incentives to embrace the status quo limit the capacity of public agencies to be innovative.[4]

To bring expectations for performance, standards of behavior, and outcomes into closer alignment, we have three options: (1) lower standards;

2. Wilson (1887).

3. For good discussions of these institutional designs and the conditions that gave rise to them, see Barzelay (1992, chapter 1); and Skowronek (1982).

4. Altshuler and Zegans (1990) identify three particularly strong disincentives to bureaucratic innovation: absence of competition; harsh treatment for failures at the hands of legislators and reporters without compensating rewards for success; and deep suspicion of bureaucratic innovation and creative initiative by powerful constituencies across the political spectrum.

(2) promote innovation within the framework of existing constraints, which would, in effect, lower expectations; or (3) strike a new balance between the pursuit of innovation and the values with which it may conflict.

Our choice among these means can be improved by careful deliberation. And, in three ways, research can facilitate these deliberations. First, research can clarify the nature of the policy challenge we face. Second, research can provide a framework for deliberation based on careful and systematic appraisal of the decisionmaking context. Third, research can focus these deliberations on specific proposals for addressing the potential trade-offs between innovation and accountability.

Such research is most fruitfully rooted in strong baseline measures of key group norms concerning innovation in public agencies. For example, in designing administrative reforms it would be helpful to know what legislators, elected executives, public managers, journalists, and individual citizens believe are the values at stake, the outcomes sought, and the choices they would make when faced with specific trade-offs. Unfortunately, such a baseline does not exist. Therefore, a central and policy-relevant challenge to scholars interested in advancing the debate is to produce this understanding of group norms.

Method

In this preliminary investigation of group norms, I chose to concentrate on career civil servants in senior management positions. I felt that this group would be among those who best reflect the core values of American public administrators.

My strategy for data collection was straightforward. I held two focus group discussions with nine career civil servants, each a current senior manager in state or local government. I used focus groups because I wanted to pick up on the language that managers used to discuss innovation. For this purpose, an interactive group offered several advantages: First, my presence would be less felt than in one-on-one interviews; second, a group discussion, built around shared examples, might surface points of agreement, disagreement, and confusion that would not emerge in one-on-one interviews; third, a focus group would give the managers an opportunity to grope toward common understandings of issues that perplexed them; and fourth, a focus group would enable the managers to comment on and to refine each others' observations.

I drew the focus group participants from the June 1991 session of the State and Local Executive Program at Harvard University John F. Kennedy School of Government. They included seven agency heads and two deputies, all from large public agencies. They had on average seventeen years of public sector experience. Five participated in the first group and four in the second. They were not informed in advance about the discussion topic.[5]

In conducting the focus groups, I used a mix of prepared questions and spontaneous probes. Prepared questions centered on qualities of the excellent public manager; how best to define innovation; the relative importance of innovation to public management; appropriate and inappropriate behavior in pursuing innovation; and examples of successful, unsuccessful, and controversial innovations. When a consensus appeared to evolve, I told the group what I thought I had heard and polled the participants for their reactions.

As this work was exploratory, I used an open coding strategy, labeling categories that emerged from the data and reducing data around these categories. Three broad descriptive categories resulted from this process, each containing a variety of themes around which individual manager's views were distributed.[6] These categories are: (1) innovation in the public manager's world view, (2) the politics of innovation, and (3) the management of innovation.

The nine managers by and large shared the same basic orientation in each of these topic areas. In particular, they voiced consistent views about the meaning of innovation, describing its essence as implementing ideas or technologies new to a given situation and its purpose as advancing policy. These views were uniformly reflected in the examples they

5. Note a caveat: Public managers who attend advanced training for three-week periods are a self-selected group and may have a bias in favor of innovative thinking and creative initiative. Nonetheless, with an average of seventeen years of public sector experience culminating in a senior management position, these managers were clearly part of the bureaucratic culture and had done well in it. As such, they seemed to be a reasonably good pool on which to draw for a pilot probe.

6. Because the attitudes that emerged were widely shared, I considered two hypotheses: that the apparent consensus was an artifact of the data collection process, and, alternatively, that it genuinely reflected the participants' settled views. Two reasons might have existed for doubting the validity of the consensus findings. First, the findings might have been random artifacts resulting from an essentially arbitrary "groupthink" process; second, the groups might simply have been following my unconscious lead toward predetermined conclusions. I rejected "groupthink" because the views expressed did not appreciably vary between the two groups. I rejected the power of my unconscious suggestions both because the participants revealed themselves as savvy, opinionated individuals, and because much of what they said genuinely surprised me.

provided of successful, unsuccessful, and controversial innovation. They argued that the pursuit of innovation, as they defined it, has become an important part of their work because of budget cutbacks and rapid demographic and technical changes. They expressed concern, however, that innovation is increasingly seen as an end in itself instead of a means to an end. In addition, they shared common views about the appropriate sources of new ideas and avenues for expressing them and about how legislators would be likely to respond to innovative bureaucratic initiatives. Finally, they expressed similar views about how to encourage innovation in public agencies without violating traditional norms about the distinction between policy and administration.

Innovation in the Public Manager's World View

In describing how innovation in government fit into their world view, these managers focused on three key issues: (1) the meaning of innovation; (2) the factors that motivate a career public manager to innovate; and (3) the relative importance of innovation as a managerial activity.

What does it mean to innovate? When these managers talked directly about what innovation meant to them, four ideas emerged:

—Innovation is the process of implementing an idea, or enacting a technology, novel to a given situation;

—Successful innovation depends more on implementation skills and political savvy than on creative thinking;

—Innovation is a tool for improving agency performance, not an end in itself; and

—Innovation is an intrinsic part of the public manager's job.

When they talked about the purpose to which this tool was put, they cited three aims: improving productivity, increasing proficiency, and advancing policy.

The many examples offered by these managers were in accordance with their ideas about innovation. Their examples had four common features: (1) a difficult and often complex implementation challenge; (2) a clear, tangible link to agency mission; (3) an idea or technology novel to the situation but not new to the world; and (4) stakeholder anxiety that, if not handled properly, could harden into active resistance to the program.[7]

---

7. The single example in which creative thinking plays a critical role concerns a janitor who developed a markedly cheaper way to replace school windows.

As these views suggest, to these managers, innovation meant better implementation. Some managers took pains to distinguish explicitly between innovation and policymaking. They described innovation as developing the means by which public agencies fulfill broad purposes and policymaking as the process of establishing these purposes. They claimed that public managers as a class had primary responsibility for innovation but conceded exclusive responsibility for making policy to elected officials. To these public managers, innovation was about means, not about ends.

From an academic's perspective, the most striking feature of their comments and their examples was the lack of emphasis on creativity and originality. Not one of their examples was distinguished by a particularly creative concept or idea, and not one of the managers' stories emphasized the creative aspects of the process by which the idea came about. Instead, these managers' stories focused consistently on the challenges of implementing locally novel ideas that would enable them to better meet their policy mandates.

Their lack of emphasis on creativity was striking because, like many academics who think about innovation, I associate innovation with creativity. In contrast to these managers, who emphasize implementation, when talking about innovation, my colleagues and I place as much weight on the generation of novel ideas as on their implementation. What accounts for this difference in emphasis?

Scholars who take an interest in innovation typically think about it as a kind of *process*—a creative process by which a novel idea is developed and implemented. By contrast, public managers (both those who participated in this study and many others with whom I have spoken since these data were first published) think about innovation in terms of adaptive change that occurs within a *domain of responsibility.*

Specifically, the managers' comments about innovation tend to refer to any sort of adaptive change that advances mission within the framework of existing public policy. Implementing useful change within this domain, whether the ideas are original or not is what concerns them. When talking about innovation, scholars and public managers emphasize different phenomena because they are attaching the word to markedly different concepts.

What motivates public managers to innovate? These managers described their principal motivation to innovate as putting useful ideas into action. They also cited funding crises, technical changes, and burgeoning demands for public services as important spurs to innovation. But they did not suggest that a personal need for creative expression or public credit for their ideas were important stimuli. The first group did consider whether "pride of ownership" was an important motivator; after some debate, they agreed it was important but much less so than the desire for task accomplishment.

Is innovation important? The managers generally saw innovation as an important part of their work. Members of the second group tried to quantify this view, observing that they typically spend about 40 percent of their time thinking about innovation or trying to innovate. Noted one:

> I think of it a lot. All the time, I'm trying to rack my brain, trying to come up with some cheaper, better way of trying to do some of the stuff that we're supposed to be doing. . . . But I'd say, oh, at least 40–50 percent of what I do is either trying to think up things or . . . trying to implement some innovation that I'm trying to do.

Although the managers described innovation as an increasingly important part of their work, they did not view it as a defining characteristic of excellence in their profession. When asked to describe the attributes of excellent public managers and public agencies, they did not— with one exception—spontaneously cite innovation or closely related ideas such as entrepreneurship, adaptive change, or continuous improvement. Instead, the qualities of excellence among public servants, both elected and appointed, which they cited were: commitment to public service, vision, drive, integrity, people skills (particularly the capacity to build consensus), capacity for organization, team play, and the ability to successfully challenge an organization. They also saw "firmness," rapid "turn-around time," finding "excitement in life," and willingness to take risks as particular attributes of excellent public managers. Noted one:

> There's a lot of guys who kind of go along—get-along type of people who don't really move an organization around—and maybe try to avoid taking some tough decisions. So I admire in the public manager someone who's willing to take a tough decision, willing to take some risks—but then has the ability of pulling it off.

Describing a personal role model, another commented:

> This is a person who truly and honestly believes and lives public service, thinks strategically, thinks about people, sensitive to people management, handles the up and out and [the] down and in equally well and balances the two.

They described excellent public agencies as fulfilling the public trust in carrying out services that citizens want the government to perform. One noted that excellent public agencies are "clear about what the public values are and reflective of those values." They also felt that excellent public agencies routinely met performance expectations and that they communicated effectively with citizens about the nature of their work and more generally about how government functions. Consistent with this view, they stressed that the best public agencies see themselves as part of a larger governmental system and their job as doing what is best for that system, instead of adopting a parochial, agency-centered concept of their service mission. Observed one:

> If everybody is really global in their thinking—rather than "I need to make my department great and take care of business here and feel good about what I'm doing"—I think it works better. I think you really get a more functional or efficient type of system.

When asked directly whether pursuit of innovation was a quality shared by excellent public managers, they agreed that it was. But they were quick to express concern that the recent vogue for innovation was creating perverse incentives. Said one:

> For some time now, I have [had] a thing about the word "innovation." I'm uncomfortable with it; I think it intimidates people. I think that it is *trendy* [speaker's emphasis]. Looking at what you do and whether you're doing the right things, and then looking at how you do them—that's innovation. But I think the word "innovation" is too much pressure laden and sort of intimidating.

Collectively, this evidence suggests that public managers have a particular set of ideas in mind when they talk about innovation. Innovation for these managers defines a domain in which they have both the right and responsibility to make novel interventions. It is both a domain of discretion and a domain of obligation, and as such, for these managers, innovation is both exciting and "intimidating."

The Politics of Innovation

The nine managers had strong views about the proper allocation of bureaucratic and legislative responsibilities, about how politicians respond to innovative initiatives by public managers, and about what prompts these responses.

Roles and Responsibilities

The managers argued that creative ideas can come from anywhere in the political system and should be encouraged whatever their source.[8] Different types of innovative ideas, however, ought to be subject to different types of screening. Civil servants, they believed, should be authorized to implement ideas that advanced established policies without making major claims on new resources, but new ideas altering basic purposes or requiring significant new resources should be implemented only with prior legislative approval. The managers did not suggest how distinctions among innovative ideas are to be made in practice. They did note, however, that, when dealing with borderline cases, successful civil servants engage in regular, informal consultation with legislative overseers.

When asked about the fundamental responsibilities of civil servants as innovators, the managers described three: (1) to produce and promote useful ideas; (2) to inform political overseers about changes in the policy environment and flaws in policy assumptions revealed in the course of normal practice; and (3) to routinely improve the operating performance of their organizations in a manner consistent with current policy.

With these responsibilities, they assert, come five basic rights: (1) to inquire into and analyze current operations and the policies on which they are based; (2) to report findings to elected officials; (3) to propose new ideas that stem from these findings; (4) to implement innovations that advance policy, within program and within budget; and (5) to undertake small-scale trials of productivity-enhancing initiatives.

By contrast, the managers believed that a civil servant's discretion over pilots for new programs was subject to negotiation. "All depends on your local situation," said one. "I'm sure all of us have certain things we

---

8. They observed, however, that ideas for innovations were the most likely to come from civil servants. Noted one:

> Obviously the people who are paid, the worker bees, the people who are in the bureaucracy, are probably the people . . . [with] some type of expertise or technical background. And that's where you would think the actual ideas would generate from. It might be spurred by public policy that came out of a legislative body or whatever. But those would be the broad parameters, and it would be the working out the details, and the rules and the regulations that have to go along with it [the policy].

can do, without having to check with anybody. That may be big, it may be smaller. Just depends." They felt that informal authorization was generally sufficient for most changes within programs and noted that the public managers who are most effective at obtaining and exercising discretion seek informal authorization long before taking precipitate action. "It's like a garden," said one manager. "You prepare the groundwork."

These nine senior civil servants believe that public managers, by right and responsibility, are both innovators and policy actors. They advise on, promote, and interpret policy. In direction setting, however, they defer to elected officials. Noted one manager:

> For what it's worth, I think major new policy initiatives have to come from elected officials. I mean, staff can have ideas, maybe bounce and buzz off of them. But, ultimately, if you're going to affect segments of your public, either in offering a new service or taking something away that's been there before . . . that's their [the legislature's] call.

Political Responses to Bureaucratic Initiative

The nine managers agreed that politicians are sensitive to controversy, cost, and electoral cycles.[9] Consequently, innovations that save money, that are noncontroversial, and that offer a quick pay-back and opportunities to claim credit will garner support more readily than innovations lacking these qualities. Politicians also tend to be more supportive of innovations with which they have a personal connection. Managers who consult political overseers early in the innovation process, and who manage such consultation effectively, will do better than those who do not.

The Management of Innovation

Choices concerning organizational strategy, structure, and methods of implementation are shaped to some degree by the framework of societal norms within which an agency operates. Such norms may be conducive

---

9. This is consistent with John W. Kingdon's argument that those in Congress use controversy as a basis for deciding which voting decisions require attention and which do not. He observes, "Congressmen begin their consideration of a given bill or amendment with one overriding question: Is it controversial? For virtually every participant, legislative matters are immediately divided into two categories as a first step in the decisional process: controversial and non-controversial." Kingdon (1989, p. 244).

to the bureaucratic pursuit of innovation, or they may hinder such initiative. When asked whether external norms of accountability were consistent with the increasing pressure that they were feeling to innovate, the nine managers, for the most part, saw little conflict. While they did cite a few aspects of the control system that could be improved, they argued that the existing rules governing bureaucratic action were not a significant impediment to innovative initiative.[10] Well-managed public agencies, they argued, could achieve high levels of innovation within existing institutional constraints.

When discussing the management of innovation, the nine public managers focused on four issues: grants of discretion to public employees; innovation strategy as a management tool; factors that distinguish healthy and unhealthy approaches to innovation; and the manager's role in making innovation part of routine practice.

Is discretion to innovate an asset or a liability? The managers argued that granting discretion to their employees is both necessary and desirable but that such discretion must be managed. When weighing the benefits to be obtained from intelligent grants of discretion to employees versus the risk of being held personally accountable for employee error, they consistently came down on the side of granting discretion. These managers saw it as their job to protect their employees from unfair attacks in the media and vindictive legislative inquiries. One manager observed that "[we] figure out ways to achieve our objectives without exposing our employees to that kind of abuse. We have a responsibility to do that."

These managers also agreed that employees who brought forward proposals for specific innovations should be encouraged. In their view, then, the problem of managing discretion is one of making appropriate assignments, not of overcoming barriers to trust. The basic decision rule with respect to assignments appeared to be that discretion should be lodged with the members of the organization who have the best combination of relevant knowledge and professional capacity.[11]

10. According to the nine managers, aspects of the control system that could be improved included inflexible work rules and narrow job descriptions; seniority rules that resulted in a poor connection between pay and performance; limited capacity for reprogramming budget dollars; and requirements that small purchases be centrally processed. The managers observed that these particular rules hindered their efforts to implement policy and discouraged employee initiative, without improving accountability.

11. Related to the question of how much discretion to grant public employees is how hard public managers should push employees to innovate. The managers were unequivocal in their responses: First provide the required supports, next push employees until they begin to feel uncomfortable, then back off. One described this as a "barometer approach."

Should managers have an innovation strategy? These managers claimed that they did not pursue formal innovation strategies. They described their approaches to innovation as ad hoc and opportune. They talked about searching constantly for ways to improve performance and wanting their employees to do likewise.

Their comments about encouraging innovation in the ranks, however, do suggest a clear strategy—one built around process instead of policy objectives. These managers sought to design organizational systems that would enable employees to use their creative energies effectively. These efforts centered on socializing employees to internalize management objectives and establishing open lines of communication. They considered it vital, however, to be receptive to good ideas whatever their source. Said one, "Role modeling has an awful lot to do with how communications does work in an organization."

The strategy articulated by these managers was grounded in a deeper set of beliefs about how to produce innovation in what I call "healthy" public agencies and how in "unhealthy" agencies efforts to innovate were systematically thwarted. In healthy public agencies, they argued, employees throughout the organization seek to innovate as a part of normal practice without subverting routine. Noted one manager, "If they feel like there's a need to be creative or innovative, or push the envelope, or whatever, and it's something they can justify from their own experience, . . . I have enough faith in their ability, that they should go up and do that." By contrast, they said, in dysfunctional organizations, employees generally show little initiative, and the rare innovator finds it necessary to end-run colleagues to accomplish his or her objectives. These managers concluded that rule-obsessed organizations turn the timid into cowards and the bold into outlaws.

They also identified several obstacles to innovation in public agencies: entrenched middle managers highly resistant to change, "closed door" commissioners and department heads who fail to maintain frequent and open communications with employees at all levels of hierarchy, and "rigid boxes" (rules) that stifle initiative without contributing to efficiency or accountability. They argued that these obstacles are so profoundly embedded in most public organizations that employees, who have often been subjected to years of abusive treatment, find grasping opportunities for initiative extremely difficult. Commented one:

I guess after eleven years that message has been imprinted so hard, that if you do stick out your [nose], we punish [you] for it. But it might take eleven years to turn that around. But I try to offset that with saying, "Look, I take into account that you are a person, a professional, that you have a reason for being where you are. You have got ideas that are important, that are of substance. And I'm going to give you sufficient latitude, and I'll back you up all the way." And I try to offset that and allow that to be a management style that not only goes to the deputies, but also as they deal with the people under them.

The managers used two basic methods for overcoming complacency. The first was to hold employees accountable for producing results that mattered in the outside world. They noted that this objective was best accomplished by combining well-defined organizational goals with a customer-service orientation. The second, which they called "empowerment," was aimed at overcoming employees' fear of reprisals for taking initiative, by providing credible and sustained support for employee-initiated projects that were consistent with agency goals. They hoped, by taking these steps, to create climates in which employees felt comfortable coming forward with ideas and in which they anticipated support from their superiors when taking a creative risk.

Realigning the Public Administration Model

The nine managers' views are grounded in the "public administration model" established during the administrative reform era, which had its conceptual roots in 1887 with Woodrow Wilson's call for a new theory of administration and which peaked in the first decades of the twentieth century. This model has two defining elements: a fundamental norm that assigns politicians the authority to make policy decisions and civil servants the responsibility to implement them; and a theory of administrative practice that prescribes a rigid system of control as the most appropriate means by which civil servants may fulfill their obligations.

This theory reflects a belief that effective policy implementation is defined by three basic virtues: honesty, fairness, and efficiency. The challenge was to develop a system that, above all, protected these virtues. The recommended solution was a system of control characterized by hierarchy, functional segmentation, and rigorous task accountability.

The nine public managers embraced the first element of the public administration model—the basic distinction between policy and administration. But they regarded the model's approach to effective implementation as shopworn, and they were quick to propose alternatives. We might therefore describe these managers' pattern of belief as an adaptation of the public administration model aimed at bringing its methods into closer alignment with current realities.

The classic model assumes in part that (1) the means of fulfilling policy objectives are known and unvarying; (2) environmental change is sufficiently slow and predictable for legislative policy to keep pace; (3) policy shapes methods, never the reverse; (4) resources are adequate to mandates; and (5) the personal development of public employees is irrelevant to organizational effectiveness. In contrast, the nine managers described their world as characterized by rapid change, broad policy mandates, and resources inadequate to their legislatively mandated responsibilities. In their view, therefore, a manager's fundamental obligation to implement policy effectively cannot be fulfilled by adhering to the old methods.

Consequently, to the traditional model's virtues of honesty, fairness, and efficiency, these managers added flexibility, ingenuity, and adaptivity. Unfortunately, these newer virtues do not bloom in an environment that actively suppresses bureaucratic discretion. Given this obstacle, they judged that public managers must satisfy their commitment to effective policy implementation by cultivating the new virtues in ways that do not compromise the old ones.

The ideas concerning bureaucratic innovation conveyed by these nine managers reflect a serious effort to grapple with this challenge of integrating new virtues into an old framework. During our discussions, they engaged it in two ways. First, they asserted a strong claim to discretion in carrying out their assigned missions, while limiting themselves to an advisory role with respect to ends. Their concept of innovation firmly embraced this distinction: They defined innovation in terms of better implementation, not better policy. Second, they expressed trust in the capacity of their employees to handle discretion and sought to build this trust by delegating broadly and opening channels of communication.

Clearly, these managers are seeking to cultivate adaptive change in their organizations. But, ultimately, what assessment should be made of the methods they advocate and the role they choose to play?

In areas where technical adaptation is the primary challenge, these managers' ideas offer strong prospects for genuine improvement. Where

basic technical invention is required, their ad hoc approach is likely to
work less well. In such cases, a deliberate strategy for reinventing core
technologies would appear to be more appropriate. In areas where policy
innovation and technical change are necessarily intertwined, the
approach these managers advocate is not likely to stimulate civil servants
to make useful contributions.

Here lies the crux of the problem: Government cannot meet society's
demand for improved policy and practices by limiting the public
manager's role to policy implementation only. Much useful change, no
matter what term we use to describe it, is likely to come from a process
of learning-by-doing through which we discover the packages of values,
policies, technology, and practices that satisfy us best. To the extent,
therefore, that the innovation gap is measured by a need for simultaneous technical and policy change, and to the extent that this gap cannot be
closed within the existing division of responsibility between administrators and elected officials, we will have to look for new models.

It is time for the search to begin.

References

Altshuler, Alan, and Marc D. Zegans. 1990. "Innovation and Creativity:
Comparisons between Public Management and Private Enterprise."
Cities, vol. 7. no. 1 (February): 16–24.

Barzelay, Michael. 1992. *Breaking through Bureaucracy: A New Vision
for Managing in Government.* University of California Press.

Dumaine, Brian. 1991. "The Bureaucracy Busters: How They're Breaking the Corporate Chains." *Fortune* (June 17): 36–50.

Kantor, Rosabeth Moss. 1983. *The Change Masters: Innovations for
Productivity in the American Corporation.* Simon and Schuster.

Kingdon, John W. 1989. *Congressmen's Voting Decisions,* 3d ed. University of Michigan Press.

Skowronek, Stephen. 1982. *Building a New American State: The Expansion of National Administrative Capacities, 1877–1920.* Cambridge,
England: Cambridge University Press.

Wilson, Woodrow. 1887. "The Study of Administration." *Political
Science Quarterly,* vol. 2 (June): 197–222.

CHAPTER SIX

Innovation in the Concept of Government Operations:
A New Paradigm for Staff Agencies

Michael Barzelay and Babak J. Armajani

TROUBLED BY A HOST of problems plaguing industrial society and outraged at the deep penetration of partisan politics into executive branch operations, early twentieth-century reformers fashioned a bold vision of state government as an efficient, competent, and virtuous institution. Animated by this vision, reformers waged campaigns to create civil service systems and to reorganize the growing number of state commissions, institutions, and agencies into a handful of executive departments with top leaders appointed by the state's chief executive. These advocates of state government reorganization also pinned their hopes for honest and efficient government on the creation of staff agencies, which were to exercise continuous control over line agencies by performing their administrative functions for them in a centralized fashion. Reformers

An earlier version of this chapter was published as Barzelay, Michael, and Babak J. Armajani. 1990. "Managing State Government Operations: Changing Visions of Staff Agencies." *Journal of Policy Analysis and Management* 9(3): 307–38. Reprinted by permission of John Wiley & Sons, Inc. For a more detailed account, see Barzelay, Michael, with the collaboration of Babak J. Armajani. 1992. *Breaking Through Bureaucracy: A New Vision for Managing in Government*. University of California Press.

The authors thank David Bishop, John Brandl, Lee Friedman, Larry Grant, Elaine Johnson, Peter Katzenstein, Linda Kaboolian, Robert Leone, Mark Moore, Catherine Moukheibir, Connie Nelson, Judy Pinke, Alasdair Roberts, Rogers M. Smith, Georgina Wyman, Jim Verdier, Raymond Vernon, Jeff Zlonis, the attendees of the John F. Kennedy School of Government conference on Managing State Government Operations: Changing Visions of Staff Agencies, and Fred Thompson.

were convinced that centralizing the accounting, purchasing, budgeting, and personnel functions was the best way to curtail political favoritism in hiring and buying, to limit expenditures to appropriated levels, to increase gubernatorial control of government operations, to eliminate waste, to reduce duplication of effort, and to capture economies of scale.

In the 1920s and 1930s, this bureaucratic reform vision became dominant in many American states.[1] When reformers began to gain political power, they often pressed for the creation of civil service commissions and boards of control, which were to be composed of accounting, budgeting, and purchasing divisions. Significant elements of the bureaucratic reform vision were institutionalized in each of these centralized staff functions. After successive waves of reorganization, many states created departments of administration and finance, which grouped together most, if not all, centralized staff functions under a single gubernatorial appointee. These organizations became the chief embodiments of the bureaucratic reform vision in state government.

For decades, this vision persisted. Governors took seriously the idea that, as chief executive, they were responsible for making state agencies economical and efficient. Backed by the recommendations of economy and efficiency commissions, chief executives often pressed for greater centralization and control. Beginning in the 1930s, schools of public administration educated their students about economical and efficient systems for budgeting, accounting, purchasing, and personnel administration and, in the process, socialized them into the bureaucratic reform vision. Meanwhile, this vision escaped serious challenge. Subsequent demands that government be fair and equitable, instead of merely economical and efficient, were easily rebuffed by centralized staff agencies through their control over line-agency purchasing and hiring decisions. The objects of control—line-agency managers—could not successfully challenge a system that regarded their complaints about bureaucratic red tape as evidence that the system worked.

Inventing a New Vision

In the 1990s, more than any time in the last fifty years, the bureaucratic reform vision is vulnerable to challenge. Many politicians are

1. White (1933, pp. 176–209).

looking for ways to increase the public's satisfaction with government services while not raising taxes. Some recognize that substantial changes in the way state employees and overseers relate to one another may be necessary to increase the quality and cost-effectiveness of state services.

In Minnesota, when Governor Rudy Perpich returned to office in 1983, he explicitly abandoned the conventional vision and created a climate in which political appointees and career officials could experiment with new ways of managing the relationships among overseers, line-agency employees, and staff-agency employees.[2] Some of these experiments required the tacit and explicit support of legislative committees, which in most cases was forthcoming. The experiments resulted in significant experience with managing certain staff functions (including internal services, purchasing, staffing, and information systems) in ways that depart from the bureaucratic reform tradition.

The Bureaucratic Reform Vision

For years, those who work in staff agencies have believed that, as specialists in administration, their job was to keep line agencies from wasting taxpayers' money, from evading political control, and from treating employees or vendors unfairly. This vision of good government is rooted in American civic culture and democratic theory, in classical administrative theory, and in widely used mechanistic images of organizational life. The following beliefs are central to this vision:

— Administration and politics should be distinct domains of governmental activity.

— The responsibility of the bureaucracy is to execute the state's laws economically and efficiently.

— State departments and agencies should be accountable to the legislature, governor, and courts, and they should discharge their responsibilities in an impersonal manner. The centralization of overhead functions and the uniform application of statewide rules and procedures are essential for impersonal administration and conducive to economical and efficient government.

— Line functions should be staffed largely by career employees who possess technical or clerical skills; their charge is to apply technical

2. Hale (1989).

expertise and rules to particular contexts. Staff functions should employ career public servants who possess specialized knowledge of administration and use this knowledge in controlling line agencies.

—When issuing orders to line agencies, staff agencies act in the name of the chief executive; hence staff agencies operate according to the doctrine of the "unity of command." The top officials of staff agencies are also accountable to the legislature, just like their line-agency counterparts.

Animated by these understandings, generations of civil servants and top officials strove to make government work like a good, clean, and efficient machine. For most of these civil servants, doing good meant eliminating divergences between uniform rules and agency behavior and reducing the measured costs of government activity.

During the early part of the twentieth century, the bureaucratic reform vision reflected a deep sense of outrage against the corruption and inefficient use of resources in government. Because this sense of outrage had been directed, in large part, at people who worked for the executive branch, the first generation of staff-agency employees naturally assumed that their line-agency counterparts were looking for every chance to subvert the public interest and the law. This frame of mind, supported by the emerging theory of public administration, encouraged staff-agency employees to think of themselves as legitimately exercising unilateral control over line agencies to eliminate malfeasance, wastefulness, and other improper behavior.

The assumption that line-agency employees should be subjected to unilateral control persists. In the 1980s, managers of Minnesota's central purchasing function emphasized the importance of guarding against the wasteful tendencies of line-agency employees. They asserted that line-agency employees would acquire Cadillacs if central purchasing did not force them to buy Chevrolets. From 1938 (when the Department of Administration was created) to 1980, line agencies were not permitted to purchase items costing more than $50 without approval from central purchasing.

Line-Agency Performance

The most important difference between the old and new visions of overhead agencies is that the new vision holds the performance of line agencies to be a prime value, whereas the old vision either subordinated this value to others—such as fiscal accountability, impersonal administration, or economy—or simply did not include it.

Although it is hard to believe, staff agencies, operating under the old vision, did not value line-agency performance; this tendency is clear from their operating style. In Minnesota's procurement function, for example, two values monopolized the attention of buyers and their supervisors: treating vendors fairly and economizing. Treating vendors fairly meant soliciting competitive bids and in some cases favoring small or socially disadvantaged businesses. To achieve economies, buyers often procured a less expensive good, even if it did not fully perform the intended function and even if the purchase was delayed to aggregate many agencies' requests for a similar item. For example, several years ago, a Minnesota community college requested that central purchasing procure numerous personal computers for a course on computing that was to be offered in six months. This course was listed in the college catalogue and soon became oversubscribed. By the semester's start, these personal computers had not yet been obtained. To minimize unit costs, central purchasing had delayed ordering them until enough other requests had accumulated. No one compared the forgone value of buying less appropriate materials or of imposing extensive delays in delivery with the cost savings generated. The focus was on measured cost savings, not on the trade-off between actual value and actual cost.

Cooperatively integrating competitive values does not require that conflict between staff and line organizations would or should disappear. An employee of the personnel agency, for instance, will ordinarily be more committed to preserving the values of the state's civil service system and labor relations than the line manager, who is normally committed to his or her program goals. In both the old and new visions, such structured conflict is useful; it engages actors with different (but valid) perceptions, normative commitments, and interests in a process of mutual adjustment. Advocates of the new vision, however, deny that the old vision's process of noncooperative mutual adjustment is very functional. They challenge overseers and managers to focus on enhancing line agencies' performance, to take into account the opportunity cost of exercising central control, to regard line-agency and staff-agency managers and overseers as partners, to infuse staff-line interactions with the spirit of joint problem solving, and to hold state agencies accountable for their performance.

Elements of a Post-Bureaucratic Vision

The post-bureaucratic vision challenges staff-agency employees to regard their participation in various kinds of mutual adjustment processes as essential to improving governmental performance.[3] To help staff-agency employees understand this responsibility, the post-bureaucratic vision uses the conceptual network of service management.[4] Even before this conceptual network becomes part of their work experience, staff-agency employees, as members of a post-industrial society, tacitly understand service management. Consequently, specialized training may not be necessary for staff-agency employees to imagine how they could use service-management ideas to engage in mutual adjustment with line agencies or overseers.

The bureaucratic reform vision was crafted during the rise of the manufacturing sector. In contrast, America's contemporary economy, values, and rationality myths are heavily influenced by the service sector.[5] Consequently, many staff-agency employees eventually realize that the public interest will be better served when they use their expertise to provide quality and cost-effective services to customers as does a service sector business.

The principal customers for some staff-agency employees are their political overseers; for others, the managers of line agencies. In some circumstances, both are their customers. In either case, the satisfactions and complaints of these customers reveal how well they are performing their staff function. In the new vision, the general public is not the customer of staff agencies but the ultimate beneficiary of the interactive process among line, staff, and overseers.

Staff-agency employees should be accountable to their customers, which means that the customer is entitled to judge what constitutes value. Because staff agencies were formerly understood to be accountable only to the public and to overseers, being accountable to customers requires a paradigm shift. While being accountable to overseers as customers is consistent with the bureaucratic reform vision, being accountable to line-agency managers as customers directly contradicts this older view. Once staff-agency employees make the paradigm shift, however, they accept the concepts of both accountability and service management.

---

3. Lindblom (1965).
4. Lakoff and Johnson (1980); Albrecht and Zemke (1985); Heskett (1986); Heskett (1987); and Barzelay and Kaboolian (1990).
5. Meyer and Rowan (1977).

Because people in government characteristically wish to serve those to whom they are accountable and because society honors such efforts, the acceptance of this presumption gives rise to a strong desire to meet customers' needs and expectations.[6]

A fundamental strategic choice is whether the principal customers of particular staff-agency employees are overseers or line agencies. When overseers are the principal customers, staff-agency employees are in the business of assuring the people in these roles that state managers and employees take into proper account the public's interests, which include democratic accountability of the bureaucracy; financial accountability; honest, fair, and equitable administration; the forging of value-creating links among agencies; and informed policy decisions. In contrast, when line-agency managers are the principal customers, staff-agency employees are in the business of meeting each line agency's budget-constrained demands for productive inputs, such as qualified personnel, physical facilities, equipment, information, supplies, and professional services.

The services that staff agencies should offer overseers as customers include the following: financial control, or assurances that governmental funds are managed according to financial and budgetary policy; state agency leadership, to assure that managers and employees understand and comply with statewide norms of honesty, fairness, and equity; linkage formation among the production strategies of individual agencies, to take advantage of economies of both scale and coordination; information and analysis, to help overseers hold line agencies accountable for aligning their production strategies and mandates; and policy advice.

In providing leadership and forging productive linkages, staff-agency employees should focus their attention on the public's interests in government operations (including honesty in government, quality service, strengthened civic norms, fairness, efficient use of resources, and social equity), instead of on rules and procedures.

Staff-agency employees who serve overseers should also recognize that line managers are more likely to cooperate with statewide norms of government operation if they understand, tolerate, and accept those norms. To build such understanding and acceptance, staff-agency employees should involve line-agency managers, as well as overseers, when developing norms. Once the norms are developed and understood, line-agency managers bear the responsibility for devising the means to

6. Peters and Waterman (1982).

comply with them, thereby bringing mandates and production into closer alignment. Staff-agency employees should be willing and able to assist line-agency managers with their compliance planning. Once formulated, compliance plans should be reviewed by staff-agency employees to ensure that they conform to the statewide norms. Sample audits should be conducted to assure that line agencies are implementing their compliance plans and to obtain remedies for noncompliance. In addition, the post-bureaucratic vision urges overseers (and the staff-agency employees who serve them) to conduct periodic performance reviews, apart from the appropriations process.

When staff-agency employees are accountable to line-agency managers as customers, they should respond to line managers' conclusions about how to bring their mandates and production into alignment. Staff-agency employees may try to influence these judgments, using a variety of marketing strategies, but should not substitute their own. For example, if line-agency managers believe that, to achieve their mandate, they need to use more data processing services, staff agencies should not stand in the way. The service levels or expenditures of these staff-agency activities should be set not by overseers but by line agencies' appropriations.

While overseers hold line agencies accountable for serving the public and meeting other expectations in their mandates, they should hold staff agencies accountable for developing and implementing service enterprise strategies that are successful in the state government environment. Such strategies should be focused on creating value for customers, net of cost.

In a few instances, staff-agency employees should regard both line-agency managers and overseers as their customers. The activities of procurement and personnel, for example, need to reflect line agencies' mandate-driven needs, as well as the public's interests in central control. Under the new vision, service-management concepts should be used in developing strategies even for these nonprototypical service enterprises. Furthermore, overseers should hold the managers of such activities accountable for meeting the needs of line-agency customers, balancing the public's interests in accomplishing line-agency mandates and in central control.

A Strategy for Managing Staff Agencies

The management strategy of Minnesota's Department of Administration (DOA) made a sharp distinction between "control" and "service" activities.[7] For prototypical control activities, the customers were overseers, such as the governor and the members of relevant legislative appropriations and policy committees. For prototypical service activities, the customers were line-agency managers. This strategy placed a high value on the efforts of staff-agency employees to decide whether they were engaged in service or control. DOA executives used the post-bureaucratic vision to coach their employees as they decided who their principal customers were.

As a result of this process, numerous activities were classified as service activities, including the central supply store, the typewriter repair service, the central motor pool, building maintenance, travel management, printing and mailing, management consulting, and the state documents center. Many other activities, such as inventory and property management, were classified as control activities. In one crucial case at the Information Management Bureau (IMB), attempts at categorization led to a formal reorganization. Department executives and key legislators decided to divest IMB of its oversight responsibilities for data processing and telecommunications and to transfer them to a newly created Information Policy Office (IPO). (In addition, IPO was granted authority to review all agency requests for legislative appropriations for the development or purchase of information systems equipment or software.) Thus DOA's information-technology responsibilities were divided between IMB's service function and IPO's control function.

For procurement, however, this tension between service and control was not so easily resolved. DOA recognized the need to improve line-agency managers' satisfaction with the department's buying and contracting services as well as to meet its overseers' demands for honest, fair, and equitable treatment of vendors and for economies of scale. In devising a strategy for procurement, DOA undertook to specify to whom each buyer and contracting agent was accountable and for what.

One reason the post-bureaucratic strategy places great emphasis on the service-control tension is that people are powerfully motivated when they have a sense of purpose. For many people, satisfying others provides an engaging purpose.[8] Exercising leadership in state government on behalf of one's overseers is an engaging purpose, as is serving the production needs of line-agency managers. In contrast, serving and control-

---

7. Minnesota Department of Administration (1986).
8. Hackman (1986).

ling the same line-agency managers is not a particularly engaging purpose, because the value system that orients human action in a control relationship undercuts the value system that orients work in a service relationship. By clarifying who the customer is, the Minnesota strategy sought to foster work-unit cultures in which employees take personal responsibility for producing results that either line-agency managers or overseers will value. A clear choice also enables staff-agency employees to create mutually understood and more satisfactory relationships with the people with whom they interact most often—their counterparts in line agencies.

To a greater extent than before, staff-agency employees engaged in service activities and their line-agency customers now interact through the process of buying and selling. In this process, internal service providers gather firsthand information about what product attributes are of greatest value to their customers as well as how their performance is judged by those customers—information that comes through customer contact, the use of surveys and focus groups, periodic visits by DOA executives to line agencies, and other marketing devices. The results of these attempts to understand customers' needs are then used by the service providers to adjust their products and how they do business. In the same process, customers learn how DOA can accommodate their particular needs; they become aware of the range and depth of the product lines offered by service activities; and they may discover new ways of organizing their own production processes.

The Minnesota strategy also used revolving funds to structure and manage the process of buying and selling internal services. (Service activities that operate on revolving funds do not receive general fund appropriations; instead, sales are the source of revenue.) To illustrate how revolving funds work, suppose that the Department of Natural Resources (DNR) decides to employ the printing operation to produce a brochure. In return for services rendered, the DNR pays a fee to the printing operation based on the unit price and volume of the services sold. Payment takes place through a transfer from the DNR's appropriated funds (or its revenues from users fees) to the printing operation's revolving fund account. The amount of funds transferred represents the revenue earned by the printing operation. The same revolving fund account is charged for all the expenses incurred, including overhead, in producing the brochure. This system of exchange and payments makes it possible for service managers to spend as much as they deem necessary to satisfy the demands of line agencies for such internally produced products and services. The exchange of funds for services rendered also supports the idea that internal service activities are enterprises, accountable to line agencies as customers. It potentially undermines the notorious general fund mentality, which focuses on executing planned budgets, not on meeting customers' needs and controlling costs. In addition, the use of accrual instead of cash accounting yields one measure of value-cost leverage, namely net income.[9] Thus, in implementing this strategy, the Minnesota state legislature agreed to finance two major service activities, telecommunications and plant management, with revolving instead of appropriated funds.

Still, legislative overseers were worried that a unit with both control and service responsibilities might, in response to pressures by line-agency managers for better service at lower rates, reduce the resources devoted to oversight. This was of particular concern when IMB possessed both control and service responsibilities while financed by revolving funds. Thus the legislature funded some control activities—such as those previously assigned to the IMB—by appropriations, not revolving funds. Paying for control activities with appropriated funds also improved the working relationships between staff and line agencies, for the rates that line agencies paid for service no longer included the cost of controlling them.

A Strategy for Control Activities: The Case of IPO

The post-bureaucratic strategy of control was most clearly developed in Minnesota in the Information Policy Office. IPO's customers—the legislature—articulated their needs and expectations in the statutory language that created the office:

> The office must develop and establish a state information architecture to ensure that further state agency development and purchase of information systems equipment and software is directed in such a manner that individual agency information systems complement and do not needlessly duplicate or conflict with the systems of other agencies. The development of this information architecture must include the establishment of standards and guidelines to be

9. Heskett (1987).

followed by state agencies. . . . The office shall assist state agencies in the planning and management of information systems so that an individual information system reflects and supports the state agency's and the state's mission, requirements, and functions. The office must review and approve all agency requests for legislative appropriations for the development of information systems, equipment, or software. Requests may not be included in the governor's budget submitted to the legislature unless the office has approved the request.[10]

The specific operating strategy for satisfying overseers as customers was fourfold.

First, much effort was devoted to formulating a commonly understood and jointly valued set of principles that constituted the state's information architecture. Principles were usually cast in broad language, such as the principle that all data are the property of the state and not of individual agencies. These principles were debated and voted on by an information policy council, composed of deputy and assistant commissioners who represent the major users of information technologies.

Focusing attention on principles, instead of rules, created flexibility in implementation and kept the purpose of coordination more clearly in view. In addition, through the overall design of an information architecture, IPO's staff attempted to persuade legislators that IPO understood information management from a statewide perspective and that a set of general, guiding principles existed that the legislators could also use to make better budgeting decisions.[11]

Second, IPO sought to communicate these principles, as well as the overall vision, to all those involved in making information-related decisions. It published a guide for planning new information systems, "Charting Your Course: Strategic Information Planning for the 90s," and issued a monthly newsletter, *Inside Information.* These and other communication media, in addition to training seminars, helped line-agency managers learn how to relate with IPO during the appropriations process.

Third, a consulting and implementation section of the office provided agencies with a framework for probing the implications of the statewide architecture for their information management and acquisition decisions. In preparing for the biennial budget process, this section required state

10. Minnesota Statutes, 1987 Supplement, Section 16B.41, subdivision 2.
11. Grant (1989, p. 7).

agencies to submit an organizational mission statement, an information vision, a strategic information plan, a conceptual information architecture, a tactical information plan, and information systems–related budget requests.

Fourth, while most of IPO's human and financial resources are devoted to developing, negotiating, communicating, and implementing the state's data and telecommunications architecture, some resources are allocated to enforcement. The job of enforcement personnel is not to audit all agencies to determine whether they are conforming to statewide norms for information systems, but to audit relatively few agencies to determine whether they are conforming to their own IPO-approved plans.

To measure IPO's performance, the staff held periodic performance appraisal meetings with the legislative overseers who were most interested in information technology, including the chairperson of the House Appropriations Committee's State Departments Division. In addition, after the conclusion of the 1989 legislative session, IPO held focus groups with agency managers. According to *Inside Information,* the words most frequently used by the state's managers to describe IPO's work included "client-oriented," "nonbureaucratic," "educative," "personable," and "credible."

IPO's model of control is a response to the failings of the old vision's enforcement model of control, which understood successful performance to involve promulgating numerous detailed rules, granting large numbers of discrete permissions to act, and performing extensive audits. In the new vision, the "control function shifts from focusing on preventing managers from making mistakes and punishing those that do not abide by the rules, to focusing on helping managers succeed."[12]

A Strategy for Managing Internal Service Activities

The strategies of Minnesota's internal service activities include service-oriented missions and accountability relationships. In composing mission statements, internal service providers articulate a common concept that gives direction and meaning to their work. These mission statements, along with memories of composing them, influence the way service-activity

12. Grant (1989, p. 6).

employees understand and resolve operational issues. Service providers' operational actions and decisions are also influenced by their accountability relationships with line-agency employees and overseers.

For example, one of the most prominent internal service organizations is the InterTechnologies Group, formerly the Information Management Bureau. During the transition to a service orientation, IMB partly described its mission as "providing centralized management of computer applications and facilities, telecommunications, and records for state agencies." The InterTechnologies Group's revised mission was "to provide results from information assets which customers value."[13] This shift symbolized a much greater concern for the results of information-related service activities—in the future as well as the present—as perceived by InterTech's customers in line agencies and elsewhere in government.

In 1988 the Operations Management Bureau, which groups together such activities as printing, mailing, travel management, the central supply store, the state documents center, and materials management, had the following mission:

> The Operations Management Bureau provides efficient and effective general services to state agencies. The bureau is efficient when quality services are provided at costs which are less than the private sector. It is effective when agencies are satisfied with its services and standards. The mission is to provide support to the operating agencies of state government by helping them get more from their budget dollars.[14]

Within the bureau, the travel management division established a mission to provide safe transportation and travel services for state employees on official business at the lowest possible cost to the state. The printing and mailing services division sought "to provide quality printing, copying, mailing, and rental services to meet the graphic communication needs of all three branches of state government."

To hold internal service activities accountable for pursuing their missions, department executives and operating managers used the practices of both service management (agency-relations visits, measuring customer satisfaction, marketing, sales-trend analysis, and competitive analysis) and financial management (financial reporting, business planning, capital project evaluation, and price setting).

---

13. Pinke (1989, p. 2).
14. Minnesota Department of Administration (1988, p. 2).

Identifying and Listening to Customers

One basic feature of an accountability relationship is the obligation to listen to criticism. To create an accountability relationship between service providers and line agencies, Admin executives scheduled and participated in annual agency-relations visits, beginning in 1983.

> The agency relations visits reports in the fall of 1984 were quite controversial. These reports, printed on colored paper to attract attention, included the comments of line-agency managers, and were distributed throughout the department. Negative comments were not edited, except to remove overly abusive language. Some of the department's managers complained bitterly about line managers' criticism of their services being published for others in the department to see. This was precisely the idea, however. We wanted to create a climate in which the line managers' opinions had a good deal of value and impact.[15]

Managers were also encouraged to develop their own means for measuring satisfaction with their services, such as customer comment cards and surveys. In addition, during 1985, the department as a whole developed and administered a survey to eleven hundred managers in state government.

Marketing

In the Department of Administration, marketing included two-way communication aimed at a mutually satisfying exchange of something of value. Department executives made marketing management a key responsibility of activity managers. For example, as part of annual performance plans, activity managers are asked to devise marketing programs. As a result, the printing division began to focus on the needs of particular market segments; the central store formulated plans to expand its share of the public sector market for supplies; and the documents center greatly increased its range of publications.[16]

The Role of Competition

Furthermore, internal service activities were held accountable for examining and adjusting to a competitive environment. Each year as part

15. Zlonis (1989, p. 2).
16. Zlonis (1989, p. 3); Ordahl (1989); and Barzelay (1988, p. 7).

of the price- or rate-setting process, activity managers compared their prices with those outside of state government.[17] Competitive pressures also came from substitute ways to meet line agencies' needs. For example, office photocopies competed with the services of the central printing operation, and state employees conducting official business could either use motor-pool vehicles or their personal cars. Collective bargaining agreements specify the per-mile rate of private vehicle reimbursement. In this case, service providers became accountable for increasing their share of the total state market for vehicular transportation and for keeping the cost-per-mile below the private vehicle reimbursement rate.

The Minnesota strategy exposed to private competition many service activities, including data entry, micrographics services, central stores, management consulting, and typewriter repair. Because line agencies were authorized to contract with outside vendors, internal service activities had to continuously strive to meet the needs of line-agency customers better than the competition. The managers of these marketplace activities were held accountable by DOA executives for developing strategies that built on sources of competitive advantage, such as familiarity with state government systems, norms, and people. They were also accountable for meeting financial performance plans (for example, net income targets).

Financial Management of Utilities

When the public's interests in central provision and control (for example, the realization of statewide economies of scale and coordination) were believed to outweigh the public's interests in using open competition among internal and external providers, services activities were not subjected to private sector competition. In Minnesota, activities that fit this description included the statewide telecommunications network and office space management in the capital area. Such activities—known as utilities—were held accountable to customers by revolving fund governance as well as by service-management practices.

The cost of providing services was a major issue in relations between the managers of utilities and their customers. Before the new strategy was adopted, line-agency managers complained that these utility rates

17. Zlonis (1989, p. 6).

increased much faster than did their agencies' appropriations. At that time, line-agency managers argued that the state's internal service activities were not accountable for the decisions that affected the rates line agencies paid. In creating a provider-customer accountability relationship, the Department of Administration chose to involve line-agency executives in the governance of utilities, with customers participating in the process that determined rates. The resulting annual rate packages were constrained by two policies: charging on the basis of fully allocated costs, and equating expected revenues and expected expenses during each fiscal year. Within these constraints, rate review panels had discretion over customization and standardization decisions as well as over investments and divestments—all of which affected costs and, therefore, rates.

The tools used by staff-agency executives and legislative appropriations committees to oversee utility revolving funds included the annual rate packages and quarterly financial statements.[18] The annual rate packages delineated all of the key factors that affected rates, including agreed-upon service levels, planned investments, spending plans, and adjustments to retained earnings. Revolving fund financial statements included a balance sheet, income statements, and sources and uses of cash.

Financial Management of Marketplace Activities

Most marketplace activity managers were accountable for offering valuable products and services to their customers and for doing so profitably. Prices for activities that competed directly with private vendors were based on a number of factors, including the cost of providing the service, trends in the marketplace, the development of market incentives, and customer resources. Department executives carefully reviewed and approved annual business plans that projected revenues, expenses, and profit. These plans also identified investment and market-growth opportunities, which were funded either from retained earnings or from loans granted by the Department of Finance.

The department's policy was that retained earnings from marketplace activities were to be returned to the general fund. The amount targeted for return to the general fund was negotiated with and approved by the Department of Finance, which also approved annual business plans and investment decisions.

18. Minnesota Department of Administration (1986, p. 23).

Some Consequences

The clarification of operating-unit missions and accountability relationships, along with the strategic use of service and financial management concepts, altered the organizational cultures and practices of Minnesota's internal service activities. For example, at InterTech:

> Managers and other staff have readily picked up the challenges of looking at their function and methods differently from what they ever were in the organization's history. Great inroads have been made in the four key emphasis areas of creating customer service relationships, adopting marketing concepts, strengthening financial management, and price competitiveness. The new mission and its four concepts are used to guide decision-making in the new environment. New customers are being drawn to work with InterTech staff, and ongoing customer relations have been strengthened. Some customer/InterTech relationships have become the partnership envisioned in the new mission.[19]

In many cases, the morale of internal service providers also substantially improved, especially when their purposes and accountability relationships were clarified. In plant management, the confluence of shifting the funding base and asking for customer evaluations helped employees understand that they were accountable for improving the satisfaction of line-agency personnel and for keeping plant management's rates comparable to those of privately owned and managed buildings. In the change, plant management acquired the tools needed to meet this challenge, including better cleaning equipment and higher quality supplies. Within a few years, plant management had visibly improved facilities, received positive evaluations by customers, achieved rate stability, and accumulated modest retained earnings.

The financial performance of internal service activities improved markedly after 1983. In fiscal year 1982, the retained earnings of nine of fourteen revolving fund activities were negative. By fiscal year 1989, all but one revolving fund had positive retained earnings. Yet such progress was not achieved at the expense of another financial objective: controlling rate increases. Before the strategy evolved, line agencies complained that rates were increasing faster than their budgets. Between fiscal years 1985 and 1989, in contrast, the average yearly rate increase for revolving

19. Pinke (1989, p. 10).

fund activities was only 1.77 percent, and average rates in fiscal year 1990 were only 0.86 percent higher than in fiscal year 1989.

Furthermore, the volume of services increased significantly. For example, once department executives decided to meet the pent-up line-agency demand for motor-pool cars, they increased the fleet from eight hundred to one thousand vehicles. When the highly respected management consulting activity was financed by revolving funds, it virtually tripled the volume of its services. In contrast, the conversion of the financing of telecommunications to a revolving fund led to a 50 percent decrease in volume; after customers had to pay for these services, they found ways to economize.

The new strategy also altered the range and quality of products. The central store modernized its selection of supplies (for example, by stocking Post-it notes) while terminating its the sixty-year-old typewriter repair service. The documents division liquidated obsolete titles and began to stock many new books about Minnesota or by Minnesota authors.[20] InterTech chose not to develop new, major systems.[21] Plant management experimented with differentiating its product into three levels of quality and cost. The printing operation began to offer quick-turnaround photocopying services at locations near its customers. And the motor pool upgraded its vehicles by, among other things, acquiring front-wheel-drive cars equipped with air conditioning and cloth upholstery.

A Strategy for Managing Central Purchasing

Working out the strategic implications of the post-bureaucratic vision is especially challenging when the staff function resembles both the service and control categories. Central purchasing is a classic example. Historically, its dominant orientation was to control line agencies' purchases of good and services from the private sector and to keep the administration of state government nonpartisan, efficient, legal, and fair to vendors. If, however, purchasing is a service activity, then its business is to provide centralized professional buying services to line agencies. In this view, the buyers who work for central purchasing are professionals who know how to evaluate vendors' product offerings and ensure that pur-

20. Ordahl (1989, p. 4).
21. Pinke (1989, p. 3).

chases are made in accordance with state policies. Centralization creates specialization that makes it easier for buyers to evaluate product quality as well as to judge whether a vendor is a responsible bidder. Because the procurement operation negotiates statewide contracts for many product lines, centralization also provides an opportunity for line agencies to purchase many of the same commodities and services for less money.

Calling procurement both a service and control function is consistent with the post-bureaucratic vision. Procurement's business is to perform the professional work of buying products and choosing vendors on behalf of line agencies and to ensure that these purchases are made in accordance with state laws and policies.

When asked to identify their principal customers, employees of Minnesota's purchasing operation—after four months of extended discussion—chose line agencies. The designation of line-agency managers as purchasing's main customers did not mean, however, that this organization was striving to become a prototypical service activity. Unlike internal service activities, which were financed by revolving funds, central purchasing was funded by appropriations. This arrangement signals that buyers were not accountable to line-agency managers in precisely the same way as, for example, providers of data processing services, who sold their services to line agencies. Because appropriations committees reviewed general fund activities more closely than revolving fund activities, central purchasing had regular contact with overseers, essentially as customers. Thus central purchasing was enmeshed in a more complicated set of customer relationships than are prototypical service activities.

Mission and Accountability in Central Purchasing

The mission of the purchasing operation in Minnesota was "to purchase products and services that best meet the necessary quality requirements for the needs of our customers, at the best possible price from responsible vendors, within the required time frame, in accordance with all applicable statues and in an ethical and professional manner." James Kinzie reports that many of the words contained in this statement were debated and fought over with a passion.[22]

In response to many internal changes, purchasing employees grew to understand and accept this mission. These changes included examining

22. Kinzie (1989, pp. 10–11).

how the work of the office was conducted (using process flow analysis), collecting information about processing times, hearing and responding to line agencies' criticisms voiced at agency relations meetings, hiring a few individuals who had not been socialized into the old vision of procurement, focusing attention on bigger purchases (by increasing line-agency authority for small purchases), expanding training opportunities, redesigning the office facilities, rewriting job descriptions, increasing buyers' signature authority, traveling regularly to line agencies to meet with customers, holding regular staff meetings, establishing specialized units for awarding contracts and for managing vendor relations, and recognizing successful employees with achievement awards. These sweeping internal changes were motivated by a desire among many purchasing employees to improve their ability to respond to line agencies' needs. Dealing with line agencies' criticisms was the point of departure:

> It took me two or three meetings to get the group to stop being defensive and to listen to what the agencies were trying to say. The comments in the survey about us were extremely graphic and at times bitter, which would almost automatically cause people to get defensive. This was, of course, a natural reaction because to them it made their work of the last twenty years seem wasted—a tough pill for anyone to swallow. What I attempted to do was to get them to see that our customer agencies were complaining about the system rather than about them personally. When that sank in, we started addressing ways to change the system to allow us to give the agencies the level of service they needed.[23]

Changing the system also involved efforts by Department of Administration executives to work with some of purchasing's other customers: legislators on the government operations committees. These overseers gradually approved legislation that enabled purchasing to meet many of the line agencies' demands for improved service.

The performance of the central purchasing activity is measured in numerous ways. One indicator is the average amount of time elapsed between the arrival of a materials requisition form and the issuance of a purchase order. In July 1986 the average elapsed time was fifty-one days, with only 22 percent of materials requisitions processed in less than twenty-five days. In contrast, during fiscal year 1989, the average pro-

---

23. Kinzie (1989, p. 12).

cessing time was twenty-one days, with 57 percent of incoming requisitions fully processed in less than twenty-five days.[24]

A Strategy for Managing Central Staffing

Employees of central staffing activities are traditionally devoted to the idea that their expert administration of recruiting, classification, and examination standards is crucial for making state government an efficient, clean, and fair institution. They are highly invested in the mission of defending the system against the particularistic demands of line-agency personnel and overseers. One aim of the new strategy for managing this activity in Minnesota was to decrease staffing employees' guardianship of the system and to increase their sense of accountability for the results of their work. The mission statement of the staffing division of the Department of Employee Relations's personnel bureau reflected this change in outlook:

Our mission is (1) to assist state agencies in maintaining the quality and continuity of their workforce by ensuring that staff needs are met on a timely basis and (2) to ensure that consistent relationships exist among positions statewide as a foundation for an equitable compensation system.[25]

With the new mission and strategy, staffing employees are asked to care about the customer needs and public policies—but not a mention of the system. Furthermore, managers of the staffing activity portrayed the system as an evolving tool for accomplishing public policies (for example, merit employment, open access, affirmative action, and line-agency mandates) instead of a bulwark against chaos and corruption.

Once staffing activity managers decided that their unit served customers and that the primary customers were line-agency managers and supervisors, the department created an agency services section. The members of each agency services team were responsible for coordinating all personnel knowledge and actions necessary to resolve customers' problems according to statewide staffing norms.[26]

---

24. Kinzie (1989, p. 27).
25. Johnson, Kurcinka, and Vikmanis (1989, p. 45).
26. Johnson, Kurcinka, and Vikmanis (1989, p. 22).

As part of the strategy leading service-agency employees to experience accountability to line-agency managers, each team's responsibilities were broadened to include identifying qualified candidates as well as classifying positions, thereby enabling a single team to handle virtually all the work that the central staffing activity must perform in structuring and filling positions. Staffing managers created three distinct agency service teams: one for social service agencies, one for scientific and technical agencies, and one for administrative agencies. This move focused the attention of agency services employees on assisting particular customers; it also concentrated expertise within a team for the subset of position classification, in each group of agencies. When team members needed special assistance in making classification or examination decisions in accord with statewide norms, they drew on the resources of the staffing division's experts, who were assigned to the technical services section. Agency services teams were also to draw on the resources of the applicant services section, whose job was to schedule and score tests, certify highly qualified candidates, and provide employment information to prospective applicants.

Defining the Quality of Staffing Services

After redesigning the activity's jobs and organizational structure, staffing-division managers worked to develop standards of quality performance within the framework of its complex accountability relationships. In doing so, they attempted to clarify exactly what behaviors were expected from staffing employees. In part, they defined quality as meeting a number of standards for responding to fully documented customer requests. Standards included producing within one day lists of already certified candidates for an opening, providing copies of candidates' applications within three days, and assigning vacant positions to a class within two weeks.[27] These standards were formulated by staffing employees in consultation with line-agency managers, tested during a four-month experiment, subsequently publicized in a newsletter distributed to all state managers, and then tracked to see that they were being met on a consistent basis.

Quality performance was also defined, in part, as demonstrating to customers that the staffing division cared about their needs. It also meant

27. Minnesota Department of Employee Relations (1988).

contributing to realistic and informed customer expectations about the services that the staffing division could, given its operational capacity and public policies, deliver. Staffing managers reassured their employees that responding positively to managers did not necessarily mean saying yes to their requests.

Improving Working Relationships

The staffing-division managers used service-management concepts to improve the working relationships among line-agency managers, line-agency personnel officers, and themselves. Through focus groups and informal conversations, staffing managers discovered that line managers' knowledge of the staffing process was highly fragmented and distorted. Most of their limited knowledge came from interactions over specific requests with line-agency personnel officers. Neither line-agency personnel officers nor the central personnel bureau had attempted to inform line managers about how the system operated.

A key element of the new staffing strategy was to provide information to line managers—over time and through multiple channels—that would improve their ability to work with line-agency personnel officers and centralized agency services teams in resolving staffing problems. As part of this campaign, service teams visited their customers and made presentations. A regular newsletter, *Smart Staffing: An Information Series for Managers and Supervisors,* was also developed. Written in nontechnical language, it provided practical information that managers could use in approaching problems with their agency personnel officers and the central staffing division. Several issues of *Smart Staffing* described less familiar hiring options such as short-term hiring, temporary appointments, provisional appointments, reinstatements, exceptional qualifications appointments, work-out-of-class assignments, interagency mobility assignments, temporary unclassified appointments, transfers, and demotions.

One reason that line managers had previously not possessed the information they needed to plan their staffing efforts or solve staffing problems was that agency personnel officers viewed their specialized knowledge of the system and their role as the sole channel for agency communications with the Department of Employee Relations as sources of power and organizational standing.[28] These agency-based personnel professionals

---

28. Johnson, Kurcinka, and Vikmanis (1989, p. 30).

historically did not seek to be held accountable to the line managers in their agencies for meeting their staffing needs in a timely and convenient fashion. The staffing division's use of service management concepts in relation directly to its customers in line agencies was designed, in part, to empower operating managers and supervisors to hold their own personnel officers accountable for providing quality services.

Some Consequences

When line-agency managers were surveyed in March 1988, 50 percent said they were satisfied with the staffing division's efforts to make the system understandable; in a survey in January 1989, this number increased to 90 percent. Similarly, but less dramatically, line-agency managers' satisfaction with the staffing division in "helping to solve problems" increased from 53 percent to 72 percent over the same short interval. In the later survey, a new dimension of quality was identified: effectively helping managers to hire staff to serve the public. On this dimension, 74 percent of respondents in January 1989 said they were satisfied.[29]

The new strategy has also gained measurable support from the legislature. Funds were appropriated for upgrading information systems and for hiring five new staffing division employees. Legislation was passed authorizing the commissioner of employee relations to suspend laws and rules to experiment with procedures that would speed the hiring process.

Conclusion

The post-bureaucratic vision promises staff-agency employees clearer and more meaningful accountability relationships, as well as the tools required to succeed in satisfying the customers to whom they would become more clearly accountable. It also offers staff-agency employees ways to explain the value of their work to themselves and to others— ways that fit the broader culture's evolving system of meaning.[30] Another attraction of post-bureaucratic operational missions and accountability relationships is that the work effort oriented by these ideas tends to generate palpable responses from the people who are affected by what staff-

29. Johnson, Kurcinka, and Vikmanis (1989, p. 48).
30. Meyer and Rowan (1977).

agency employees do. The expectation of receiving positive feedback, or even feedback of any reasonable kind, is engaging, especially when compared with the feedback experienced by people operating under the bureaucratic reform vision. Furthermore, the idea of "accountability to customers" can be of interest to employees who would otherwise be accountable only to superiors, providing them with a conceptual system other than the "chain of command" for discerning what actions are valuable or virtuous. This alternative conceptual system can change for the better an employee's relations with hierarchical superiors.

The Minnesota experience reveals that the search for greater meaningfulness in the everyday life of public service can motivate staff-agency employees to undertake the unsettling process of examining their work from a different vantage point.

References

Albrecht, Karl, and Ron Zemke. 1985. *Service America: Doing Business in the New Economy.* Homewood, Ill.: Dow Jones–Irwin.

Barzelay, Michael. 1988. "Introducing Marketplace Dynamics in Minnesota State Government." Case Program. Harvard University, John F. Kennedy School of Government.

Barzelay, Michael, and Linda Kaboolian. 1990. "Structural Metaphors and Public Management Education," *Journal of Policy Analysis and Management,* vol. 9, no. 4 (Fall): 599–610.

Grant, Larry. 1989. "Leadership as a Model for Control in a Bureaucratic Organization." Paper prepared for the conference on Managing State Government Operations: Changing Visions of Staff Agencies. Harvard University, John F. Kennedy School of Government, June 13–14.

Hackman, Richard J. 1986. "The Social Psychology of Self-Management in Organizations." In *Psychology and Work: Productivity, Change, and Employment,* edited by Michael S. Pallak and Robert O. Perloff. Washington, D.C.: American Psychological Association.

Hale, Sandra. 1989. "Creating and Sustaining and Environment for the New Vision." Paper prepared for the conference on Managing State Government Operations: Changing Visions of Staff Agencies. Harvard University, John F. Kennedy School of Government, June 13–14.

Heskett, James L. 1986. *Managing in the Service Economy.* Harvard Business School Press.

_____. 1987. "Lessons in the Service Sector." *Harvard Business Review,* vol. 65, no. 2 (March-April): 118–26.

Johnson, Elaine, Joe Kurcinka, and Julie Vikmanis. 1989. "From Personnel Administration to Human Resource Management: Changing Visions of the Central Staffing Function." Paper prepared for the conference on Managing State Government Operations: Changing Visions of Staff Agencies. Harvard University, John F. Kennedy School of Government, June 13–14.

Kinzie, James. 1989. "From Economy and Efficiency to Creating Value: The Central Purchasing Function." Paper prepared for the conference on Managing State Government Operations: Changing Visions of Staff Agencies. Harvard University, John F. Kennedy School of Government, June 13–14.

Lakoff, George, and Mark Johnson. 1980. *Metaphors We Live By.* University of Chicago Press.

Lindblom, Charles E. 1965. *The Intelligence of Democracy: Decision Making through Mutual Adjustment.* Free Press.

Meyer, John W., and Brian Rowan. 1977. "Institutionalized Organizations: Formal Structure as Myth and Ceremony." *American Journal of Sociology,* vol. 83, no. 2 (September): 340–63.

Minnesota Department of Administration. 1986. *A Strategy for Managing and Funding DOA Activities.*

_____. 1988. *Agency Overview.*

Minnesota Department of Employee Relations. 1988. "Turnaround Times for DOER's Services." *Smart Staffing* (July): 3.

Ordahl, Stephen. 1989. "Managing Internal Services: The Documents Center." Paper prepared for the conference on Managing State Government Operations: Changing Visions of Staff Agencies. Harvard University, John F. Kennedy School of Government, June 13–14.

Peters, Thomas J., and Robert H. Waterman. 1982. *In Search of Excellence: Lessons from America's Best-Run Companies.* Warner Books.

Pinke, Judy. 1989. "Managing Internal Services: The Inter-Technologies Group." Paper prepared for the conference on Managing State Government Operations: Changing Visions of Staff Agencies. Harvard University, John F. Kennedy School of Government, June 13–14.

White, Leonard. 1933. *Trends in Public Administration.* McGraw-Hill.

Zlonis, Jeff. 1989. "Internal Service Activities." Paper prepared for the conference on Managing State Government Operations: Changing Visions of Staff Agencies. Harvard University, John F. Kennedy School of Government, June 13–14.

CHAPTER SEVEN

Innovation in Public Sector Human Services Programs:
The Implications of Innovation by 'Groping Along'

Olivia Golden

MANAGERS IN state and local human services agencies are trying to solve problems for which routine government practice is failing; thus they cannot do without innovation. For example, when Greg Coler took office as director of the Illinois Department of Children and Family Services, he found a "crisis in adoption" of African American children—and he found that his agency's routine practices and its isolation from the African American community were part of the problem.[1] When Jean Ekins, director of the Family Learning Center in Leslie County, Michigan, started worrying about teen pregnancy and its connection to dropping out of school, she found that her rural community had always assumed that young mothers would drop out. She had to find her own way to a new set of practices that might change that outcome.[2]

Professional practice and academic research offer at least two models for successful innovation in the public sector. The first model, "policy planning," emphasizes the importance of an innovative idea carefully refined into statute and policy, a comprehensive effort to foresee and

An earlier version of this chapter was published as Golden, Olivia. 1990. "Innovation in Public Sector Human Services Programs: The Implications of Innovation by 'Groping Along.'" *Journal of Policy Analysis and Management,* vol. 9, no. 2 (Spring): 219–48. Reprinted by permission of John Wiley & Sons, Inc.

1. Warrock (1988).
2. Brunetta (1988b).

avoid implementation problems, and the use of control and incentives to ensure that actions conform with the original policy. The second and contrasting model deemphasizes the initial policy idea in favor of rapid action modified by experience. In Robert D. Behn's vision of management as "groping along," a public agency's ability to solve a difficult problem in a new way comes from adaptation to the environment.[3] If this second picture is correct, we might expect that successful public sector innovations frequently do not arise from a single clear statute or executive policy but from a messy process of evolution and adaptation, featuring many changes and wrong turns.

To see which of the two models best characterizes effective innovations and to find possible implications for human services agencies, I examined seventeen successful innovations in human services, identified through the Ford Foundation and John F. Kennedy School of Government Awards Program for Innovations in State and Local Government.[4] These seventeen programs were the 1986 winners and finalists in human services, broadly defined to include education, employment and training, and health (see table 7-1). For four of the seventeen examples, I could rely on research by other authors; for the other thirteen, I have used material in the awards program files.

The Ford Foundation cases have an important advantage over samples more typically used for studies of public sector innovation: They allow us to work backwards from innovative operating programs and ask how they developed. Thus, for these cases, the implicit definition of an innovation is an innovative operating program, not an innovative idea. Consequently, these programs could have developed from a clear innovative idea or from many adaptations that add up to an innovative program (as one might expect under the groping-along model).

By contrast, most previous studies of public sector innovation have drawn a sample from jurisdictions adopting either federally supported innovations or programmatic or technological innovations that

3. Behn (1988); and Behn (1991, chapter 7).
4. The Awards Program for Innovations in State and Local Government was established in 1985 by the Ford Foundation, in conjunction with the John F. Kennedy School of Government at Harvard University. Applications were solicited for programs of all types from state and local jurisdictions across the country. Kennedy School faculty and staff screened the applications in several stages producing a pool of about twenty-five finalists per year, which each received a site visit by evaluators with related academic or professional expertise. The final selection of ten winners was made by the Ford Foundation's National Committee on Innovations in State and Local Government.

Table 7-1. Winners and Finalists in Human Services, Ford Foundation and John F. Kennedy School of Government Awards Program for Innovations in State and Local Government, 1986

Program	Sponsor	Description
Winners		
Block Nurse Program	St. Paul, Minn.	Home health care and home care services for the elderly, provided by neighborhood residents
Case Management for At-Risk Children	Department of Juvenile Justice, New York, N.Y.	Case-management services to identify needs of individual children in detention and to follow up into the community
Family Learning Center	Leslie public schools, Ingham County, Mich.	Comprehensive services for pregnant and parenting teens
FoodNet	Los Angeles County, Calif.	Food distribution system for surplus foods and other food assistance
One Church, One Child	State of Illinois	Cooperative arrangement with black churches for adoption of African American children
Quality Incentive Program (QUIP)	State of Illinois	Nursing home payment system with payments scaled by quality of care
Rehabilitation Engineers Program	State of North Carolina	Field-based engineers travel to homes and workplaces of disabled individuals to make customized modifications
Finalists		
Emergency Homes for Families	Memphis, Tenn.	Transitional housing and social services for homeless families
Employment and Training (ET) Choices	Commonwealth of Massachusetts	Comprehensive employment and training program for welfare recipients
Hartford Action Plan for Infant Health	Hartford, Conn.	Public-private partnership including insurance companies, banks, local foundations, and government with the aim of reducing infant mortality in Hartford

Table 7-1. (continued)

Program	Sponsor	Description
Homeless Services Network	St. Louis, Mo.	Public-private partnership providing comprehensive services for the homeless, including coordinated referral and intake for shelters, case management, counseling, and other services
Medicaid Demonstration Project	Santa Barbara County, Calif.	Alternative approach to organizing and paying for medical care, with a focus on physician case management and on cost containment
Mobile Construction Crew	Kansas City, Mo.	Provides training in the building trades for minority youth through the rehabilitation of homes owned by low-income residents
Prison Pet Partnership	State of Washington	Vocational training program in dog obedience training and kennel management, which is also intended to improve inmate behavior through their affection for the dogs
Progressive Property Management	Suffolk County, N.Y.	Makes properties owned by the county because of tax arrears available to the Department of Social Services for homeless families
Sound School	New Haven, Conn.	Public high school that uses the marine environment as the focus for teaching
Washington Service Corps	State of Washington	Community service program that matches unemployed young people with community agencies that have unmet needs

researchers specified in advance.[5] Such studies then trace the evolution of the federal policy or the technology in a local operating setting. While these studies employ a sharper, less subjective definition of innovation, they run the risk of overemphasizing the original policy idea and under-sampling examples of groping along. Thus the Ford cases offer a broader range of examples of the development of innovation.

Two Models of Innovation in the Public Sector

Two contrasting models of innovation exist in the public sector, with contrasting implications for managers who need to innovate to solve problems or accomplish results.

The Policy Planning Model

Observers, practitioners, and scholars frequently assume that most ben-eficial changes come about through new policy ideas, typically adopted through legislation. From this assumption flow a number of suggestions for innovators: The public manager who wants to innovate should pay a great deal of attention to the development of good ideas and to their refine-ment into excellent and implementable policies. Then the manager should use incentives and controls to induce compliance with the innovative policy. The manager might also rely on a group of analysts who are pro-tected from day-to-day concerns to develop and refine the ideas and to give these analysts power to force the bureaucracy to carry out their ideas.

The naive version of this view assumes that a good new idea enshrined in statute or in an authoritative executive policy decision is the first and the single key step in producing change. Despite the more complex picture developed by the implementation literature, scholars and practi-tioners often employ this simple idea. Robert T. Nakamura notes, for example, that the "textbook policy process," with its neat categories and sequential ordering, "is widely incorporated into our vocabulary"—the vocabulary of both "scholars" and "policy actors"—despite its clear inaccuracies.[6] One reason is that the political environment surrounding

---

5. Berman and McLaughlin (1978); Levin and Ferman (1985); Mazmanian and Sabatier (1983); and Yin (1979).
6. Nakamura (1987, p. 143).

practitioners and the training and self-image of analysts and academics overemphasize ideas, formal policies, and program design.[7]

The sophisticated view, reflected in the "top-down" or "planning and control" elements of the implementation literature, recognizes the many obstacles to converting a policy idea into an operating program but argues that authoritative policy decisions, frequently in statutory form, are crucial to major change; that the quality of planning reflected in those policy decisions is crucial to their successful implementation; and that the implementation strategy should aim to control subsequent actions to conform as much as possible to the original policy. For example, Daniel A. Mazmanian and Paul A. Sabatier argue that, in most important cases, it is possible to identify both a legislative decision that is a key starting point for policy change and a stage of policy formulation. And they disagree with what they call a "pessimistic" finding that implementation in practice results in considerable adaptation of the original policy.[8] Reviewing the implementation literature, Giandomenico Majone and Aaron Wildavsky note that this model emphasizes the initial policy design and "prescribes clearly stated goals, detailed plans, tight controls and—to take care of the human side of the equation—incentives and indoctrination."[9]

For public managers committed to innovation, the practical implications of both the simple and the sophisticated versions of this model are similar. First, managers should concentrate energy, time, and resources on identifying the best ideas and developing them into excellent statutes, policies, or programs. For the implementation theorists, this recommendation includes refining an idea to take implementation issues into consideration when designing policy. In a review of implementation prescriptions, Laurence J. O'Toole, Jr., describes the conventional wisdom among these researchers with a top-down perspective: "(1) design policies to keep the degree of required behavioral change low . . .; (2) simplify the structure of implementation and minimize the number of actors . . .; (3) seek more consideration of the problems of implementation during the initial stages of policy formulation . . .; and (4) take care to leave the responsibilities of implementation among units sympathetic to the policy."[10]

7. Levin and Ferman (1985, pp. 25–26).
8. Mazmanian and Sabatier (1983, pp. 79, 766).
9. Majóne and Wildavsky (1984, p. 165).
10. O'Toole (1986, p. 200).

Second, as suggested by Majone and Wildavsky, this model prescribes bringing choices made during action into line with the original policy. Thus Mazmanian and Sabatier "sought to identify a number of legal and political mechanisms for affecting the preferences and/or constraining the behavior of street level bureaucrats and target groups."[11]

Third, organizations should create a special unit of analysts freed from operational tasks and given power over bureaucratic action. For example, Arnold J. Meltsner proposes that to achieve innovation, it may be necessary to isolate analysts from day-to-day pressures and give them strong budgetary enforcement powers that enhance their control over the rest of the organization.[12]

The Groping-Along Model

A sharply contrasting view of innovation in public organizations, which is much closer to recent analyses of change in private organizations, argues that a good policy idea is the result of a stream of experience, not the starting point.[13] Therefore, as Behn argues in "Management by Groping Along," successful public managers concentrate on gaining experience by translating ideas quickly into action and then changing course as needed.[14] What these managers start with, according to Behn, is a sense of mission or direction but not a well-defined policy: "An excellent manager has a very good sense of his objectives but lacks a precise idea about how to realize them. . . . Despite years of experience and study, even the best manager must grope along. He tests different ideas and gauges their results. Then he tries different combinations and permutations of the more productive ideas."[15]

The theory behind this vision is made more explicit by writers in the tradition of "implementation as exploration."[16] The complexities of the real world cannot be anticipated, and ideas divorced from rich operational experience are so general that they are likely to be systematically wrong; thus the results cannot be known ahead of time. Consequently, ideas need to be tried out so that experience can become a teacher. Based on that

11. Sabatier (1986, p. 25).
12. Meltsner (1976, p. 294).
13. Mintzberg (1987, pp. 66–75).
14. Behn (1988); and Behn (1991).
15. Behn (1988, p. 645).
16. Browne and Wildavsky (1984a).

learning, not only actions but also the policy idea and the original objectives may need to be modified. According to Browne and Wildavsky,

> What an organization devoted to learning can do about implementation failure is to utilize it as a route to implementation success—successful exploration. Rather than seeking to make tractable eternally intractable social problems, or designing detailed problem-solving policies, a learning organization must . . . analyze its policies for their informational yield. It should evaluate its implementation of these policies, not against prospectively stated objectives alone, but in light of discoveries made during implementation.[17]

The prescriptions implied by this view of successful innovation are different from those of the policy planning model. Instead of planning ahead, managers ought to act quickly, pay attention to the results of their actions, and then modify them based on experience. Behn writes that managers ought to "establish a goal and some intermediate targets. Then get some ideas and try them out. . . . You will never really know which ones are productive until you experiment with them." Furthermore, managers ought not to spend their time planning: "Do not spend your time attempting to plot out carefully your exact course, with all the details. You can never get it right."[18]

Several other authors have offered evidence that these prescriptions—particularly the emphasis on flexibility and adaptation—are associated with successful innovations. For example, Martin A. Levin and Barbara Ferman found that reassessment and "error correction" were characteristic of effectively implemented programs under the Youth Employment Demonstration Projects Act.[19] Paul Berman and Milbrey McLaughlin found that "mutual adaptation"—that is, changes in both the federally proposed policy and the local school district's operations—characterized successful implementation of federal innovations in education.[20]

Phyllis Ellickson and others found support for a second element of the groping-along model: brief initial planning periods. For the local innovations in criminal justice that they studied, long planning periods were

17. Browne and Wildavsky (1984b, p. 255). For more on the reasons that the results of implementing ideas cannot be known in advance, see Levin and Ferman (1985, pp. 14–16); Mintzberg (1987, p. 69); Lindblom (1959, pp. 86–87); and Etheredge (1985, pp. 141–43).

18. Behn (1988, p. 652).

19. Levin and Ferman (1985, p. 101).

20. Berman and McLauglin (1978, pp. 14–15).

less successful than short ones, because they diverted energy from action and led to rigidity in operations: "Contrary to the expectations of adoption theory, initial characteristics of the innovation itself rarely provide useful information about its eventual success. This is because most criminal justice innovations change over time as they are adapted to their institutional environment."[21]

The differences between these models are significant for both practitioners and academics because they lead to different prescriptions for improving program innovation and therefore program performance. The policy planning perspective advises the manager to concentrate energy on framing an initial statute and policy design, to plan carefully and comprehensively with attention to implementation as well as policy, and to work to keep others in line with the initial policy plan. In contrast, the groping-along model involves much less attention to the original idea or policy—a number of different policies might start an organization down a useful path—and advises the manager to act quickly (perhaps even without specific statutory authority), to test ideas through experience (gathering operational information along the way), and to regard the divergent actions of implementors as reason to adjust the policy, not just to change the actions.

Four Detailed Case Studies

The following detailed case studies of successful, innovative managers offer an opportunity to try out the two contrasting models in four real situations.[22]

Family Learning Center

In 1986, when it won the Innovations award, the Family Learning Center—sponsored by the Leslie public schools in rural Ingham County, Michigan—offered pregnant and parenting teen-agers a comprehensive program of education, day care, social and mental health services, and health care with the aim of keeping them in school.[23] The impressive

21. Ellickson and others (1983, pp. 43–44).
22. These cases date from the Ford Foundation's 1986 award year, more than ten years ago, and have not been updated or contacted for this chapter.
23. Brunetta (1988).

program results included more than 90 percent graduation rates, better than average birth outcomes, and a low rate of repeat pregnancies.[24]

The program was founded in 1974 by Jean Ekins, a schoolteacher who had left teaching while her own children were young. As she began looking for an opportunity to return to work, she became aware of teen pregnancy as a general issue and, more specifically, as the reason that many Leslie residents failed to finish high school. Working with Leslie's first adult education director, she developed a proposal for a program for teen parents and took it to the school board. Because of the religious and political conservatism of Leslie, she anticipated considerable resistance to providing services to pregnant girls. But once she demonstrated that no local funds would be required—state reimbursements for the additional students would pay for the program—the board allowed her to go ahead.

In the program's first semester, the comprehensive and integrated services that earned it an Innovations award twelve years later did not exist. The strictly educational program consisted of one teacher (Ekins) and eight students. Ekins saw quickly that the students' needs went far beyond education and that to succeed the program would have to address those needs: "It just hit with both barrels because there were so many needs out there."[25] She continued, "It was real clear that we had to make some changes immediately, and the first change was we had to figure out how we were going to transport these young people to the educational program. . . . The second thing became very clear: these young people could not go to school on a daily basis if they did not have child care."[26]

As she found new supporters, many outside of Leslie itself, Ekins expanded services. She added a day-care center with a volunteer supervisor in the school's second semester; weathered a bitter community dispute over sex education in the schools later that year (a dispute so bitter that her mailbox was bombed twice); added a second full-time teacher in the fall of 1975, drawing on funding (and credibility) provided by a neighboring school district that offered to pay for its students to attend the center; achieved state licensing of the day-care center, which enabled the volunteer supervisor to become a full-time, paid staff member; persuaded the Leslie public health nurse to become part of the program; got involved in teen-pregnancy issues at the state level and

24. Schorr (1988, p. 204).
25. Brunetta (1988a, p. 7).
26. Brunetta (1988a, p. 6).

decided to expand her services further; persuaded a social worker to offer some social services on-site; and eventually received state funds to hire a third full-time teacher and a mental health counselor.

One Church, One Child

In 1986, One Church, One Child sought adoptive homes in the African American community for African American children through a partnership with black churches.[27] After the state of Illinois committed to make the adoption process more responsive to the African American community, the pastors began urging families within their congregations to adopt a child. Along with changes in adoption policies and procedures, One Church, One Child reduced the number of African American children awaiting adoption in Cook County (Chicago) from more than 700 in 1979, to 212 in 1983, to 45–65 in 1988.

When Greg Coler became director of the Illinois Department of Children and Family Services (DCFS) in 1978, he faced "a crisis in adoption" of African American infants and children.[28] About twice as many African American as Caucasian children were awaiting adoption in Cook County, even though it was about three-quarters Caucasian.

Coler's initial effort—publicizing the availability of the children for adoption—did not work. His agency provided funds for a nonprofit clearinghouse for information on adoption information and enlisted support from newspapers and television. "The department produced public service announcements promoting adoption. But . . . they ran at odd times of the day and night, not necessarily during DCFS office hours. Later the department learned that people had responded to the ads and phoned the department on the spur of the moment, only to reach a telephone that was never answered."[29]

In the early summer of 1980, the idea of working with the black churches came up in a meeting and, in July, Coler followed up by meeting with the well-respected African American pastor of a Chicago Catholic Church, Father George Clements. Over the next several months, they defined the program and built a network of pastors. The program became operational in Cook County that November, when Father Clements urged families in his congregation to step forward to adopt a

27. Warrock (1988).
28. Warrock (1988, p. 1).
29. Warrock (1988, p. 4).

child; when no one responded, he announced that he would adopt a child himself—a step that received considerable publicity.

Next, Coler addressed legislative and bureaucratic issues. In the program's first eighteen months, he financed it through flexible funding in his own budget. For fiscal year 1982, however, he made the case to the governor that, compared with foster care, adoption saved money, and the governor proposed a substantial increase in adoption funds. In 1981 the state legislature enacted several changes in adoption procedures proposed by Coler.

At the same time, it became clear that the program could not work without major changes in staff attitudes and procedures within the adoption agency. DCFS had tended to exclude African American families through both formal agency regulations, such as requirements for the number of rooms in an apartment, and unofficial practices, which screened out prospective parents who seemed unsophisticated or uneducated. Consequently, Coler and his deputy, Gordon Johnson, changed agency operations by offering pay and compensatory time incentives to workers, hiring new African American adoption workers who did not share the assumptions of existing staff, encouraging staff to use their own creativity to carry out the new mission, and backing up that sense of mission with new quotas for placements as well as new procedures that emphasized responsiveness to prospective parents. Several of the ideas for changing procedures—for example, the use of group processes to prepare and counsel families—came from individual adoption staff.

In 1982–83 the program expanded statewide producing another round of changes, most notably in organizational structure and staffing. The program continued to change and adapt, responding in part to new issues raised by its success. Johnson recalled: "We woke up one morning and we had more white and Hispanic kids needing adoption placement than black."[30] In 1988, One Church, One Child added a Caucasian Catholic priest and a Hispanic priest to the board and produced brochures targeting these groups.

Case Management for At-Risk Children

In 1986, Case Management for At-Risk Children was a set of innovations at New York City's Department of Juvenile Justice (DJJ) that

---

30. Warrock (1988, epilogue 6).

together aimed to identify children's individual needs (medical, educational, and other), offer services to address those needs during the (sometimes brief) time that the child is in DJJ, and follow the child back to the community with "aftercare" services.[31] The innovation lay in applying the idea of case management (which is common for long-term social services programs) to an agency that detains youth pending disposition by the courts and, therefore, has custody of them for indeterminate and often brief periods.

When Ellen Schall became DJJ commissioner in January 1983, she found a history of violence and escapes at the department's one secure detention facility (Spofford); racial tensions, turf wars, and low morale among the staff; and no common sense of the agency's mission. Moreover, she found staff paralyzed by a perceived incompatibility between two conceptions of their role: custody and care. As Schall recalled, the staff aggressively challenged its new leadership: "What are we? Guards or caretakers? . . . What is it? Are we this or that? Tell us, and don't sort of smoosh it in the middle."[32]

According to the Innovations application, the evolution of case management as a concept that might bring together the two sides of the dilemma happened over about six months. It began in April 1983 with the implementation of the Aftercare program, funded by a federal grant. Over the next two years, DJJ took a dozen specific actions including a major organizational development effort drawing on outside consultants and a reorganization of Spofford to better fit case management. Along the way, the senior staff debated whether to create a single concept of case management and apply it throughout the agency but decided to work with the various operating units (secure and nonsecure detention, for example) to develop individualized approaches based on each unit's needs.

Collecting information from formal systems and from the experience of case managers and then adapting the program to that information was part of DJJ's philosophy of innovation. In the beginning, information as basic as the length of stay of the youth in detention or the youths' reading levels or health needs was not available. According to the application,

> We have been lucky to have had the time to try something, to fix it, to learn from our mistakes. . . . We are institutionalizing not just service delivery systems for children but also a systematic

31. New York Department of Juvenile Justice (1986); and Varley (1987).
32. Varley (1987, p. 13).

approach to change. What we have developed is a careful and iter-ative process of raising questions; collecting data to answer those questions; developing mechanisms and forums for involving staff at all levels in program design and redesign; building consensus about the best program options; and institutionalizing new pro-grams into the operating and management structure of the agency.[33]

At the beginning, the mandate for change was uncertain. When she was appointed, Schall recollects: "The mayor said two things to me: 'Don't let any of them get out,' and 'Do as much as you can for them.' "[34] Thus, in the beginning, DJJ asked for as little explicit political authorization as possible; then, as evidence of success began to show, it requested more. The early stages of the innovation were funded by federal money and foundation grants, with no request for additional city funds until July 1985, fifteen months after pilot implementation. As the program demon-strated success, DJJ asked for more city funds. According to the applica-tion, support from the mayor and deputy mayor came about "in part because . . . we have turned around the agency."

ET Choices

Employment and Training (ET) Choices, a finalist in the 1986 Inno-vations awards, provided education, training, day care, and other support services to welfare recipients in Massachusetts with the aim of helping recipients attain self-sufficiency.[35] The program differed from other state work-to-welfare programs (particularly those in existence when it began) in the voluntary nature of recipient participation, the comprehensiveness of program services, and the program's commitment to day care and other support services.

Behn proposes ET as an example of "management by groping along." Welfare Commissioner Charles Atkins, writes Behn, "knew where he wanted to go. But he did not know how to get there." His agency "had little expertise in helping welfare recipients find jobs; nor had it exhib-ited much desire to do so."[36] Atkins, however, chose neither detailed advance planning nor a pilot program. Instead, "just six months" after

33. New York Department of Juvenile Justice (1986, application II, questions 19 and 29).
34. Varley (1987, p. 4).
35. Behn (1991).
36. Behn (1991, p. 128).

Atkins became commissioner, "ET began operating statewide."[37] Atkins
established placement goals for each local office, encouraged considerable improvisation in how local offices achieved these goals, and then
learned from effective and ineffective approaches. Atkins's managerial
philosophy was clear: "Get it up and running, and then fix it."[38]

Behn mentions many readjustments and adaptations. For example:

—The department adjusted its marketing strategy for welfare recipients once it learned from focus groups that they were not responding to
participants' success stories.

—The department fought for and won a long list of changes in worker
salaries, job assignments, and working conditions to enable workers to
carry out the new mission.

—Over time, the department increased emphasis on the hard-to-serve,
developed a broader network of service providers and thereby expanded
services available, and changed its standards for the types of jobs into
which recipients are placed.

—After being an Innovations finalist, the department developed a
case-management system that goes beyond ET to ask workers to develop
self-sufficiency plans for the families on their caseloads.

As in the Family Learning Center, the qualities for which the program
was recognized by the Innovations program developed only over time. As
Behn notes, "The ET of year one was an extremely primitive program
compared with the case-management system developed for year five."[39]

Findings

To decide if an example of innovation fits the policy planning or
groping-along model, a determination must be made of how one process
of innovation would differ from the other. At least four detectable differences exist between the two models: (1) the role of initial legislation, (2)
the timing and development of the innovative idea, (3) the role of planning in advance of implementation, and (4) the level of change during
program operation.

First, the expectation is that innovations developed through policy
planning would most often begin with legislation, while legislation would

37. Behn (1991, p. 127).
38. Behn (1991, p. 127).
39. Behn (1991, p. 129).

not be evident as an initial element of innovations that developed through groping along. Legislative action would more likely occur after program development in groping-along innovations—in the same way that, according to Henry Mintzberg, strategies in the private sector are often formally adopted after, instead of before, they are expressed in action.[40]

Second, in innovations that developed through policy planning, a clearly specified policy idea would be expected to be present from the early stages of the innovation, before implementation, and this initial idea would remain a constant throughout the program's development. In contrast, groping-along innovations would not be characterized by a well-specified initial idea. Instead, a very sketchy concept would emerge, probably in the form of a broadly expressed goal (a sense of where the agency should go), which is fleshed out with clearer programmatic content (a sense of how to get there) during implementation. Also to be expected is a multitude of programmatic ideas aimed at the same goal, all to be tried in the hope of identifying the most promising. After several years of development, the central idea of a groping-along innovation would not necessarily align closely with the original concept.

Third, in innovations that came about through policy planning, an extended planning period could be discerned during which the program design and the best implementation process are developed. By contrast, groping-along innovations should be characterized by a brief planning period before implementation, to get the idea into operation as soon as possible.

Finally, in successful policy planning innovations, limited change would take place during operations. While all innovations will change somewhat during implementation, change in the policy planning model ought to be less fundamental and less frequent than in the groping-along model. In addition, different managerial attitudes would be evident toward change, with policy planning innovators focusing on bringing implementation back in line with the original plan, through controls or incentives, while groping-along managers focus on learning from experience about how to change the plan. That is, in innovations that are fully consistent with the groping-along model, managers would seek out and welcome change, not merely accept it.

The programs described in the four detailed case studies offer the best evidence for distinguishing between the two models, because the addi-

40. Mintzberg (1987, p. 69).

tional evidence collected by the casewriters fills in the gaps in the appli-cations material and provides a knowledgeable outside perspective. For the other thirteen programs, the application files appear to offer reliable evidence on certain specific facts, such as the presence or absence of leg-islation and the dates of implementation. The files offer suggestive but considerably less complete and reliable evidence on more subtle points, such as the completeness of the original idea or the commitment of the managers to a culture of change. For these more subtle distinctions, I draw most fully on the four complete case studies and rely on the other thirteen programs primarily to provide a context, a general and prelimi-nary sense of the limits or the strength of the findings drawn from the four primary cases.

The Role of Initial Legislation

Innovation did not typically begin with legislation. Only one of the seventeen examples started with legislative action. In this single excep-tion, the Washington (state) Service Corps, state legislators concerned about youth unemployment and lack of funding for community services initiated the innovation by passing legislation to recruit unemployed youth, match them with community agencies, and pay their salaries through state funding with a match from the employing agency. This example fits fully the policy planning model.

However, none of the other cases fits so well. In four, the innovation did not begin with legislation, but it received at least some legislative support early in the process. The four examples represent a range from limited and perhaps grudging acquiescence (the Leslie School Board voting to allow the Family Learning Center to go ahead, provided that it would not cost money) to enthusiastic endorsement (the local community council voting to support the St. Paul Block Nurse Program). Still, in these four cases, the legislative action came after the program design.[41]

In the remaining twelve cases, either the applications did not record any legislative action or such action came much later. In the One Church, One Child and the Case Management for At-Risk Children programs, program managers did not seek legislative action at the beginning, when

41. The other two examples are that the Memphis City Council voted funding for the Emer-gency Homes for Families and that the California legislature passed legislation needed by the Medicaid Demonstration Project in Santa Barbara.

it might have delayed program operation. They sought legislative assistance and budgetary authority after the program had some momentum and, ideally, some successes.

The Initial Innovative Idea

A more fundamental difference between the two models than the role of legislation is the role of an initial, well-specified idea. As a group, the four detailed cases suggest, consistent with the groping-along model, that the innovative idea is rarely fully present at the beginning but develops through action. The thirteen less detailed cases offer a couple of counterexamples as well as considerable support for this view of the innovative idea as a culmination, not a first step.

Among the four detailed cases, the Family Learning Center, ET Choices, and Case Management for At-Risk Children offer the clearest examples of the limitations of the initial idea and of its development through action. In the Family Learning Center, the initial idea—to teach a special class to pregnant teen-agers to keep them in school—was neither fully specified nor innovative. It was substantially different from the final idea of comprehensive and integrated services for the whole family.

In ET Choices and Case Management for At-Risk Children, the initial idea was useful but broad, and the programmatic content of the idea—the sense of how to get there from here—developed only through action. The initial idea of ET Choices included general principles that remained key, such as voluntary participation and a variety of services, but the details of how to carry out those principles were worked out through implementation. As a result of this continual refinement of the initial ideas through operational experience, Behn notes, the 1988 (fifth-year) ET Choices program looks substantially different from the program Atkins started in 1983.[42] Similarly, in Case Management for At-Risk Children, the initial idea was simply to "do something for kids" that would move away from the custody-versus-care dichotomy; the next stage of the ideas, "case management," was not much more specific until it was fleshed out by actions.

The fourth of the detailed cases, One Church, One Child, originally seemed (based on the application) to represent the policy planning end of

42. Behn (1991, pp. 127–50).

the continuum. But the casewriter's further research revealed considerable development and change in the central idea as a result of operational experience. In particular, the idea of involving the churches itself emerged through Coler's groping along toward a way of involving African American families in adoption of African American children: He tried out a portfolio of ideas, including such failures as the public service announcements, and this was the one that worked. Furthermore, involving the churches, central as it appears to the innovation, is far from the whole of it. In the end, the role of the ministers in reaching their congregations turned out to be only half the real innovative idea; the other half was the agency's adaptation to the needs of African American families, through changes in policy, personnel, and agency culture.

The application files for the other thirteen programs offer somewhat mixed evidence on this point. At least two seemed to have had a well-specified and complete idea in place before operation began:

—The Medicaid Demonstration Project in Santa Barbara County, California, a 1986 finalist, provided health care to MediCal recipients through a case-managed system with each recipient having a primary care provider (a physician or hospital) who approved access to health care and was paid per capita by the county. Before operation, the program idea appears to have been developed to a specific level, making it possible to put in place federal medicaid waivers, state enabling legislation, a contract with a fiscal agent, and contracts with health care providers.

—North Carolina's Rehabilitation Engineers Program, a 1986 winner, supplemented the usual counseling, training, and medical services offered to the disabled with five circuit-riding engineers. These engineers traveled throughout the state to design and build equipment that enabled disabled individuals to function at home or at work. While the program managers were receptive to program adaptation and change, this idea of where the program was going and how to get there seems to have been constant from the beginning.

One caution in interpreting these examples is that applications written retrospectively might be expected to overstate the coherence of the innovative idea over time and to smooth away some of the wrong turns and blind alleys. Such selective memory could bias descriptions toward the policy planning model.

Despite this possible bias, a number of the applications describe how ideas developed in action in ways that resemble the groping-along model. For example, the central idea of the Illinois Quality Incentive Program (QUIP) incorporated both a key element that was present from the beginning and a key element that developed unexpectedly through action. The initial idea was to pay nursing homes based on their quality, rated from one to six stars so that the public would immediately understand the meaning of the score. The idea that developed through action was the key role of the nurse case managers (who visited the homes and evaluated quality) in educating and motivating nursing-home owners to provide better care.

On balance, these successful public sector innovations offer considerable support for the groping-along model—not as the only possible route for innovation, but as one important route. In many cases, the innovative idea was not well specified at the beginning but became so gradually, as the program evolved.

Planning for Implementation

As predicted by the groping-along model, the 1986 finalists and winners were characterized by rapid implementation instead of extended planning. For fifteen of the seventeen winners and finalists, the time from the first discussion of the idea to initial (sometimes pilot) operation was about a year or less. In Case Management for At-Risk Children, DJJ's aftercare program began six months after Schall's appointment as commissioner; One Church, One Child began within six months after the idea first came up; and ET Choices began operating statewide about six months after Atkins began working on it. A few other examples:

—Illinois's QUIP is striking for the speed with which it was carried out in a large, statewide medicaid bureaucracy. The idea came up during 1984 negotiations between the state and the nursing homes and was written into their December 1984 settlement; the staff was hired and the program written and designed in January and February 1985; and the first round of assessments was conducted in June of 1985, just six months after the idea was first ratified.

—The Block Nurse Program reported six months between the first neighborhood meetings and brainstorming and the first clients served.

—The Emergency Homes for Families program reported two months from the time of the idea until the first leases were signed and renovations begun, and six months before the first family was placed in a house.

—The St. Louis Homeless Services Network reported ten months from the time the mayor appointed a task force on the problem until the network began operation.

One of the two programs with a longer planning period was the Medicaid Demonstration Project in Santa Barbara County, which (to receive waivers and clearances from federal and state governments) had to resolve many operational issues during planning. It also had to negotiate various contracts. As a result, the period from the receipt of the first planning grant to operation was about three years. Possibly, the groping-along approach is harder to adopt in a program so tightly linked to the requirements of higher levels of government; Santa Barbara's demonstration was part of a state program (MediCal), which in turn was part of a national program (medicaid), whereas many of the other innovations fit into the gaps between other programs.[43]

The Role of Change

Consistent with the groping-along model, the four detailed case studies illustrate frequent and substantial change. The Family Learning Center evolved from a solely educational program to a comprehensive one. DJJ developed and modified its case-management program in response to perceptions by individual units of their operating needs. One Church, One Child adjusted organizational structures and internal policies as it went along (and, at the end, adapted to success by trying to expand to Caucasian children). And ET Choices changed its services, the nature of its job goals, and the structure of worker jobs. In all four cases, the culture of change comes through as well in the voices of the managers: in ET Choices, "Get it up and running, and then fix it"; in the Family Learning Center, "there were so many needs out there"; in the Department of Juvenile Justice, "We have been lucky to have the time to try something, to fix it, to learn from our mistakes."

The application files reveal widespread consistency but at least one possible counterexample: the Medicaid Demonstration Project, which again appears to better fit the policy planning model. The application form did not note any program modifications since implementation and

43. Irwin Feller and Donald C. Menzel discuss the influence of intergovernmental relations on innovative behavior. They hypothesize that new federal mandates, attention, and money may all encourage innovative behavior by state and local jurisdictions; they do not discuss the issue raised here about the more extended advance planning that may be required by networks of intergovernmental regulation. Feller and Menzel (1977, pp. 61–62).

predicts continuation or "continued improvement" instead of substantial change or modification. Questions on program obstacles and shortcomings elicited primarily descriptions of obstacles outside the program rather than anticipated changes in the plan. This evidence, while sketchy, makes sense given the program's context; its extraordinarily complicated regulatory environment might make change more difficult and more costly than for more free-standing programs.

For the most part, however, the application files confirm that successful innovations change frequently and substantially during program operation and that innovative managers actively question their experience and seek out change. In response to an application question asking for milestones in the program's history, many of the programs cited events occurring since the beginning of implementation as well as before—even though the sample answers given in the question itself emphasized events up to the point of implementation (initial legislative authorization, serving the first client). In response to other questions (about program shortcomings, obstacles encountered, and future expectations), many applications offered a generous list of actual or intended changes. And some managers found yet other places on the application form to discuss both the changes they had made and their general managerial philosophy about change:

—St. Louis's Homeless Services Network (a 1986 finalist and 1987 winner) linked up a whole range of services for the homeless, operated by different community groups across the city, into a unified network. At the time of its 1986 application, it had been operating only five months and therefore reported no modifications since implementation. But the culture of change came through in a report of a major modification made right at the point of implementation: "Rather than put a flawed plan into operation and oversee its inevitable failure, everyone worked to revise the plan so that it would succeed. Thus, a major obstacle or pitfall was transformed into a beneficial program modification."

—North Carolina's Rehabilitation Engineers Program has displayed considerable consistency over time. Nonetheless, the program managers seem to possess the same culture of change, even if they find their program to need less fundamental overhaul. For example, according to the application, "It has . . . been vital to re-write internal policies and procedures early in the Program." In response to the question on program shortcomings, the application offers three, all identified through operations, along with solutions to two of them. And at a Ford Foundation seminar for the 1986 winners, the North Carolina manager spoke powerfully about the role change and adaptation played in the program's success.

One final piece of evidence for the managerial culture of change is that the process of learning through experience appears not to stop when the program is recognized as successful by the Innovations award but to go on indefinitely. In a seminar for the 1986 and 1987 winners, the 1986 winners emphasized not only the modifications that they had made before winning the award but also the modifications during the year since the award. The studies of ET Choices and One Church, One Child (by researchers who followed the programs after they received the awards) support those impressions.

Thus, in many of the seventeen cases, the groping-along model of frequent, substantial, and deliberately sought-out change fits closely. In these examples, the innovations are out on the street rapidly in some form, but no one views that form as final; initial implementation is only the beginning of a process of constant change in response to information. Compared with what would be expected from the policy planning model, most of these innovations reveal not only frequent change but also a managerial culture of change that sees continual reassessment as desirable.

The Ford Foundation winners and finalists offer some variety in the model of innovation that they follow, with at least one example characterized by policy planning. But most of these successful innovations, including the four with the most researched evidence, evolved by groping along.

Applicability of the Findings and Limitations of the Sample

Even if these seventeen cases of human services innovation are overwhelmingly of the groping-along type, the nature of case study evidence raises questions about their applicability to the broader world of public sector innovations. Because these finalists and winners are not a random sample, the finding that these human services innovations are characterized by groping along can only be suggestive.[44] However, the suggestion

44. In addition, because I have not examined the initial applications to the awards program, a distinction cannot be made between two interpretations of the finding that human services finalists and winners are characterized by groping along. The first interpretation is that innovations in general, both successful and less successful (that is, initial applications as well as finalists and winners), are frequently characterized by groping along. The second interpretation is that successful innovations (the finalists) are more frequently characterized by groping along than less successful innovations (the applications weeded out at earlier stages). Both of these hypotheses, however, would suggest that managers learn how to grope along.

will be stronger if the cases have been selected by a process that, so far as can be determined, is unbiased—and weaker if the entry and selection process already leans toward groping-along programs.

Candidates for the Ford Foundation awards were self-nominated. To generate these nominations, the Kennedy School of Government mailed applications to lists provided by the major organizations of state, county, and municipal governments, to alumni of all Kennedy School programs, and to anyone who requested information. The mailings included, in addition to executive branch officials, state legislative leaders (majority and minority leaders, committee chairs, speakers) and city council members in large cities. The legislative mailings are important because they suggest that the outreach did not bias the group of applications against programs initiated by legislatures. Little is known about what kinds of programs were most likely to respond to these mailings, although the program brochure encouraged initiatives in human services and economic development as well as public-private and public-non-profit partnerships. Within human services programs, the evidence does not suggest that either groping-along or policy planning innovations would have been systematically more likely to enter.

The outreach effort generated more than thirteen hundred applications. Then, to produce the twenty-five finalists, teams of people associated with the Kennedy School and the Ford Foundation screened the applications. The available information about the criteria used by the screening teams and the impressions of Innovations program staff do not suggest that either groping-along or policy planning innovations were systematically favored. Because neither the entry nor the selection process seems to favor one or the other type of innovation systematically (at least within the group of human services programs), little reason exists to believe that the winners and finalists are systematically different from other successful state or local innovations in human services.

But do these winners and finalists offer a basis for hypothesizing about programs outside human services and about programs at the federal instead of the state and local level? Here the suggestion seems much weaker and the need for caution much greater. Programs in human services might differ from those in other fields in several ways that are systematically related to their style of innovation. For example, human services innovations require little initial investment compared with, for example, innovations in more capital-intensive fields (such as revamping a highway system or a governmentwide computer system). Possibly, programs that require more up-front investment have to devote more time to advance planning and are less able to adjust after implementation than human services programs, leading them to the policy planning model. The chain of cause and effect also could be easier to predict in some other fields. If that were the case, policies developed in advance might lead to fewer unanticipated consequences than in human services and have less need of adjustment through groping along.

Similarly, federal programs may be different from state and local programs in systematic ways that affect the development of innovation. First, as suggested in the Santa Barbara medicaid innovation, a program's links to complex intergovernmental systems might restrict the ability of managers to grope along by increasing the requirements for predictability. This restriction might be true for federal programs looking down the intergovernmental system as well as for state and local programs looking up. Second, after a certain point, the size of a program could restrict the ability to grope along (though several of the state and local programs, such as ET, are large). Third, the focus on operating programs means that the evidence does not address federal legislative or regulatory innovations that are important for their symbolic power, as ideas, instead of for their operations.

Overall, then, winners and finalists in human services may be different from innovations in other fields and at the federal level, but they do not seem likely to be systematically different from other state and local innovations in human services.

A Time-Phased Model of Innovation by Groping Along

These seventeen cases support Behn's prescriptions for "management by groping along." The next step is to refine these prescriptions to make them more valuable as a guide to managerial action. What exactly is meant by advising managers to act quickly with limited planning? Managers should not act thoughtlessly or entirely give up the tools of analysis. But they should not try to plan out too many details—whatever "too many" means in practice—and that they should act before they are sure that they are right. How can someone be advised on how to walk this difficult line, achieving the right balance of analysis and action? One possible answer is that the balance between analysis and action is in part a matter of timing, with the most important role for analysis coming after experience, not before.

In the early stages, the innovative managers in the case studies developed a conception of the problem, including the broad purpose of agency action and a broadly defined approach; built some level of consensus around that conception; gathered "craft knowledge" about the problem and agency capacity in the area; and put together the minimal plans needed to get a specific idea implemented in some form.[45] For example, in One Church, One Child, Coler developed a conception of the problem as the absence of African American adoptive homes. As he talked with many different people about the problem and tried out his early ideas, he both built consensus and developed craft knowledge—for example, knowledge about the role of the church in the African American community and about obstacles that African American leaders thought his agency put in the way of adoption. Once the ministers were on board, he assigned high-level staff to spend an intensive few months working with them to put together the limited plans required to make the first presentation.

In this start-up phase, the role of analysis—at least in its more specialized forms—seems limited. Possibly analysts could help in framing the conception (as Schall's planning office did for the DJJ) or gather useful craft knowledge (for example, by interviewing workers or clients). Certainly, they could develop the basic plans, although program or field staff may be more likely than analysts to understand the bare-bones nature of what should be planned out this early. But the central lesson of the innovation-by-groping-along story is that the manager should not at this stage pay much attention to comprehensive policy analyses or elaborate contingency plans.

After the program is operating, however, the focus changes. Now the manager is trying to quickly learn from experience and is greedy for information—information that is reliable, relevant to the real problem, highly detailed, reasonably comprehensive, and available quickly. As if finding and collecting such information were not enough of a challenge, once the information comes in, the manager must determine its implications for changing program operations.

Not surprisingly, given the size of these tasks, the cases suggest that the successful managers spend a great deal of time and energy on them and motivate others to do so as well. In all three of the large organizations, for example, the managers developed new types of outcome and

---

45. Henry Mintzberg describes the kind of knowledge managers need as "personal knowledge, intimate understanding, equivalent to the craftsman's feel for the clay." Mintzberg (1987, p. 74).

performance measures (adoptive placements, job placements, measures of children's health and education status) and new channels for collecting and reporting the information. The Department of Juvenile Justice offers the most formal and explicit process for acting on this new information, but the others insist equally strongly, if more informally, on a serious response. This serious attention to new information suggests that Behn's choice of the term "groping along" instead of "experimenting," while making vivid the excellent manager's bias toward action, may obscure another characteristic: the excellent manager's bias toward information, rich information that conveys as much experience as possible.[46] And that bias toward information provides a potentially important role for analysis: identifying alternative sources for information; devising ways of collecting it; making sense out of it; bringing overall quantitative measures of success into conjunction with the individualized responses of workers and managers; and prodding operating managers when they become complacent or defensive or ignore evidence of failure or incomplete success.

These human services managers did not achieve their innovations through extended planning and development of an initial policy idea. Instead, innovation developed through action, over time, so that the idea at the time of the award often bore little resemblance to the idea at the beginning of the program. These managers acted quickly, so that they could start gaining operational experience as soon as possible. They did not act without thought, without consultation, or without a sense of direction, but they did act without detailed plans. After acting, they cared intensely about the information to be gained from those actions, and they were able to carry their organizations with them in mulling over the information and in responding to it, over and over again. For them, operational experience provided the material for continuous innovation.

The challenge for scholars is to figure out what it means to improve practice in a world of groping along. For one thing, it means putting less emphasis on skillful prediction and more on skillful learning—on the retrospective analysis of experience. In a world of groping along, teaching future Jean Ekinses about comprehensive and integrated services is less important than helping them recognize when the teen-agers need day care. The task is to enable other managers—less willing by temperament than Ekins to acknowledge a wrong start, or less able than she to coax

46. Behn (1988, p. 645).

the most useful information out of the system—to find the evidence that is so compelling that it hits with both barrels.

References

Behn, Robert D. 1988. "Management by Groping Along." *Journal of Policy Analysis and Management,* vol. 7, no. 1 (Fall): 643–63.

_____. 1991. *Leadership Counts: Lessons for Public Managers from the Massachusetts Welfare, Training, and Employment Program.* Harvard University Press.

Berman, Paul, and Milbrey McLaughlin. 1978. *Federal Programs Supporting Educational Change.* Santa Monica, Calif.: Rand Corporation.

Browne, Angela, and Aaron Wildavsky. 1984a. "Implementation as Exploration." In *Implementation,* 3d ed., 232–56. University of California Press.

_____. 1984b. "Implementation as Mutual Adaptation." In *Implementation,* 3d ed., 206–31. University of California Press.

Brunetta, Leslie. 1988a. "Jean Ekins and the Family Learning Center." March 15.

_____. 1988b. *Jean Ekins and the Family Learning Center,* Parts A, B, and Epilogue. Case Program. Harvard University, John F. Kennedy School of Government.

Ellickson, Phyllis, and others. 1983. *Implementing New Ideas in Criminal Justice.* Santa Monica, Calif.: Rand Corporation.

Etheredge, Lloyd S. 1985. *Can Governments Learn?: American Foreign Policy and Central American Revolutions.* Pergamon Press.

Feller, Irwin, and Donald C. Menzel. 1977. "Diffusion Milieus as a Focus of Research on Innovation in the Public Sector." *Policy Sciences:* 49–68.

Levin, Martin A., and Barbara Ferman. 1985. *The Political Hand: Policy Implementation and Youth Employment Programs.* Pergamon Press.

Lindblom, Charles E. 1959. "The Science of Muddling Through." *Public Administration Review,* vol. 19, no. 2 (Spring): 79–88.

Majone, Giandomenico, and Aaron Wildavsky. 1984. "Implementation as Evolution." In *Implementation,* 3d ed., 163–80. University of California Press.

Mazmanian, Daniel A., and Paul A. Sabatier. 1983. *Implementation and Public Policy.* Glenview, Ill.: Scott, Foresman and Company.

Meltsner, Arnold J. 1976. *Policy Analysis in the Bureaucracy.* University of California Press.

Mintzberg, Henry. 1987. "Crafting Strategy." *Harvard Business Review,* vol. 65, no. 4 (July/August): 66–75.

Nakamura, Robert T. 1987. "The Textbook Policy Process and Implementation Research." *Policy Studies Review,* vol. 7, no. 1 (Autumn): 142–54.

New York Department of Juvenile Justice. 1986. Applications materials. Ford Foundation and John F. Kennedy School of Government Awards Program for Innovations in State and Local Government.

O'Toole, Laurence J., Jr. 1986. "Policy Recommendations for Multi-Actor Implementation: An Assessment of the Field." *Journal of Public Policy,* vol. 6, part 2 (April–June): 181–210.

Sabatier, Paul A. 1986. "Top-Down and Bottom-Up Approaches to Implementation Research: A Critical Analysis and Suggested Synthesis." *Journal of Public Policy,* vol. 6, part 1 (January–March): 21–48.

Schorr, Lisbeth B., with Daniel Schorr. 1988. *Within Our Reach: Breaking the Cycle of Disadvantage.* Anchor Press/Doubleday.

Varley, Pamela. 1987. *Ellen Schall and the Department of Juvenile Justice.* Case C16-87-793.0. Harvard University, John F. Kennedy School of Government.

Warrock, Anna M. 1988. *Finding Black Parents: One Church, One Child,* Case and Epilogue. Case Program. Harvard University, John F. Kennedy School of Government.

Yin, Robert K. 1979. *Changing Urban Bureaucracies: How New Practices Become Routinized.* Lexington, Mass.: Lexington Books.

Part Three

INNOVATION AND
THE MEDIA

CHAPTER EIGHT

Why Government Innovation Is Not News:
The View from the Newsroom

W. Lance Bennett

EVEN A CASUAL LOOK at the news suggests that government innovations are not covered much at all. What may be worse in the eyes of
policymakers, when innovations are covered, the news stories tend to be
dramatized, playing up failures or exaggerating the hopes for miracle
solutions to chronic public problems. The experiences of both public
officials and journalists involved in the Ford Foundation and John F.
Kennedy School of Government Awards Program for Innovations in
State and Local Government produced these questions: "Are the news
media and pubic officials natural antagonists? Are there ways the public
interest can be pursued by both parties more consistently?"[1] The questions arise from remarks such as this from a successful innovator:

> When you're a bureaucrat, you're incredibly vulnerable because you
> stand to absorb public disdain for government. There's basically a neg-
> ative attitude toward government in the press. There's a tendency for

The author would like to acknowledge the financial support of the Ford Foundation, along
with the valuable assistance of Andrea Beal, John Young, and Nancy Stark in gathering data for
this analysis. John Klockner provided key help in all stages of data gathering and analysis.
Thanks to Margaret Gordon for the encouragement to think about the subject, and to Robert
Entman for commenting on an earlier draft of this chapter.
1. Margaret Gordon, Edward Bassett, and Michael Fancher to the author, July 12, 1991,
letter of invitation to the Ford Foundation conference on Public Innovation and the Media: Stimulus or Barrier?

the press to jump on small mistakes you make. You're easy to criticize. It's easy to trigger negative feelings about the bureaucracy, no matter how high-minded and public-spirited a job you think you're doing.[2]

In a study of 250 policymakers, John W. Kingdon found that only 26 percent mentioned the media as being important to their work, and only 4 percent regarded the media as very important in setting their agendas.[3] According to Kingdon's informants, the trouble with media coverage is the tendency of the press to enter a developing policy process abruptly, sensationalize the story for a brief period, and then drop it before the policy community itself had concluded its work, much less agreed upon how to publicize the results. Other research shows that policies can be damaged when coverage highlights conflicts between the agencies involved, or gives too much credit or blame to some actors and not others. As a result, participants often see news coverage as a sign of the failure of the process itself.[4] The growing conclusion seems to be that journalists have become active political players, with the potential to wreak havoc on government policy.[5]

By moving the analytical camera back from a close-up on public officials and taking a wide-angle shot of the larger newsmaking process, things appear differently. Antagonism (or its slightly more ritualized counterpart, adversarialism) still plays a part, but not as the center of attention. In the wide-angle shot, cases exist in which politicians cope successfully with the press, often exercising a good deal of control over the development of news stories. A substantial body of literature is available that looks at the interactions between reporters and officials as a balance of adversarialism and mutual dependence with politicians most often in control.[6]

At the very least, politicians can be the high-power actors in the news game. And far from being simply antagonists, reporters and officials also live in a state of mutual dependence, each needing the other to satisfy their respective, if different, goals. Officials may try to manage the news to promote various ends, including personal advancement, protecting their agencies, shielding some policies from unwanted public scrutiny, and actively promoting others. On the media side, behind every journalist is a bureaucratic organization trying to operate efficiently by gather-

2. Husock (1991, p. 3).
3. Kingdon (1984, p. 61).
4. Ripley and Franklin (1987, chapter 4).
5. Linsky (1986).
6. Fishman (1980); and Sigal (1973).

ing required amounts of news within the constraints of fixed budgets, limited personnel, and intense competition with other organizations.

When viewed as the product of organizations at work, the news becomes both less mysterious and harder to reduce to any single factor such as antagonism between reporters and politicians. Depending on how governmental and journalistic organizations mesh in a given situation, the result may be news that satisfies all parties, or news that leaves reporters or officials or both feeling that they have been disadvantaged. At other times, the bureaucratic fit between press and government is so remote that little or no news results at all.

This latter pattern—the sheer lack of fit between news-gathering routines and innovative policy processes—may account for the absence of good news about innovations. The basic explanation goes something like this: Because news organizations are set up to gather fixed daily or weekly amounts of news as efficiently as possible, the obvious bureaucratic solution is to look in the most obvious and accessible places and rely on the most available and cooperative official sources. Sending reporters to the usual places (beats, press conferences, scheduled events) to gather information from the usual suspects (government officials, civic and interest group heads) turns out to be a successful strategy for securing a reliable supply of what most people accept as news. Furthermore, the pressure of many reporters (the press pack) covering much the same territory may increase the chances of finding leaks and uncovering scandals. One ironic result is that leaks and scandals have become more or less routine features of the news, which no doubt adds to the wariness of politicians around the press.[7] For all of their obvious journalistic efficiency, these organizational routines may not be good for at least one thing: gathering news about government innovations.

Consider the possibility that most innovations develop off the beaten press path, involving cooperation between different public agencies, across different levels of government, and sometimes between the private and public sectors. In addition, large numbers of actors may be involved, few of whom seek to take the credit (or the heat) for the entire operation. In other words, as the very idea of innovation implies, something is going on outside of normal government routines. This also means that news organizations set up to cover those government routines have to go out of their way to assemble the pieces of those stories.

7. Molotch and Lester (1974).

Even when news organizations make the effort, and officials are willing to talk about an innovative policy, another problem may enter the picture. Stories about, for example, solid waste treatment, pollution monitoring, library automation, controlling land development, detecting discrimination, removing garbage, and other subjects of innovation may be important, but they are hard to tell as dramatic, human interest stories that make up the core of the news. Research by Shanto Iyengar shows that the personalized, human interest angles that dominate the news may not be useful for communicating detailed or impartial information about politics and society.[8] However, as long as these are the kinds of stories journalists are trained to write, editors expect, and marketing consultants say the audience wants, they will remain news. As a result, innovations present reporting challenges even when other obstacles are overcome.

In short, press antagonism and officials' fears of failing may keep some innovations out of the news, but a more general and useful explanation involves simple bureaucratic neglect, or the disconnection of news gathering routines from the people, places, and plots of innovation stories. Framing the problem in this way may be useful because it opens up the possibility of bureaucratic solutions on both sides that would increase the coverage of innovations. If better fits between government and news organizations can be engineered, actors on both sides of the news line may discover that it is relatively easy to cooperate in producing news that better informs citizens about how government policy is made.

When Do Innovations Become News?

The prediction is that innovation stories are reported most often because they happen to mesh well with the way news organizations are set up to gather, write, and distribute their product. Just what are the chief properties of these news routines? At or near the top of the list is location, or where the story occurs. Things that happen on beats, at press conferences, or as scheduled events—in other words, things that take place where reporters are already stationed or where they can easily get to— are more likely to be reported as news. The trouble with innovations is that they are likely to be happening in between the cracks in political and journalistic bureaucracies: away from beats, and in places that reporters

8. Iyengar (1991).

and assignment editors have to go out of their way to find. According to this organizational logic, most innovations that do make the news are the sort that are easy to find, either happening on or close to regular beats, or presented as media events complete with invitations telling journalists when and where to show up.

As important as the location of news is its source. The most common sources in the news are prominent officials such as mayors, governors, city council members, senators, presidents, and police chiefs, along with spokespeople for civic and interest groups.[9] The whole system of beats, press conferences, and scheduled media events is designed to bring the usual sources in contact with the press in routine, efficient ways. The trouble is that the vast majority of newsmakers are not likely to be innovators. To the contrary, mayors, presidents, and interest group spokespeople, for example, are more likely to represent established political routines, ongoing agendas, and the viewpoints of government and business as usual. Thus the prediction is that innovative news happens when innovative projects drift to the attention of already prominent news sources, or in the even rarer case when an innovator has the media skills to become a news source.

Then there is the factor of time. The news is timely not only by being contemporary, but also by developing quickly for journalists who have other assignments to cover and by being reportable on the short deadlines that prevail in the news business. Innovations may be timely in the first sense, but they probably require more time from reporters with less guarantee of meeting deadlines than other news assignments. Covering an innovation story can get a news organization into a situation where the ending of the story may not be written for some time, and the ending likely will be an anticlimactic fizzle instead of a more newsworthy triumph, tragedy, or scandal. The prediction, then, is that innovations that make the news are likely to be those most fully developed, most easily wrapped up, or, best of all, already in operation.

Timely topics that have solid narrative endings (triumph, tragedy, scandal, or farce) suggest that the plot possibilities of a situation have a great deal to do with whether it gets reported as news. The news tells stories about society and the world, a fact that is easy to overlook. If the dramatic angle is not clear, translating social reality into news is difficult.[10]

9. Sigal (1986).
10. Darnton (1975).

Consider, for example, this part of a memo from the executive producer of a network news program to his editors and reporters:

> Every news story should, without sacrifice of probity or responsibility, display the attributes of fiction, of drama. It should have structure and conflict, problem and denouement, rising action and falling action, a beginning, middle, and an end. These are not only the essentials of drama; they are the essentials of narrative.[11]

The dramatic requirements of news are more demanding all the time in this age of infotainment. According to the news doctors hired by papers and TV stations to tell them how to stay competitive and profitable, the kind of news that people tune into is quick, easy to grasp, starring compelling actors, and having obvious personal consequences for the news consumer.[12] While breakthroughs in solid waste treatment may be important, they are hard to dramatize in ways that people can, or even want to, understand. The prediction, then, is that the innovation stories most likely to be covered will have plot possibilities that connect quickly to life concerns and feature compelling actors within the news frame. For example, endangered species monitoring programs may become news because stories can feature cute animals, beautiful nature scenery, and an occasional craggy scientist or environmentalist wandering through as a source of technical information. By contrast, upstream innovations such as pollution abatement programs that might save species from having to be monitored are less newsworthy on all counts.

However, the sheer importance of an innovation is not discounted in making news decisions. Talking about importance in some higher, objective sense is difficult because of the bureaucratic constraints of news organizations. The measure of a story is often taken by applying implicit formulas (disasters, crashes, the status of the actors involved, and so on), along with journalists' practical judgments about the newsworthy topics of the day.[13] These judgments play a large part in whether or not a potential story clears the final bureaucratic hurdle, the editorial "so what" or "why?" question: Why does this story matter? As an executive producer of the *ABC Evening News* said in a memo to his staff:

11. Epstein (1973, pp. 4–5).
12. Smith (1986); and Zorn (1986).
13. Gans (1979).

The *Evening News,* as you know, works on elimination. We can't include everything. As criteria for what we do include, I suggest the following for a satisfied viewer: (1) "Is my world, nation, and city safe?" (2) "Is my home and family safe?" (3) "If they are safe, then what has happened in the past 24 hours to make that world better?" (4) "What has happened in the past 24 hours to help us cope better?"[14]

On many days, the news hole is filled by answering the first two questions, with little time left over for things such as innovations that fall into the last two categories. Then there is the problem that most government innovation stories do not fall within the twenty-four-hour time clock built into these questions.

Given all the ways that important events can escape being defined as news, the life of the journalist is simplified by not having to explain in detail why something is newsworthy. Thus the easiest news to report arises from existing beats. The rest is primarily topical, triggered by the latest fears, fads, fashions, and events in society. Even when they become topical, innovations may be at the mercy of those puzzling features of a mass-mediated society, the changing cycles of public and media attention.[15] A potential news topic that fits neatly into the upswing of one of these cycles makes it easy for the press to avoid the question of why it matters, looking, instead, to the sheer volume of media coverage to justify the story. According to this simplifying rule of media logic, hot topics take on lives of their own, making it possible for journalists to avoid existential struggles over their significance.[16] During an education crisis, for example, stories on educational innovations are naturals. At other times, their importance becomes harder to justify. During periods when crime is in and air quality is out, it is easier to report on innovations in criminal justice procedures than to cover new pollution programs. By their very definition, the trouble with most innovation stories is that they require journalists to convince, first, themselves and then the public of their importance. The prediction here is that the innovation stories most likely to become news are those most easily linked to ongoing social crises and public concerns, not the ones most likely to educate people about new problems or radical solutions to old ones.

14. Paletz and Entman (1981, p. 17).
15. Downs (1972).
16. Altheide and Snow (1979).

By now it may have become clear that these conditions for explaining which innovation stories are most likely to be reported as news are the familiar journalistic criteria of who, what, when, where, and why? in disguise. However, these five journalistic rules of thumb were presented in the more qualified terms of source, plot possibilities, time, location, and so what? to make a point. Not just any event or innovation with a who, what, where, when, and why attached makes the news. The problem in the case of innovations is that most of them lack the right kinds of whos, whats, wheres, whens, and whys to satisfy the bureaucratic requirements of news production. To put this in the more positive formulation favored by science, the kinds of innovations that become news:

— Happen in places routinely covered by reporters;

— Come from official sources with regular press contact;

— Fit within time frames dictated by deadlines and the need to wrap up features;

— Have dramatic plot possibilities; and

— Connect easily with social trends, attention cycles, or topics that have already become running news stories.

Consider a simple example of how this works. The story is from the *New York Times*. The headline reads: "For Oregon's Health Care System, Triage by a Lawmaker with an M.D."[17] The story is long, with twenty-eight paragraphs, totaling 30.5 column inches of text and running 50.5 inches overall with photo and headline. The subject is an innovation in the Oregon state health insurance system that will restructure the kinds of treatments covered, eliminating coverage for some treatments that are both expensive and have little chance of saving lives, and freeing up funds so that basic health care can be extended to citizens previously not covered at all. An innovative program that would make Oregon the first state to provide health insurance for all its citizens certainly seems like a natural for a news story. Yet a closer look suggests that this story had the signs of routine news written all over it, making its intrinsic importance as an innovation less the reason for becoming news than that, for an innovation story, it happened to fit all the requirements of routine news.

As a state capital story, it was easily covered by a reporter on assignment. A single source provided all but four paragraphs of the story, and that source was the president of the Oregon state senate, one of the most

17. Timothy Egan, "For Oregon's Health Care System, Triage by a Lawmaker with an M.D.," *New York Times,* June 5, 1991, p. 12.

accessible officials in the state, who conveniently happened to be the author of the plan. The large photo above the text shows senate president and physician Dr. John Kitzhaber perched on the gallery rail above the senate chamber in the capitol building.

And, speaking of the source, the star of the story is not a typical innovator, but as president of the state senate, he was already a prominent news source who is doubly newsworthy in a health story by virtue of being "a lawmaker with an M.D." Moreover, Dr. Kitzhaber is a newsworthy character, being described in the text as "wearing jeans and a floral tie," facts confirmed in a photo in which he is striking a casual pose, tie loosened. The good doctor is also a good news source because he speaks the language of sound bites, telling the reporter that his plan differs from other health programs because it rations treatments instead of rationing people. Like most routine news, this is Dr. Kitzhaber's story; it is "his health bill" and "his idea." The other three sources cited in the article receive a total of three paragraphs, while the doctor-lawmaker gets twenty-three.

The economy of sources helped make this a manageable, timely assignment for the reporter to complete as part of a series on different state health plans. On the matter of time, the story was neat, easily wrapped up, with few surprises or unexpected loose ends. One long interview, several phone calls, a photo shoot, and that is it. All in a day's work for a reporter on the road. Not that there is anything wrong with this. To the contrary, the story was useful and informative, but it also happened to be easier to research and tell than stories about more typical innovations involving more people scattered over more territory with less interest in promoting their causes.

The dramatic qualities or plot possibilities of the story further recommend it as news. As the word "triage" in the headline suggests, this story is about life and death, and how governments dispense health care. The source being both politician and doctor also helps the plot, enabling the reporter to open the story with this line: "As an emergency room physician, Dr. John Kitzhaber has spent much of his professional life in the fast-motion treatment of bleeding patients." With these plot developments, a potentially dry topic is turned into a more compelling one. The stage is set around Dr. Kitzhaber and his personal policy crusade for five paragraphs before the reader is given the first hint about the policy. Only eight paragraphs of the story can be construed as explaining the plan itself. The other twenty paragraphs provide scene setting, character development, and dramatic conflict in the form of congressional approval that must be obtained for a state such as Oregon to alter its use of medicaid funds and national politicians opposed to the idea of rationing treatments. (In the end, Congress rejected the plan.)

In addition to fitting the definition of routine news, the story was topical. A national health care crisis had been on the political agenda for several years, receiving considerable attention in opinion polls and from the media. As further evidence that health care already had a place on the news agenda, the reporter was on special assignment covering health policy in various states. While the Oregon innovation angle made for a nice twist on a running story line, the innovation probably did not make it news. The subject of health care first made the news agenda, a reporter was assigned to look at state programs, and an innovation story happened to get caught in this news net.

When an innovation is served up as neatly as it was in this case, it is likely to become news. And it was a good news story at that. It probably would have been missed without all the special factors required to turn political innovation into routine news.

Recycling News

The studies reported here are aimed at answering two questions: First, to what extent did an innovation (recycling) become a big news story because it acquired the characteristics of routine news on its way to the headlines? Second, how did successful local innovation programs make the leap into the national media? A series of related studies of the *New York Times* (the *Times,* or *NYT*), the *Seattle Times* (*ST*), and the national news and public relations wire services provided answers to these questions.

The core study was a ten-year look at recycling coverage in the *New York Times* from 1980 to 1990.[18] The *Times* was selected for several reasons, not the least of which is its role as the leading national news organization, probably contributing more to the daily news agenda of both print and broadcast mass media than any other source.[19] Among

18. The Nexis database used in this research begins in June 1980. Thus coverage for 1980 was available only for the last six months of the year. In analyses requiring a full year for baseline comparisons, 1981 was used as the first year of the time series.

19. Gans (1979).

other things, this means that the *Times* coverage is more likely to involve investigative methods and background documentation that go beyond routine journalism, thus making it a good, critical test of the hypotheses about innovation coverage. If recycling made the *NYT* because of routine news characteristics, then it likely was a routine story in much of the rest of the mass media as well. In addition, the *NYT* is the major local paper in a metropolitan region (Connecticut, New Jersey, and Long Island) that was suffering a variety of environmental and waste removal problems that gave its coverage of recycling both local and national angles.

Several studies were run on *Times* coverage. Using the Nexis full-text database, the first study was simply a ten-year trend analysis of the number of articles, including editorials and opinion pieces, that mentioned the terms "recycling" (also "recycled," "recycle," and so on), "environment" (and cognates), "garbage," "trash," and combinations of these. While covering considerable territory (72,500 stories), such high-level searches are inevitably crude and error prone. A term such as "recycling," for example, became a widely used word in the American vocabulary, meaning that many news articles were about recycling things other than waste products (such as politicians, baseball players, jokes, and movies). In addition, a computer search is hard pressed to make judgments about the kinds of sources and plots used in stories. These and other problems were handled by reading individually three and one-half years of recycling stories (July–December 1980 and all of 1981, 1987, and 1988) both to determine how many of the stories were about recycling things other than waste products and to pick up more precise data on sources, plot themes, and news locations appearing in the relevant recycling stories.[20]

Two coders were trained to recognize (1) the use of recycling in a story as referring to the recycling of waste products (if not, the story was coded as not appropriate); (2) in the case of appropriate stories, source attributions made to government officials, business spokespersons, interest groups, and other voices in the stories; (3) plot themes or problem statements as environmental, garbage-related, and other; (4) all alternatives to recycling, definitions of materials being recycled, and political

20. The years 1980 and 1981 were chosen to establish a baseline at the beginning of the ten-year period. The choice of 1987 and 1988 reflects both their placement toward the end of the study period and that they fell around a dramatic upswing in the number of recycling stories, providing a nice insight into the characteristics that turn a subject into a big story.

initiatives and conflicts surrounding recycling programs; and (5) references to innovative recycling programs in other locations around the country (and in a few cases, around the world). In all, 1,489 stories were hand-coded, and coder reliability was 80 percent or above on all tasks, with disagreements resolved by mutual discussion under the guidance of a referee (not the author) familiar with the coding scheme. In all cases, the coding was performed with no knowledge of the hypotheses underlying the research.

In addition to the story structure data, the *New York Times* coverage was also searched for references to the Seattle recycling program, arguably the most successfully innovative of the many recycling programs that went into effect around the nation during the decade.[21] A comparison study of the coverage in the *Seattle Times* during the period surrounding implementation of the Seattle program (1986–90) made it possible to determine which story features (who, what, where, when, why) were common at local and national news levels, and which ones were different. Another study (again, using the Nexis database) of references to the Seattle program in the national news and public relations wire services provided an even more general look at what features of a local innovation became selected for national news distribution. Taken together, these data provided rich material for an anatomy of a news story on government innovation.

Anatomy of an Innovation

Recycling launched its news career in the 1980s with part of the "so what?" question already answered in the public mind, giving it an immediate journalistic advantage over many other innovations. As a result of the environmental movement of the 1970s and the growth of individual and curbside recycling programs with primarily an environmental emphasis, recycling had become a household word. That is, people were already familiar with the concept, thereby taking much of the pressure

21. For example, Seattle won the Top Urban Program Award from the National Recycling Coalition in 1989. At the time, the city was recycling 35 percent of total waste and 45 percent of residential. See "Seattle Recycling Called Best in the U.S.," *Seattle Times,* October 11, 1989, p. c3. In the same year, the Institute for Local Self-Reliance selected Seattle as the Best Overall Program in a Large City. And in 1990 Seattle's program was one of ten winners of the Ford Foundation and John F. Kennedy School of Government Awards Program for Innovations in State and Local Government and the only recycling program to receive an award.

off journalists to answer the "so what?" question in news reports.[22] By the beginning of the 1980s, the word "recycle" had entered the everyday vocabulary of America to the extent that reporters were using it casually to refer to any number of subjects that had nothing to do with waste products. Individual coding of stories in the last half of 1980 and all of 1981 shows that fully 74 percent of the stories using the term "recycle" referred to things other than waste products. The percentage of nonwaste uses of the term had dropped to 60 percent by 1987–88, suggesting both that the novelty of the word was beginning to wear off and that the news focus was beginning to sharpen around more clearly defined story themes.

The numbers of *NYT* stories in 1981 were used as baseline figures, and growth patterns were charted in different story categories over the decade in figure 8-1. Recycling news followed the path of environment coverage fairly steadily until 1987, when the *NYT* proclaimed that its metropolitan region, and more generally, the nation, was having a garbage crisis.[23] The garbage theme created a focused political problem for news writing, while recycling fit the "so what?" bill neatly as the leading solution. Recycling stories grew rapidly from 1987 on, carrying both garbage crisis and environment-related themes to new heights. A clearer picture of just how much recycling coverage was boosted when the garbage crisis hit the news agenda comes from looking at figure 8-2, which is based on changes from one year to the next in the numbers of stories linking recycling to various other topics, including the garbage crisis.

A detailed theme analysis of stories in the 1980–81 period compared with the 1987–88 interval offers further evidence that recycling gained a new relevance because of its neat fit in problem-solution stories about the garbage crisis. The recycling stories in the later period made increasing references to waste removal breakdowns, the need for state and metro-

22. This may have mixed effects on reporting, because the large-scale programs of the 1980s had many technical and economic aspects that differed from the grass-roots efforts of earlier years. "Easy" news coverage glossed over complicated new wrinkles in favor of keeping descriptions of the idea of "recycling" simple.

23. Figure 8-1 depicts growth rates, not numbers of stories. Environment stories outnumbered recycling stories during this period by a factor of more than ten (52,599 to 4,794). This is not surprising given both the generality of the term "environment" and the high numbers of stories making reference to the nonnatural environment (for example, architectural environment, work environment, and so on). The important comparison, therefore, is the relative rate of growth of stories showing the levels of environment references holding steady across the decade, while recycling references grew rapidly in the last few years, led by linkages to the garbage crisis.

Figure 8-1. *Rate of Change from Base Year 1981 in* New York Times *Articles Containing Selected Recycling-Related Words, 1981–1990*

Percent

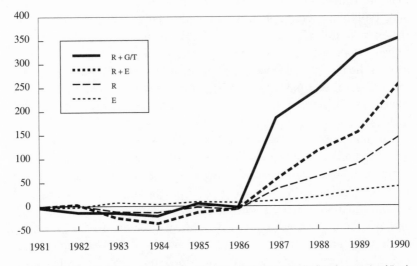

Note: R + G/T = "recycling" (and cognates), "garbage," and "trash"; R + E = "recycling" (and cognates) and "environment" (and cognates); R = "recycling"; and E = "environment." Rate of change is calculated as the percentage increase or decrease in coverage from 1981 base year.

politan recycling programs, the existence of successful programs in places such as Seattle, and the need for more political attention to the crisis.[24] The most dramatic change was in the percentage of stories that referred to garbage problems. In the 1980–81 period, only 21 percent of the recycling stories made the link to garbage problems, compared with 63 percent of the recycling stories in the 1987–88 period that made the connection. With the discovery of the garbage crisis, the *New York Times*

24. Data from the theme analysis show that, by the end of the decade, recycling became the leading alternative to metropolitan trash disposal via land filling and incineration. In the 1980–81 period, only 6 articles (or 4 percent of all recycling articles in the period) mentioned recycling as an alternative to disposal, compared with 43 articles (or 11 percent of all recycling articles) during 1987–88. Recycling was discussed as an alternative to landfilling in 27 articles (7 percent) in the later period, compared with only 4 (2 percent) at the beginning of the decade. References to large-scale state and metropolitan recycling programs grew even more dramatically, from 26 (18 percent) in the early years to 135 (36 percent) in the later period. And, not surprisingly, the *NYT* covered political angles more as the story grew into a possible solution to a recognized social problem. In the later period, 27 stories (7 percent) mentioned formal political angles such as budget battles or election campaign statements, compared with zero references to these things at the beginning of the decade.

Figure 8-2. *Year-to-Year Rate of Change in* New York Times *Articles Containing Selected Recycling-Related Words, 1981–1990*

Percent

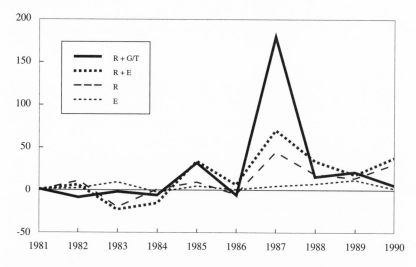

Note: R + G/T = "recycling" (and cognates), "garbage," and "trash"; R + E = "recycling" (and cognates) and "environment" (and cognates); R = "recycling"; and E = "environment." The year-to-year rate of change is calculated as the percentage increase or decrease in coverage from the year before.

had two big, long-running, easy-to-grasp themes on which to peg recycling stories. Few innovations come so neatly packaged or with such sustained topical momentum behind them. But when they do, they are likely to become big news.

If the journalist's "so what?" question was simplified by the early link between recycling and the environment and was made easier by the problem-solution formula that emerged in writing about the garbage crisis, these factors alone do not account for the dramatic jump in recycle/environment stories and the even more dramatic increase in recycle/garbage stories during the year 1987. What explains the magnitude of those leaps then? The most obvious answer is that the dramatic potential or plot possibilities of the recycling story became particularly rich in 1987.

In that year, a garbage barge from Long Island sailed the Atlantic and the Caribbean for 155 days, looking for a place to unload its trash. The garbage barge became something of a news icon, summing up the various dimensions of the garbage crisis in a single, long-running serial story about a derelict ship, unwanted at all ports of call, running out of places to unload its odiferous cargo either at home or abroad. In all, the garbage barge sailed into the news a total of sixty-eight times during 1987, strengthened its icon status with twenty more showings during 1988, and made thirteen cameo appearances in the 1989–90 period.

As a news icon, the garbage barge dramatized many aspects of the entire garbage crisis. The morals of the garbage barge saga were clear. Neither New York nor the nation could ignore the garbage problem any longer. Traditional solutions had failed, and the time had come to try something innovative. *NYT* coverage increasingly mentioned successful recycling programs such as the one in Seattle and made more direct comparisons between the low rates of recycling in the metropolitan New York region and the high rates of waste handled by Seattle's programs. Recycling had become something of an off-the-shelf, formula news story with a series of predictable angles that all helped turn innovation into routine news. Were there successful programs operating somewhere? How many waste products (ranging from ordinary household trash to chemicals, plastics, and nuclear wastes) could reasonably be handled by such programs? And what were politicians doing to get recycling programs up and running in areas hardest hit by the garbage crisis?

With the emergence of a familiar political plot line, information attributed to government officials not surprisingly increased over time. The increase in official information and the dominant role of government were measured in two different ways. First, the hand coding of stories in the 1980–81 and 1987–88 periods showed that government officials were cited as information sources in 53.8 percent of the stories in the earlier period, a figure that grew to 65.5 percent in the later period. The second measure looked more broadly for government as the backdrop or setting for the story. A computer search matched references in the same story to recycling, garbage, or trash, along with the term "government" or any of a list of various official titles.[25]

The computer-coded results show that as recycling stories grew in number over the years, so did the part scripted for government and official

25. The computer search looked for references in the same news story to "recycle" (and its cognates), the words "garbage" or "trash," along with any of the following terms (and their cognates): "government," "official," "mayor," "council," "representative," "senator," "director," "agency," "governor," or "president." The differences in the methods used in the two searches are important to understand. In the hand coding, the coders looked only for attributions of information to particular officials. The computer, by contrast, was programmed to look for more general references to government and official titles, whether or not they added specific infor-

Figure 8-3. *Rate of Change in* New York Times *Articles Containing Selected Recycling-Related and Government-Related Words, 1981–1990*

Percent

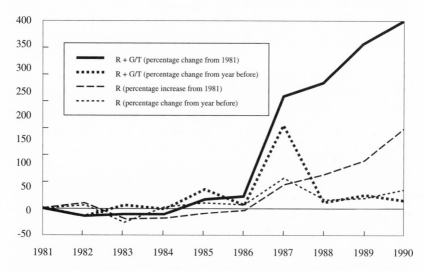

Note: R + G/T = "recycling" (and cognates), "garbage," and "trash"; R + E = "recycling" (and cognates) and "environment" (and cognates); R = "recycling"; and E = "environment"; plus, in each category, "government," "agency," "official," "governor," "director," "mayor," "council," "president," "representative," and "senator" (and their cognates).

actors, increasing more than 200 percent above 1981 levels by 1987 and rising almost 350 percent above 1981 levels by 1990. Figure 8-3 illustrates these trends with two growth curves, one using 1981 as a baseline, while the other shows changes from each year to the next, graphically emphasizing the jump between 1986 and 1987. Comparing figure 8-3 with figure 8-1, the growth of the role of government paralleled the growth of the story itself over the course of the decade. The two measures support much the same conclusion: Routine news formulas prevailed from the beginning, but as the dramatic form of the story became clearer, coverage was further routinized by giving increasing say to government officials.

---

mation about recycling to the story. The computer-generated trends shown in figure 8-3 thus provide an indication of the extent to which the dramatic scene, or backdrop of the news story, was set around government, while the hand-coded data show the degree to which government officials provided material for the story. The implication of the two measures seems to be that, with the addition of statements by government officials in larger numbers and the scene set almost entirely around government, the innovation story resembled routine news more as it became big news.

The pattern of news sources from the private sector provides a more intriguing indicator of the extent to which coverage of recycling succumbed to journalistic routines. Recycling as an innovation almost always involved partnerships between governments and private businesses or revenue-generating public corporations. As recycling became adopted in more places around the country, the market for the sale of recycled products grew more competitive and, in some cases, became so saturated that recycling companies could not sell their wares—a development that might argue for shifting the news focus to the business angle. Yet the amount of news space devoted to business voices dropped as recycling news became both bigger and more routinized. Data from the hand-coded *NYT* articles reveal that business voices appeared in 25 percent of the articles on recycling during the 1980–81 period but dropped to appearances in just 10.6 percent of the articles in the 1987–88 period after recycling had become a big story. These trends all confirm the source patterns that appear in routine news.

Another source pattern worth noting is the percentage of *NYT* articles reporting the views of different kinds of actors. Like many innovations, recycling involved initiatives from government, business, and citizens' groups working together (and, at times, entering into conflict). To capture these interactions, source patterns were examined for the hand-coded stories by scoring sources in four categories: government, business, interest groups, and other (including person-on-the-street interviews and opinion polls). The data showed that *NYT* coverage seldom contained voices from multiple source categories, meaning that business stories were almost exclusively about business issues, government stories about government, and interest group stories about issues concerning the interest groups cited. The average number of source categories per recycling story was 1.04 in the 1980–81 period and rose only slightly to 1.15 by 1987–88. Complex interactions among government, business, and interest groups that commonly take place in an innovation such as large-scale recycling programs were not reported. Typical of routine news, most coverage in the *New York Times* was source-driven, not reporter-driven. Reporters seldom left their routine beats to cover the story.

Coverage in the *Seattle Times* of Seattle's recycling program between 1986 and 1990 illustrates the difference between source-driven and reporter- or organization-driven coverage of an innovation. In the thirty-six articles written with "recycle" (and cognates) in their headlines during this period, an average of 2.02 different source categories came into play per article, and fully 22 percent of the articles made reference to three or more (out of a possible four) different categories of sources.[26] In part, this departure from routine journalism reflected a deliberate policy of the *Seattle Times* as a news organization to define its own agenda of local issues, resulting in more reporter- and editor-driven, and fewer source-driven, stories. However, the source diversity in *ST* coverage must be credited, in part, to successful efforts by players in the Seattle recycling story to be available to the press. In addition, at the time, Seattle had a working program to cover, and New York did not. Because the Seattle program was forged from the efforts of (and conflicts among) government, business, and interest groups, many stories included citations of sources from more than one of these categories.

Stories written around a restricted range of sources, as were most of the *NYT* reports during the decade, make it easier to locate the news and file reports in a timely manner. A reasonable question, however, is whether locating a place such as Seattle, where a successful innovation already existed, represented a point of departure from routine national news. Closer inspection of Seattle coverage both in the *NYT* and the national wire services suggests that several factors were at work to make the Seattle recycling program an exceptionally easy one to locate and write up in a timely fashion. The main reason is that key actors from government, business, and citizens' groups involved with the Seattle program were skillful at publicizing their success, making it easier for both local and national news organizations to find Seattle on the recycling map and to have something dramatic or interesting to write about the Seattle program.

A search of *NYT* articles with "recycle" (and cognates) in their headlines between November 1987 and January 1991 produced fifteen reports and editorials that made reference to Seattle, two of which were not about recycling wastes. Of the thirteen appropriate stories, twelve cited

26. Typical of the *ST* coverage were stories rich with multiple sources and—more important for the present concern about routine versus nonroutine news—sources from the different categories of business, government, and citizens' groups. For example, one story reported the views of Craig Benton, consultant for Seattle's composting program and the King County recycling program; Ed Steyh, project manager of the Seattle Solid Waste Utility; Jonathan Howe, of Metro Center YMCA, which ran West Seattle Recycle; Greg Kinnear, of Kitchen Distributing Co.; and two Seattle residents. Another article included Armen Stepanien, of Fremont Recycling Co.; Jerry Powell, a recycling expert; Nora Smith, director of the Washington State Recycling Association; Virginia Galle, Seattle city councilwoman; Don Kneass, head of Seattle's waste reduction program; Susan Smith, owner of Rainbow/Seattle Recycling; and Al Friedman, chair of a local Sierra Club chapter.

Seattle as a model for possible New York programs. Several referred to specific Seattle success estimates ranging from 25 percent to 45 percent of Seattle wastes removed by recycling programs. Four articles offered details of the Seattle plan, complete with source citations to the bureaucrats in charge of city and metropolitan programs. In part, the *NYT* may be credited for reaching into a distant urban bureaucracy to find knowledgeable sources about an innovative program. However, those Seattle bureaucrats also managed to put themselves on the national source list by other means, as part of the local effort to put their program on the national news map.

A study of the national news and public relations wire coverage from November 1985 (well before the *NYT* began its dramatic coverage of recycling in the context of the garbage crisis) to May 1991 shows that Seattle stories were ripe on the wires for the picking. Seattle had become the location of media events created by press-seeking bureaucrats to lead both national and local journalists to the story. In 1986, for example, the city put itself on the national media map by hosting the Fifth Annual Recycling Congress, complete with an address by New York's director of recycling. Typical of the media orientation of local citizens' groups, Washington Citizens for Recycling gave out annual Packaging Awards and Booby Prizes, an event that landed a feature story in the venerable *New York Times*. The Seattle program won the National Recycling Award in 1989 from a group called the National Recycling Coalition, another story that went out over the United Press International (UPI) wires, on November 27, 1989.

In general, the wire stories tell a tale of Seattle politicians, businesses, and citizens' groups promoting the local success story and basking in the reflected media coverage. Prominent politicians at all levels of government (mayor, county executive, governor, state commissioner of public lands, Seattle port commissioners, and one of the state congressional representatives) joined bureaucrats on the news and public relations wires, explaining how the program worked, taking credit for its success, promising even bigger results in the future, and, inevitably, proclaiming Seattle "Number One."[27]

The media sensitivity of actors involved with the recycling story is perhaps best captured by Diana Gale, then the director of Seattle's Solid Waste Utility and the person responsible for implementing the new

27. Seattle mayor Norm Rice, quoted on the Business Wire, November 11, 1990.

program. Gale hired a marketing research firm to conduct focus groups with consumers. She also retained a public relations firm to design a public opinion campaign to address potentially volatile issues. In addition, she hired a full-time public relations specialist to handle press relations for her agency. From the marketing experts, Gale learned that the utility "needed to have a better press image, that we needed more consistency in our image and logo." The consultants told her that, to sell the new program, the utility had to "get a logo, get colors, get an image, have a personality." An important part of selling the image involved press relations. Part of the job for the full-time public relations expert was, in the words of Gale, "to get on a friendly, first-name basis with reporters."[28]

As the halo of media attention grew, actors outside of the public-private partnership that defined the Seattle program took advantage of the publicity surrounding the local success. For example, the business community in a rival city in the region put out a press release announcing its own program. Westin Hotels announced the beginning of a recycling program in Seattle on Earth Day. Another press release proclaimed that U.S. West telephone had printed its annual report on recycled paper produced by a Seattle paper mill. Reynolds Aluminum, with large facilities in Washington state and a checkered history of environmental battles, announced a foil recycling venture in Seattle and several other cities. Boeing engineers told a UPI reporter about plans to recycle garbage in outer space. Seattle datelines figured in forty-eight wire service stories during the four-and-a-half years studied.

Equally impressive is how the Seattle news managers responded when the story took a negative turn. A problem with recycling is that large-scale programs depend on markets for recycled products so that private firms involved can turn a profit. As programs in Seattle and other locations around the country went into full swing, some markets became saturated with recycled products. Prices collapsed, creating an element of doubt about the viability of the Seattle plan and, more generally, about the hopes for large-scale diffusion of the innovation. Helping to keep the story on its appointed positive plot were rapid responses from a variety of actors on the local scene. Following reports that the recycling industry was in trouble in Washington state, a coalition of government, citizens', and business groups held a press conference and sent out a press release on the wires under the headline "Washington Recycling Industry

28. Husock (1991, p. 3).

Has Sound Future."[29] As a result of this public relations repair work from local actors involved, Seattle remained an easy location for national reporters to find. The Seattle story was packaged to be reported in a routine way.

Conclusion

The studies reported here tell a tale of sources and reporters working together to produce a routine news story. As innovators became successful in telling their story, more people made themselves available to the media, including many news sources who arguably had little to do with the innovation itself. Thus a sort of critical news mass was created in Seattle, with more available sources producing more quotable material, resulting in more news, attracting the attention of more newsmakers, and so on. In each of its characteristic respects (that is, the who, what, where, when, and why), the recycling story became big news less because of investigative journalism breaking through some barrier of mistrust and adversity between reporters and innovators, than because at every juncture of the story a series of routine interactions emerged between journalists and newsmakers. These interactions proved for the most part beneficial to the actors connected to the innovation and, more important, meshed nicely with the daily routines of news organizations (in this case, the wire services and the *New York Times*).

Only at the local level is greater evidence found of more complex, multisourced stories with detailed accounts of how the innovation worked and more critical questions about its potential problems. In part, this was to be expected for a variety of reasons having to do with the availability of the local sources; a fair amount of friction between business, government, and citizens' groups as the program was implemented; and the greater need for the Seattle news audience, as users of the program, to understand how it worked—all factors likely to motivate closer investigation in the press. An important element of the local reporting was the *Seattle Times'* editorial policy of targeting a group of local agenda issues to cover in depth. Such policies on the part of news

29. Public Relations Wire, May 15, 1990. The groups were the State Committee for Recycling Markets, the Washington State Recycling Association, Washington Citizens for Recycling, Seattle Chamber of Commerce Solid Waste Committee, and the Department of Trade and Economic Development Business Assistance Center.

organizations increase the chances of coverage that goes beyond the routine.

The prescription that comes from this analysis is deceptively simple. News organizations will report more government innovations if they are looking for them. However, the way the news organization does its looking also matters. To cast a more favorable light on *NYT* coverage of recycling, the sustained coverage and the big increase after 1987 clearly reflected some agenda setting within the paper. The *NYT* had long before elevated environmental coverage to something close to a beat, and its coverage of the metropolitan New York garbage crisis reflected a sustained commitment to address an important problem. Within those broadened horizons, however, many aspects of the story were driven by journalistic conveniences. One result was that the complex question of whether a Seattle-style program had much applicability to New York was not given the critical attention it deserved, particularly, and perhaps most ironically, when Seattle sources were incorporated in *NYT* stories. For all its sustained coverage of both regional and national garbage problems during the 1980s, the predominant content of *NYT* stories reflected what one would expect from a news organization following routine procedures for covering a crisis: dramatization of the problem; reliance on a narrow range of public officials as primary sources; and the tendency to compartmentalize stories around reporters' beats and source-driven information.

By contrast, the *Seattle Times* balanced its enthusiasm for a local success story with a high volume of critical coverage. Fully 52 percent of *ST* articles mentioned problems with the program. This level of critical coverage is important because it runs counter to the assumption that a negative press drives innovators under cover. If media criticism is of the routine journalistic variety, looking for scandals and failures, that may well be the case. However, the tone of most *ST* articles was constructively critical, inviting officials, business leaders, and citizens to have their say in response to various problems. It clearly helped that the key political actors were practiced in media relations skills and prepared with a "media mind-set" described by Gale's basic message to her staff: "Don't let the press become an adversary. You want it to be a friend. You're not a victim. You, too, can handle the press."[30] What emerged from this interaction between nonroutine journalism and savvy media relations at the local level was something of a dialogue in the press, with

30. Husock (1991, p. 4).

innovators becoming familiar voices allowed to talk their way through the bumpy beginning of a program, instead of having to defend themselves against charges of failure.

One moral of this story is that, when a news organization departs from its routines, criticism also becomes less routine as it is tempered by greater sensitivity to the story. At the same time, innovators may feel less embattled and media-averse as they are given the opportunity to explain their program and its problems to the public. The result may be more informative news and a more positive role for the press in the policy process.

All of this suggests that several things are involved when news organizations make a commitment to cover innovations. The first is making the commitment itself—deciding that innovations are worth putting on the agenda and that covering them requires out-of-the-ordinary journalism. Breaking with routine in this case includes, among other things, staying with an innovation as it develops, assigning reporters for the long haul, resisting easy adoption of dramatized plots and news formulas (for example, crises, scandals, failures) that do little justice to innovations or innovators, and building the network of sources required to follow a story off the beaten path. These departures from the routine may still involve adversarialism between reporters and their sources, but it is likely to be a less ritualized and more useful sort of adversarialism. By playing the role of constructive critic, the media can facilitate something of a public dialogue in which innovators are able to explain themselves and citizens can learn something about policy in the process.

References

Altheide, David L., and Robert P. Snow. 1979. *Media Logic.* Beverly Hills, Calif.: Sage Publications.

Darnton, Robert. 1975. "Writing News and Telling Stories," *Daedalus,* vol. 104: 175–94.

Downs, Anthony. 1972. "Up and Down with Ecology: The Issue Attention Cycle." *Public Interest,* no. 28 (Summer): 38–50.

Epstein, Edward Jay. 1973. *News from Nowhere: Television and the News,* 1st ed. Random House.

Fishman, Mark. 1980. *Manufacturing the News.* University of Texas Press.

Gans, Herbert J. 1979. *Deciding What's News: A Study of* CBS Evening News, NBC Nightly News, Newsweek, *and* Time. Vintage.

Husock, Howard. 1991. *Please Be Patient: The Seattle Solid Waste Utility Meets the Press.* Case Program. Harvard University, John F. Kennedy School of Government.

Iyengar, Shanto. 1991. *Is Anyone Responsible? How Television Frames Political Issues.* University of Chicago Press.

Kingdon, John W. 1984. *Agendas, Alternatives, and Public Policies.* Little, Brown.

Linsky, Martin. 1986. *Impact: How the Press Affects Federal Policymaking.* W. W. Norton.

Molotch, Harvey, and Marilyn Lester. 1974. "Accidents, Scandals, and Routines: Resources for Insurgent Methodology." In *The TV Establishment: Programming for Power and Profit,* edited by Gaye Tuchman. Prentice-Hall.

Paletz, David L., and Robert M. Entman. 1981. *Media Power Politics.* Free Press.

Ripley, Randall B., and Grace A. Franklin. 1987. *Congress, the Bureaucracy, and Public Policy,* 4th ed. Chicago: Dorsey Press.

Sigal, Leon W. 1973. *Reporters and Officials: The Organization and Politics of Newsmaking.* Lexington, Mass.: D. C. Heath.

_____. 1986. "Who? Sources Make the News." In *Reading the News,* edited by Robert Karl Manoff and Michael Schudson. Pantheon.

Smith, Desmond. 1986. "You Can Go Home Again: The New Attractions of Local News." *Washington Journalism Review* (June): 44–47.

Zorn, Eric. 1986. "The Specialized Signals of Radio News: Giving Listeners What They Want." *Washington Journalism Review* (June): 32.

CHAPTER NINE

Mass Media and Policy Innovation

Opportunities and Constraints for Public Management

Robert M. Entman

A PARADOX exists in society's desires regarding the behavior of the news media in the policy process. Policy advocates want agencies and leaders to have effective press offices. Media cooperation has become vital to innovative leadership; news coverage helps determine whether the public, politicians, and other elites will support policy change. Yet citizens generally desire media skepticism and independence; the hope is that the news will let the public know when to demand that officials alter—or not initiate—bad policy. Citizens do not want news management to be too effective, journalists too cooperative. This ambivalent normative context structures the relationship of journalists and policymakers. Neither side knows the most ethical or most effective way to handle the other.

Journalists tend to suspect calls for a more cooperative and tolerant press corps, even as officials tend to resent the skepticism, bordering on cynicism, that journalists often bring to their encounters with policymakers. Hence the persistent tension between officials and journalists, even under the best of circumstances. Given the importance of the media to the democratic accountability of government, this is not a wholly bad thing. But many in government seem to believe the tension is often more destructive than creative.[1]

1. This judgment was rooted in numerous discussions with public officials whom I have taught in media relations seminars at the Federal Executive Institute and elsewhere as well as in

Current media practices do tend frequently to impede policy innovation.[2] Though the values and biases that shape policy reporting are neither ideological in the left-right sense nor ill-intentioned, they nonetheless establish disincentives and barriers to innovative leadership. The standard operating procedures of the news business create an uncontrolled dynamic that threatens constantly to undermine those government executives who refuse to play the media game or play it poorly.

The scanty academic literature, consisting almost entirely of case studies, suggests that journalists insufficiently appreciate their power to shape the policy process and catalyze citizenship. They need to recognize that reaching their highest calling requires transcendence of standard news formulae; they need to enforce a rule of reason and proportionality in the news. This turns out to be a more revolutionary goal than it sounds. Until such behavior is the norm for journalism, however, it is only practical—and in general ethically desirable—that public managers consider news management an integral component of public management. To be sure, in some cases, hindsight will teach that more critical, distanced reporting would have served the public interest—and even officials— better than a compliant press corps. Where the processes and personnel of both enterprises are imperfect, no infallible algorithm can be found to ensure a proper balance of aggressive journalism against aggressive, media-savvy public management. Citizens will simply have to live with the tension of their conflicted desires for media performance.

Values

Journalists tend to identify themselves as skeptical and independent watchdogs, standing in for the public at the citadels of government. The professional values that govern journalists' behavior tend to make this self-image real—to a point. Journalists do not treat every official's utterances and acts with high and perpetual suspicion. They have personal and career incentives to get and stay close to the highest officials, so that, in many circumstances, journalists' lapdog instincts triumph over the watchdog.

---

observations on this point aired at the conference on Public Innovation and the Media: Stimulus or Barrier?, held at the University of Washington in Seattle, September 1991. That conference provided the inspiration for this chapter. See also Linsky (1986); Entman (1989); and O'Heffernan (1990).

2. See chapter 8.

But officials of executive branch or independent agencies enjoy neither the legitimacy nor the staff resources to coddle and cow the press the way presidents or governors often can. For them, the press's bite can be painful, its skeptical approach more consistent and less manageable.

A philosophical base exists to the standards that journalists apply in critically assessing government: Progressivism. Herbert Gans has identified journalism's "enduring values," most rooted in journalists' application of Progressive, "clean politics" standards to public officials.[3] The Progressive movement grew out of a desire to apply business management principles to government. Ironically, in journalism these values have produced expectations of government efficiency that exceed standards journalists apply to business. A business can put a new product out in the marketplace, experience large start-up costs, and see the product fail, without its executives facing charges of profligacy and inefficiency (unless they strike out repeatedly). Government managers, operating under the skeptical media gaze, tend not to enjoy such leeway with their new or experimental projects.

Among the specific judgments that the Progressive value base produces is a strong commitment to governmental openness, a belief that the public deserves full and immediate disclosure of officials' plans, motivations, and actions. Openness is not a principle business managers adhere to, except when it suits their broader strategic objectives. Yet openness often works against efficiency; for example, revealing a proposed program to the public before details have been worked out can mobilize ill-informed opposition, which can complicate decisionmaking, delay implementation, or otherwise waste time.[4]

The Progressive stance has also led journalists to demand a match between officials' words and deeds that few business operations could meet. If Lee Iaccoca promised unsurpassed quality from Chrysler's automobiles, journalists forgave his hyperbole; not so for government executives, whose rhetorical exaggerations newspeople often assume to be nefariously motivated. In practice, then, journalists are simultaneously deeply cynical and highly romantic about the possibilities of governance. All in all, officials may rightly feel buffeted by unrealistic and incompatible expectations enforced by journalists oblivious to the contradictions.

Beyond this obvious source of conflict, other aspects of public man-

---

3. Gans (1979).

4. The press drastically curtails its expectation of openness in covering foreign and defense policy, however. See Entman (forthcoming).

agement clash with the ways journalists define and judge newsworthy events. Government officers who want to change the status quo must often engage in practical trade-offs that many journalists, with their squeaky clean, Progressive values, judge as hypocritical or corrupt. Journalists sometimes sneer at the ordinary give-and-take of adjustment, compromise, and coalition building as "politics," as if politics were unsavory and unnecessary. Yet journalists also judge officials harshly if they fail to play the levers of political power skillfully, to see policy ideas through to enactment and implementation. Again, the media tend to apply conflicting, hence frustrating, standards to officials.[5]

Furthermore, public officials often need to negotiate with affected interests in private, especially during the formulation and decision phases of policymaking. Publicity at such junctures can subvert delicate agreements. But, always facing deadlines and competition, journalists tend to disregard the possible effects of publicity on outcomes; if they find out something newsworthy today, they want to report it today, not wait until the decision is made. They do not want to write history.

A similar clash arises in expectations for success once innovations are approved. Public officials believe they deserve the benefit of the doubt when they try an innovative program. They want enough time and leeway to experiment and tinker, just as business executives do. Yet journalistic practices are such that a perceived policy failure, however prematurely determined, tends to be news. The publicity in turn can become self-fulfilling, for example, by arousing legislative opposition to continued funding of a program.

Finally, the suspicion that journalists apply to public servants is so ingrained that it can fairly be described as a professional norm. Politicians and bureaucrats are considered suspect categories, and the news frequently exhibits a cynical undertone suggesting that most public servants are incompetent, venal, or both. This stereotype induces hypersensitivity in the public, so that it tends to interpret anything that might remotely qualify as incompetence or corruption as such. To be fair, politicians themselves have promoted this negative view of government and bureaucrats, so it is hardly the media's fault that they have taken political leaders at their word and started treating most public servants with undisguised cynicism.

5. Entman (1981).

Biases

Operating along with the enduring values are several institutional biases that govern the framing of news. These biases are not ideological in the left-right sense but are rooted in constraints imposed by the nature of the news industry and its competitive markets. The most important of these "production biases" are personalization, symbolization, and simplification.[6] Operating separately and together, these biases shape the frames that journalists impose; that is, they help determine what elements of a situation are selected and made salient to the news audience. Most events and issues are ambiguous, subject to multiple interpretations or frames.[7] The frames journalists tend to employ, the emphases and implications their coverage promotes, often make innovation more difficult.

Among the most irksome effects of the biases to public officials is the way journalists seem often to depict issues and events that might be viewed as scandals. In major part because of their unrealistic expectations for antiseptic politics, what journalists frame as scandalous conflicts of interest or derelictions of duty, public executives may regard as simply getting things done in the real world. Florida's former secretary of health and rehabilitative services, Gregory Coler, experienced several instances of damaging publicity that typify the excessive standards of purity the media sometimes apply.[8] These standards exemplify the personalization bias. One instance arose from Coler's friendship with two computer experts from Illinois, whom he hired as outside contractors to help in modernizing computing facilities and services. Reporters tended to see the two only as friends and therefore suspected Coler's motives in employing them. Coler saw the same act as employing persons he personally trusted and whose work he knew well (from his previous stint as director of the Illinois Department of Children and Family Services). News reports framed the hiring as a story of friendship determining personnel decisions. They failed to give Coler the benefit of the doubt and rejected his frame of the same choice as based on his confidence in the contractors' ability. Without dismissing the suspicion as totally irrational, it is fair to ask whether Coler would hire incompetents merely for the

6. Entman (1989).
7. On the nature and power of framing, see Kahneman and Tversky (1984); and Entman (1993).
8. Scott (1992).

sake of friendship, especially because he had made upgrading the computer facilities a centerpiece of his reform program.[9]

The focus of the media on a personal explanation for an action that could have been framed as rational public management reveals the personalization bias: the systematic tendency for journalists to magnify attention to stories that involve well-known personalities and to explain events and policies by reference to persons and their relationships instead of to more abstract, impersonal structures and forces.

A second spate of bad publicity for Coler illustrates the symbolization bias. Coler stayed at an expensive hotel while on government business in Miami. He paid the cost of the room in excess of the government per diem allowance himself and explained that he stayed there because he was accompanying a prominent Florida attorney who preferred posh accommodations. For the media, this was a potent symbol. It suggested a clash between Coler's words (his claim to care about serving Florida's needy and about saving taxpayers money) and his deeds.

The symbolization bias is the media's tendency to be drawn to stories in which an action seems to symbolize a larger and culturally familiar theme and to emphasize the symbolism as opposed to another framing of the event. In this case, the act of staying at a swank hotel symbolized the familiar stereotypes of bureaucratic hypocrisy and excess. Coler admitted he should have been more sensitive to the symbolism.[10] But it is also reasonable to wonder whether a government official gives up all rights to indulge private preferences, even if no extra cost is borne by the taxpayer, merely because a newsworthy symbol has been created. And even more pertinent is whether Coler's personal tastes in hotels did bear in any logical way on his commitment or capacity to improve delivery of human services in Florida. Public officials can all too easily run afoul of the media's symbolization bias, and it is sometimes difficult to see how reporting driven by this practice informs the public or prevents serious corruption.

Beyond symbols, the news is heavily influenced by the third bias, simplification. The media tend to emphasize those stories and interpretations

9. Feeding the disbelief was the report that the Federal Bureau of Investigation (FBI) had one of the friends under investigation in connection with consulting contracts awarded back in Illinois. However, journalists should certainly have learned from the government investigations of the 1970s that FBI reports and probes are often based on low-credibility allegations and may themselves be rooted in corrupt politics. In other words, journalism could treat the FBI as it does other bureaucracies and question its actions and motivations but in this case apparently did not.

10. Coler (1991).

that are easy for news organizations to cover and simple for audiences to understand. To take one example, even as the Florida papers were devoting considerable space to Coler's hotel habits, which were simple to report and fathom, they were largely neglecting the complex schemes employed by Florida banks for laundering billions of dollars in drug money. Comprehending and gathering data on those corrupt actions required much time and labor as well as a grasp of technical banking regulations and accounting practices, complexities daunting to reporters and readers alike.

What the biases appear to produce is an inability of the media to apply a rational sense of proportion to scandal coverage. Granted, Coler's hotel choice and other minor trespasses might have been newsworthy to some degree. The question is how newsworthy they were when viewed in competition with many other, unreported scandals or, for that matter, with other news, good and bad. Media organizations have no real mechanism for calibrating scandal coverage—or news in general—to some explicit and reasoned judgment of public importance. Instead they seem to be propelled along by the three biases and by competition: Once somebody has discovered one newsworthy peccadillo, other news organizations may feel driven to uncover others, and a "feeding frenzy" may ensue.[11] Such displays may not only distract the public and the affected officials or agencies from more important issues, but they may also contribute to making public service unattractive to talented people.

Aside from the problem of excessive publicity for minor or dubious scandals, perhaps the other major frustration arising from the three biases, especially simplification, involves "technical details." What are minutiae to journalists often constitute the heart of the analysis for public managers. The simplification bias reflects and reinforces reporters' beliefs that technical details are boring to audiences (and journalists often find details dull themselves). But the reasons for decisions that might on their publicized surface seem unwise may rest in technicalities (such as legal codes, cost-benefit analyses, or discounted present value) that journalists are not trained to understand and tend to regard as audience-numbing trivia. The simplification bias works against careful, prominent, and sympathetic attention to such analytical details. Journalists are probably right to assume strict limits on the mass audience's tolerance for technical explanations. Still, reporting that fails to acknowl-

11. Sabato (1991); O'Heffernan (1990); and Linsky (1986).

edge the complexities of a policy issue can wind up damaging government's ability to handle it.

In sum, the media seem to exhibit a tendency—under conditions not yet fully specified in academic research—to undermine the power and legitimacy of innovative officials and programs. The officials in question may be dishonest or incompetent; the policies, ill-advised. Part of the problem is that media coverage is not closely calibrated to whether officials are crooks or saints, or whether the programs are turkeys or potential winners. The media tend—again, not always, but too often—to disembody their coverage of innovation from judgments about the underlying character and quality of the official, or the policy analytical rationale.

Hidden Impacts on Innovation

This is not the whole story of innovation and journalism. The media's biases may undermine innovation in subtle ways not so far discussed: Instead of thwarting an official who wants to innovate, the media may bolster conditions that permit officials who do not pursue innovation to get away with their passivity. Media practices may unintentionally collude with an official desire to preserve the status quo. As an example, for reasons beyond the scope of this paper, news is largely constrained to reflect elite discourse.[12] If political elites or government agencies are not actively addressing a problem in a way that fits the simplification, symbolization, or personalization biases, the typical news organization will neglect or ignore it, reducing pressure for an innovative solution.

In some cases, though they are the exception, independent reporting can assist the innovation process. Investigative journalism can educate the public and officials themselves to the existence of policy problems. Sometimes the stories call forth citizen demands to innovate, other times they spur official steps even without arousing a public reaction. In these cases, the media take on a quasi-governmental, policy-analytical function, alerting public executives even before the news is published.[13] But most news organizations devote few resources to investigating problems that merit government attention, unless a public official fits them to the

12. Gans (1979); Entman (1989); and Bennett (1990).
13. Protess and others (1991).

biases and makes news of them. Even when the media do independently push an issue, if high-level political elites are not pressing for an innovation or discussing a policy problem in public and if agency heads are unconcerned, most news organizations can do little to force it onto the agenda. At most they can run an investigative story or two, along with an editorial. Nothing automatically compels government to respond.

But more frequently, the three biases lead to reporting that emphasizes government failure and scandal, feeding cynicism and dampening public expectations for elected officials to innovate. Moreover, by slighting policy substance and according generous coverage to symbolic media events, by pouncing on creative proposals that can generate juicy stories of personalities in dramatic conflict, by neglecting many positive innovations as too dull or complicated, the media's biases create disincentives for innovative risk taking.[14] Why bother to innovate if the political rewards are low and the risk—of being labeled a failure, a wastrel, even a fool—is high? To be sure, this context leaves considerable room for innovation by risk-seeking officials. But for all the reasons suggested, news organizations are rarely in the forefront of those forces that encourage elected or appointed officials to tackle tough problems, to support daring and creative public management, and to risk political capital in the name of innovative public policy.

At the same time, news practices may help insulate agencies and officials whose unwise decisions are not framed as "innovations." A new policy of government inaction—for example, a failure to enforce previously implemented regulations—can be an important innovation. Inaction is generally not news. Or the innovation might consist of an agency encoding a new, tortured interpretation of legislative intent in their implementing rules; administrative regulations are usually classified as technical details and escape media notice. Another kind of innovation involves judicial appointments that substantially alter prevailing legal doctrine, with major impacts on policy. These too often remain the province of specialized publications, outside the purview of the general public. And then there are the announced policies that have unannounced or unintended "innovative" but harmful consequences, outcomes that agencies generally do not publicize. In general, if officials or agencies fail to trumpet a policy change but merely start behaving differently, or if they announce the departure in an obscure place such as the *Federal Register,* the decision is

14. See chapter 8.

likely to remain unpublicized unless a powerful actor (such as the chairman of a legislative committee) complains publicly.

Consider the innovative savings and loan (S&L) policies of the early and middle 1980s. Publicity was limited almost entirely to the business press or business sections of newspapers, where few in the mass audience learned of their existence. A more vigilant media might have alerted the wider public to the potential risks of S&L deregulation, but for reasons already suggested (the complexity, the absence of well-known personalities to vilify or lionize, the failure of elites to raise a fuss) the press neglected the story—until the disaster was too far along for publicity to make much difference.[15] The press's failure here is to some extent understandable. Ten years later, the scandal remains so complicated and vast that few outside the industry itself are likely to have more than a partial grasp of it.

An even more subtle media effect on innovation comes through news organizations' cooperation with officials in manufacturing public spectacles. A typical example of such media events occurs when presidents go on pageant-filled overseas trips to distract the public from intractable domestic problems. The media find these events irresistible. Their fulsome coverage symbolizes official attention to problems while often masking genuine incapacity or uninterest in solving them.[16] This is another way of describing the dangers of an overly docile press.

This last point suggests again that, much like public officials, journalists are held simultaneously to incompatible standards. They might fairly claim that observers want them to scrutinize official actions critically, even when they are not packaged as an innovative policy or when the innovation appears purely technical. Yet critics also want journalists to assist in the innovation process, to help government executives promote their proposals and implement their new projects. The issue is precisely where to draw the line and how. Journalists are not in conscious control of this line-drawing. No single rational actor controls the process, which is propelled by the operation of the three biases. This situation necessitates public managers' attempts to impose a guiding hand. If applied systematically, a consistent approach to media management by public officials along with some introspection by journalists might help move the process toward a more rational balance between media passivity and uncalibrated aggressiveness.

15. Kurtz (1992).
16. Edelman (1988).

Managing News to Promote Innovation

Public officials have the capacity to affect the course of media cover-age. Under some circumstances, for example, government may be able to head off scandals by addressing them directly and quickly instead of letting them fester. And, under some conditions, the media treat officials and their acts positively, if not credulously or even worshipfully.[17]

Where innovations are under way, the media can perform an educative function, explaining to an often-impatient and skeptical public the benefits while preparing them for the likely costs and setbacks. In some circumstances, not yet specified, journalists do portray innovative programs and officials sympathetically, and that may buy government the time and support to launch a successful new policy. This process often involves favorable editorials, which can stimulate support among the public and other government agencies while signaling to the reporters and editors who fill the news columns that the program deserves the benefit of the doubt.

One example is provided by a case study on the director of the Seattle Solid Waste Utility, Diana Gale. She guided the agency through a series of significant and potentially controversial innovations designed to reduce the environmental impacts of garbage. These included instituting fees for collection and requiring a variety of time-consuming measures by individual residents such as placing different types of trash in sepa-rate containers. Gale and her program succeeded in part because of the favorable publicity that she self-consciously orchestrated.[18]

As another example of proactive media management, the Employment and Training (ET) Choices welfare employment program in Massachu-setts avoided premature publicity condemning it as a failure by using authority under existing legislation to craft an unannounced innovation that was not publicized for a year while kinks were being ironed out.[19] The managers of that program recognized the institutional biases of jour-nalism and used them to defend against arousing bad publicity. Then, when ready for coverage, the managers turned the biases to advantage in promoting the program by supplying simple, symbolic, and personalized stories of success.

An important case in which a high-level federal executive made media management a central part of a strategic plan to promote innovation

17. Hertsgaard (1988).
18. Husock (1991).
19. Behn (1991).

involved the Reagan-era secretary of the Navy, John Lehman. He understood the importance and means of building media-planning into policy analysis and adroitly promoted his central innovation, a six-hundred-ship Navy, and other objectives by maintaining supportive coverage. Even when controversy inevitably developed, Lehman's carefully cultivated relationship with reporters on the national security beat protected him from the development of feeding frenzies, providing him a strong presumption of competence and innocence.[20]

Yet Lehman's career also illustrates the danger of media management, and here the other side of the contradiction in desired media behavior arises. Beyond the skittishness journalists rightly express about becoming propagandists for government, overly cozy relationships among reporters and officials can ultimately harm policymakers themselves. Independent and feisty journalism can serve as an early warning system that illuminates the need for and energizes innovation, prevents bad policy changes, or provides feedback on how some new policy is working. In the Lehman case, the former Navy secretary himself later called for an active Navy of far fewer than six hundred ships and, upon sober reflection, admittedly aided by (though not dependent upon) hindsight, suggests that the crumbling Soviet empire's navy could have been checked with far less depletion of the American Treasury.[21] Aggressive reporting might have prevented the talented Lehman from squandering both U.S. resources and his own historical standing on the six-hundred-ship idea.

These examples reveal that news management is both necessary and fraught with risk. Certainly the experiences in Seattle with recycling and Massachusetts with welfare reform suggest it can often be ethical and helpful to approach policy innovation as a marketing problem and to include news management as one of the vehicles. Yet the Lehman tale is more cautionary, and the proper balance in the relationship between media and public officials will require case-by-case judgments.

From public managers' perspective, neglecting the public relations angle makes them and their programs vulnerable to undermining by opponents—persons who have no superior claim to representing the public interest—or by ill-informed public opposition. An example comes from

20. Linsky (1989).

21. Lehman's changing recommendations are described in Bernard Trainor, "Ex–Navy Chief Offers a Plan to Cut Spending," *New York Times,* March 28, 1990, p. A18. For contemporaneous evidence of the weakness of the justification for the U.S. buildup, see Stubbing (1986).

the Department of Health, Education, and Welfare (HEW) under Joseph A. Califano, which suffered from adverse publicity of a carelessly crafted though administratively innovative management audit. Because the agency failed to package the results of its audit with the likely media response in mind, journalists, operating predictably according to the simplification and symbolization biases, framed the report with headlines exclaiming that HEW wasted billions of dollars annually. A demagogic political reaction ensued in Congress, which ultimately imposed a $1 billion budget cut that only made it harder for the agency to root out fraud and waste.[22]

Because such terms as "waste," "success," and "innovation" are so imprecise, some kind of framing or cognitive anchoring with respect to any policy decision is inevitable. It might as well be the innovating official who provides the frame or at least tries to. No a priori reason exists to think either journalists or political opponents of the innovation will offer a more accurate or objective way of framing the issue. If others have a different understanding of the matter, they will usually speak up and, because journalists relish stories of conflict, receive coverage.

Innovations in the News Process

Are there any innovations that news organizations might implement to enhance their contributions to the policy process? Here is one proposal: Journalists should keep in mind that the underlying goal of the watchdog role and of journalistic assertiveness generally is to make democracy work better. Promoting that shared goal may involve making some trade-offs among values that journalists have generally taken as sacrosanct. It may require a modification of traditional journalistic assumptions, for example, that official openness is always a good thing to be demanded in virtually all conditions or that all events fitting the biases for a scandal story must be blared to the public without regard to the consequences for individual careers or for the success of policy innovation. Democracy could work better, on balance, if in some instances officials are given leeway to close the aperture of reporter access or if some minor scandals are slighted to foster innovations that augment the efficiency of government services desired by the public.

22. This example is described by Whitman (1982). Publicity examples are in "$6 Billion Is Misspent by H.E.W.," *New York Times,* April 4, 1978, p. 18; and "Mr. Califano's Mini-Scandals," *Wall Street Journal,* July 16, 1979, p. 16.

Journalists are likely to find this modification difficult to accept. Most reporters and editors believe that the journalist's job is reporting what happens, as much of it and as soon as possible. Weighing potential consequences before deciding how to write a story in their view assaults the commitment to objectivity and threatens to turn media into tools of government. But if shaping the news to advance some public interest goal sounds subversive of journalistic ideals, in practice it happens all the time. Research consistently shows a significant positive relationship between a newspaper's editorial policy and its news slant.[23] Moreover, editors do routinely screen stories for possible negative consequences, most frequently arising from concerns about privacy, libel, and national security. The point here would be not to construct stories that promote a specific policy or leader but to shape news practices so that they advance a more procedural goal: allowing government to work under conditions of more public support, patience, and trust.

23. See, for example, Entman (1989, chapter 6); and Halberstam (1979).

References

Behn, Robert D. 1991. *Leadership Counts: Lessons for Public Managers from the Massachusetts Welfare, Training, and Employment Program.* Harvard University Press.

Bennett, Lance. 1990. "Toward a Theory of Press-State Relations." *Journal of Communication,* vol. 40, no. 2: 103–25.

Coler, Gregory. 1991. Remarks made at the conference on Public Innovation and the Media: Stimulus or Barrier?, University of Washington, Seattle, September.

Edelman, Murray J. 1988. *Constructing the Political Spectacle.* University of Chicago Press.

Entman, Robert M. 1981. "The Imperial Media." In *Politics and the Oval Office: Toward Presidential Governance,* edited by Arnold J. Meltsner, 79–101. New Brunswick, N.J.: Transaction Books.

_____. 1989. *Democracy without Citizens: Media and the Decay of American Politics.* New York: Oxford University Press.

_____. 1993. "Framing: Toward Clarification of a Fractured Paradigm." *Journal of Communication,* vol. 43, no. 4 (Autumn): 51–58.

_____. Forthcoming. *Projections of Power: Media and the National Defense.* University of Chicago Press.

Gans, Herbert A. 1979. *Deciding What's News: A Study of* CBS Evening News, NBC Nightly News, Newsweek, *and* Time. Pantheon.

Halberstam, David. 1979. *The Powers That Be.* Knopf.

Hertsgaard, Mark. 1988. *On Bended Knee: The Press and the Reagan Presidency.* Farrar, Straus, and Giroux.

Husock, Howard. 1991. *Please Be Patient: The Seattle Solid Waste Utility Meets the Press.* Harvard University, John F. Kennedy School of Government.

Kahneman, Daniel, and Amos Tversky. 1984. "Choice, Values, and Frames." *American Psychologist* 39: 341–50.

Kurtz, Howard. 1992. "Asleep at the Wheel." *Washington Post Magazine* (November): 10ff.

Linsky, Martin. 1986. *Impact: How the Press Affects Federal Policymaking.* Norton.

_____. 1989. *John Lehman and the Press.* Harvard University, John F. Kennedy School of Government.

O'Heffernan, Patrick. 1990. *Mass Media and American Foreign Policy: Insider Perspectives on Global Journalism and the Foreign Policy Process.* Norwood, N.J.: Ablex Publishers.

Protess, David L., and others. 1991. *The Journalism of Outrage: Investigative Reporting and Agenda Building in America.* New York: Guilford Press.

Sabato, Larry. 1991. *Feeding Frenzy: How Attack Journalism Has Transformed American Politics.* Free Press.

Scott, Esther. 1992. *Managing a Press "Feeding Frenzy": Gregory Coler and the Florida Dept. of Health and Rehabilitative Services.* Harvard University, John F. Kennedy School of Government.

Stubbing, Richard A. 1986. *The Defense Game: An Insider Explores the Astonishing Realities of America's Defense Establishment.* Harper and Row.

Whitman, David. 1982. *Fraud, Abuse and Waste at HEW.* Harvard University, John F. Kennedy School of Government.

Part Four

INNOVATION IN POLICY FIELDS

CHAPTER TEN

State Innovation in Health Policy

Deborah A. Stone

THE LITERATURE on innovation in the public sector seems to agree on one thing: Innovation is more likely to bubble up from below than to be planned and implemented from above. Innovations in public sector human services programs do not often follow the "planning model," in which the innovation starts with a clear and well-specified idea, goes through a lengthy planning period, and encounters limited change during the period of operation. More common are innovations that follow a "groping-along" model, in which a public manager has only a general goal, tries many alternatives, puts ideas into action without much planning, learns from experience, and modifies both the core idea and the strategies for achieving the goal as the innovation proceeds.[1] Innovative organizations, too, tend to be ones that allow freewheeling, discretionary authority and that tolerate experimentation and failure by their employees, rather than ones with strict hierarchical control, tight rules, and heavy oversight.[2]

In a similar vein, scholars of intergovernmental relations are looking

---

"State Innovation in Health Policy" originally appeared as "Why the States Can't Solve the Health Insurance Crisis," in *American Prospect,* no. 9, Spring 1992, pp. 51–60, and the material is used here by permission of *The American Prospect.* The article has been substantially updated and revised for this book.

1. Behn (1988); and Golden (1990).
2. Behn (1988); Golden (1990); and Altshuler and Zegans (1990).

to lower levels of government as the most promising sites of innovation. Some scholars of federalism assert that the states in general are "reinvigorated, resourceful, energetic, assertive and innovative" sources of knowledge and change for the federal government.[3] Some, but not all, analysts of health policy think innovation in health policy is more likely to come from the states than from the federal government.[4] States, according to those analysts, are highly motivated to innovate in health policy because they are pressured from all sides. From above, the federal government mandates states to provide more benefits to more people while cutting its own contributions to state revenues. From below, the cities and counties come to the states for fiscal relief as their uncompensated care bill grows. And from within, the business community complains to state government about the escalating costs of insurance or the inability to obtain employee coverage at all. States are the payer of last resort.

Since the failure of President Bill Clinton's nationally directed health care reform, expectations and hopes for the states as innovators have run even higher than in the period before 1994. The faith in state capacity rests on two claims: First, the states were sources of major innovations in the absence of much national policy on cost containment and access to health insurance before Clinton tried to nationalize the issue; and second, now that national reforms are largely out of the picture, states have no choice but to solve the problems on their own.

Given the tremendous responsibilities now being thrust on the states, as well as the larger political culture of federalism that places so much faith in state experimentation, creativity, leadership, flexibility, and responsiveness, the historical record of states and health policy innovation is worth examining. A close reading of history suggests that most innovations often credited to the states did not originate in the states, nor were they carried out by states independent of resources and political authority from outside the states. Moreover, the theory of "bottom-up" innovation prevalent in the literature is belied by the reality of "top-down" policy change in health policy. (Although health policy includes issues of technology, manpower, and service delivery, my argument is restricted to issues of financing and access, for the central dilemma of contemporary U.S. health policy lies in how to provide universal access

    3. Reeves (1990); Elazar (1990); Rovner (1988); and Bowman and Kearney (1986).
    4. Schneider (1989); Shortell and McNerney (1990); Kosterlitz (1990); Mashaw (1993–94); Leichter (1996); and Marmor, Mashaw, and Oberlander (1996).

to health services while controlling costs.) Historically, states have not been major innovators in finance and access, nor are they likely to produce innovative solutions given current political arrangements.

State Innovation by Carrot and by Cudgel

At first glance, health appears to be a policy arena with an extraordinarily high rate of innovation. For the area of medical technology, this is certainly true. But, on close inspection, most of the financing and access innovations were started at the center and were often forced on the states either through legislation or slightly more gently through strings attached to federal medicare and medicaid money. These innovations are near-perfect specimens of the planning model, with an initial statute, a lengthy planning period, a clearly specified idea, and pursuit of the original idea with reasonable constancy.

The major reforms in state and local health policy during the 1960s and 1970s were mandated by federal legislation. Neighborhood health centers, those quintessentially local health institutions of the 1960s, did not bubble up from neighborhoods but were conceived and established by the federal Office of Economic Opportunity (OEO) starting in 1965. To be sure, OEO sought to stimulate local institutions and community groups to propose and operate the centers, but the requirements and the monetary strings all came from and led back to Washington. Health maintenance organizations (HMOs)—a new label coined by a policy entrepreneur in Minnesota for an old concept of prepaid group practices—could scarcely be said to have germinated in Minnesota, unless the idea of marketing prepaid group practices as simultaneously preventive health policy and cost containment is considered an innovation.[5] In any case, the HMO policy entrepreneurs begged the federal government to consider HMOs eligible for reimbursement from medicare and medicaid. Before long, Congress obliged by defining what sort of organization could be a "federally qualified HMO," giving tremendous fiscal impetus and legal guidance for the homogenization of the concept.

A 1972 federal law required states to set up utilization review boards known as Professional Standards Review Organizations. The National Health Resources Development Act of 1974 required states to establish

---

5. Starr (1982, pp. 395–97).

health planning agencies with mandates to review proposed capital expenditure projects and deny the unnecessary ones a certificate-of-need. These agencies had a novel form of governance by a board of which at least 50 percent of the members were representatives of the community. In both reforms, the federal government used these new organizational mechanisms to pass judgment on monies that it, ultimately, would be giving to the states through the federal medicare and medicaid programs. And so the story goes. Reform after state reform was a federally initiated, if not federally mandated, affair.

What about diagnosis related groups (DRGs)? DRGs were a genuinely new hospital payment system based on a fixed price per disease instead of a per diem rate. The system was first introduced in New Jersey in the late 1970s and was eventually adopted by medicare. In many ways, the DRG payment method looks like a bottom-up innovation success story. New Jersey's newly appointed state health commissioner found herself at the head of a system with rising hospital costs, financially precarious urban hospitals, and a mechanism of hospital rate-setting controlled by the hospitals. She had clear goals: to replace the per diem reimbursement system and to bring all hospitals under a single rate-setting system to prevent them from shifting costs to unregulated hospitals. Beyond those goals, her plan for reaching them was not well articulated. After considerable tinkering, she instituted an innovative payment scheme designed at the Yale University School of Public Health.

The New Jersey DRG story, however, is another tale of innovation by federal carrots and constraints. The commissioner's innovation was politically blocked three times, and each time, intervention by the Health Care Financing Administration (HCFA) came to the state's rescue.[6] In 1976 a bill that would have granted the Department of Health authority to regulate all payers was blocked by Blue Cross and the New Jersey Hospital Association and was never even reported out of committee. Nevertheless, the bill caught the attention of people at HCFA, who were looking for states to conduct rate-setting experiments with alternatives to per diem reimbursement. HCFA stepped in with a $3 million demonstration grant to the Department of Health to design the system. The grant enabled the commissioner to hire a team of experts somewhat outside the normal civil service rules and to pay for them.

6. For details of the DRG story, see Dunham and Morone (1983); and Morone and Dunham (1985).

In 1978 the Department of Health proposed another bill necessary to implement the DRG innovation; it would have allowed the department to pay hospitals for uncompensated care by splitting the costs among all payers. This provision was designed to win the support of the hospitals. The bill faced significant opposition, however, until HCFA promised a waiver of normal medicare rules so that New Jersey would have approximately $60 million in medicare money to put in its fund for uncompensated care. With the lure of $60 million, the law passed easily, only to be challenged once more by the Hospital Association, which claimed that the department had no authority to implement DRGs because they were nowhere mentioned in the bill. Before the legislature could hold hearings on the controversy, HCFA made its third appearance, this time with a letter to the Department of Health: HCFA wanted a DRG experiment; and if New Jersey abandoned the plan to use DRGs, HCFA would delay the waiver, perhaps never grant one, and reconsider its commitment to funding an experiment in New Jersey.

The New Jersey DRG innovation illustrates a crucial point about state health politics: The political environment for health policy was (and is in every state) extremely dense. The affected interests were well organized and carried significant political clout. Virtually any payment or regulatory reform would affect each interest group in its pocketbook. In that situation, the state health agency had little room for maneuver. Only the intervention of a federal agency—a big "heavy" from outside the state political arena—could enable the Department of Health to win against the strong, local, entrenched interests.

State reform in the 1980s was not much different. The Omnibus Budget Reconciliation Act of 1981 (OBRA), much heralded as a stimulus to state innovations in medicaid policy, did permit states more flexibility in defining eligibility, services, and rates in their medicaid programs.[7] But in an important sense, OBRA, as well as subsequent budget acts of the 1980s, simply lengthened the states' medicaid leash a bit. Many states exercised some of the new options available to them, but those options (such as expanding eligibility to pregnant women or to the medically needy who did not receive aid to families with dependent children (AFDC)) were carefully circumscribed by the federal statutes. There was scarcely room for anything worthy of the name innovation.

Another set of 1980s state and local policy experiments—the medic-

7. Schneider (1989); and Fraser (1987).

aid "competition demonstrations"—was just as surely controlled from the center. The Health Care Financing Administration solicited proposals to test "innovative health care financing and delivery approaches" and, in 1982, approved seven demonstrations in six states.[8] The new approaches were hardly new. Competition between HMOs, payment on the basis of per-capita fees instead of fee-for-service, and case management (the buzzword for a variety of mechanisms to control and monitor physician referrals and hospitalization) had all been around for a long time. What was new was that state medicaid programs were encouraged to try them, but only after careful planning and submission of the plans to HCFA for approval. (No sign of groping along here.)

Another innovation of the 1980s deserves particular mention because it was avowedly community-based. There was an effort to form local coalitions of insurers, providers, professionals, and business and labor groups that would operate as a "third force" between the boundaries of the traditional private and public sectors.[9] Because of their commitment to the community and the creative energies that they would release, these community coalitions would, it was hoped, be able to arrive at local solutions to the conundrum of cost-containment and access.

Where did the strategy come from? Not the communities. The idea of local coalitions found fertile soil in the general antiregulatory and anti-Washington mood of the late seventies and early eighties.[10] For all the anti-Washington appeal of the strategy, however, it got its real push from national organizations, even if not always Washington-based ones. The U.S. Chamber of Commerce and the Business Roundtable's Task Force on Health began urging their members to become involved in local health care issues. Six national organizations under the leadership of former secretary of labor John Dunlop formed "Dunlop's Group of Six" to promote the coalition strategy. They were the AFL-CIO, the American Medical Association, the American Hospital Association, Blue Cross/Blue Shield, the Health Insurance Association of America, and the Business Roundtable.

On close inspection, the coalitions turned out to be overwhelmingly initiated and dominated by business as a response to their concerns about the cost of providing health care to their employees.[11] In the largest

8. Anderson and Fox (1987).
9. McLaughlin, Zellers, and Brown (1989); and Brown and McLaughlin (1990).
10. McLaughlin, Zellers, and Brown (1989, p. 72).
11. Meyerhoff and Crozier (1984, p. 121).

survey, covering 215 coalitions, almost half (45 percent) were employer-only coalitions; that is, only employers had voting membership.[12] Employers were members in 94 percent of all coalitions, and the next most active groups were physicians and hospitals, each with voting membership in 40 percent of the coalitions. Only 28 percent of the coalitions were broad-based—that is, having voting members from the physician, hospital, insurance, labor, and business sectors. These could hardly be said to be community coalitions. Moreover, they were not terribly active in cost-containment (the predicate of the coalition strategy). More than 70 percent said their main goal was education, and almost half said education was their only goal. The two most frequent projects of coalitions were education (67 percent) and data collection (53 percent).[13]

The Robert Wood Johnson Foundation, attracted by the idea of community coalitions, established a program to stimulate them. In 1981–82 the foundation invited communities to apply for about $15 million in seed money. Sixteen communities were eventually funded with multiyear planning grants (no sign of groping here), and eleven of these with implementation grants. Thus these coalitions could not easily be characterized as community innovations; they were called into being by a national grants program and designed to the specifications of its application process. But even conceding them the status of a community innovation, a careful evaluation (which to its credit, the foundation funded) found little evidence that they succeeded in doing what they were supposed to do: contain costs.[14]

Virtually all of the deliberate small-scale, state experimentation on design and management of medicaid is done at the behest of the federal government. Section 1115 of the Social Security Act provides for "research and demonstration waivers" to enable states to experiment with innovative ways of controlling costs and expanding coverage under medicaid. (Because federal statute imposes strict requirements on how states run their medicaid program, including a requirement that each state program have uniform rules throughout the state, states need waivers from these requirements if they are to deviate from federal rules, even for a small-scale experiment.) However, the whole waiver process lodges control of experimentation in the federal executive branch. The Health Care Financing Administration develops an agenda of projects proposed

12. McLaughlin, Zellers, and Brown (1989).
13. McLaughlin, Zellers, and Brown (1989).
14. Brown and McLaughlin (1990).

by its staff and members of Congress, and it then solicits proposals from
state medicaid agencies for demonstrations that fulfill its agenda. HCFA
rarely receives unsolicited proposals, and the whole program sends
signals that state agencies are much more likely to succeed if they
respond to federal requests rather than initiate their own demonstration
ideas.[15]

In sum, most of the big innovations addressed to the cost and access
dilemma in health policy are not initiated by states. States are prodded
into new initiatives by federal mandates, by the lure of federal money for
demonstration grants, by threats of withdrawal of federal money, and by
national organizations (such as HCFA and the Robert Wood Johnson
Foundation) seeking to test their innovative ideas. By and large, states
are the testing grounds for innovations in health policy, but they do not
control the innovation process. They are guided and constrained by the
requirements of federal funding sources and are probably somewhat
restricted in their vision by the constant barrage of ideas-in-vogue from
more national institutions.

From late 1992 to 1994, when the possibility of federal health insurance reform loomed likely, the insurance sector (both for profit and nonprofit) prepared itself to deal with a federal statute and a strong federal
regulatory authority. The pace of insurance company mergers picked up,
as did the expansion and marketing of managed care plans. Since that
time, the states have found themselves facing a far more concentrated
and powerful health insurance industry. In trying to solve problems of
access to health care, states can no longer worry only about the difficulty
of getting more people covered by health insurance policies; they now
have to cope with the various strategies of managed care plans to limit
care for people they do cover.

In this new environment, especially after 1994, state initiatives in
health policy have been largely directed to mitigating some of the perceived abuses and negative effects of powerful managed care plans.
There has been a spate of "backlash legislation"—state laws whose only
purposes are to restrain managed care plans from denying necessary care
and to increase the rights and power of patients vis-à-vis their plans.[16]
The new laws often deal with minute details of health-care delivery and
coverage for those who are already covered; for example, laws that

15. Dobson, Moran, and Young (1992).
16. Serafini (1996); and Milt Freudenheim, "HMOs Cope with a Backlash on Cost
Cutting," *New York Times,* May 19, 1996, p. A1.

mandate forty-eight-hour hospital stays for childbirth, laws that mandate hospital stays (as opposed to day surgery) for mastectomies, and laws that prevent an insurer from denying payment for emergency care if the patient reasonably thought he or she needed urgent care. Most of these legislative efforts have sidetracked state legislatures from trying to control health care costs and increase access to health insurance for the uninsured.

State Innovations: Fingers in the Dike

At the state level, a cadre of dedicated public servants and advocates is willing to devote enormous energies and even pay high political costs to relieve the health insurance crisis in the absence of federal leadership.[17] Many of these initiatives do succeed in making health services available to people who need them and who were not getting them before. Yet at the same time, many of these reforms perpetuate the institutions, rules, and practices of the current system. By supporting and extending the current paradigm of health insurance, they intensify the very practices that create high costs and low access in the first place.

At the heart of the problem of medical insurance is a structure that gives everyone incentives to withdraw from risk-pooling and cost-sharing arrangements.[18] Employers, in seeking the lowest-cost insurance package for their employees, withdraw from large community programs such as Blue Cross/Blue Shield. Instead of pooling the risks of their employees with other (sometimes less healthy) employee groups, they self-insure or purchase commercial policies priced according to the risks of their employees. Commercial insurers, seeking a larger market share in health insurance, design products priced according to the risks of specific employee groups and target particularly healthy groups in their marketing efforts. Especially in the small business market, insurers are increasingly using medical underwriting techniques to screen potential policyholders and to price policies according to precise medical risks. Employers shift more of the costs of illness onto employees and subdivide their employees into groups with more homogeneous risks. As a result of all these factors,

17. Demkovich (1990); Lemov (1990); Coye (1991); Alpha Center (1991); and Leichter (1996).

18. Stone (1991); and Stone (1993).

health insurance risk pools are segmented, leaving more people to pay very high prices for their health insurance and often unable to obtain any insurance at all.

Consider one of the major state innovations to deal with this problem. More than half the states have created high-risk pools to cover people who have been denied insurance by private companies for medical reasons. Because these plans by definition include only people who already have or are likely to have costly diseases, the premiums and copayments must be high. The pools simply cannot provide affordable insurance for the average person. Even with significant state subsidies, the states are forced to raise the premiums for this coverage, and premium increases stimulate people to disenroll from the pools.[19] Some states subsidize their high-risk pools from state revenues; others assess insurance companies based on their pro-rata share of business in the state; and some states use a combination of these two methods. Most states allow insurance companies to credit their high-risk pool assessments against their state taxes. Because state tax revenues are thereby reduced, the net effect is the same as subsidizing the pools from state general revenues.[20]

High-risk pools in effect continue to segment broad-risk pools into smaller pools with more homogeneous risks. Subsidies from state general revenues do broaden risk-pooling by requiring all citizens in a state to contribute to the costs of medical care for the very sick. But several other features of high-risk pools effectively narrow risk-pooling. First, these pools admit only people who are likely to have very high medical costs, and so they have sick people sharing their (very high) costs with other sick people. Second, because employers who self-insure are exempt from state insurance regulation, they cannot be required to contribute to high-risk pools. They also do not pay any premium taxes to state coffers. Hence, employers and their employees do not share in the medical care costs of the high-risk pool, except insofar as they contribute in other ways to state general revenues. Third, but politically most salient, because state legislatures restrict eligibility for high-risk pools to people who have been rejected by private insurers, the very existence of these pools reduces political pressure on private insurers to relax their underwriting standards. By creating high-risk pools, states actually make

19. Stearns and Mroz (1995–96).
20. U.S. General Accounting Office (1988, p. 16).

it easier for insurance companies to continue their competitive strategy of medical underwriting and insuring only the healthy. The repair reinforces precisely the structural feature that causes the problem in the first place.

Most of the other state innovations to deal with the access problem could be analyzed along similar lines. Typical strategies, each used by several states, include:

—Exempting insurers from state legislative mandates to offer certain benefits when they design policies specifically for small businesses;

—Creating special state pools for some uninsured workers, pregnant women, or children;

—Establishing trust funds or special accounts to cover hospitals' costs of uncompensated care;

—Providing tax credits or subsidies to small firms that offer health insurance;

—Providing state subsidies to lower the cost of private companies' insurance policies for low-income people; and

—Paying the administrative costs of organizing small businesses into purchasing pools so they can receive lower prices from private insurers.

Because each of these strategies addresses only a small part of a large systemic problem, and because many of them effectively use public money to subsidize private insurers without requiring any changes on the insurers' part, each stopgap measure lets the overall system continue to escalate costs and reduce insurance coverage.

States, then, do seem to be bursting with motivation and energy to innovate in health policy. But the big problems of health care transcend state boundaries and require more political power than state governments have.

Barriers to State Innovation: Federalization of Health Policy

The federal medicare program is the payer for about 40 percent of hospital costs. States and community coalitions can try to do something about controlling hospital costs, but the lion's share of the costs is controlled by a lion outside their jurisdiction. The federal government's chief cost-containment strategy for itself has been to use DRGs and other methods to curtail its own costs and to withdraw from sharing the costs of uncompensated care with other payors.

Medicaid accounts for a major portion of state budgets.[21] Although it is nominally a federal matching program for expenditures the states decide to make, in practice the states have less and less autonomy to decide what they will expend on medicaid, let alone how they will manage it. Federal mandates have continually increased the types and income-level of people covered, first through the federal supplemental security income (SSI) program, then through mandates built into budget acts of the 1980s.[22] What started out in 1965 as a physician and hospital insurance program for the poor has become, through the SSI program, primarily a funder of long-term care services for the elderly, disabled, and blind. These three groups account for about a quarter of the medicaid population but two-thirds of medicaid expenditures. Other adults and children (mostly those who qualify via a means test and state AFDC programs) comprise about two-thirds of the medicaid population but receive only 25 percent of the expenditures.[23] While medicaid covered about 65 percent of the poor in 1976, eight years later, in 1984, it covered only 38 percent.[24] By 1991 medicaid coverage of the poor had increased to 44 percent, still considerably short of the 1976 level.[25] Yet, despite medicaid's expanded coverage, the proportion of uninsured continued to grow, largely because employer-based coverage has declined. States, then, are relatively powerless to control the size of the uninsured population in their jurisdiction or the expenditures they must lay out for medicaid. Rather, they respond to the hands they are dealt by federal medicaid legislation and employer behavior.

Although medicaid is supposed to be a joint federal-state program, states are highly constrained by federal program rules and, worse, by stalemates in the rulemaking procedures for statutory revisions to medicaid. Since 1984 the general trend has been for Congress to pass expansions to medicaid. Meanwhile, HCFA is notoriously slow (from the states' point of view) at enacting implementing regulations. In 1985 Congress enacted benefit expansions for pregnant women and children as

21. Estimates vary depending on the measurement used, but they are about 19 percent of total state expenditures in the measure preferred by the National Association of State Budget Officers or about 12 percent of state tax revenues, excluding gasoline taxes earmarked for highway spending. All measures indicate that medicaid spending as a share of state resources has risen dramatically since the mid-1980s. Gold (1996).

22. For a useful summary, see Coughlin, Ku, and Holahan (1994, pp. 47–55).

23. Coughlin, Ku, and Holahan (1994, p. 19).

24. Fraser (1987, p. 5).

25. Coughlin, Ku, and Holahan (1994, pp. 57–58).

well as new standards for intermediate care facilities for the mentally retarded. The legislation made these new provisions effective immediately, and though it also required HCFA to promulgate appropriate regulations, two years passed before HCFA actually did.[26] Similarly, HCFA was very slow to go through the rulemaking process to provide implementing rules for numerous congressional medicaid reforms, often taking more than three years.[27]

This tug-of-war among Congress, HCFA, and the states is more than a matter of bureaucratic red tape or lack of coordination among multiple institutions responsible for medicaid. As professor Eleanor D. Kinney notes, it represents a deep structural problem in the political system when the executive and legislative branches are controlled by different parties with different goals for a state-federal program. During the 1980s, as the Reagan and then the Bush administration became concerned with medical cost containment, Congress became increasingly Democratic—the Democrats gained control of the Senate as a result of the 1986 election and increased their share of House seats after both the 1982 and 1984 elections—and more concerned with expanding access for the poor and standardizing the program across the states. Congress, Kinney suggests, began the practice of requiring states to implement its statutory reforms without regard to the existence of regulations because it grew increasingly frustrated with HCFA's foot-dragging.[28] With respect to medicaid at least (the most important state health-financing program), the states are the proverbial punching bag while Congress and the executive branch duke out their conflicting visions of what medicaid should be.

Since 1995, with the Democratic party in control of the White House and the Republican party in control of Congress, states have been forced to wait out the fights between legislative and administrative branch proposals for medicaid reform. The positions are roughly reversed. Congress, and especially its Republican majority, favors deep cuts in medicaid spending, even to the point of ending the medicaid entitlement, while the Clinton administration and congressional Democrats generally favor broader population coverage. Currently, though, in contrast to the 1980s, there is virtually no political possibility for medicaid expansion. Democrats are consigned to fighting off Republican proposals to delegate many eligibility and benefit coverage decisions to the states—a devolution that

26. Kinney (1990, p. 877).
27. Kinney (1990, p. 899).
28. Kinney (1990, pp. 875–82).

would invariably result in medicaid contractions, given the states' fiscal constraints and their increasing fiscal burdens under the 1996 welfare reform law. In this environment, congressional delegation of more authority to the states would be a license to contract their role in providing access to health care. This situation will likely foster a great deal of innovation in ways to cut back expenditures, but at the cost of effective solutions to the access problem.

Precisely because medicaid is a joint federal-state program, designed originally to induce states to make greater fiscal efforts on behalf of health care for the poor, Congress established national standards for state programs. These include not only eligibility requirements and minimum service packages, but also other design requirements, such as offering recipients a free choice of medical provider, making all program rules applicable across the state, and using particular forms of provider reimbursement. National standards may be laudable (and highly effective) in certain ways, but they seriously constrain the ability of states to innovate. If a state wants to restructure health insurance in any way that implicates medicaid (the most important vehicle states have to deal with low-income uninsured people), the state needs a "programmatic waiver" from the federal rules. (These waivers are different, and more difficult to get, than the "research and demonstration waivers," which apply to temporary and small-scale demonstration projects.) If a state wants to experiment with more centralized budgeting and planning by combining all revenue sources for health care, it needs waivers from HCFA to include medicare and medicaid in its plans. If it wants to experiment with using managed care for its medicaid population to generate cost-savings, it needs a waiver from the freedom-of-choice requirement.

The federal waiver process has by all accounts been at least a discouragement if not an obstacle to state innovation. Even though the 1981 Omnibus Budget Reconciliation Act encouraged states to experiment with different cost-containment strategies and authorized waivers that would permit states to limit recipients' choice of providers, subsequent congressional acts and amendments gave conflicting signals to the states, and obtaining federal waivers has been one of the great frustrations of state governors.[29]

Perhaps the most vivid example of how the federal waiver process inhibits state innovation is Oregon's experience. The Oregon Health

29. Spitz and Abramson (1987).

Plan, proposed in 1990, was designed to manage the cost and access dilemma by establishing a priority list of medical procedures according to cost-effectiveness criteria, denying coverage to medicaid enrollees for low-priority procedures, and using the savings to insure more people for primary care.[30] Oregon's leaders conceived of the plan as incremental. Initially the rationing would apply only to poor adults and children in medicaid, but not to the elderly, disabled, and blind recipients of medicaid or to state employees or anyone else in the state. Because the Oregon plan called for eliminating some services from the federally specified basic medicaid benefit package, the state needed a waiver to implement the plan. HCFA was reluctant to use its administrative authority to grant a waiver for such a major change, so the state turned to Congress for a legislative waiver.

Once the waiver request entered the congressional arena, it became highly visible and a matter of interest to national policy actors. Sara Rosenbaum from the Children's Defense Fund, seeing inequities for poor women and children, teamed up with Representative Henry A. Waxman, Democrat from California, and other liberal health policy advocates to oppose the waiver. National organizations such as the American Academy of Pediatrics, the National Association of Community Health Centers, and the Association of Catholic Hospitals allied with opponents of the Oregon plan. The plan was quickly embroiled in national politics. Bob Griss, a researcher at the United Cerebral Palsy Fund and a national advocate for the disabled, argued persuasively that the plan discriminated against the disabled by assigning lower priority to medical procedures that did not restore full functioning to patients and, therefore, that the plan violated the Americans with Disability Act of 1990. Largely on the strength of this argument, the Bush administration denied the waiver. Not until President Clinton took office was a waiver finally granted, and then only with some twenty-nine restrictions, including a requirement that the state get federal approval for its priority list of medical procedures.[31] Under the Clinton administration, several additional states have received

30. Garland and Hasnain (1990); Crenshaw and others (1990); Timothy Egan, "Oregon Lists Illnesses by Priority to See Who Gets Medicaid Care," *New York Times,* May 3, 1990, p. A1; and Timothy Egan, "Oregon Shakes Up Pioneering Health Plan for the Poor," *New York Times,* February 22, 1991, p. A12.

31. Brown (1991); Timothy Egan, "Problems Could Delay Proposal by Oregon to Ration Health Care," *New York Times,* July 30, 1990, p. A8; *State Health Notes* (p. 2); and Robert Pear, "U.S. Backs Oregon's Health Plan for Covering All Poor People," *New York Times,* March 20, 1993, p. A8.

waivers, including Minnesota, Tennessee, and Rhode Island, but the process has by no means been simple or short.[32]

One dramatic lesson of this political history is that states are not their own masters when it comes to innovation in health policy. Medicaid is the biggest program with which states can address the health problems of the poor, yet national regulations ensure that states cannot modify their programs without submitting their plans to a national audience. Health care for the poor is so high on both state and national policy agendas that any state innovations receive instant national attention, if not in the national newspapers, at least in the highly developed network of issue-specific reports and newsletters (such as *State Health Notes* and National Governors' Association reports). States are so hungry for solutions that they begin imitating a promising innovation before it has gotten off the drawing boards in its home state. Within months of Oregon's introduction of its plan, several state legislatures debated proposals patterned on it. Thus the states' desperate search for solutions and for information brings national exposure to a fledgling state innovation, rendering it an object of national political conflict before it is off the ground.

Another major barrier to state innovation in health policy is a federal statute that was never conceived or considered as a piece of health legislation: The Employee Retirement Income Security Act of 1974, known as ERISA. ERISA exempts employers who self-insure from state insurance regulation, as well as from state premium taxes on insurance. This "preemption" (so called because ERISA is said to preempt state laws and regulations as they relate to self-insured plans) has weakened state authority over health insurance as more employers have ceased purchasing employee coverage from private insurers and decided to self-insure instead—in large part because ERISA gives them a huge financial incentive to do so. In 1974 only 5 percent of people with employee health insurance were covered under self-insured plans; now, more than 50 percent are.[33]

Hawaii offers the crucial lesson here. In 1974, slightly before ERISA was enacted, Hawaii passed its Prepaid Health Care Act requiring employers to provide coverage at least as good as a state-defined benefit package and to pay at least half the cost of coverage for their employees. When the state tried two years later to increase the minimum benefit

32. Holahan and Nichols (1996).
33. Gabel and Jensen (1989); and Sullivan and Rice (1991).

package by adding treatment for substance abuse, Standard Oil Company of California sued, claiming ERISA preempted the states from regulating self-insured companies. In 1981 the U.S. Supreme Court agreed with Standard Oil.[34] Hawaii managed to negotiate a special congressional exemption from ERISA permitting it to keep the original plan and benefit package, but it can make no further changes in requirements on self-insured companies. Congress was clear, too, that it was granting a one-time exception to Hawaii and that no other states need apply.[35]

Because of the ERISA exemption, states cannot stipulate coverage requirements for self-insured plans. They cannot, for example, even require self-insured employers to cover pregnancy, emergency care, treatment of mental illness, preventive care, or anything else. The ERISA exemption of self-insured employers from these mandates has been a major impetus for business exodus from the commercial and Blue Cross/Blue Shield insurance markets. Moreover, courts have interpreted ERISA as giving employers an absolute right to change the terms of coverage they offer, so they are free to reduce coverage, for example, by ceasing to cover expensive diseases such as acquired immune deficiency syndrome (AIDS) or cancer or by putting ceilings on the amounts they will pay for treatment of any diseases.[36] If self-insured plans can shed their coverage of expensive—or any—medical care, states will find themselves being asked to pick up the tab for this uncovered care.

The same ERISA exemption that fueled the breakup of large risk pools in health insurance also prevents state governments from taking actions to rectify the disintegration. Because they cannot regulate self-insured businesses, they cannot reach the major insurers. States cannot restructure health financing in any way that would mandate employers to provide health coverage or that would require employers to pay taxes to support coverage for the uninsured.

The combination of judicial interpretation of ERISA and congressional unwillingness to extend the Hawaii precedent means that states have almost no leverage over employers who self-insure. Minnesota's 1994 MinnesotaCare Act depends on setting expenditure limits for health care, which in turn depends on having good data about health care spending from all sources. Implementation was delayed significantly when several labor union trust funds (unsuccessfully) used the ERISA pre-

---

34. *Standard Oil Company of California* v. *Agsalud,* 454 U.S. 801 (1981).
35. Fox and Schaffer (1989); and Mariner (1992).
36. *McGann* v. *H&H Music Company,* 946 F.2d 401 (5th Cir. 1991); and Mariner (1992).

emption to challenge the state's authority to collect data from self-insured plans.[37] Some states are seeking to mandate that employers provide health insurance, but to avoid ERISA problems, they offer employers the option of "play or pay." That is, either employers may buy health insurance that meets state criteria or they must pay into a state pool to cover people without health insurance. Massachusetts, Oregon, and Washington have each passed "play or pay" legislation, and though each has asked for a waiver or a congressional amendment to ERISA, none has received one. Reportedly, failure to get an ERISA waiver was the "turning point" that prompted provider groups to withdraw their support for Washington state's 1993 plan, and the Oregon state legislature wrote an automatic repeal into its plan for an employer mandate if the state could not get an ERISA waiver by January 1, 1996.[38] Congressional unwillingness to change the ERISA preemption has been a major stumbling block to state reforms.

Two court rulings in 1995 suggest a trend toward more judicial sympathy with states. Most important, the U.S. Supreme Court unanimously held that a New York state law requiring commercial insurers and self-insured plans to pay a surcharge on inpatient care did not trigger the ERISA preemption.[39] New York had instituted its surcharges in 1988 to woo large employers back to Blue Cross/Blue Shield. (Because Blue Cross/Blue Shield was exempt from the surcharges, it could offer lower premiums.) In a significant victory for the states, the Court gave great weight to the states' traditional role in regulating health care and declared that the ERISA preemption might not apply to state laws and regulations that had only an "indirect economic influence" on self-insured plans. Later the same year, a federal court allowed Minnesota to fund its expanded health insurance coverage with a tax on health care providers, despite an ERISA challenge.[40]

Nevertheless, ERISA is still a formidable obstacle to state reform, for several reasons. First, no court has yet allowed a state to tax self-insured plans to raise revenue for expanded health insurance coverage. In the cases discussed above, states have taxed or charged health care providers, not self-insured plans themselves. Second, the ERISA pre-

37. Blewett (1994).

38. Crittenden (1995).

39. *New York State Conference of Blue Cross and Blue Shield Plans* v. *Travelers Insurance Company,* 115 S.Ct. 1671 (1995).

40. *Boyle* v. *Anderson,* F.3d (8th Cir. 1995).

emption has helped foster strong political opponents to state reforms. Because large insurance companies often act as administrators for self-insured plans, they have a huge stake in preserving the ERISA exemption, and they can pour enormous financial resources into litigating against the states. In New York, Travelers Insurance Company was the lead plaintiff for a group of commercial insurers who together tied up the state in litigation for seven years. Unions are another interest with a stake in fighting state legislation that would in any way tax self-insured plans. And third, Congress has refused to grant any waivers since the one for Hawaii, to amend ERISA to change the preemption, or to create a regular process for states seeking waivers. So states have no choice but to pass legislation, wait for the inevitable legal challenge, and put themselves at the mercies of the courts.

Barriers to State Innovation: Big Problems Need Big Innovators

Even if the federal government were not an obstacle through its control of a major share of health revenue sources and its national rules and legal requirements, states still might not be able to craft innovations to address the significant problems in health care.

Probably the most widely used metaphor in health policy is the balloon. Squeeze health care costs in one part of the system, and they whoosh to another. If one payer musters the power to constrain its costs (say, by firmly fixing its rates, as medicare did, or by getting a state to cap its hospital rates, as Blue Cross/Blue Shield did in New Jersey), hospitals will shift their costs and charges onto other insurers and self-paying patients. If a state sets up hospital cost controls, doctors will move more of their work into nonhospital settings, such as offices or outpatient surgery centers. If states try to increase employers' share of health care costs and citizens' access to services by mandating that all insurance policies carry certain benefits, employers will switch to self-insurance. If employers are caught between pressures to insure their employees and the rising costs of doing so, they will shift more of the costs onto their employees. The lesson of the balloon metaphor is that regulating the health system effectively is impossible if only a part of it can be regulated.

Political conflict in health policy almost always takes the form of what political scientist James Q. Wilson calls interest group contests, in which one set of intense, concentrated interests squares off against another set of equally intense, concentrated interests.[41] The fates of the key interests—hospitals and physicians, commercial and nonprofit insurers, business and state government—are inextricably intertwined, and they are each exquisitely sensitive to proposed policy changes. In Wilson's classic model, policy arenas with this type of conflict are generally characterized by alternating victories or by stalemates. In health policy, the stakes for each group are so high that even a temporary political loss seems unthinkable. From the point of view of state governments, permitting temporary losses might mean destruction of institutions—hospitals that go out of business, physicians who flee the cities, insurers who stop writing business in the state, or employers who move their operations and their jobs out of state. In this type of political contest, one player in the system can block a proposal and effectively bring the situation to a stalemate.

States are hamstrung in part because they are only states. In a federal system, political actors who are unhappy with a state regulation always have the possibility of exit, and the threat of exit is developed to a fine art. If a state tries to regulate insurers, insurers can and do threaten to withdraw from the state. Insurers used this tactic when a few states and Washington, D.C., tried to prohibit health and life insurers from using AIDS antibody tests, and they succeeded in rolling back every state prohibition except California's ban on using AIDS tests in health insurance underwriting.[42] When Massachusetts sought to require businesses to provide health insurance to their employees or pay into a state fund for the uninsured, the threat of exit by both businesses and insurers was an ever-present, if usually unspoken, factor.[43]

Threats of exit are so potent that state policymakers are sometimes discouraged from even attempting reforms. Even states with healthy economies that have the fiscal potential and political will to increase their taxes feel impotent to proceed. The director of Maine's state planning office noted that, although states have the formal power to raise property and sales taxes, they are "constrained in how aggressive [they]

41. Wilson (1974).
42. Hiam (1987–88); and Bruce Lambert, "Insurance Limits Growing to Curb AIDS Coverage," *New York Times,* August 7, 1989, p. A1.
43. Kronick (1990).

can be. We can't go to a 6 percent sales tax when New Hampshire doesn't have one."[44]

The corollary of the exit threat in a federal system is the "magnet fear." States fear that by offering more generous benefits to the poor than neighboring states, they will induce more poor people to move into the state.[45] To avoid this possibility, states might engage in a "race to the bottom," cutting their health insurance programs instead of expanding them. Observers in health policy note that Hawaii is so far the only state to have implemented a universal access health insurance program—and they attribute Hawaii's ability to do this to its insularity and its lack of worry about an influx of uninsured.[46] Social scientists have tried to measure the impact of differentials in state social benefits on individuals' location decisions and have generally found only a small influence, if any.[47] But even if academics cannot find much evidence of magnet effects, if state policymakers believe that is how the world works, they will make policy based on their beliefs and assumptions, so the race to the bottom may be an important phenomenon.

Some Lessons and Questions about Innovation

Innovation in health policy in the United States does not fit the model of bottom-up, groping-along innovation currently in favor in the innovation literature. Historically, states have more often been the testing ground for federal agencies and national foundations to try out their ideas—laboratories for the federal government rather than basement tinkerers in their own right. When states do try to innovate at their own initiative, they are constrained by several factors: a deep penetration of state programs by federal money and federal rules; a corresponding lack of autonomy over health programs; and a centralized waiver process, which, combined with a strong intergovernmental health policy network and a desperation among states, catapults still-fragile state ideas into rough national political fights.

One striking feature of innovation in state health policy is the extraor-

44. Quoted in Kosterlitz (1990, p. 714).
45. Peterson and Rom (1990).
46. Erik Eckholm, "Health Care Plan Falters in Massachusetts Slump," *New York Times,* April 11, 1991, pp. A1, A16; and Sagar and Socolar (1990).
47. For a review of the literature, see Kenyon (1996).

dinary extent and rapidity of diffusion to other states. State hunger for answers and ideas is fed by a rich network of intergovernmental actors and information sources. Diffusion of innovations is generally considered to be a good thing, but it is worth questioning whether rapid diffusion can sometimes be a hindrance to innovation.

Diffusion might block innovation in two ways. First, the dissemination of ideas from an individual state to a national institution (such as HCFA, the National Governors' Association, or the Robert Wood Johnson Foundation) and then to other states may be so rapid that state-level public managers are more inclined to copy another state than to grope along finding their own solution. With such rapid diffusion, states may copy an innovation before its shortcomings have been revealed or evaluated. Second, in a system with strong federal oversight over state programs, once a federal agency or national foundation latches onto an idea (such as competition or case management) and offers states money to test it, further innovation at the state-level may be short-circuited as states scurry to acquire the new money attached to the federally favored innovation.

Some policy problems may simply be too big for states to handle. Health policy perhaps is one of them. What are the elements that make for big problems requiring big, planned, centralized, top-down, federal innovation? Such big problems might be found in the following circumstances.

First, big problems are likely to occur when a policy system is "tightly coupled." Virtually any change in any part of the system affects some other part of the system. Others have sometimes called this situation a "dense" or "crowded policy space."[48] The many policy actors affected by any change in this arena are also well organized; well plugged into the network of related officials, agencies, and groups; and well positioned to receive any new information about contemplated or actual changes. In this kind of policy system, there is no possibility for low-visibility bargaining, backroom deals, or rough-and-ready implementation of experiments and trial balloons.

Second, big problems are likely when a policy system is regulated loosely enough so that actors in the system can escape regulation or at least shift the burdens of regulation onto other segments of the system. We know enough about social regulation to know that there is almost always

48. Wildavsky (1979, pp. 62–85); and Majone (1989, pp. 158–61).

wiggle room for the regulated parties. When a policy system is structured along federal lines, with a division of authority among the states, these multiple jurisdictions inevitably create opportunities for highly motivated interests to play others off against themselves and to escape the control of one jurisdiction by moving to another. In this situation, it is hard for any one jurisdiction to muster sufficient authority to make major policy changes. Innovation will have to come from some authority large enough to exercise control over the smaller constituent entities.

Third, big problems are likely when political conflicts are characterized by intense, apparently life-threatening fights among concentrated powerful interests. When organizations and interest groups believe their existence, the livelihood of their members, and their raison d'être are at stake in even minor policy changes, government agencies will require enormous power to dominate or resolve the conflicts. When policymaking in that arena is highly fragmented, government agencies will not have sufficient power, and policy innovation may require some kind of prior political reconstitution of authority.

Ironically—and detrimentally—the U.S. health policy system is federally dominated. The federal government directs and constrains state government innovations, even as the reigning ideology celebrates the importance of state and local innovation. Meanwhile, the federal government lacks enough power to control the health system. It tries to operate through the states and shifts many of the big problems of financing and access to them. In the end, neither the states nor the federal government is capable of solving the core problems. Perhaps the most fundamental issue for future innovation research is how to design political and policy structures that are capable of reform in the face of big problems.

References

Alpha Center. 1991. "Health Care for the Uninsured: State Initiatives." Washington (December).

Altshuler, Alan, and Mark Zegans. 1990. "Innovation and Creativity: Comparisons between Public Management and Private Enterprise." *Cities* (February): 16–24.

Anderson, Maren, and Peter D. Fox. 1987. "Lessons Learned from Medicaid Managed Care Approaches." *Health Affairs,* vol. 6, no. 1 (Spring): 71–86.

Behn, Robert D. 1988. "Management by Groping Along." *Journal of Policy Analysis and Management,* vol. 7, no. 4 (Fall): 643–63.

Blewett, Lynn A. 1994. "State Report: Reforms in Minnesota Forging the Path." *Health Affairs,* vol. 13, no. 4 (Fall): 200–09.

Bowman, Ann O'M., and Richard C. Kearney. 1986. *The Resurgence of the States.* Prentice-Hall.

Brown, Lawrence D. 1991. "The National Politics of Oregon's Rationing Plan." *Health Affairs,* vol. 10, no. 2 (Summer): 28–51.

Brown, Lawrence D., and Catherine McLaughlin. 1990. "Constraining Costs at the Community Level: A Critique." *Health Affairs,* vol. 9, no. 4 (Winter): 5–28.

Coughlin, Teresa A., Leighton Ku, and John Holahan. 1994. *Medicaid since 1980: Costs, Coverage, and the Shifting Alliance between the Federal Government and the States.* Washington, D.C.: Urban Institute Press.

Coye, Molly Joel. 1991. "Health Care for the Uninsured." *Issues in Science and Technology* (Summer): 56–62.

Crenshaw, Robert, and others. 1990. "Developing Principles for Prudent Health Care Allocation: The Continuing Oregon Experiment." *Western Journal of Medicine,* vol. 152 (April): 441–46.

Crittenden, Robert A. 1995. "Rolling Back Reform in the Pacific Northwest." *Health Affairs,* vol. 14, no. 2 (Summer): 302–05.

Demkovich, Linda K. 1990. *The States and the Uninsured: Slowly but Surely Filling the Gaps.* George Washington University, National Health Policy Forum and Intergovernmental Health Policy Project, October.

Dobson, Allen, Donald Moran, and Gary Young. 1992. "The Role of Federal Waivers in the Health Policy Process." *Health Affairs,* vol. 11, no. 4 (Winter): 72–94.

Dunham, Andrew, and James Morone. 1983. *The Politics of Innovation: The Evolution of DRG Rate Regulation in New Jersey.* DRG Evaluation, Volume IV-A. Princeton, N.J.: Health Research and Educational Trust of New Jersey.

Elazar, Daniel J. 1990. "Opening the Third Century of American Federalism: Issues and Prospects." *Annals of the American Academy of Political Science* 509 (May): 11–21.

Fox, Daniel M., and Schaffer, Daniel C. 1989. "Health Policy and ERISA: Interest Groups and Semi-Preemption." *Journal of Health Politics, Policy and Law,* vol. 14, no. 2 (Summer): 239–60.

Fraser, Irene. 1987. *Medicaid Options: State Opportunities and Strategies for Expanding Eligibility.* Washington, D.C.: American Hospital Association.

Gabel, Jon R., and Gail A. Jensen. 1989. "The Price of State Mandated Benefits." *Inquiry,* vol. 26, no. 4 (Winter): 419–31.

Garland, Michael, and Romana Hasnain. 1990. "Community Responsibility and the Development of Oregon's Health Care Priorities." *Business and Professional Ethics Journal,* vol. 9, no. 3/4: 183–200.

Gold, Steven. 1996. "Health Care and the Fiscal Crisis of the States." In *Health Policy, Federalism, and the American States,* edited by Robert F. Rich and William D. White, 97–125. Washington, D.C.: Urban Institute Press.

Golden, Olivia. 1990. "Innovation in Public Sector Human Services Programs: The Implications of Innovation by 'Groping Along.' " *Journal of Policy Analysis and Management,* vol. 9, no. 2 (Spring): 219–48.

Hiam, Peter. 1987–88. "Insurers, Consumers, and Testing: The AIDS Experience." *Law, Medicine, and Health Care,* vol. 15, no. 4: 212–22.

Holahan, John and Len Nichols. 1996. "State Health Policy in the 1990s." In *Health Policy, Federalism, and the American States,* edited by Robert F. Rich and William D. White, 40–70. Washington, D.C.: Urban Institute Press.

Kenyon, Daphne A. 1996. "Health Care Reform and Competition Among the States." In *Health Policy, Federalism, and the American States,* edited by Robert F. Rich and William D. White, 253–74. Washington, D.C.: Urban Institute Press.

Kinney, Eleanor D. 1990. "Rule and Policy Making for the Medicaid Program: A Challenge to Federalism." *Ohio State Law Journal* 51: 877–911.

Kosterlitz, Julie. 1990. "Seeking the Cure." *National Journal* (March 24): 708–14.

Kronick, Richard. 1990. "The Slippery Slope of Health Care Finance: Business Interests and Hospital Reimbursement in Massachusetts." *Journal of Health Politics, Policy, and Law,* vol. 15, no. 4 (Winter): 887–913.

Leichter, Howard. 1996. "State Governments and Their Capacity for Health Reform." In *Health Policy, Federalism, and the American States,* edited by Robert F. Rich and William D. White, 151–79. Washington, D.C.: Urban Institute Press.

Lemov, Penelope. 1990. "Health Insurance for All: A Possible Dream?" *Governing* (November): 56–62.

Majone, Giandomenico. 1989. *Evidence, Argument, and Persuasion in the Policy Process.* Yale University Press.

Mariner, Wendy K. 1992. "Problems with Employer-Provided Health Insurance—The Employee Retirement Income Security Act and Health Care Reform." *New England Journal of Medicine,* vol. 327, no. 33: 1682–85.

Marmor, Theodore, Jerry Mashaw, and John Oberlander. 1996. "National Health Reform: Where Do We Go from Here?" In *Health Policy, Federalism, and the American States,* edited by Robert F. Rich and William D. White, 277–92. Washington, D.C.: Urban Institute Press.

Mashaw, Jerry. 1993–94. "Taking Federalism Seriously: The Case for State-Led Reform." *Domestic Affairs,* vol. 2 (Winter): 1–21.

McLaughlin, Catherine G., Wendy K. Zellers, and Lawrence D. Brown. 1989. "Health Care Coalitions: Characteristics, Activities and Prospects." *Inquiry,* vol. 26, no. 1 (Spring): 72–83.

Meyerhoff, Allen S., and David A. Crozier. 1984. "Health Care Coalitions: Evolution of a Movement." *Health Affairs,* vol. 3, no. 1 (Spring): 120–28.

Morone, James, and Andrew Dunham. 1985. "Slouching towards National Health Insurance: The New Health Care Politics." *Yale Journal on Regulation,* vol. 2, no. 2: 263–91.

Peterson, Paul E., and Mark C. Rom. 1990. *Welfare Magnets: A New Case for a National Standard.* Brookings.

Reeves, Mavis Mann. 1990. "The States as Polities: Reformed, Reinvigorated, Resourceful." *Annals of the American Academy of Political Science,* vol. 509 (May): 83–93.

Rovner, Julie. 1988. "Welfare Reform: The Issue that Bubbled up from the States to Capitol Hill." *Governing,* vol. 2 (December): 17–21.

Sagar, Alan, and Deborah Socolar. 1990. "Advancing toward Health Care for All: Lessons for Illinois from Other States." In *Paying for Health Care in Illinois: Chicago Assembly Background Papers.* University of Chicago, Center for Urban Research and Policy Studies.

Schneider, Saundra K. 1989. "Governors and Health Care Policy in the American States." *Policy Studies Review,* vol. 17, no. 4 (Summer): 909–26.

Serafini, Marilyn Weber. 1996. "Reining in the HMOs." *National Journal* (October 26): 2280–83.

Shortell, Stephen M., and Walter J. McNerney. 1990. "Criteria and Guidelines for Reforming the U.S. Health Care System." *New England Journal of Medicine,* vol. 322 (February 15): 463–67.

Spitz, Bruce, and John Abramson. 1987. "Competition, Capitation, and Case Management: Barriers to Strategic Reform." *Health and Society* 65: 348–70.

Starr, Paul. 1982. *The Social Transformation of American Medicine.* Basic Books.

State Health Notes. "Intergovernmental Health Policy Project," no. 103. George Washington University.

Stearns, Sally S., and Thomas A. Mroz. 1995–96. "Premium Increases and Disenrollment from State Risk Pools." *Inquiry,* vol. 32, no. 4 (Winter): 392–406.

Stone, Deborah A. 1991. "How Should We Pay for Medical Care: Pooling Risks or Charging the Sick?" In *Paying for Health Care: Public Policy Choices for Illinois,* edited by Lawrence B. Joseph. University of Chicago, Center for Urban Research and Policy Studies.

———. 1993. "The Struggle for the Soul of Health Insurance." *Journal of Health Politics, Policy, and Law,* vol. 18, no. 2 (Summer): 287–317.

Sullivan, Cynthia B., and Thomas Rice. 1991. "The Health Insurance Picture in 1990." *Health Affairs,* vol. 10, no. 2 (Summer): 104–15.

U.S. General Accounting Office. 1988. *Health Insurance: Risk Pools for the Medically Uninsured.* GAO/HRD-88-66BR. April.

Wildavsky, Aaron. 1979. *Speaking Truth to Power: The Art and Craft of Policy Analysis.* Little, Brown.

Wilson, James Q. 1974. "The Politics of Regulation." In *The Politics of Regulation,* edited by James Q. Wilson, 357–94. Basic Books.

CHAPTER ELEVEN

The Paradox of Innovation in Education:
Cycles of Reform and the Resilience of Teaching

Richard F. Elmore

EDUCATION IN THE UNITED STATES has regularly been judged to need fundamental change. The idea of mass public education originated with social movements, modeled explicitly after evangelical religious movements and mobilized to extend learning to all children.[1] During the Progressive era, the modern structure of public education evolved from a reform agenda directed at wresting control of the schools from parochial interests and giving it to administrators and community elites.[2] At the onset of World War I, the federal government, concerned about the failure of schools to contribute to the country's industrial health, undertook to introduce vocational training on a broad scale. From the early twentieth century to the early 1950s, schools were subjected to repeated study and reform as they grappled with vast expansions in enrollment and diversification of the social background of students.[3] In the 1950s and early 1960s,

This chapter is based on a paper prepared, with support from the Ford Foundation, for the Conference on the Fundamental Questions of Innovation, sponsored by the Governors Center at Duke University, May 3–5, 1991. The paper draws upon research supported by the Consortium for Policy Research in Education, composed of Stanford University, the University of Wisconsin at Madison, Michigan State University, the Eagleton Institute of Politics at Rutgers University, and Harvard University. The consortium's work is funded by the Office of Educational Research and Improvement in the U.S. Department of Education. I was assisted in the preparation of this paper by Richard Fossey and Mark Melchior.

1. Tyack and Hansot (1982).
2. Tyack (1974).
3. Cohen (1985).

the U.S. government, stimulated in part by the launching of the Soviet satellite *Sputnik,* sought to improve math, science, and foreign language instruction. By the mid-1960s, reformers were again pressuring schools as the main cause and remedy for social inequality.[4] Starting in the late 1970s, a concern that the United States was losing its international political and economic position encouraged wide-scale attempts by states and localities to increase academic standards for students, to improve the quality of the teaching force, and, lately, to change fundamentally the governance and delivery structure of public education.[5]

Within these repeated cycles of policy innovation have revolved many smaller epicycles of innovation in instructional practice, school organization, and management: progressive education, the junior high school and the middle school, new curricula, teaching techniques based on behavioral science, and teaching techniques based on cognitive science. Since early in the twentieth century, these ideas and more have regularly buffeted the schools.

The Paradox of Innovation in Education

Despite this history of constant innovation, education reform advocates in each period have characterized schools as intransigent and resistant to change, blaming the failures of particular innovations on the incapacity of schools to respond to new, self-evidently useful, ideas.[6] On one level, innovation in education is a simple, if somewhat discouraging, story about how a large-scale public enterprise responds, or fails to respond, to innovative ideas. Almost any innovative idea can find a place in public education—in some specific schools, in some localities—and these innovations often prove to be as successful as their purveyors suggested. Yet educational innovations have a short half-life. They often disappear and reappear in predictable, short-term cycles, and the sponsors of new innovations are usually unaware that their ideas have already been tried.

On another level, the story has a darker, more perplexing side. While education is awash in innovation, most innovations originating from public policy have little impact on its core technology: the processes of teaching and learning. Policy innovations usually work around the edges

---

4. Elmore and McLaughlin (1988).
5. Firestone, Fuhrman, and Kirst (1989); and Fuhrman, Clune, and Elmore (1988).
6. Elmore and McLaughlin (1988).

of instructional practice, often affecting it in perverse and unpredictable ways, but seldom directly improving it. Similarly, innovations in instructional practice are seldom embodied in public policy and hence have little effect beyond the schools in which they are developed.

In instructional practice, education has a tradition of cottage industry innovation. Individual practitioners and researchers develop new practices, often based on sophisticated, empirically grounded ideas, and test them in selected settings. This form of innovation dates at least from the early decades of the twentieth century when John Dewey demonstrated that inquiry and practice could be connected in powerful ways.[7] These cottage industry innovations in instructional practice seldom apply to schools other than the ones in which they are developed and tested, and, if they do, they are often adopted in an eviscerated, watered-down form that bears little resemblance to the original.

Thus the story of innovation in education is two stories—one about periodic cycles of policy innovation around predictable themes and the other about a cottage industry of innovations in instructional practice. Yet neither has had much sustained effect on the enterprise as whole. A central paradox of education, then, is that schools, possibly more than any other institution in society, are constantly changing in response to external pressures but never seem to satisfy reformers. So much changes, but so little changes.

In modern society, innovation is generally thought to be a good thing. Innovation is the major social process by which organizations sort out relations with their markets and publics. In the private sector, innovation determines how firms make, exploit, and protect a market niche for their products.[8] In the public sector, innovation performs analogous, but more complex, functions of clarifying relationships with key publics, strengthening accountability links with those publics, and explaining the value of what public agencies produce.[9]

Not surprisingly, research on innovations usually takes change as the dependent variable and assumes, at least implicitly, that the objective of any good organization or policy is to maximize innovation, subject to certain constraints on authority and budget. This "pro-innovation" bias diverts attention from more basic questions about whether particular innovations improve the output or efficiency of public services.[10] Are

---

7. Dewey and Dewey (1915).
8. Dosi (1988).
9. Barzelay and Armajani (1990); and Barzelay and Armajani (1997).
10. Zegans (1990).

the most innovative organizations the highest-performing organizations? The paradox of innovation in education provides an opportunity to test prevailing conceptions of the value of innovation in improving public services.

A serious consideration of innovation in education undermines some conventional convictions: that innovation is an unalloyed good; that policy innovations necessarily improve the performance of public organizations; and that public sector innovation consists simply of designing good policies and successfully implementing them. Examining education raises questions about the purposes of innovation in the public sector and the institutional context that determines how innovations arise and affect public organizations. What is the value of innovation in the public sector? What are the social conditions that underlie successful innovation in knowledge-intensive enterprises such as education?

To address these questions, three types of innovation that have been stable and recurring themes in American education are examined. These are attempts to improve: (1) the technical core of education through the dissemination of new instructional materials and practices; (2) the performance of teachers by introducing new incentives and career structures; and (3) the performance of schools by altering the structures and incentives under which they operate.[11]

Innovations in Instructional Practice

In the early twentieth century, the idea of changing schools by changing instruction emerged in the fledgling enterprise of public education. The basic idea was simple: As the composition of the student population changes, as external demands on public education shift with changes in society and the economy, and as new academic knowledge develops, schools should respond. To stay current with changes in their environment, then, schools must change their basic processes of instruction.

Also from this period emerged the main structural features of American education that have since attracted the scrutiny of reformers: the age-grade structure for organizing instruction, tracking and ability grouping within age groups, the comprehensive secondary school with its diverse and sprawling curriculum, and teacher-centered instruction.

11. Elmore (1990).

Generally, classes were taught as a group. Teacher talk dominated verbal expression during class time. Student movement during instruction occurred only with the teacher's permission. Classroom activities clustered around teacher questions and explanations, student recitation, and the class working on textbook assignments. Except for laboratory work done in science classrooms, uniformity in behavior was sought and reflected in classroom after classroom with rows of bolted-down desks facing the blackboard and the teacher's desk.[12]

Such instructional practice was well adapted to the task that schools had assumed and to the dominant view of teaching and learning at the time. Teachers, who were likely to be young, female, recent graduates of schools in which they taught, and working under tight male supervision, were encouraged to impose order on unruly students and expected to teach an explicit curriculum tailored to teachers' and students' limited capacities.[13] The administrative progressives who oversaw this new system were heavily influenced by theories of scientific management that attached high value to "bureaucratic efficiency, organizational uniformity, [and] standardization" and by "the infant science of educational psychology that believed children learned best through repetition and memorization."[14]

Educational progressives soon produced an appealing alternative to this view of teaching. Called child-centered or student-centered instruction, it continues to exercise a powerful influence on instructional practice. Reformers of this persuasion

wanted instruction and curriculum tailored to children's interest; they wanted instruction to occur as often as possible individually or in small groups; they wanted programs that permitted children more freedom and creativity than existed in schools; they wanted school experiences connected to activities outside the classroom; and they wanted children to help shape the direction of their learning.[15]

For the advocates of student-centered instruction, the best response to student diversity was to tailor education to the individual student, instead

12. Cuban (1984, p. 30).
13. Tyack (1974, pp. 59–71).
14. Cuban (1984, p. 31).
15. Cuban (1984, p. 31).

of forcing all students to fit the same mold. They, too, appealed to psychological theories, most of the developmental sort, to support their views of how students learn best. For most of the twentieth century, the tensions between teacher-centered and child-centered instruction, between behavioral and developmental views of learning, and between standardized and individualized ways of organizing instruction have been a continuous theme of educational reform.

As student-centered instruction began to gain popularity in the 1920s and 1930s, several school systems launched ambitious reform initiatives. In the 1930s, New York City made a systemwide attempt to introduce new student-centered instructional practices that included designating 10 percent of the city's elementary schools as sites for the development of new practices, training for teachers by local universities and professional associations, and major support from the city's administrative staff. In the early 1920s, Denver launched a broad-scale effort of instructional reform by giving teachers leadership roles to develop new curricula and teaching practices. Teacher-led committees, on which principals and central administrators also served, worked with university specialists and national reformers to develop a new student-centered curriculum. Principals were then given responsibility for implementing the new curricula. In the 1920s, Washington, D.C., also undertook ambitious reforms of instruction that was organized separately for African American and Caucasian schools, often with the same people providing training on alternate days for African American and Caucasian teachers.[16]

These innovators used organizational and managerial practices that were enlightened, even by today's standards. The results, however, were, at best, mixed. Larry Cuban estimates that at the peak of the reform period only one-fourth to one-third of classrooms in these cities had successfully implemented some version of student-centered instruction. And the effects of the reforms tended to trail off quickly after districts moved away from the reform initiatives.[17] Furthermore, the late 1940s and early 1950s saw a major political backlash against student-centered or progressive education, led by business interests and conservative politicians, who ridiculed the instructional practices associated with student-centered learning.

In 1951 the University of Illinois launched a cooperative venture between its mathematics and engineering faculties to develop a new sec-

16. Cuban (1984, pp. 41–111).
17. Cuban (1984, pp. 41–111).

ondary school mathematics curriculum. A few years later, Jerrold Zacharias at the Massachusetts Institute of Technology formed the Physical Science Study Committee (PSSC) to develop a new secondary school physics curriculum. These projects were based on the widely shared convictions among university faculties that, because high school curricula were based on outmoded conceptions of content and failed to interest students in math and science, college students were unprepared for serious work in these fields. In 1956 the National Science Foundation (NSF) funded Zacharias and PSSC to develop and disseminate their ideas to American public schools. NSF sponsored a similar effort in life sciences—the Biological Sciences Curriculum Study (BSCS)—and, in the 1970s, extended its reach into the social sciences by sponsoring Man: A Course of Study (MACOS).[18]

These curricula embodied a distinctive view of knowledge, teaching, and learning, derived from a sweeping critique by prominent university scholars of instructional practice in elementary and secondary schools. These critics observed that public school curricula were not based on current scientific knowledge, that heavy reliance on textbooks as the main source of knowledge for students undermined the idea that science was primarily a matter of inductive inquiry, that teachers were poorly prepared to teach serious academic content and to lead students in an inquiry-focused learning, and that content was typically presented in a disjointed fashion, leaving students with no overall understanding of the subject. The new curricula stressed ambitious notions of course content, a high degree of integration between traditional classroom study and laboratory (or inquiry-oriented) work, an integrated view of the subject matter, and a heavy reliance on summer workshops to retrain teachers in new content and techniques.[19] Over two decades, tens of thousands of teachers participated in NSF-sponsored summer workshops to learn the new curricula, hundreds of millions of dollars were spent on the development and pilot testing of new materials, and thousands of university faculty were engaged in either curricular development or training.

These NSF-sponsored curriculum efforts were impressive examples of public sector entrepreneurship and institutional innovation. They mobilized university faculty, who traditionally disdained elementary and secondary school teachers, to improve instructional practice. They provided

18. Alkin and House (1981).
19. Dede and Hardin (1973).

models of curriculum that embodied ambitious conceptions of knowledge and teaching, compared with the watered-down versions in most textbooks. They reached large numbers of teachers and provided them with new professional networks. By 1977 about 45 percent of high school science teachers, one-third of junior high science teachers, and 10 percent of elementary teachers had attended at least one NSF-sponsored workshop, and about 40 percent of science teachers had used one or more NSF-sponsored materials. According to a 1977 NSF-sponsored survey, NSF-sponsored materials were in use in about 30 percent of elementary schools and about 60 percent of secondary schools, while mathematics materials were in use in less than 10 percent of elementary and secondary schools.[20]

In an enterprise that involves about 2.5 million teachers, close to 100,000 schools, and more than 15,000 local school districts, these percentages appear impressive. Yet they conceal a decidedly modest effect on instructional practice. The NSF-sponsored innovations had only a short-term and extremely limited impact. Textbooks continued to be the exclusive vehicle of instruction for virtually all science, math, and social studies teachers. One of the ironies of the NSF-sponsored innovations was that they markedly affected the content of traditional textbooks, as commercial publishers readily captured the new materials and converted them to traditional forms.[21] Lecture and recitation, not active inquiry, continued to be the dominant mode of instruction. Instructional units were taught in isolation from each other with little integrating structure. And lectures and labs continued to be conducted separately.[22] As an innovation strategy aimed at the core technology of schools, the NSF initiative was broad but shallow.

These attempts to change instructional practice illustrate some themes common to many similar efforts: Innovation seems to occur readily at the level of entrepreneurship and institutional invention.[23] Big-city superintendents are among the major innovators pushing for changes in organization and instruction, inventing ingenious strategies for mobilizing their school systems around ambitious new ideas of teaching and learning. Outsiders, such as university faculty and NSF staff, can be enlisted to invent new approaches to teaching and learning, coupled with ingenious

20. Weiss (1978); and Elmore and McLauglin (1988, pp. 15–17).
21. Wirt and Quirk (1977).
22. Stake and Easley (1978).
23. Elmore and McLaughlin (1988); and Atkin and House (1981).

processes of dissemination. No shortage of good ideas exists about how to improve school organization and instruction. Nor is there any shortage of entrepreneurial interest in inventing new ways to influence schools.

However, the difficult problem remains of influencing the basics of instructional practice—such mundane matters as what kinds of materials are used, how students are engaged in learning, and how multiple activities are structured around common purposes. Innovators have little difficulty demonstrating that these activities can be done differently in a few settings. But innovations seldom change such commonplace practices as teacher-centered instruction, textbook-driven content, and compartmentalized knowledge. Recent comprehensive studies of school organization and instructional practice reveal that the basic patterns of organization and instructional practice of the first few decades of the twentieth century still dominate secondary schools today.[24]

Innovations in the Occupational Conditions of Teaching

A second recurring theme in educational innovation is changing the conditions of teachers' work. Specifically, reformers have focused on two innovations: offering monetary rewards to teachers based on performance, usually called merit pay; and giving successful teachers greater status and broader responsibility, usually called career ladders or differentiated staffing.

Early in the twentieth century, the idea of merit pay for teachers emerged from the principles of scientific management. As Susan Moore Johnson observed: "The rationale behind merit pay is simple. If teachers are paid competitively on the basis of performance, they will work harder. The system will reward effective teachers and encourage them to remain in classrooms while nudging ineffective, unrewarded teachers to leave. As a result, . . . schools will improve."[25] In the 1920s, somewhere between 20 and 50 percent of American school districts (depending on which districts were surveyed and how merit pay was defined) granted salary increases based on merit. Yet within a decade merit pay was swamped by another, more enduring innovation: the uniform salary scale. From the 1930s to the mid-1950s, interest in merit pay waned and

24. Goodlad (1984); Powell, Farrar, and Cohen (1985); and Sizer (1984).
25. Johnson (1984, p. 176).

most plans adopted in the 1920s were gradually displaced by uniform salary scales based on seniority and educational attainment. In the mid-1950s, merit pay returned to the political agenda, and, by the early 1960s, about 10 percent of local districts had merit pay systems. With the growth of collective bargaining and political mobilization among teachers in the mid-1960s and 1970s, interest again waned. The proportion of districts adopting merit pay dropped to around 5 percent, and those plans lasted less than five years. Only one American school district—Ladue, Missouri—managed to maintain the same merit pay plan for thirty years, from the early 1950s to the mid-1980s.[26]

In the early 1980s, with renewed concern about the performance of American schools, merit pay was again on the political agenda, this time coupled with career ladder proposals to link increases in both compensation and status to evidence of teacher performance. At the peak of this reform period, as many as thirty-three states considered merit-based compensation and career ladder proposals. Yet only a handful of states adopted programs—Arizona, Florida, Tennessee, and Utah were the main ones—and most were either pilot programs that were not expanded (Utah and Arizona) or programs that were abandoned altogether (Florida). Only Tennessee maintains a statewide program initiated in the early 1980s.[27]

Over these numerous cycles, merit-pay experiments revealed a few recurring problems. First, "schools found it difficult to devise defensible criteria of meritorious teaching."[28] The key word here is "defensible." Developing performance measures is not particularly difficult, using such technologies as standardized achievement tests, classroom observation protocols, and principals' ratings. Much more difficult is to defend the link between such measures and "good" teaching. If the link between performance measures and prevailing notions of good teaching is weak, as it is in all of the assessment technologies developed thus far, teachers perceive the process to be arbitrary; thus, instead of increasing motivation, rewarding teachers on the basis of performance undermines motivation and morale.

A second recurring problem is that merit pay is inconsistent with cooperative, egalitarian workplace norms that characterize relations among teachers and with the necessity for collegiality in basic school functions. Merit pay, which is based on individual, competitive concep-

---

26. Johnson (1984, p. 176).
27. Firestone, Fuhrman, and Kirst (1989).
28. Cohen and Murnane (1985, p. 5).

tions of motivation, makes maintaining positive working relations among teachers extremely hard.[29]

Yet another problem is that the designers of merit-pay schemes usually lacked any real understanding of what motivates teachers. Teachers consistently rate conditions of employment that are directly related to teaching and learning—manageable class sizes, good materials, collegial interaction, support and validation from administrators for their practice—as motivating in their work.[30] They tend to rate compensation as a "dissatisfier." Thus pay can be a drag on morale and engagement if it is perceived to be inadequate, inequitable, or unfair, but, by itself, it seldom motivates.[31]

The merit-pay schemes that survived for any time were the ones that solved these recurring problems. In the early 1980s, David Cohen and Richard Murnane looked closely at six of the one hundred or so surviving merit-pay plans and found four main characteristics: (1) They gave extra pay for extra work, instead of for higher performance. (2) They solved the problem of defensible criteria "in political, rather than scientific terms," by asking teachers to state their own criteria or letting them formulate criteria cooperatively. (3) They defined rewards to minimize competition and conflict, by keeping the amounts small, keeping the differences between awards small, and giving awards to almost everyone. (4) They kept the plans unobtrusive by making participation voluntary and not calling conspicuous attention to recipients. These strategies undermine the main purposes of merit pay and suggest less that the examples were successful than that they managed some accommodation between the theory behind the innovation and the realities of the workplace.[32]

Significantly, merit-pay plans seemed to survive longest where they were least needed—in affluent local school districts that had been successful in recruiting strong teaching staffs. In localities where teachers' salaries are already high and where labor-management relations are good, small merit increments that are widely distributed through processes that have little or nothing to do with student performance are seen by teachers as an affirmation of community support for good teaching, instead of as a divisive or competitive influence. The existence of merit pay also helped "school administrators justify spending money on

29. Cohen and Murnane (1985, p. 5).
30. Darling-Hammond, Wise, and Pease (1983).
31. Johnson (1986); and Herzberg (1968).
32. Cohen and Murnane (1985, p. 9).

education to their boards, and it helped both boards and administrators to make the same argument to their communities."[33]

These conclusions, while undermining the theories behind merit pay, are consistent with more enlightened theories of compensation and performance. A lively debate has taken place in the management literature about whether employees' performance is enhanced more by strategies that rely on intrinsic sources of motivation, such as job enrichment and access to decisions affecting one's work, or by extrinsic sources, such as pay. The general conclusion is that extrinsic motivation can enhance short-term performance when the task to be performed is well specified, individual performance is central to the achievement of goals, and the individual controls conditions that lead to performance. As the task becomes more uncertain, as cooperation becomes essential, as individual control is attenuated, and as long-term commitment becomes more important to organizational success, intrinsic motivation becomes more important.[34]

Career ladders and differentiated staffing are, in some respects, designed to compensate for the weaknesses of merit pay. Career ladders create differentials in status, often with differential compensation, by introducing multiple teaching ranks, from novice to advanced practitioner. Sometimes differentiated staffing arrangements are indistinguishable from career ladders, and sometimes they involve a job enrichment component, in which teachers are offered opportunities to participate in special assignments, such as curriculum development projects, for which they are given either released time from their regular duties or additional compensation.

Career ladders and differentiated staffing are designed not only to reward teachers for good performance, but also to attract and keep good teachers and to acknowledge that teaching requires expert knowledge. Teacher advocates complain that teaching is a careerless occupation in which success and experience do not lead to recognition and increased status (except when teachers leave teaching to become administrators). These advocates recommend an occupational structure in which some

33. Cohen and Murnane (1985, p. 9).
34. For a general management perspective, see, for example, Herzberg (1968); Beer and Walton (1989); Levinson (1990); and Vroom (1989). For economic analyses of merit pay that reaches similar conclusions, see Cohen and Murnane (1985); and Richards (1985). For a discussion of management issues specifically addressed to education, see Bacharach, Lipsky, and Shedd (1984).

teachers with demonstrated competence and experience assume broader responsibility for research, curriculum development, supervision of novice teachers, and coordination of collegial activities. Such arrangements, advocates argue, would reward talented teachers and encourage them to remain in the profession.[35]

The history of career ladder and differentiated staffing experiments closely parallels that of merit pay. Differentiated staffing experiments emerged in the late 1960s and early 1970s, yet only a few survived into the 1980s.[36] Two examples—in Temple City, California, which started in the late 1960s, and Charlotte–Mecklenburg, North Carolina, which started in the early 1980s—seemed successful, at least in sustaining themselves. Both models involved a series of career stages, ranging from provisional teacher through senior, or master, teacher. Both required, as a condition for advancement, additional academic training as well as evidence of classroom success and leadership. Both clearly defined the responsibilities of teachers at each stage and left them little discretion. And both involved small amounts of released time and additional compensation for teachers in the higher ranks.

In the early 1980s, building on these examples, a number of states enacted career ladders. Some of these programs—notably in Arizona, Florida, and Georgia—were soon abandoned or scaled back, as policymakers discovered the problems in developing defensible criteria for judging teacher performance. Two examples—in Tennessee and Utah—survived beyond the early stages of implementation.

The patterns that emerged from the implementation are familiar. The additional money that came with the programs was broadly distributed among teachers, often in increments as small as $500 per year. Participation in activities funded by the programs was also widely distributed. In Utah, teachers typically allocated funds as widely as possible within schools, in some cases to virtually all teachers. In the early years of the Tennessee program, two-thirds of eligible teachers received project support or summer stipends. Enhanced status, insofar as it accrued at all to participating teachers, seemed to come from collegial recognition rather than permanent changes in formal role or position. Some teachers perceived that the programs further burdened overworked teachers. Many teachers who did not receive rewards felt that the amounts were

35. Holmes Group (1986).
36. Freiberg (1985).

too small to be of any value and questioned the motives of teachers who did receive them. Some evidence existed that teachers who did not receive rewards reduced their contributions to their schools. And, while reward recipients generally responded positively, teachers did not think that the programs were a particularly good way of recognizing good teachers. Overall, minimal evidence was available of either serious job expansion or redesign. Abundant evidence confirmed the patterns of earlier merit-pay schemes: rewarding extra work rather than conferring permanent status, using political instead of technical means of allocating rewards, minimizing the visibility of rewards, and distributing them widely.[37]

In attempts to change the conditions of teaching, political and administrative entrepreneurship was not lacking. Regular cycles of innovation occur around the issues of teacher competence, motivation, and performance, just as they do around other educational issues. Policymakers and administrators seem ready to invent solutions with each cycle, and these solutions take root, if only temporarily, in a number of settings. There is neither a shortage of innovative ideas nor a lack of capacity to innovative. The system is awash in innovations.

These innovations are based, however, on common-sense theories about what the system needs. In this case, the theory is that the system needs better teachers who are more attentive to student performance. The problem with this common-sense theory is that it leaves out most of the complexity of constructing a mass profession of people dedicated to teaching and learning, and of constructing a collection of organizations—schools—that are decent, stimulating, and rewarding workplaces for people who choose teaching as a career. Teaching is a complex and uncertain task. Conditions of work that support good teaching—access to new knowledge, collegial support, active engagement in the creation of new ways to teach—cannot be influenced by policies based on the sort of common-sense theories that appeal to innovators. Such policies require deep understanding of the special characteristics of teaching and learning.

Unfortunately, little cumulative learning takes place from one cycle of innovation to the next. Innovations in education seem to be driven largely by political demands, which cause the same types of solutions to resurface each time the problem of teacher performance comes around

---

37. Malen, Murphy, and Hart (1988).

without a serious consideration of what happened to last cycle's solutions. This treadmill effect occurs even though social science knowledge about human motivation, job satisfaction, and performance is becoming more sophisticated. So the treadmill effect is probably not attributable to a lack of new knowledge with each repeat of the cycle but to the lack of impact of such knowledge on policy.

Changing Incentives for Schools

The third recurring theme of innovation in education is changing schools by changing the incentives under which they operate. Two current versions of this theme are educational choice and school-based management. School choice is a mechanism for substituting parental and student control for administrative control. Choice is based on the idea that, if schools are forced to compete for clients, their performance will improve as they become more responsive to the needs and preferences of students and parents. School-based management is a strategy of administrative decentralization, in which schools are given greater discretion and control over budget, personnel, and program within a structure of regular performance evaluations and consultations with the communities they serve. School-based management stems from the idea that schools will perform better when they can shape their own responses to educational problems and are required to develop a closer working relationship with their immediate communities.[38]

These reforms reflect America's historic ambivalence about centralized bureaucracy. From the inception of public education, reformers have opposed centralized administrative control. Every fifteen to twenty years, urban school systems have gone through regular cycles of centralization and decentralization, involving bruising political battles around the growing political influence of emerging minority populations. In the 1960s, the Ocean Hill–Brownsville conflict in New York City resulted in the creation of the current thirty-two community districts. The 1985 political battle in Chicago produced a system of elected boards for each of the city's more than five hundred schools. At the same time, Americans have been reluctant to change the basic structure of educational

38. For an elaboration of the distinction between systems of choice and systems of decentralized administrative control, see Raywid (1990).

governance that emerged in the early twentieth century: locally centralized political and bureaucratic control by elected boards of education,
board-appointed superintendents, and central offices.

Similarly, various versions of school choice have been present in
American education at least since the early twentieth century, when
mushrooming enrollments and increasing student diversity created pressures to educate children with different backgrounds, aptitudes, and predispositions for learning. Since at least the early twentieth century, for
example, most urban educational systems have had schools that were
accessible to students only through examinations. During the 1960s,
when curricular diversity was an asset, not a sign of intellectual flabbi-
ness, many urban systems created a range of alternative schools with distinctive and different forms of education. And under the dual pressures
of desegregation and "white flight," many urban school systems established magnet schools to attract racially integrated student bodies.

While some current critics portray local school systems as monolithic
bureaucracies with little or no sensitivity to the diverse needs and preferences of their clients, the realities are more complex.[39] Certainly, as the
critics argue, the basic governance structure of locally centralized control
has remained essentially the same throughout the twentieth century. It is
probably not true, however, as the critics also argue, that this system has
lacked sensitivity to the diverse needs and preferences of its clients.
Schools are, in regular cycles, alternately criticized for being not responsive enough and for being too responsive to students and their parents.
The progressive reforms of the 1920s and 1930s, which were designed to
allow for a more nurturing, child-centered approach to learning that
accommodated the diverse interests and backgrounds of children, were
followed by a major political backlash in the 1940s and 1950s, designed
to bring back order and traditional academic values. Similarly, reforms
of the early 1980s reflected a backlash by political leaders against what
they perceived to be the excesses of the 1960s and 1970s. So while centralized bureaucratic and political control has been a constant of American education, the public schools have not been unresponsive to pressures to diversify their programs. Recent analyses suggest that public
schools have been so sensitive to external pressures at times that they
have lost a coherent sense of mission.[40]

39. Chubb and Moe (1990).
40. Powell, Farrar, and Cohen (1985); and Cohen (1990).

When, in the 1960s, Milton Friedman began advocating educational vouchers, choice began to emerge as a serious policy innovation.[41] By the late 1960s, the Office of Economic Opportunity (OEO) had formulated a proposal to introduce educational vouchers in communities across the country.[42] While several communities, with OEO support, conducted feasibility studies of vouchers, and three or four states passed enabling legislation for voucher experiments, only one community—Alum Rock, California—launched a full-fledged experiment, which it abandoned after three years. Choice disappeared from the national political agenda for about fifteen years but not from the administrative agenda of local school systems. The 1960s and 1970s were a period of considerable local experimentation with alternative and magnet schools, although these experiments seldom went beyond a handful of schools in each district.[43] In the early 1980s, choice emerged again as a serious political issue when the governors of the fifty states endorsed a proposal to experiment with choice arrangements.[44] Nearly thirty states have enacted legislation to experiment with choice, including allowing high school students to enroll in postsecondary institutions for part of their coursework and allowing parents or students to choose schools within their district, in neighboring districts, or, in the case of Milwaukee, private schools.

Serious analysis of the implementation and effects of educational choice is scarce. Preliminary studies suggest a few early and tentative patterns. First, the design of choice arrangements is subject to complex political pressures. Alum Rock, for example, permitted alternative programs within existing public schools but provided no opportunity for teachers to organize schools outside the existing structure. Minnesota allows students to transfer to schools in neighboring districts but provides no transportation subsidies, other than requiring the "sending" district to transport students to the district line, and allows any district to refuse students from other districts. Washington state allows profit-making or nonprofit organizations to organize education clinics outside the existing public school system to help secondary school dropouts complete school. To receive reimbursements from the state, clinics must meet stringent performance criteria and all their teachers must be state certified just like regular public school teachers. These and other examples suggest that choice arrange-

---

41. Friedman (1962).
42. Jencks (1970).
43. Raywid (1985).
44. National Governors' Association (1986).

ments are shaped less by abstract principles about incentives that promote performance than by competing political interests.[45]

Second, choice arrangements take time to develop. Over the three years of the Alum Rock experiment, parents—many of them poor and Hispanic—showed a steadily increasing understanding of their options and an increasing willingness to choose schools outside their immediate neighborhoods. But the educational programs from which they could choose showed little differentiation in content or pedagogy and no significant impact on achievement.[46] Community District 4 in New York City, one of longest-running intradistrict choice programs in the country, started with one alternative school in 1973 and grew gradually to more than twenty alternative programs. This gradual process of growth reflected the belief that only high-quality programs should be allowed to participate and that the development of such programs required starting small and expanding only as teachers and administrators were confident that they could succeed.[47] If the aim of choice programs is to increase quality and performance by making teachers and parents more conscious of what they are choosing and why, then it seems plausible that the process of redesigning programs and introducing parents to the complexities of choice will take time.

Third, no necessary relationship exists between choice and high-quality educational programs, where quality is judged by students' exposure to academic content. The educational programs that emerge under choice arrangements reflect what educators know how to do, what parents and students want, and what resources are available. If educators do not know how to provide high-quality education, introducing choice may provide them with an incentive to learn, but it will not guarantee that they have the time or resources. If students and parents prefer athletics to academics, or if they prefer Rosacrucian Vegetarian Spiritualism to mathematics and science, choice will not necessarily improve academic learning. If both parents and educators prefer strong academic content but school resources are inadequate, choice will not necessarily improve academic performance. Consequently, educators experienced with choice stress the importance of developing strong alternatives before choice is introduced.[48]

45. Elmore (1991b).
46. Elmore (1991a).
47. Elmore (1991b).
48. Elmore (1991b).

Fourth, choice programs that treat parents and students from different social backgrounds equitably are difficult to design and typically result in a high level of administrative control.[49] Probably the most common complaint against school choice is that it perpetuates—even aggravates—existing inequities in American education. Nevertheless, intradistrict choice programs can provide equitable access to educational programs. In Cambridge, Massachusetts, which to desegregate its schools runs an intradistrict open choice program, large amounts of information, tailored to the language and culture of parents, reduced differences in the propensity of parents from different backgrounds to choose alternatives.[50] If the aim of choice programs is to increase the responsiveness of schools to all parents, not just those parents who would be active choosers within any system, then information is key. But providing information about alternatives is a form of administrative control; thus choice may change the type of administrative control but probably not the level.

School-based management is a mainstream managerial approach for simultaneously increasing flexibility and accountability by delegating detailed decisions to schools within a structure that provides direct community influence and periodic monitoring of school performance.[51] It typically involves some combination of three features: (1) a deliberate attempt to devolve decisionmaking authority on such matters as budget, personnel, and curriculum from central administration to the school; (2) a school-site council, usually composed of school administrators, teachers, parents, and sometimes members of the broader community; and (3) a process of periodic assessment of school performance that allows elected officials and central administrators to provide oversight and guidance. Although reforms that devolve authority from central offices to administrative subunits have a long history in public education, school-based management is a recent phenomenon.

Specific school-based management plans vary greatly. In some cases, schools are given significant control over substantial budgets. Other plans simply formalize school-level responsibility for small discretionary budgets that already existed. In some cases, formal administrative authority is lodged with the principal; in other cases, authority is placed, at least nominally, with the school-site council. In some cases, district policies and collective bargaining contracts are modified to allow

49. Levin (1987).
50. Elmore (1991a).
51. Clune and White (1988, p. 11).

for greater school-level decisionmaking; in other cases, plans are implemented without modifying existing policies, often at the expense of any
real devolution of authority.[52]

School-based management seems to "create opportunities to be
involved in decisionmaking, but it does not substantially alter influence
relationships."[53] That is, school-site councils discuss decisions of all types,
but the informal processes of decisionmaking remain unchanged. In
schools where the principal made most routine decisions without consulting teachers or parents, the same pattern persisted after school-based management, although more people did have an opportunity to be heard. Furthermore, parents and teachers, who are traditionally excluded from
participation in decisions affecting school operations, are also less likely to
participate in deliberative discussions under school-based management.[54]

School-based management seems to result in a high level of new
activities in schools, but most of the activities—social events, discipline
policies, newsletters, tutorial projects, fund-raising activities, and
extracurricular programs—have, at best, an indirect connection to the
basic instructional program. The closer activities get to the instructional
core of a school, the less school-based management affects them. On
matters such as textbook adoption, teaching practices, and curriculum
content, little evidence exists that school-site decisionmaking has any
impact. Hence "systematic investigations suggest that school-based management does not precipitate major adaptations [or] innovations in the
instructional component of schools."[55]

Changing the incentives under which schools operate has had little
direct impact on teaching or learning for two reasons. First, the changes
themselves are often not designed around any explicit theory of how they
will relate to the core technology of schools. Choice, for example, is a
theory about how organizations ought to respond when they are subjected to the pressures of competition, but it fails to identify how competitive pressures are translated into new teaching practices, new modes
of student learning, and increased performance. Advocates of choice
seem simply to want all schools to do whatever it is that effective schools
do, without knowing exactly what that is. School-based management is a
theory about how organization affects performance, but it, too, lacks an

52. Malen, Ogawa, and Kranz (1990).
53. Malen, Ogawa, and Kranz (1990, p. 309).
54. Malen, Ogawa, and Kranz (1990).
55. Malen, Ogawa, and Kranz (1990, p. 317).

explicit explanation of how changes in organization translate into changes in instructional practice and thus student learning. Second, changes in incentives are always marginal modifications to existing structures and incentives. These new systems do not change teacher knowledge, existing political relationships, or the way people think about their work. Thus these reforms get quickly neutralized by the constraints under which they are implemented.

Some Explanations and Prescriptions

The problem in education is not an absence of innovation; education is awash with innovation. Nor is the problem an absence of entrepreneurship; innovations seem to arise regularly from both policymakers and high-level administrators as well as through isolated cottage industry innovators. Yet these innovations do not affect, in any enduring or systematic way, the core technology of teaching and learning. The innovation paradox reflects an ability of public education to absorb or deflect almost any attempt at innovation without much discernible, long-term impact on its core processes.

At least three explanations can be found for the paradox. First, instructional practice is intractable and inherently complex: The forces that determine teaching practice—most notably, teachers' knowledge, their exposure to teaching, and constraints on the quality of people who can be attracted to teaching as a mass occupation—are far more powerful determinants of what happens in classrooms than the ideas of innovators or the conventional tools of policy.[56] If this is true, education cannot be changed fundamentally without altering the social conditions that determine access to teaching and the organizational conditions of teaching practice.

If, as research suggests, one of the most powerful influences on how teachers teach is how they themselves were taught, changing teaching is, to a significant degree, a generational problem. The task is not simply to affect how today's teachers teach, but to ensure that enough students in any generation are exposed to good teaching so that they will teach differently when they become the next generation of teachers. If, as research also suggests, teachers' knowledge of the subject matter is a key

56. Cohen (1988); and Cuban (1984).

constraint on their ability to adopt new teaching practices, then changing teaching practice requires the cultivation of subject-matter knowledge among existing teachers plus selection and compensation measures that make hiring more knowledgeable teachers in the future possible. Policymakers and managerial innovators are not accustomed to thinking in these broad terms. They want specific fixes that work now, or least in the next electoral cycle, instead of solutions that take generations to design and implement.

Second, the political and institutional structure of public schooling guards against change. One version of this explanation suggests that the political structure of public education creates powerful forces for stability that cannot be altered except by eliminating the structure itself. This requires state and local governments to shift from the direct provision of education to licensing and regulating (in some minimal way) the providers of education.[57] Another version of this explanation is that the institutions of public education have legitimated themselves with society by performing certain key functions, such as providing credentials for people for entry into the work force. If schools perform these functions acceptably, they can buffer their core technology—teaching practice—from outside interference.[58] This argument suggests that schools will not change their core practices unless the basic social function of schooling is changed.

In either case, the kinds of innovations that are required to change schooling are different from those tried by policymakers and administrators. These are more likely to be "institution changing" policies that alter the mission, incentives, and structures of education, not the mandates and inducements used in the past.[59] Changing the mission, incentives, and structures of institutions that are politically well entrenched is a kind of policymaking with which very little experience exists. (The experience that can be pointed to—major reforms of federal regulatory agencies in the 1970s, for example—does not inspire confidence.) Nonetheless, institutional explanations emphasize that making fundamental changes in the details of an organization without changing its relationship with the broader society will have little impact.

Third, the innovations themselves are poorly designed and implemented. Policy innovations are usually based on common-sense theories

57. Chubb and Moe (1990).
58. Meyer and Rowan (1978).
59. McDonnell and Elmore (1987).

about what the system needs, instead of on a deep understanding of the core processes of teaching and learning, how they work, and how they might be made to work differently. Furthermore, as common-sense theories recur in regular cycles of reform, they fail to become more sophisticated, even when social science knowledge is increasing. So innovation in education tends to be a monotonous repetition with little long-term improvement. In the absence of clear, consistent policy direction, schools will continue to respond episodically and incoherently to innovations.[60]

This view suggests that education will change only with dramatic changes in the design and implementation of policies directed at schools. For example, the basic purposes and systems under which schools operate could be significantly simplified: clear guidance on key goals, testing and assessment policies consistent with those goals, alternative curriculum frameworks that address the main subjects to be tested, teacher education and professional development to prepare teachers to teach within these curriculum frameworks, and financial incentives for schools that show greater-than-expected achievement of the goals. If the basic policy structure of education were simplified in this way, then schools (with some additional financial support) could concentrate on developing teaching practices to achieve these more fundamental and coherent goals. This is how other industrialized countries approach public education. It is not, however, a formula for maximizing innovation in public education; it is a formula for focusing schools on a set of policy goals and putting innovation in the service of these goals.

Learning from the Education Paradox

What can be learned about innovation throughout the public sector from the paradox of innovation in education? The most obvious point is that a high rate of innovation does not mean that a public enterprise is functioning well or that performance is improving. If education is any guide, innovation can be nothing more than random responses to external stimuli. Schools have adapted well—too well—to a political environment that requires evidence of innovation as an indication of political responsiveness.

Public enterprises, such as education, that have complex core technologies—practices that require a high level of knowledge and judg-

---

60. Fuhrman, Clune, and Elmore (1988); and Smith and O'Day (1991).

ment—are difficult to change in any enduring way using the traditional instruments of public policy and management. Most educational innovations that originate with policy or management do not reach the technical core of schools. Those innovations that start in the technical core seldom, if ever, generalize to the realm of policy and management. Policies that might affect the core technology of schooling are not the sort that policymakers and high-level administrators find interesting. They focus on mundane issues such as what teachers know about academic content. Such policies cannot be stated in simple common-sense theories. They require a deeper understanding of the enterprise than most policymakers are able to acquire.

Finally, innovation in education reveals a more fundamental problem with innovation research. The management and policy literature on innovation suggests that if the world were populated by clever people with good ideas and ingenious implementation strategies and who operated in organizations that promote innovation, public enterprises would steadily improve in their efficiency and effectiveness. Over the past century, American education has had at least its fair share of such people, often working in organizations that supported them. Yet these people and their organizations have not improved the overall performance of public education. Almost anything can be done in American education, as long as it is not done on a large scale, over a long period of time, or in a way that threatens the basic patterns of instructional practice. In other words, a theory of entrepreneurship and innovation that works at the smallest level of aggregation in a complex system does not necessarily generalize to the system as a whole. Furthermore, innovating in the smallest unit, without a system for generalizing to the whole, creates political rewards for random innovations instead of real, sustained improvement in the delivery of public service.

References

Alkin, Marvin, and Ernest House. 1981. "The Federal Role in Curriculum Development, 1950–80." *Educational Evaluation and Policy Analysis,* vol. 3: 5–36.

Bacharach, Samuel B., David B. Lipsky, and Joseph B. Shedd. 1984. *Paying for Better Teaching: Merit Pay and Its Alternatives.* Ithaca, N.Y.: Organizational Analysis and Practice.

Barzelay, Michael, and Babak J. Armajani. 1990. "Managing State Government Operations: Changing Visions of Staff Agencies." *Journal of Public Policy Analysis and Management,* vol. 9, no. 3 (Summer): 307–38.

_____. 1997. "Innovation in the Concept of Government Operations: A New Paradigm for Staff Agencies." In *Innovation in State and Local Government,* edited by Alan A. Altshuler and Robert D. Behn.

Beer, Michael, and Richard Walton. 1989. "Harvard Business School Note: Reward Systems and the Role of Compensation." In *Manage People, Not Personnel,* 15–30. Harvard Business School Press.

Chubb, John E., and Terry M. Moe. 1990. *Politics, Markets, and America's Schools.* Brookings.

Clune, William, and Paula White. 1988. *School-Based Management: Institutional Variation, Implementation, and Issues for Future Research.* Rutgers University, Eagleton Institute of Politics, Center for Policy Research in Education.

Cohen, David. 1985. "Origins." In *The Shopping Mall High School: Winners and Losers in the Educational Marketplace,* edited by Arthur G. Powell, Eleanor Farrar, and David Cohen, 233–308. Houghton Mifflin.

_____. 1988. "Teaching Practice, Plus Que Ce Change . . ." In *Contributing to Educational Change: Perspectives on Research and Practice,* edited by Phillip Jackson, 27–84. Berkeley, Calif.: McCutchan.

_____. 1990. "Governance and Instruction: The Promise of Decentralization and Choice." In *Choice and Control in American Education,* edited by William H. Clune and John F. Witte. New York: Falmer Press.

Cohen, David, and Richard Murnane. 1985. "The Merits of Merit Pay." *Public Interest,* vol. 80: 3–30.

Cuban, Larry. 1984. *How Teachers Taught: Constancy and Change in American Classrooms.* New York: Longman.

Darling-Hammond, Linda, Arthur Wise, and Sara Pease. 1983. "Teacher Evaluation in the Organization Context: A Review of the Literature." *Review of Educational Research,* vol. 53: 285–328.

Dede, Christopher, and Joy Hardin. 1973. "Reforms, Revisions, Reexaminations: Secondary Science Education since World War II." *Science Education,* vol. 57: 485–91.

Dewey, John, and Evelyn Dewey. 1915. *Schools of Tomorrow.* Dutton.

Dosi, Giovanni. 1988. "Sources, Procedures, and Microeconomic Effects of Innovation." *Journal of Economic Literature,* vol. 26 (September): 1120–71.

Elmore, Richard F. 1990. "Introduction: On Changing the Structure of Schools." In *Restructuring Schools: The Next Generation of Educational Reform*, edited by Richard F. Elmore, 1–28. Jossey-Bass.

_____. 1991a. "Choice as an Instrument of Public Policy: Evidence from Education and Health Care." In *Choice and Control in American Education*, edited by William H. Clune and John F. Witte. New York: Falmer Press.

_____. 1991b. "Public School Choice as a Policy Issue." In *Privatization and Its Alternatives*, edited by William Gormley. University of Wisconsin Press.

Elmore, Richard F., and Milbrey Wallin McLaughlin. 1988. *Steady Work: Policy, Practice, and the Reform of American Education*. Santa Monica, Calif.: Rand Corporation.

Firestone, William, Susan Fuhrman, and Michael Kirst. 1989. *The Progress of Reform: An Appraisal of State Education Initiatives*. Rutgers University, Eagleton Institute of Politics, Center for Policy Research in Education.

Freiberg, H. J. 1985. "Master Teacher Program: Lessons from the Past." *Educational Leadership*, vol. 42: 22–27.

Friedman, Milton. 1962. *Capitalism and Freedom*. University of Chicago Press.

Fuhrman, Susan, William Clune, and Richard Elmore. 1988. "Research on Education Reform: Lessons on the Implementation of Policy." *Teachers College Record*, vol. 90: 237–58.

Goodlad, John. 1984. *A Place Called School: Prospects for the Future*. McGraw-Hill.

Herzberg, Frederick. 1968. "One More Time: How Do You Motivate Employees." *Harvard Business Review*, vol. 46: 56–57.

Holmes Group. 1986. *Tomorrow's Teachers: A Report of the Holmes Group*. East Lansing, Mich.

Jencks, Christopher. 1970. *Giving Parents Money to Pay for Schooling: Education Vouchers*. Harvard Graduate School of Education, Center for Education Policy Research.

Johnson, Susan Moore. 1984. "Merit Pay for Teachers: A Poor Prescription for Reform." *Harvard Educational Review*, vol. 54: 175–85.

_____. 1986. "Incentives for Teachers: What Motivates, What Matters." *Educational Administration Quarterly*, vol. 22: 54–79.

Levin, Henry. 1987. "Education as a Public and Private Good." *Journal of Policy Analysis and Management*, vol. 6: 628–41.

Levinson, Harry. 1990. "Asinine Attitudes toward Motivation." In *Manage People, Not Personnel,* 77–88. Harvard Business School Press.

Malen, Betty, Michael Murphy, and Ann Hart. 1988. "Restructuring Teacher Compensation Systems: An Analysis of Three Incentive Strategies." In *Attracting and Compensating America' Teachers: Eighth Annual Yearbook of the Education Finance Association,* edited by Kern Alexander and David H. Monk. Cambridge, Mass.: Ballinger.

Malen, Betty, Rodney Ogawa, and Jennifer Kranz. 1990. "What Do We Know about School-Based Management? A Case Study of the Literature—A Call for Research." In *Choice and Control in American Education,* edited by William H. Clune and John F. Witte, 289–341. New York: Falmer Press.

McDonnell, Lorraine, and Richard Elmore. 1987. "Getting the Job Done: Alternative Policy Instruments." *Educational Evaluation and Policy Analysis,* vol. 9: 133–52.

Meyer, John, and Brian Rowan. 1978. "The Structure of Educational Organizations." In *Environments and Organizations,* edited by Marshall W. Meyer and others. Jossey-Bass.

National Governors' Association. 1986. *Time for Results: The Governors' 1991 Report on Education.* Washington, D.C.: National Governors' Association, Center for Policy Research and Analysis.

Powell, Arthur G., Eleanor Farrar, and David K. Cohen. 1985. *The Shopping Mall High School: Winners and Losers in the Educational Marketplace.* Houghton Mifflin.

Raywid, Mary Anne. 1985. "Family Choice Arrangements in Public Schools: A Review of the Literature." *Review of Educational Research,* vol. 55: 435–67.

_____. 1990. "Rethinking School Governance." In *Restructuring Schools: The Next Generation of Educational Reform,* edited by Richard F. Elmore, 152–205. Jossey-Bass.

Richards, Craig. 1985. "The Economics of Merit Pay: A Special Case of Utility Maximization." *Journal of Education Finance,* vol. 11: 176–89.

Sizer, Theodore R. 1984. *Horace's Compromise: The Dilemma of the American High School.* Houghton Mifflin.

Smith, Marshall, and Jennifer O'Day. 1991. "Systemic School Reform." In *The Politics of Curriculum and Testing: Yearbook of the Politics of Education Association,* edited by Susan Fuhrman and Betty Malen. New York: Falmer Press.

Stake, Robert, and James Easley. 1978. *Knowing and Responding to the Needs of Science Education.* Case Studies in Science Education 19. Champaign-Urbana, Ill.: Center for Instructional Research and Curriculum Evaluation.

Tyack, David. 1974. *The One Best System: A History of American Urban Education.* Harvard University Press.

Tyack, David, and Elisabeth Hansot. 1982. *Managers of Virtue: Public School Leadership in America, 1820–1980.* Basic Books.

Vroom, Victor. 1989. "Preface." In *Manage People, Not Personnel,* ix–xvi. Harvard Business School Press.

Weiss, I. R. 1978. *Report of the 1977 National Survey of Science, Mathematics, and Social Studies Education.* Research Triangle Park, N.C.: Center for Educational Research and Evaluation.

Wirt, John, and Susan Quirk. 1977. *National Curriculum Projects and Development in Education.* Washington, D.C.: Rand Corporation.

Zegans, Marc. 1990. "Strategy, Innovation, and Inertia: Unbundling Some Old Assumptions." Paper prepared for the Annual Research Conference of the Association for Public Policy and Management, San Francisco.

CHAPTER TWELVE

Innovations in Policing:
From Production Lines to Jobs Shops

Mark H. Moore, Malcolm Sparrow, and William Spelman

SINCE THE MID-1980s, we have been observing innovations in policing from three vantage points. First, through our involvement in Harvard University's Executive Session on Policing, we have kept abreast of the ideas, experiments, and visions of the nation's leading police executives.[1] We have heard them discuss the important challenges facing their organizations and how the field is likely to develop in the future.

Second, with assistance from the Ford Foundation Program on Innovations in State and Local Government, we developed and tested general methods for identifying the most important innovations in a policy field, be it policing, welfare, or defense.[2] To discover how important innovations are developed and disseminated within a field, a necessary first step is to reliably identify those important innovations. We tested three specific methods: (1) interviews with a panel of experts, (2) surveys of prac-

---

1. The Executive Session on Policing was a series of meetings (spread over several years) of a distinguished group of police executives, mayors, police labor leaders, and academics to discuss future strategies of policing. The results of these meetings are presented in a published series of papers entitled *Perspectives on Policing*. See, for example, Moore and Trojanowicz (1988a); and Moore and Trojanowicz (1988b). The series is published jointly by the National Institute of Justice (an agency of the U.S. Department of Justice) and Harvard University. It is available from the National Institute of Justice. See also Sparrow, Moore, and Kennedy (1990).

2. The results of this research appear in Moore, Spelman, and Young (1992); and Spelman, Moore, and Young (1992).

titioners, and (3) content analyses of leading professional journals. The principal aim of the project was methodological: to discover the general strengths and weaknesses of these methods for identifying the most important innovations in a field. Nevertheless, because we used policing as our "test bed," the project also produced an important substantive result: an estimate of the most important innovations in policing.

Third, through our ongoing involvement with the Innovations program, we commissioned, studied, and taught cases about police innovations.[3] Often the innovations analyzed were semifinalists, finalists, or winners in the awards program. These cases have helped us understand what policing recognizes as an innovation, how innovation occurs within police departments, and how innovations diffuse from one department to another.[4]

From these activities, we have not only learned what innovations have been important in policing, but also how important questions about innovations in other fields can be framed and investigated. More particularly, we have learned to distinguish strategic innovations that fundamentally reposition organizations in their environments, from smaller, less significant programmatic, administrative, and technological innovations that simply allow organizations to be more efficient or effective in pursuing previously established missions. We have also learned that a significant aspect of particular programmatic, technological, or administrative innovations is their likely impact on the future strategic direction of the organization. Some small-scale innovations facilitate, even force, strategic change; others anchor organizations more solidly in their current mission and strategy.[5] And we have learned that one of the most important kinds of strategic innovations that public sector organizations make is to become committed to continuous adaptation and innovation to meet unusual or changing circumstances.[6]

We cannot be sure that any of these observations are valuable to those studying innovations in other fields. Policing may be unusual. But our casual knowledge of such fields as welfare, community economic development, environmental protection, and defense policy suggests that some important comparisons and challenging analogies, if not powerful gener-

3. Cases developed about innovations in policing include Arnold and Leone (1990); Kennedy (1990b); Kennedy (1991a); and Kennedy (1991b).
4. Moore and Sparrow (1988); and Spelman, Moore, and Young (1992).
5. Moore and Sparrow (1988).
6. Moore (1994).

alizations, exist. Still, we leave the task of generalizing to the reader and stick to what we know best: analyzing innovations in policing.

Defining, Categorizing, and Evaluating Innovations

One challenge in innovations research is to operationally define "innovation" and to categorize the various kinds of innovations.[7] A simple definition works well: An innovation is any reasonably significant change in the way an organization operates, is administered, or defines its basic mission.

Qualifying Changes as Innovations

Not all organizational changes qualify as innovations.[8] Some are simply too small, obvious, or idiosyncratic to warrant much analytic attention. Those changes worth recognizing as innovations should be globally (or at least locally) new to the organization; be large enough, general enough, and durable enough to appreciably affect the operations or character of the organization; or be consciously designed or adapted as a response to a perceived problem by some level of the organization.[9]

Some would also insist that an innovation worth analyzing should improve the performance of an organization. Such a definition would exclude innovations that failed. To study the process of innovation—in particular, to analyze how organizations distinguish successful from unsuccessful innovations—failures as well as successes must be examined. To explore how innovations improve organizational performance, the criterion of success must be included in the operational definition.

How stringently should scholars define innovation? How high should they should set the hurdle that any particular organizational change must surmount to count as an innovation? The answer depends upon their analytic purpose. To explore how the most important innovations are con-

7. Authors in this book offer other definitions. Alan A. Altshuler and Marc D. Zegans, in chapter 3, define innovations as "novelty in action." See also Altshuler and Zegans (1990, p. 20). In contrast to this broad definition, Laurence E. Lynn, Jr., in chapter 4, proposes a much narrower one: "Innovation is properly defined as an original, disruptive, and fundamental transformation of an organization's core tasks. Innovation changes deep structures and changes them permanently."

8. Governors Center (1993, p. 11).

9. Leonard (1986).

ceived, implemented, and diffused—to focus attention on the small number of truly significant innovations in a field—scholars should set the standard very high. To examine how small-scale innovations occur, they should to set the standard much lower. And to get a sample size large enough to study the process of innovation quantitatively, scholars will need to set the standard low.

We set the standard low for two reasons. First, to study which innovations were important, it was necessary to avoid incorporating the idea of importance into the definition of innovation. We wanted to learn how to discriminate among a heterogeneous class of innovations, not purify the category so that everything inside it was already significant. Second, to examine how small-scale innovations occurred and accumulated within organizations and how particular innovations diffused across a field, it was necessary to include both small-scale, local innovations and large-scale, global innovations.

Categorizing Innovations

Using this definition, a wide variety of changes were swept into our analytic net. The challenge was to organize them into different types of innovations, as well as to decide which were more important than others. Four distinct categories emerged: programmatic, administrative, technological, and strategic.

Programmatic innovations establish new operational methods of using the resources of the organization to achieve particular results. In policing, recent examples include setting up stakeouts of likely robbery targets to apprehend and deter robbers, arresting fences as a way of discouraging burglaries, using police officers to provide drug education in schools, and offering victim-resistance training to women.

Administrative innovations are changes in how police organizations prepare themselves to conduct operations or account for their achievements. These include changes in personnel policies and practices such as new methods for recruiting or screening officers, new training approaches, new supervisory relations within the department, and new career tracks for officers. Administrative innovations also include new ways of measuring the performance of individual police officers or the overall performance of the entire department. The development of a national accreditation process for police departments is also an administrative, not a programmatic, innovation because, even though such efforts undoubtedly have important operational effects, they are often under-taken primarily to establish the credibility of the organization with its overseers.

Technological innovations depend on the acquisition and use of some new piece of capital equipment. These might be simple equipment changes such as lightweight body armor, nonlethal weapons, or more secure radio communications equipment. Other recent technological innovations involved new forensic aids such as deoxyribonucleic acid (DNA) typing to uniquely identify suspects and more accurate methods in the automated identification of fingerprints. Still others involved the application of computer technology to report writing, to more secure communications, and to more realistic and challenging weapons training courses.

Strategic innovations foreshadow, reflect, embody, or in some signifi-cant way lead to a fundamental change in the overall philosophy and ori-entation of the organization. These changes could involve important redefinitions of the primary goals or objectives of policing, the range of services and activities they could supply, the principal means they would use to achieve their goals, the key internal and external working rela-tionships, or the methods used to finance the organization's activities.

For example, the shift from the goal of "controlling" crime to a focus on "fear reduction" or the "provision of emergency medical and social services" is an important strategic innovation in policing.[10] So is the shift from "law enforcement" to "problem solving" as the police's primary means of responding to incidents.[11] Other strategic innovations include working partnerships with community groups as a primary tactic for dealing with street-level drug markets and long-term contracts with developers to provide foot patrols at fixed locations in new shopping areas.[12] These innovations are strategic because they change some of the basic understandings about the ends or means of policing or the key structures of accountability that now shape the overall efforts of police departments.

These categories are not clearly separated from one another; thus assigning any particular innovation to one category or another is often a judgment call. Nonetheless, these distinctions are useful to capture the variety of innovations that occur and to serve as a reminder of innova-

10. Sparrow, Moore, and Kennedy (1990).
11. Eck and Spelman (1987).
12. Kennedy (1990a); and Reiss (1985).

tions that might be forgotten or underemphasized. A panel of twenty people, nominated by their peers as experts in policing, also divided police innovations along these or closely related dimensions. Furthermore, all of these experts could understand and deploy our scheme once it was presented to them.[13]

RELATIONSHIPS AMONG THE KINDS OF INNOVATIONS. These abstract categories helped us to sort the huge variety of innovations presented in the field's professional journals. Moreover, by struggling to assign each particular innovation to a specific category, we came to understand the logical relationships among the different kinds of innovations.[14]

For example, every innovation classified as a technological innovation could be further characterized as either programmatic, administrative, or strategic.[15] The defining characteristic of a technological innovation is not its purpose but the material in which the innovation is embodied. This means that in defining an innovation as technological, we have not yet characterized its purpose; thus every technological innovation is also a programmatic, administrative, or strategic innovation.

Innovations involving new uses of computers were particularly difficult to categorize. In some instances (for example, using computers to support firearms training programs or to search for fingerprints), the classifications were straightforward. (Firearms training would be classified as administrative; fingerprint searches as programmatic.) But in many other cases involving laptop terminals, mobile digital terminals, or computer-aided dispatch systems, the technological innovations affected both operational and administrative arrangements. Although these innovations were more difficult to classify, they were more important to analyze because their implications were so wide-ranging.

Sometimes the current or potential effects of technological innovations were large enough to count as strategic, even though the direction was unclear. For example, cellular telephones could be used to establish much closer contact between police officers and individual citizens, because citizens would be able to call individual officers in their cars directly. In contrast, mobile digital terminals seemed valuable principally because they increased the reliability and security of communications within the police department and gave officers quick access to depart-

13. Moore, Spelman, and Young (1992, pp. 18–20).
14. Moore, Spelman, and Young (1992, pp. 64–70).
15. Moore, Spelman, and Young (1992, pp. 66–68).

mental databases. As a result, cellular phones wired officers more closely to citizens, while mobile digital terminals wired them more closely to their organization and their cars. Each communications technology encouraged particular working relationships and thus had different but important strategic implications.

By far the most difficult distinction to make was between strategic innovations and all the others.[16] By definition, a strategic innovation has large implications for the overall position of the organization in the society. It changes the basic paradigm or gestalt of policing. A strategic innovation does not simply improve performance within an existing structure of goals, operational methods, and administrative structures. Instead, it recasts the overall framework by redefining the purposes, inventing new methods, or establishing new external or internal working relationships to help the organization achieve its newly defined purposes. Our research challenge was to decide which particular innovations had this strategic quality.

In determining what innovations were strategic, we were aided by our knowledge of the trends in strategic thinking now occurring in policing.[17] These include rethinking the ends of policing to include crime prevention, fear reduction, and emergency services that go beyond the goal of controlling crime or apprehending offenders. They also include rethinking the means of policing to emphasize the community's own role in controlling crime and promoting security, and the use of analytic problem-solving methods to identify conditions that produce repeat calls. They also include a shift in external and internal working relationships to increase the visibility and transparency of police operations to ordinary citizens, and to flatten hierarchies and decentralize initiative. Finally, they include new revenue sources for police including special taxes, the creation of local foundations, and the acceptance of gifts of training and property from local donors.

To some degree, these strategic changes all fit within the set of new ideas called community policing or problem-solving policing. When these ideas were presented in the field's journals, we categorized them as strategic. In addition, however, we also recorded as strategic innovations new activities that moved in the direction of these new ideas (usually noting whether their strategic significance was programmatic, administrative, or technological). Innovations that were not themselves strategic

16. Moore, Spelman, and Young (1992, pp. 67–70).
17. Kelling and Moore (1988); and Moore and Trojanowicz (1988b).

Table 12-1. *Distribution of Types of Innovations in* Police Chief

Percent

	Definition of "strategic" employed	
Type of innovation	Stringent	Less stringent
Programmatic	33	21
Administrative	26	21
Technological	34	33
Strategic	7	24

Source: Moore, Spelman, and Young (1992).

could, nonetheless, become strategically important because they either pointed the way toward strategic changes, unleashed forces inside or outside the organization that would further a strategic change, or permanently altered how the police conducted their business. For example, new methods of evaluating police department performance (for example, surveys measuring victimization, fear, self-defense activities, and recent experiences with the police) could be strategically important, not only because they reflect different ideas about what police departments should be accomplishing but also because they help to prompt such changes.[18]

Data on the distribution of the different kinds of innovations that were discussed since the mid-1980s in *Police Chief,* one of the most widely read journals in the field, are presented in table 12-1.[19] Because of the difficulty of deciding if an innovation is strategic, we have classified the data with two different definitions of "strategically important"—one narrow and exacting, the other broader and more lenient.

Evaluating Innovations

More difficult than categorizing innovations has been evaluating them. One major problem is conceptual: Defining what is a successful, valuable, or important innovation is suprisingly difficult. We specifically asked our expert panel to reflect on and describe the criteria they used to make these judgments. Their intuitive wisdom helped us clarify the criteria for evaluating innovations.[20]

18. Alpert and Moore (1993).
19. For an explanation for why we used the *Police Chief,* see Moore, Spelman, and Young (1992, pp. 55–56).
20. Moore, Spelman, and Young (1992, pp. 22–32).

OUTCOME-ORIENTED CRITERIA. The most consistent response we received to the question of how particular innovations should be evaluated was that the innovation should have "accomplished what it was intended to do." This statement, while general, does reveal that to our experts an innovation was important only if it produced some valuable, concrete result.

The experts often wanted to give substantive content to this abstract standard and therefore employed additional criteria that reflected their own views of the important objectives of policing. Many said that an important police innovation should "reduce crime," "reduce fears," or "increase public satisfaction." Traditionalists in the group tended to emphasize the importance of "reducing crime"; some thought this was the exclusive criterion for evaluating police innovations. Advocates of the newer strategies of policing nominated both "fear reduction" and "increased public satisfaction" as important results of police innovations.

"Increased public satisfaction" is another ambiguous criterion. Ideally, an increase in public satisfaction would be derived from the police improving their performance in dealing with issues that concern the community. To some experts, those concerns are most importantly crime and criminal victimization; therefore the only proper way for the police to earn increased public satisfaction is to reduce crime.

Other experts believed that the police could also "increase citizen satisfaction" by responding to problems that citizens thought were important, such as unruly conduct or disorderly conditions. They did not assume that crime was the only or most important problem to which the police could make a useful contribution. Instead, they imagined a wide variety of citizen problems that the police could help resolve.

Still others believed that the police could increase citizen satisfaction not by producing results but simply by improving the quality of service. The police could be more prompt, more courteous, and more helpful in responding to calls; they could also be more accessible to citizens on the street and less confrontational and defensive at neighborhood meetings. Thus some experts advocated such criteria as "improved service quality" or "increased police responsiveness."

To some of our experts, however, such criteria suggested public relations gimmicks. They worried that the police might cheat by doing nothing more than putting on a good face. That would be particularly objectionable if the good face were not earned day to day in specific, concrete encounters with the public, but on a wholesale basis through a public relations campaign that obscured the police department's real performance.

Thus our experts were divided on the question of whether "increased public satisfaction" was a proper criterion. Nearly everyone believed that it was important; yet many were concerned that this result could be produced dishonestly as well as honestly. Most experts wanted to give credit only to the honest ways.

COST-EFFECTIVENESS, EFFICIENCY, AND PRODUCTIVITY. In addition to producing some valuable result, said our experts, important innovations should reduce costs. Some explicitly nominated "cost-effectiveness" as an important criterion. Other respondents used phrases such as "increased efficiency" or "enhanced productivity." To our experts, however, these different phrases carried somewhat different connotations.

"Cost-effectiveness" was an appropriate criterion for judging both particular operational programs and those administrative innovations designed to improve the overall functioning of police departments. "Increased efficiency" and "enhanced productivity" were used in a more limited way—namely, when discussing the administrative or technological innovations designed to support the overall performance of the organization. In this pattern of responses, the concepts of "efficiency" and "productivity" were most appropriate when examining the performance of the whole organization in the pursuit of a well-established, general police objective such as controlling crime or responding rapidly to calls. In contrast, the concept of "cost-effectiveness" was most commonly used in evaluating the impact of a particular programmatic initiative to deal with a particular part of the police department's mission.

IMPLEMENTATION. The expert panel also identified several criteria for implementation. For example, a commonly cited criterion was the impact of the innovation on "officer morale and satisfaction." For many experts, this factor was important because it influenced the ease of implementation. For others, this criterion was itself an outcome. For them, the impact of the innovation on their officers' morale was as important as its impact on objective social conditions or the perceptions of citizens. For still others, this criterion was important because it affected the general climate within the organization. It helped "commit the officers" to the enterprise or readied the organization to develop and respond to other new ideas. The second most commonly identified implementation criterion was the "survivability" or "institutionalization" of the innovation. An innovation could not be important if it did not survive. In general, the expert panel preferred innovations that had a favorable impact on officer morale, fitted comfortably within the existing culture of the police, and survived. They were less inclined toward innovations that faced opposition and resistance.

But some experts sounded a different note. Important innovations were the risky ones. Instead of fitting neatly within the organization's culture, these innovations challenged it. If an innovation could influence the organization and the field by "teaching them to ask better questions," or "broadening discussions" and leading to "productive ferment," that would be as valuable as an innovation that fit comfortably. In this view, even innovations that failed could be important. But the most valuable innovations would both stretch the thinking of the field and succeed.

These observations mesh with the views of those experts who were less interested in the immediate effectiveness of the innovation in achieving its stated goals than in what one expert called its "the second and third round implications." These experts thought that some innovations had reverberating effects—like a stone tossed in the water. To evaluate an innovation required an examination not only of its immediate impact but also of its side effects. And, in some cases, these side effects would be more important than the immediate consequences.

VALUE TO THE BROADER FIELD OF POLICING. Many respondents evaluated innovations by their impact on the broad field of policing. Thus they focused attention on such issues as the "diffusion" of the innovation, its "widespread adoption," or its "diffusibility," "replicability," and "adaptability." Intuitively, they believed that the more widely used an innovation becomes and the more properties it has to foster wider use, the better it is.

Others saw innovations as experiments designed to expand the boundaries of knowledge about "what works." From this perspective, innovations were evaluated as contributions to the goal of "systematizing police knowledge," "using research to modify operational procedures," "filling gaps" in the array of police techniques, "adding to police knowledge," or both "exploiting and fitting within the cumulative development of knowledge within the field." In this view, innovations are "research and development projects" that contribute to the overall stock of knowledge about policing that is, in principle at least, broadly available to the field. The most significant innovations show how police resources may be more efficiently and effectively used to solve an important problem. Those that solve important problems are more important that those that succeed in unimportant areas or those that fail (even in instructive ways). They are important because they teach the field a new, general, and permanent lesson.

Here, too, a contrary theme arose—one that valued risk, ambition, and failure as well as replicable successes. Many respondents, for example, stressed that "novelty" was an important characteristic: If a program was not new in some important sense, it should not be called an innovation and could not be valued as one. Even more boldly, some argued that valuable innovations challenged common assumptions and beliefs. In this view, exploring new areas about which no one knows much (so that any approach seems reasonable) is less useful than upsetting and correcting a widely endorsed conventional wisdom.

PHILOSOPHICAL AND STRATEGIC IMPLICATIONS. A majority of our experts evaluated innovations not only by their effectiveness or their contributions to knowledge but also by their influence on both the future development of the organizations into which they were introduced and the overall development of the field. In describing the potential importance of innovations, these experts used phrases such as "changes the mind-set of the police," "alters the paradigm of policing," "changes definition of policing," produces a "big effect on what police do," or "shifts policing toward becoming a serious, human service enterprise."

Moreover, these experts had specific ideas of how innovations could produce such effects. They watched for the influence that one innovation had on the likelihood of additional innovations being attempted. They wanted to see how an innovation "helped ask better questions," "stimulated a climate of innovativeness," "encouraged continuous improvement," or "stretched thinking within the department."

They also considered the extent to which the innovation, or the process by which the innovation was initiated and implemented, shifted the location of decisionmaking and initiative downward in the organization. They were concerned with how an innovation diffused responsibility and authority more broadly. The more an innovation encouraged other innovations at many different levels of the organization, the more important it was.

In addition, they valued innovations that involved citizens. They liked innovations that responded to the explicit concerns of citizens or engaged them in the operational solution of the problem. Some emphasized innovations that "tapped into public concerns," "opened doors to the outside," "mobilized others to deal with crime," or "got citizens involved and distributed the responsibility for preventing and solving crimes to other agencies and to the citizens themselves."

These are characteristics of police departments that are shifting to "community-oriented" or "problem-solving" policing. Thus many respondents evaluated particular innovations by looking at their impact on the transition to this new strategy either within a particular organization or in the field as a whole. Others, however, saw in innovations only the potential for improvement within the existing frame of policing.

Assessing Award-Winning Innovations

Using this framework for defining, categorizing, and evaluating innovations, we examined the innovations in policing that have been finalists or won awards in the Innovations program. Our objective was not to evaluate the awards process but to use the award winners as a set of innovations to analyze.

Between 1987 and 1990, the finalists and winners in the awards program included six local and state police organizations with seven innovations that reflect the diversity of creative thinking within police organizations.

In 1987 the Duluth, Minnesota, Police Department won an innovations award for its Domestic Abuse Intervention Program. In the words of its award application, this program "reverses the indifference of the legal system to the plight of abused women" and "unites courts, city police, and human services agencies through a tough arrest policy, mandatory jail sentences, and mandatory counselling and follow-up for offenders."

Also in 1987 Baltimore County's Citizen Oriented Police Enforcement (COPE) Program was a finalist. COPE focused on reducing fear instead of criminal victimization. COPE did this by establishing a special unit within the police department to administer victimization surveys, to work closely with local community groups and businesses to identify the particular problems that frightened the communities, and then to resolve these problems by making arrests and by using whatever combination of traditional and innovative tactics seemed appropriate.

In 1988 the St. Louis County Police Department won an innovations award for Computer Assisted Report Entry (CARE). CARE allowed patrol officers to call in their incident reports to specially trained clerks who would type the reports directly into a computer system that would automatically send out multiple copies. These copies would go to the detectives assigned the responsibility for investigating the case, to the national databases that helped police forces around the country identify and return stolen property, and to the logs of crime incidents that were maintained at both precinct and central levels and served as the basis for reporting on crime trends and for targeting patrols.

Also in 1988 the Minneapolis Police Department's Repeat Call Address Policing Unit (RECAP) reached the finals of the award program. RECAP used computer-based analyses to identify the relatively small number of addresses in Minneapolis that accounted for the largest proportion of the calls for service. The addresses were then closely analyzed to determine the cause of these multiple calls and what could be done to solve the underlying problem. Sometimes the response involved arrests; sometimes it required different interventions by other agencies such as liquor control boards or mediation services.

In 1988 Baltimore County's COPE unit once again made the finals, this time with a special program focused on responding to and resolving "hate crimes" in which racial or religious bias seemed to be part of the motivations of the offenders and part of the experience of victimization.

In 1990 the Alaska State Police Department's Village Public Safety Officer's (VPSO) Program made the finals. VPSO trained local residents in the skills required to fight fires, enforce laws, and search for and rescue citizens lost in the arctic wilderness. It also taught the Alaska State Troopers to adapt their conventional police operations to the traditional values of Alaska's ethnically diverse communities.

Also in 1990 the Newport News Police Department's Problem Oriented Policing (POP) initiative reached the finals. In the language of the award application, POP sought to "institutionalize the concept of police officers as problem-solvers." All officers were authorized, when not responding to incidents, to work pro-actively on problems they identified on their own or with advice from the community. They were taught a four-step method to use in responding to problems: (1) scan, (2) analyze, (3) respond, and (4) assess. Over the previous year, the department identified and solved seventy-nine particular problems from local vandalism to citywide prostitution and thefts from vehicles.

Assessing the Innovations

In their impact on the current performance of the police and their significance for the future, these programs are different. Two—the Duluth Domestic Abuse Intervention Program and the St. Louis County CARE

Program—can best be viewed, respectively, as straightforward program
and technological innovations. The four others—Minneapolis's RECAP
Program, Newport News's POP Program, Alaska's VPSO Program, and
Baltimore County's COPE Program—both herald and facilitate some
important strategic changes in policing.

A CLASSIC PROGRAM INNOVATION. The Duluth Domestic Abuse
Intervention Program is, in many ways, a classic program innovation. All
over the country, police departments must decide how best to respond to
domestic assaults. The basic question is whether to arrest the offender
(almost always the husband) or to find some other means for resolving the
dispute. In the past, the police rarely made an arrest, typically because the
women refused to press charges. Even when the victim was willing to swear
out a complaint that would justify the arrest, the police still hesitated; experience had taught them that women rarely prosecuted their husbands. Moreover, the police often thought the problem could be more effectively
resolved through mediation and counseling agencies instead of by the criminal court. These domestic incidents were simply not police business.

More recently, however, three factors have spurred the police to
reconsider this common practice. First, research revealed that, for a
domestic homicide, the police had been previously summoned to the
scene an average of four to six times.[21] Clearly, the police were missing
an important opportunity to prevent murders.

Second, the women's movement gradually established a different
understanding about why women were refusing to swear out a complaint:
The abused women did not make a considered judgment about their
interests and then refuse to press charges. Instead, they were psychologically and economically dependent on their husbands, who coerced them
not to file charges.[22] Thus the police should not take the abused wife's
expressed preferences to avoid her husband's arrest as controlling; her
real preferences and interests could not be determined until the coercion
was removed. That required the police to arrest the husband and learn
later what the woman really wanted.

Third, some experimental studies, also carried out in Minnesota, indi-
cated that mandatory-arrest policies seemed more effective in reducing
the likelihood of subsequent attacks by the husband than did the alternatives of counseling or no action.[23]

21. Sherman and Berk (1984).
22. Weingart (1989).
23. Sherman and Berk (1984).

From such pressures, a police department inevitably would develop a new way of responding to domestic assaults, and this "new" approach undoubtedly would emphasize arrest and continued controls over the conduct of the offender. Duluth's program innovation was worth an award because it was a clear change from past practices and because it held some prospect for improving a police department's response to what has been a stubborn, consistent problem. If this new approach to domestic violence proved effective, it would be just the sort of programmatic innovation that should be disseminated widely.

But this innovation seems to have only limited significance for the evolving strategy of policing. Because it drags the police into the domain of domestic (as well as stranger) violence, makes them responsive to women's groups, and involves them in more collaborative efforts with prosecutors and courts, the innovation may have some strategic significance. But no one has ever doubted that the police should respond to domestic violence, and nothing is more central to the current strategy of policing than arresting violent offenders. Thus the program is nothing more (and nothing less) than an important new idea about how to use conventional police methods to deal with an important, recurrent problem.

A CLASSIC TECHNOLOGICAL INNOVATION. St. Louis County's CARE Program seems equally important—and equally limited. It is a classic technological innovation relying on computer technology to improve the routine operations of the police. By using telephones to report crimes and computers to distribute, store, and analyze the data from the reports, some old organizational routines are speeded up, and resources are saved.[24] If faster, wider response to crimes increases apprehensions and clearances (thus more effectively deterring and incapacitating offenders), such changes will be effective and will save money and time. The innovation can also be easily and widely disseminated, and it increases the overall knowledge available to the field. Thus CARE meets many of the criteria for a successful and important innovation.

Missing, however, is any significant strategic implication. Unchanged is the basic concept of policing: to respond effectively to crimes after they have occurred, and to increase the likelihood that offenders may be apprehended. CARE's faster processing of reports might, however, help precinct or departmental managers notice and respond to trends in local crime by putting more patrol officers in the vicinity of crimes when they occur.

24. Arnold and Leone (1990).

Both the Domestic Abuse Intervention Program and the CARE Program leave the essential strategic concepts of "professional policing" undisturbed. The end remains effective crime control. The means remain arrests produced through patrols, rapid response to calls, and retrospective investigation. The key working relationships remain unchanged: Citizens are nothing more than the eyes and ears of the police; patrol officers are directed to incidents reported by citizens; and their responses are monitored by their immediate superiors.

Because these programs fit so neatly within the existing strategy of policing, they may not only fail to move the field forward. They may more solidly anchor police practices in the past strategy of policing. Even as they are making the police more efficient and effective in the short run, they may become a drag on the future development of policing.

Strategically Important Innovations

The Minneapolis RECAP Program is important because it promises to use police resources more efficiently and effectively in responding to incidents and because it changes a police department's basic conception of its work.[25] A cornerstone of the traditional strategy of policing has been the development of a communication system linking citizens to police officers through telephones, centralized dispatching, and two-way radios. This has allowed the police to be available to citizens with unprecedented speed. Within most cities, the police can respond in under five minutes to an urgent call from anywhere. It is a great accomplishment.

Unfortunately, this network has also become one of the greatest obstacles to innovation and change in policing.[26] The growth of the urban population and the successful marketing of 911 emergency telephone systems have led to a dramatic increase in calls. Yet the financial problems of the cities have prevented them from responding with increased manpower and equipment. Thus the police find themselves now struggling to meet a very specific, well-defined, easily measured, and politically visible objective: to keep response times low.[27] The pressure exerted by this system has made it difficult to explore any alternative uses of police resources.

Efforts to manage response times have stimulated innovation—much of

25. Sparrow (1994).
26. Sparrow, Moore, and Kennedy (1990).
27. Kennedy (1987); Kennedy (1988); and Kennedy (1990c).

it based on technology. The most common innovations are called "differential police response."[28] The basic idea is to establish clear priorities among calls, delaying police responses to nonurgent calls, and sometimes responding with something other than a patrol car. For example, for a minor break-in that occurred long before the call was made, the police sometimes ask the citizen to mail in his or her complaint. Other responses include wringing additional efficiencies out of the available patrol force through automated vehicle-locator systems and using dispatch algorithms that find the patrol car closest to the scene. Still, the basic strategy remains unchanged: Police respond to incidents, which they then examine to see whether a law has been broken and whether an arrest is appropriate.

Traditionally, the police have accepted the demand for their services as a given—an exogenous variable that they could not influence—and attempted to respond to that demand as effectively and as efficiently as possible. When calls increased, the police sought to be more effective and more efficient. RECAP also responds to the increase in calls for service but in a wholly different way. RECAP sought to reduce the demand for service. Because a large majority of calls come from a limited number of addresses, which the police seem to visit repeatedly, RECAP seeks to reduce the demand for service by resolving the problems underlying the repeat calls.

The RECAP strategy requires the police to shift from an incident-handling to a problem-solving approach.[29] In the past, the police thought problem solving would reduce rapid-response capabilities; the only way to do problem solving was to take officers off the line. Because that threatened to increase response times and created greater burdens for those officers who remained in rapid-response units, it always seemed a difficult and risky experiment. The RECAP program links problem solving to the objective of keeping response times low. The solution to the response-time pressure is to solve the problems that are producing repeat calls. Thus the most pressing problem faced by police executives—the increase in demand for service—requires a shift in focus from incidents to problems.

The significance of this strategic change is hard to exaggerate. To eliminate problems that are stimulating calls for service requires a wholly different investigative and analytic approach.[30] Police look less

28. McEwen, Connors, and Cohen (1986).
29. Goldstein (1990); and Sparrow (1994).
30. Sparrow (1994).

for offenders and more for other precipitating causes of crime such as frustrating relationships or ongoing disputes. Police seek solutions less often in arrests and more often in other kinds of intervention that renegotiate relationships. The solutions are less likely to rely solely on police resources and more likely to draw on resources from outside the department. This has important implications for the orientation and skills of the police officers, and even for the role of the police department within city government. That makes RECAP important not just programmatically but also strategically.

The POP program in Newport News explicitly identifies the opportunities for problem solving suggested by the RECAP program and extends that approach across the entire organization. POP specifically authorizes the police department as a whole to identify problems and to work out solutions that draw upon powers other than arrest and upon resources other than those controlled by the department. Moreover, this is not an isolated staff activity located near the center and top of the department; everyone in the organization is authorized and encouraged to engage in this undertaking.

The Alaska VSOP Program is based on the complementary ideas that the community itself must do much of the work of policing and that policing is more than crime control. In Alaska, the police seek to mobilize communities not only to be their eyes and ears but also to coproduce deterrence, enforcement, and crime prevention. Moreover, these police recognize that once a vigilant, competent community has been established to deal effectively with crime, it can undertake such other tasks as fire fighting and search and rescue. Finally, VSOP recognizes that if the police are to be successful in establishing close and effective relationships with local communities, their operations will have to be adapted to meet community norms and expectations. Police cannot be entirely outside the community if they are to develop close working partnerships; they must be "of" the community as well. These ideas have challenging implications for the traditional strategy of policing that assigned citizens only a limited role, focused obsessively on crime control, and operated independently from the community.

But the innovation with the most important strategic implications is Baltimore's COPE Program. For four reasons, COPE is significant in the revolution now shaping policing.[31]

---

31. Kennedy (1990b).

First, COPE is one of the first efforts to focus on citizens' fears as a separate and solvable problem. Traditionally, police departments have viewed fear reduction as an important objective but assumed that it would result from reducing criminal victimization. Most departments thought it dangerous and cynical to seek to allay citizens' fears without reducing crime. What the field gradually learned, however, was that fear was an important problem in its own right—reducing the quality of life for individuals and degrading the cohesion of neighborhoods and their ability to defend themselves.[32] Furthermore, fear was unexpectedly disconnected from actual levels of victimization, and police could reduce fear through efforts that were different from those they employed to reduce crime.[33] The Baltimore County Police Department was one of the first departments to act on these findings and use fear reduction as an organizing concept.

Second, COPE demonstrated the causal link between close community relationships and the goal of reducing fear. To reduce fear, the police had to get into close contact with communities so that they could discover and respond to whatever frightened citizens.

Third, COPE revealed the need to rely on problem solving instead of law enforcement methods to reduce people's fears, which are most commonly stimulated by things such as graffiti, litter, and disorderly youth.[34] Against such problems, the traditional police powers to arrest and prosecute have little impact. The police need other solutions. Baltimore County's police helped to organize block groups and used their influence with other county departments to eliminate graffiti and litter. They also mediated conflicts over the use of public spaces.[35]

Fourth, COPE continues to be a laboratory for showing how these ideas of fear reduction, community relations, and problem solving begin to infect the rest of the department. Originally, COPE was a separate unit, small and vulnerable. Gradually, that unit grew. Now COPE has reached the stage where further development requires disseminating the techniques into the general operations of the department and the dissolution of the special unit. Is the COPE "culture" now strong enough to stand on its own without the protection of a special structure and powerful enough to dominate the traditional patrol culture? The answer will

32. Skogan (1990).
33. Moore and Trojanowicz (1988a).
34. Wilson and Kelling (1982).
35. Kennedy (1990b).

determine whether COPE remains an important program in the repertoire of police operations or becomes an important wedge in transforming the overall strategy of policing.

Programs such as RECAP, POP, VSOP, and COPE are simple ideas that have radical implications for the future strategy of policing. Even though their origins and purposes are different, they all push the police in the same general direction—toward a more sustained engagement with communities. The police are no longer allowed to stay at the surface of community life dealing only with criminal incidents through arrest and prosecution. Instead, they are drawn into the conflicts and frustrations that are frightening citizens and causing them to call the police. Once enmeshed in these problems, the police have to find new solutions; simply arresting someone does not solve the problem. So the police are compelled to reach outside their department. That, in turn, forces the department into a more decentralized, entrepreneurial style and draws the police into a much different relationship with the community and with other agencies of local government.

Institutionalizing Innovation: Commissioning the Officers

If problem solving and community policing are the wave of the future, then much of the concept of policing and many of the administrative arrangements that now connect individual officers to the rest of the department will have to change.[36] The notion that policing is the routine application of policies and procedures must be discarded. It needs to be replaced with the idea that policing requires invention and improvisation as officers encounter new situations and problems. The image must be abandoned of policing as a "production line" for which a few engineers have designed processes that can be used over and over again to produce a consistent result. It needs to be reconfigured with the image of a "job shop" in which each police assignment is treated as a new challenge that might require a new solution.

Correspondingly, administrative relations within a department must change. The tradition of centralized control to ensure that the officers follow the established procedures must give way to decentralized respon- siveness in which the officers themselves are encouraged to invent new

36. Eck and Spelman (1987); and Moore (1994).

Table 12-2. *Administrative Style of Police Departments*

Traditional style	Community-policing style
Bureaucratic organization	Professional organization
Centralized	Decentralized
Command and control	Commissioned officers
Control through rules	Control through values
Control through supervision	Control through after-the-fact accountability
Citywide accountability	Local responsiveness
Management as supervision	Management as coaching
Functional specialists	General practitioners
Promotions through ranks	Promotions through pay raises
Academy training	Clinical training

solutions or adapt old solutions to new circumstances. The officers must define the problems to be solved and the appropriate means for doing so. Their supervisors can be coaches in this activity but not controllers. Otherwise, too much of the necessary initiative will be lost.

This shift in strategy from professional policing to community or problem-solving policing is itself an innovation that creates a new administrative framework within which the police are asked to engage in a continuing process of innovation and adaptation. The strategies of community and problem-solving policing are innovations, representing a fundamental change in the basic strategy of policing. These strategies also commit police organizations to a continuing process of innovation and adaptation. Instead of top-down experiments with new programs, individual officers, working with the community, are authorized to define problems and find solutions. Instead of applying known technologies for dealing with a problem now embedded in the policies and procedures of the department, police officers are expected to invent a response. Each problem that is identified and solved is, in some important sense, an innovation. Thus the new strategies of policing require administrative arrangements that institutionalize innovation.

The key changes in administrative relationships and style that must accompany a shift from professional crime fighting to community or problem-solving policing and that are designed to institutionalize innovation in policing are listed in table 12-2. Dangers arise in making such changes. By giving greater initiative to officers, the organization and the community becomes much more dependent on their individual qualities. If they are skilled, the risk to the community will be less than if they are badly trained. Even more importantly, if they have the proper values, the community will be safer than if they are badly motivated.

In problem-solving and community policing, the society and the organization are asking the officers to be real professionals—to have not only the skills of their trade, but also to reflect in their actions a commitment to society's values instead of their own. In short, to implement these new strategies of policing, the society must commission the officers to act on their behalf.[37] It must trust them to have the values and the skills necessary to deal with the problems the community wants addressed. Then the potential of problem-solving and community policing can be realized without losing control of the officers. That set of changes will be the most important innovation of all—the development of a true profession of policing.

37. Sparrow, Moore, and Kennedy (1990).

References

Alpert, Geoffrey P., and Mark H. Moore. 1993. "Measuring Police Performance in the New Paradigm of Policing." In *Performance Measures for the Criminal Justice System: Discussion Papers from the BJS-Princeton Project,* edited by Lawrence A. Greenfield. Washington, D.C.: Bureau of Justice Statistics.

Altshuler, Alan, and Marc D. Zegans. 1990. "Innovation and Creativity: Comparisons between Public Management and Private Enterprise." *Cities* (February): 16–24.

Arnold, Peter, and Robert Leone. 1990. *St. Louis County Police Department.* Case C16-90-996.0. Harvard University, John F. Kennedy School of Government.

Eck, John E., and William K. Spelman. 1987. *Problem-Solving: Problem Oriented Policing in Newport News.* Washington, D.C.: U.S. Department of Justice.

Goldstein, Herman. 1990. *Problem-Oriented Policing.* McGraw-Hill.

Governors Center. 1993. *Research on Innovations in State and Local Government: The 1992 Conferences.* Duke University, Terry Sanford Institute of Public Policy.

Kelling, George L., and Mark H. Moore. 1988. "The Evolving Strategy of Policing." *Perspectives on Policing,* no. 4. Washington, D.C.: National Institute of Justice.

Kennedy, David M. 1987. *Neighborhood Policing in Los Angeles.* Case C16-87-717.0. Harvard University, John F. Kennedy School of Government.

_____. 1988. *Patrol Allocation in Portland, Oregon (A) and (B).* Cases C15-88-818.0 and C15-88-819.0. Harvard University, John F. Kennedy School of Government.

_____. 1990a. *Fighting the Drug Trade in Link Valley.* Case C16-90-935.0. Harvard University, John F. Kennedy School of Government.

_____. 1990b. *Fighting Fear in Baltimore County.* Case C16-90-938.0. Harvard University, John F. Kennedy School of Government.

_____. 1990c. *Computer Aided Dispatching in Houston, Texas.* Case C16-90-985.0. Harvard University, John F. Kennedy School of Government.

_____. 1991a. *Spreading the Gospel (A): The Origin and Growth of the DARE Program.* Case C16-91-1029.0. Harvard University, John F. Kennedy School of Government.

_____. 1991b. *Spreading the Gospel (B): DARE Goes National.* Case C16-91-1030.0. Harvard University, John F. Kennedy School of Government.

Leonard, Herman B. 1986. "Good Ideas: What Makes for Quality in Innovation?" John F. Kennedy School of Government.

McEwen, J. Thomas, Edward F. Connors III, and Marcia I. Cohen. 1986. *Evaluation of Differential Police Response Field Test: Final Report.* Washington, D.C.: National Institute of Justice.

Moore, Mark H. 1994. "Policing: De-Regulating or Re-Defining Accountability." In *De-Regulating the Public Service: Can Government Be Improved?* edited by John DiIulio. Brookings.

Moore, Mark H., and Malcolm K. Sparrow. 1988. "Institutionalizing Innovation in Municipal Police Departments." Paper prepared for the 1988 APPAM Research Conference, Seattle, Washington, October.

Moore, Mark H., William Spelman, and Rebecca Young. 1992. "Innovations in Policing: A Field Test of Three Different Methodologies for Identifying Important Innovations in a Substantive Field." Working Paper. Harvard University, John F. Kennedy School of Government, Taubman Center for State and Local Government, Innovations Research Project.

Moore, Mark H., and Robert C. Trojanowicz. 1988a. "Policing and the Fear of Crime." *Perspectives on Policing,* no. 3. Washington, D.C.: National Institute of Justice.

_____. 1988b. "Corporate Strategies for Policing." *Perspectives on Policing,* no. 6. Washington, D.C.: National Institute of Justice.

Reiss, Albert J., Jr. 1985. *Policing a City's Central District: The Oakland Story.* Washington, D.C.: U.S. Department of Justice.

Sherman, Lawrence W., and Richard A. Berk. 1984. "The Minneapolis Domestic Violence Experiment." *Police Foundation Reports.* Washington, D.C.: Police Foundation.

Skogan, Wesley G. 1990. *Disorder and Decline: Crime and the Sprial of Decay in American Neighborhoods.* Free Press.

Sparrow, Malcolm K. 1994. *Imposing Duties: Government's Changing Approach to Compliance.* Westport, Conn.: Praeger.

Sparrow, Malcolm K., Mark H. Moore, and David M. Kennedy. 1990. *Beyond 911: A New Era for Policing.* Basic Books.

Spelman, William, Mark H. Moore, and Rebecca Young. 1992. *The Diffusion of Innovations and the Creation of Innovative Police Organizations.* Working Paper. Harvard University, John F. Kennedy School of Government, Taubman Center for State and Local Government, Innovations Research Project.

Weingart, Saul. 1989. "Adding Insult to Injury: Domestic Violence and Public Policy." Ph.D. dissertation, Harvard University.

Wilson, James Q., and George L. Kelling. 1982. "Police and Neighborhood Safety: Broken Windows." *Atlantic Monthly* (March): 29–38.

Part Five

IMPLEMENTING
INNOVATION

CHAPTER THIRTEEN

Resolving the Dilemmas of Ad Hoc Processes:

Parallel Processes as Scaffolding

Thomas N. Gilmore and James Krantz

INNOVATION usually requires freedom from existing cultural constraints. Ideas often come from outside an organization, perhaps from customers or users, or from a new leader who emerges from beyond the historically dominant culture.[1] Leaders increasingly create ad hoc structures to develop ideas and plan their implementation. A creative public sector executive, Gordon Chase was one of the foremost practitioners of innovating via bypassing the existing structure. His method, according to Harvard professor Mark H. Moore, was to create a new organizational unit coterminous with the issue he wanted to focus on, place an individual in charge of it, set targets, and monitor its performance.[2] Moore concludes, "He administers the program as though it were a separate, independent program . . . [using] project management techniques."[3] Prominent examples in the private sector include Apple's development of the Macintosh computer and General Motors' Saturn car effort. In both cases, new organizations were created and deliberately buffered from the "old" corporate culture (which for Apple was less than ten years old) so

This chapter was originally published as Gilmore, Thomas N., and James Krantz. 1991. "Innovation in the Public Sector: Dilemmas in the Use of Ad Hoc Processes." *Journal of Policy Analysis and Management,* vol. 10, no. 3 (Summer): 455–68. Reprinted by permission of John Wiley & Sons, Inc.

1. Gilmore (1988).
2. Moore (1987, p. 11).
3. Moore (1987, p. 12).

that the innovation would be unfettered by the assumptions and habits of the dominant organization.

The creation of such separate entities may work well for discrete new product or project innovations, but it has drawbacks and dangers when offered as a generalized model across all types of innovation, especially when the desired result is a new mission or new organizational culture.[4] The now popular "skunkworks" model extols either deliberately created encapsulated teams or self-appointed underground ventures as vehicles for the development of transformative ideas.[5] This model frequently runs into trouble during the institutionalization phase of an innovation, however. For example, when the Vera Foundation's successful pretrial diversion project was taken over by New York City's Probation Department, it failed to sustain the pilot project's performance.[6] Furthermore, when the focus of the ad hoc group is on the functioning of the organization—its procedures, policies, strategic orientations, culture—as is often true of public sector reforms, the changes that ad hoc groups develop often fail to be completely implemented.

Unfortunately, the choice between "parallel processes" and vertical processes that use the existing roles and structure of the organization has become increasingly ideological: The former is lionized and the latter denigrated. Parallel processes refer to groups, structures, or events that bypass the existing organizational hierarchy, such as ad hoc teams; skunkworks; special multifunctional, multilevel project groups; off-site retreats; training interventions; and representative councils.[7] The creation of a special group is an implied attack on the existing structure's inability to deal effectively with the issue.[8]

The denigration of the line organization is particularly problematic in public organizations, given the current climate of contempt for bureaucrats. Journalist Daniel Schorr argues:

> One common thread connects Pentagate, Irangate, Watergate. In all three cases high administration officials, unable or unwilling to accomplish their designs through the permanent bureaucracy, created shadow governments by using allies in the private sector.[9]

4. Kazanjian and Drazin (1986).
5. Peters and Waterman (1982).
6. Friedman (1976).
7. Stein and Kanter (1980); Herrick (1985); and Bushe and Shani (1991).
8. Ware (1977).
9. Daniel Schorr, "The Bureaucracy to the Rescue!" *New York Times,* June 30, 1988, p. A23.

He quotes Melvin Paisley, deputy secretary of the Navy, arguing that the Japanese and Germans were competing so successfully against the United States because "we blew up their government 40 years ago and all the regulations that were in it." Such contempt for the formal machinery and the corollary love of the back channel can lead only to stagnation and disinvestment in changing basic governmental processes and to periodic abuse and scandal on the part of the so-called innovators.

The core issue here is how parallel processes can be used developmentally as scaffolding to enable the emergence of something more enduring, instead of as bypass approaches that collude in avoiding difficult, long-term changes. In light of short-term, appointed executives dealing with long-term civil servants, many leaders will gravitate toward a few doable, politically attractive issues rather than addressing fundamental delivery systems of the agencies they are charged with leading.[10] Furthermore, when systems issues (planning, budgeting, organizing) are addressed, they are often so identified with the particular appointed leader that successors seek to change them just to assert their own control over the agency, thereby short-circuiting any mature learning over time.[11]

Ironically, in the public sector, special units or ad hoc groups are used both to innovate and to bury deadwood. Often special units have been created to move a resister into a less damaging, make-work position. Alternatively, a new layer is created for allies, undercutting the authority of the units placed under them. In both cases, the organization is made less effective by the increased discrepancy between its formal structure and how it operates.

Resources are too scarce for an overuse of bypass strategies in the public sector to continue. By far the greatest cost is not the duplication of ad hoc and regular effort, but the long-term demoralization of the human resources as they feel written-off and disempowered. Too often overlooked in special high-performing groups is the system dynamic that links their overfunctioning to the rest of the organization's underfunctioning. This dynamic is particularly frequent when a new leader takes over and a small, inner, ad hoc group becomes ever more active, overloaded, and cut off from key resources. These in turn have been waiting for new leadership but find themselves treated merely as bystanders. No one has time to orient and direct them, and their honest contributions

10. Heclo (1977); National Academy of Public Administration (1985); and Gilmore (1988, p. 166).

11. Lynn and Seidl (1977).

about the existing culture are treated as resistance. Small initial differences grow and misunderstandings escalate, trapping human capital in the struggle between the in-group and out-group, instead of aligning and aggressively directing all resources toward the challenges the organization faces.

Dilemmas and Dysfunctions of Parallel Processes

Parallel processes free people from the existing authority structure, often allowing a creative mixing of people from different levels and functions outside of the chain of command. Yet the results of their creativity must at some point be reclaimed by the formal organization. In a session that focused on creativity in organizations, a group of middle-level executives from a wide variety of organizations addressed several themes that illuminate the difficulties this process raises.

The group was easily able to identify with the creators of new ideas and lionized their value. All the talk about innovators was positive, and no attention was directed at the disruptive aspects of innovation. A question about where new ideas "went" (in their current organizations) triggered widely shared humor, such as "into the circular file" or "into reports gathering dust on shelves," which suggested a foil to the innovator—the bureaucrat who fearfully and jealously guarded the status quo. The informal processes were spoken of positively; the formal, negatively.

One person mentioned "executing" a new idea, reflecting the reality that putting a new idea into practice often involves feelings of loss and death. These arise from the difference between the wondrous idea in the mind when contrasted to what happens when it is realized. Furthermore, to "decide" (which idea to follow) requires cutting off or killing options in favor of the chosen course of action. Those who assume the burdens of deciding and executing—essential next steps after a pool of ideas has been generated—are likely to encounter hostility and be attacked for attending to political interests in contrast to the purely substantive concerns of proposers.

The dilemma this group exposed was this: How can organizations create an atmosphere that encourages creativity and does not, at the same time, lead to dissension among their members?[12] How does one appro-

12. Miller (1983).

priately kill ideas and yet make their authors no less likely to continue to innovate? In what ways can people who have actively developed a pool of ideas participate in the screening decisions so they come to terms with the limits surrounding the choices? How can a chosen course of action be effectively implemented?

The fascination with stories of organizational insubordination in which an innovative idea has been pushed after being formally killed devalues the formal organization and its routines that, when healthy, are the means through which new ideas are ultimately brought into being.[13] Organizations, formerly valued because they enabled people to do more than they could as individuals, end up being devalued because of how they constrain individuals. But as Sir Geoffrey Vickers notes, organizations are a mixture of constraints and enablements.[14] If the push for innovation becomes separated into two parts—"we," the creative, informal, substantive, rational; and "they," the political, self-interested, conservative—the capacity of organizations to do their work is reduced.

A central issue in the creation of parallel groups concerns the linkages between them and the standing structure.

Linking Ad Hoc and Ongoing Groups: A Case Study

A recently appointed corrections commissioner was not satisfied with the initiative and creativity of his organization. He created six ad hoc task forces, each directed by someone below the executive staff level and well regarded in the organization. The executive staff assigned people from many different departments to these groups. The result was a parallel process, cutting across the major divisions at a level below the direct reports of the chief executive.

As time went on, difficulties in working out the relationships between the parallel process and the formal chain of command arose. The executive staff began to review work plans to shape the task force operations more actively. Task force leaders often felt caught between their members, who were eager to move ahead, and the executive staff, who wanted to make sure that the group was proceeding according to agreed-upon policies.

13. Kidder (1981); Peters and Waterman (1982); and Krantz and Gilmore (1990).
14. Vickers (1965).

Commitment to the Work

When one task force presented its recommendations to the executive staff, a number of critical issues in the relationship surfaced. The setting was an executive staff meeting presided over by the chief executive of the organization, and the presenter was the task force's chair. Members of the task force and the executive staff attended.

The task force chair began by introducing the members and briefly discussing their experiences in working together. He asserted that of particular value were "experiences in networking, communicating, aligning their different functions." He denigrated the substantive results somewhat by suggesting that any one person might have been able to go off alone and develop these ideas, but that the process had created some real alliances and shared understandings. He continued:

> As I was preparing for this meeting, I kept thinking of this joke about a chicken and a pig in a barnyard, looking up at a billboard that urges everyone to begin each day with bacon and eggs. The chicken says to the pig, "What a good idea." The pig replies, "That's fine for you, but for me it's a major commitment."

He then related the joke to the linking of his task force's work to the executive staff, suggesting that the executive staff faced the major commitment.

Humor often reveals anxieties. At one level the task force chair reversed the roles of his group and executive staff. A central feature of ad hoc groups is their time-limited nature. They have a deadline, after which they lose their authority to do work and face the death of their group, which has been a vehicle of satisfaction. Thus they are like the pig who must be devoured for its benefits to be realized. The executive staff, however, lives on, producing eggs day after day—some golden, some more ordinary. Might the anxiety about ending what had been a positive experience have led the ad hoc chair to reverse the group's roles? Alternatively, does the reversal underscore that the executive staff does bear the deeper commitment to following through on the recommendations, even though it did not develop as much ownership of the work as those who were centrally involved?

Responsibility for Implementation

After reviewing the recommendations, the task force leader said, "We are ready to do educational testing, beginning in June. Other areas will require more resources." Who is the "we"? Is it the task force, which has no operating mandate or capabilities? Is it the employee relations unit whose head is on the executive staff and has not been involved in the development of the plan?

In the follow-up discussion, a member of the executive staff suggested that "good management" meant that the task force should leave with "the monkey on their back for the next steps" instead of letting them dump it on the executive staff.[15] Yet, at some point, the task force's work does need to be taken in by the executive staff and reallocated, often to the line organization. Assuming that it was a good idea to begin educational assessment, some particular manager would be charged with doing the assessment, within the limits of the unit's resources. That individual would be accountable, and presumably that individual's boss would be responsible, for monitoring its progress. Conceivably the task force could be given a backup monitoring role, especially to track many parallel initiatives that might exist in many different chains of command. However, if they are the primary point of detecting compliance, then they are taking the formal chain of command off the hook. As organizational theorist Elliott Jaques points out, few groups are fired.[16] The accountability spine falls along the hierarchy.

Struggle for Resources

The task force presented its ideas but was poorly prepared to give the actual costs of undertaking them. It could not identify slack in current resources (which might have embarrassed the managers of those units that were allegedly underused) or the costs of hiring the necessary additional staff, although it did suggest a number of additional full-time equivalents necessary to do the recommended work in some areas. The members of the executive staff stressed the need to focus on the resources, especially as the annual budget was nearing a critical period. When the chief executive asked what the task force wanted, the task force leader referred the question to the members with a light comment about, "Let's sit on Santa's lap." The implication was that the decision about resource allocation was the executive staff's and the task force could only express wishes. This suggests a dependency relationship that

15. Oncken and Wass (1974).
16. Jaques (1990).

is counterproductive to the original aims of creating task forces—to empower middle managers to innovate.

Realistically, the line side of the organization had to weigh these recommendations against the resource demands of the other task forces, as well as review the priorities within their area of concern. Finally, the entire developmental budget (for new initiatives) had to be set within the context of the base budget, something that the task force could not know, given the parallel structure.

The foregoing case suggests that the relationships between a parallel structure and the existing organization need careful management across time. When formed, the parallel structure's missions and mandates must be clear—in particular, whether it is simply creating options or making recommendations or whether it will carry forward some ongoing oversight responsibilities. When given authority over an issue that normally would fall under a particular executive's command, it may undercut that executive. When multiple task forces are created, the issue of their overlap with one another must also be managed, especially when each will want new resources for its area of concern.

A Developmental Case: The Strategy Group in the Department of Juvenile Justice

The following case illustrates a successful intertwining of a parallel process with the normal vertical structure in bringing into being an innovation—case management. In early 1983, Ellen Schall became the commissioner of New York City's Department of Juvenile Justice (DJJ) and recruited a team of top executives, most notably a deputy in planning and an executive director for the detention center. In the first year, she built a strategic theme around the idea of case management as a vehicle that would link the different elements of the agency and thereby provide a whole environment for children whose lives were especially erratic and confused.[17]

In January 1984, a one-day planning meeting was held to discuss case management and to flesh out the vision and the different responsibilities for its execution. Numerous outside consultants were present, which was

17. Gilmore and Schall (1986).

later taken to suggest that the new commissioner did not yet fully trust her own staff to carry out this initiative. Parallel processes, such as this one-day meeting, often link outside consultants to organizations in transitions and at the same time serve to keep the consultants removed from some of the real difficulties in ongoing authority relationships. As a follow-up to this meeting, another one-day workshop was held in the early spring. Both events seemed loosely coupled to the daily work of the agency. However, line executives were extremely focused on their short-term agendas of getting control over the delivery of safe and humane care for the children.

After one of the consultants summarized his sense of the key achievements from the workshop at a session several weeks later, the commissioner noted, "You seem to have these results much more inside of you than I have them in me." The remark suggested that the two events, which had been widely viewed as successes at day's end, had not been effectively linked to the ongoing processes of the organization. From this conversation emerged the idea of creating a "strategy group" whose membership would reflect many of the stakeholders in the case-management system, especially those from the planning unit who had participated in the system's development. This group would meet monthly as a steering committee for the overall refinement and implementation of the strategy; membership cut across lines in the hierarchy and functional divisions in an ad hoc way, determined by the issue instead of ongoing responsibilities. Bosses and subordinates from several divisions became equal participants in the discussions. The commissioner would chair the group, and one consultant would facilitate the group's process.

A parallel process is typically employed to protect innovation from routine and often involves an elite group of staffers. At DJJ, however, a principal aim was to push busy line managers toward an ongoing focus on the strategic. In contrast to having two groups—innovative staffers in an ad hoc group versus those minding the store—the membership and mission of the strategy group created integrating pressure in participants as they struggled to link their daily preoccupations with the overall strategy.

The group proved to be enormously successful. It set deadlines for work between sessions, became a forum for others to comment on work in progress, and, most important, enabled participants to be psychologically connected to the overall strategy. Schall felt that it provided sustained pressure on line executives to think about longer-term issues. Early sessions balanced the pressure to fix immediate problems and the desire to make a difference in the long term. Furthermore, because the group was larger than the commissioner's direct reports, more people experienced her personal leadership.

In subsequent reflections on the group, people noted that during their meetings they felt less fragmented and were recharged by seeing the bigger picture, as opposed to being overcome with daily crises. Some would mistakenly refer to a previous month's meeting as having occurred "last week," indicating the sessions had a vividness that was kept alive. People felt their thinking was respected in this setting, more so than in their daily work.

In early meetings, despite the rich group discussion, the authority for the work was often felt to belong predominantly to the commissioner. At a process level, for example, she often felt that only she worried about keeping the time boundaries. She frequently had to track assigned tasks to get them submitted on schedule, as if the counterstructural feature of the group undercut its authority to set work for its members directly without invoking the commissioner's power.

Over the months, however, members became more responsible for managing the time boundaries and assumed many of the process-commenting roles that previously had belonged exclusively to consultants. After half a year of meetings, the commissioner summarized progress this way:

> It's getting easier for the group to be critical (fewer apologies, people less tentative), but cross-unit discussions are still hard. . . . We need to balance the "let's get it done" instinct with the need to put enough work in up front so we maximize our chances to actually do something and to do it well. . . . I still feel the rush of the meeting. The two hours flew by for me. . . . We have a lot to be proud of and to celebrate both strategically and operationally.

As her comments indicate, this had become a sophisticated work group in which members could confront one another, reflect on the process, balance the need to think with the need to act, and keep work in parts of the organization linked to the overall vision. But these emerging competencies were much more alive in the strategy group than in the organization's regular meetings. In the late fall of 1984, it was increasingly felt that problems about both preparation and follow-up remained. In the spring of 1985, these problems were being resolved, with much of the advance work linked to an off-site retreat (parallel process) that gave the staff a full opportunity to think about the many issues that the new case-management approach posed. During the retreat, many of the policy issues reached closure.

At this retreat, the second that the agency had taken, several levels of top management met in a variety of configurations. Schall considered the second retreat much less of a "high," less magical than the first, which the consultants attributed to the increased ability of the organization to do this kind of thinking within the regular structure. As a result, the difference between the real work and the retreat was reduced.

After the retreat, the strategy group's dominant task began to shift from developing and elaborating the case-management theme to executing the decisions that had been reached about how each unit would incorporate the strategy. In discussions with her consultants, Schall began to see a relationship between the vitality in the strategy group and the deadness in her staff meetings with her direct reports. Furthermore, she felt the necessity shift from developing the plan to the next challenge: its implementation. In late May, she made the difficult decision to disband the strategy group and reconstitute the forums through which she led the agency. She presented her decision to the staff with the following memo:

> When we embarked on this change process here at DJJ, I felt it necessary to create what was in effect a parallel organization to accompany the existing chain of command in order to develop the change and get some consensus on it. . . . Due to what I see as the developing strength of the existing administrative units, I believe the agency is in a different stage now and that it is time to merge the change and development efforts into the standing lines of authority and delegation. . . . At this point using the parallel organization seems to me to be a disservice to the organization because it tends to diminish the standing lines of communication and the ongoing role of delegation between lines and levels. . . . The senior staff, the strategy group and the current management staff meetings will cease to exist. There will be a final senior staff meeting on May 16 and a final strategy group meeting on May 30.

Appended to the memo were the memberships of each of the new groups, all of which were designed with much more respect to the hierarchy. For example, the strategy group had contained many boss-subordinate pairs that implicitly attacked the unit leaders' ability to present upward the concern of their units and downward the agency leader's concerns. The executive staff now consisted of the top staff of the major units and the corporation counsel. It met weekly and was charged with overall policy direction of the agency. The senior management group was the executive staff, plus each of their direct reports. They met monthly with the charge to work on interdivisional issues.

The decision to disband was taken unilaterally because Schall did not think people would willingly give up the strategy group. Thus its final meeting was framed not as a discussion of the new system, but as an occasion to look back on the experience and look ahead to how it might help them. A summary of the discussion follows:

> Schall explained her shift as "putting energy into the existing lines of authority . . . [and] more forthrightly facing the issues of delegation, authority, and representation versus having thoughtful people attend regardless of position."
>
> One staffer, a subordinate of the institutional director, noted that this made sense to him. "I sometimes felt like I double dipped. . . . I could work an issue with my immediate boss and get a second chance when it came up in strategy group; now policy will be set above and we will be more implementation focused." However, he acknowledged that the value was in getting to know many of his colleagues in other locations. Another noted it has served to get operating managers to take in strategy as part of their work.
>
> One expressed real regret, that he would have welcomed it being killed early in its life when it was struggling to develop, but now he felt it was needed. This was a definite place to talk about issues. It had been the vehicle of people really seeing his function differently.
>
> Another executive reassured him that he was in her mind when she made decisions about aspects of her work that had interdependencies with his unit. "We have started things here but the group does not have to continue for us to keep this up. We have internalized it now."
>
> One executive noted, "This group has helped me grow professionally and with my staff. I will carry that throughout my career."

The meeting ended with an appropriate mix of sadness and gratitude for the opportunity it had afforded to shape the agenda. People respected Schall's courage to end something when it was successful instead of having it outlive its usefulness.

The value of the decision was soon realized because it established much greater accountability in the direct lines of authority. Also, once division heads felt pressure to implement the plan and be accountable for it, they focused more on ensuring that the right talent was in place. Several of the division executives made important changes in their own teams. As the commissioner took a risk of including some and excluding others and affirming those who were her direct staff, they in turn seemed to feel her support and thereby became more potent with their own staffs.

The corporation counsel particularly responded to the new set of forums. She was the most long-tenured executive—employed there since the agency's beginning. Despite requests from the new commissioner that she take a larger role than just legal counsel, she had seemed to stay close to her technical role during the early years. Almost immediately after being chosen to be on the reconstituted executive staff, she dramatically expanded her scope, often making valuable contributions on the wide range of issues that the top staff had to address.

This case represents a developmental use of parallel processes as scaffolding to support new thinking, new strategies, and new behaviors necessary to realize the new mission. The off-site retreats were particularly valuable in protecting participants from the crush of daily problems and allowing them to think about a new mission. Yet the results of such work do not easily redirect a "dynamically conservative" large organization that is often able to be creative and innovative in the service of preserving that status quo.[18] Therefore, the commissioner used one-day workshops to refine a strategy, and when still encountering difficulties in sustaining a strategic focus, she created the transitional vehicle of the strategy group. This served as an in-between space that did not let line executives off the hook in developing the plan, as if it would or should magically come from above or from the planning unit staff. Line middle managers could not blame "them" for an unrealistic plan nor could "they" (the planners and top managers) wash their hands of the difficult implementation and follow-through issues.

Conclusion

Many of the trends that surround organizations today—empowerment, entrepreneurialism, participation—suggest real developmental difficulties

18. Schön (1971).

in the vertical relationships. In research conducted for the 3M corporation, we discovered that regular boss-subordinate meetings were the most hated, especially when compared with ad hoc task forces.[19] We suspect that one of the reasons is the difficulty that people often experience in collaborating with an authority figure.[20] In one site that had recently both implemented a major quality initiative and created a parallel council for working on issues of collaboration, a supervisor poignantly commented, "When I want to get an idea to my boss, my best strategy is to plant it with an operator who will then talk with my boss when he is 'managing by walking around,' or I will ask the operator to bring it up at one of the council meetings." This reflection vividly illustrates the interaction of the two systems and how vertical relationships can be undercut by parallel processes. Ultimately, the management machinery becomes toxic and is no longer viewed as value adding. An extreme case came to our attention in work with a factory that was attempting to change its culture and in particular the role of the first-line supervisors. One of the issues that had surfaced was the implementation of "just in time" (JIT) in the manufacturing process. The plant manager began to express his thoughts on JIT at an off-site workshop with supervisors.

> Just in time manufacturing, which I like to call common sense manufacturing, is not just a fad. Whenever I see the latest corporate hot button being pushed, I want to reach for the barf bag. We cannot treat this as a fad. You will notice that I am not asking for biweekly reports on which lines have implemented JIT, or putting it into your performance plans. How can you argue with a system that has shorter intervals, puts less product at risk, gives higher yield? It's got to be yours, it has to be self-generating, self-motivating.

His statement seems remarkable. He is saying that, because JIT is so important, he cannot use the machinery of management to drive its implementation. If he did use this machinery, people might mistake it for yet another corporate fad. Therefore, the only way he can show how seriously he is committed to the concept is to not push for it.

What does this extreme example suggest? In the wider environment, the splitting of leadership and management has led to a conception of leader as cheerleader—setting a vision, exhorting the troops, celebrating,

19. Oppenheim (1989).
20. Krantz (1989).

aligning, attuning—with less attention to the exercise of authority to control or direct subordinates' behavior. The dark side of leading is termed "management" and is laden with contempt—as if it means only bureaucratic systems that arbitrarily interfere with people's creativity and spontaneity. Management systems are presumed to have the potential to kill good ideas or turn them into fads or purposeless bureaucratic initiatives. It thus follows that an organization's capacity to involve people can be preserved only by keeping them outside of the formal authority systems, as if one cannot be committed and be a follower.

Fads are usually worrisome. Ideas are often carried in special units, while the real work continues uninfluenced by the trendy training or quality circles that are uncoupled to the line organization. Equally dysfunctional is to have the reverse situation: parallel processes being used to bypass, not to work through, the difficulties that a particular organization is facing. Many instances exist of the use of parallel process in this mode:

—Detouring a conflict that a boss did not want to address directly into a quality improvement team, with the double cost of politicizing the team's methods and letting the boss manage by indirection.

—Assigning issues (in this case morale and motivation) that are fundamentally the concern of the line executives to a cross-cut team, thereby enabling the line managers to feel less pressure to worry about the issue because others are working on it; yet the real levers for intervening lie in the vertical organization.

—Creating a permanent parallel structure for line executives to be trainers of their colleagues in areas of planning, time management, negotiation; as a consequence, people who increasingly hated their regular work could escape periodically to this pleasant oasis, without ever having to take responsibility for their inability to use what they were teaching in the running of their own units.

—Creating improvement teams that are highly satisfying to their members because people feel listened to and potent in contrast to their usual roles, in which they feel disregarded and overcontrolled.

In thinking about parallel processes developmentally, the challenge is to use them transitionally, as scaffolding, enabling some new relationships to come into being that will allow the dismantling of the supports and transition to ongoing structure and processes. The appropriate frame of reference is a life cycle, with the significant opportunities for intervention around its initial formation, its leadership, its membership, the boundaries, the relationships to the vertical structure, and, most critically, its ending.

The use of parallel processes as scaffolding resembles the phenomena that British child psychologist D. W. Winnicott conceptualizes as "transitional objects" in child development.[21] Early possessions of an infant are imbued with a specialness that enables a child to make a complicated transition such as going to sleep, leaving a parent, beginning school, losing a pet, and changing homes. Transitional objects and spaces support working through differences and similarities and, therefore, enable someone to manage change from one state to another while experiencing sufficient continuity. One feature of a transitional object is that the child has greater control over it than the wider environment and can experiment safely with it. Winnecott notes that ultimately the intense feelings associated with the transitional phenomena, when worked through healthily, become suffused over the wider environment.

In this way, the sequence of parallel processes at DJJ supported key participants in working through a complex change, beginning with a new mission, followed by strategy, and ultimately linking new behaviors back into the ongoing organizational routines. The disbanding of the strategy group at the right moment in its life cycle enabled people to spread the new insights over the wider structure. As one member said, "The group does not have to continue for us to keep this up. We have internalized it now."

At one point early on in the new executive staff meeting, after the disbanding of the strategy group, Schall, the leader, raised the question of whether the group might want to meet without her on some occasions. A thoughtful subordinate noted, "What we need is to learn to work together with you and not without you." This is one of the central issues in the development of innovation in the public sector: to marry thinking and authority.

If a developmental theory of process innovation cannot be created that integrates parallel and vertical processes, and if the ad hoc versus the ongoing is overvalued, three risks are run:

1. A self-fulfilling prophecy will be created. Because no expectations exist of the regular organization, it will fail to perform and thus be further delegitimatized.

2. The existing, formal organization will too easily be blamed for the failure of innovative ideas to get implemented, furthering a vicious cycle

---

21. Winnicott (1971); and Davis and Wallbridge (1981, pp. 58–61).

in which leaders will increase their use of parallel processes and decrease legitimation of the regular structure.

3. Many of the powerful tools of ongoing management—delegation, appraisal, reward and punishments, control systems—will be forgone in bringing into being new, more responsive, more effective organizations.

References

Bushe, Gervese R., and A. B. Shani. 1991. *Parallel Learning Structures: Increasing Innovations in Bureaucracies.* Reading, Mass.: Addison-Wesley.

Davis, Madeline, and David Wallbridge. 1981. *Boundary and Space: An Introduction to the Work of D. W. Winnicott.* New York: Brunner/Mazel.

Friedman, Lee. 1976. "The Evolution of a Bail Reform." *Policy Sciences,* vol. 7, no. 3 (September): 281–313.

Gilmore, Thomas N. 1988. *Making a Leadership Change: How Organizations and Leaders Can Handle Leadership Transitions Successfully.* Jossey-Bass.

Gilmore, Thomas N., and Ellen Schall. 1986. "The Use of Case Management as a Revitalizing Theme in a Juvenile Justice Agency." *Public Administration Review,* vol. 46, no. 3 (May/June): 267–74.

Heclo, Hugh. 1977. *A Government of Strangers: Executive Politics in Washington.* Brookings.

Herrick, Neal. 1985. "Parallel Organizations in Unionized Settings: Implications for Organizational Research." *Human Relations,* vol. 38, no. 10 (October): 963–81.

Jaques, Elliott. 1990. "In Praise of Hierarchy." *Harvard Business Review,* vol. 68, no. 1 (January/February): 127–33.

Kazanjian, Robert K., and Robert Drazin. 1986. "Implementing Manufacturing Innovations: Critical Choices of Structure and Staffing Roles." *Human Resource Management,* vol. 25, no. 3 (Fall): 385–403.

Kidder, Tracy. 1981. *The Soul of a New Machine.* Little, Brown.

Krantz, James. 1989. "The Managerial Couple: Superior-Subordinate Relationships as a Unit of Analysis." *Human Resource Management,* vol. 28, no. 2 (Summer): 161–75.

Krantz, James, and Thomas N. Gilmore. 1990. "The Splitting of Leadership and Management as a Social Defense." *Human Relations,* vol. 43, no. 2 (February): 183–204.

Lynn, Laurence E., and John M. Seidl. 1977. " 'Bottom-Line' Management for Public Agencies." *Harvard Business Review,* vol. 55, no. 1 (January/February): 144–53.

Miller, Eric J. 1983. "Work and Creativity." Occasional Paper. London: Tavistock Institute of Human Relations.

Moore, Mark H. 1987. "Gordon Chase and the Public Sector Innovation." Harvard University, John F. Kennedy School of Government.

National Academy of Public Administration. 1985. *Leadership in Jeopardy: The Fraying of the Presidential Appointments System.* Washington, D.C.: National Academy of Public Administration.

Oncken, William, Jr., and Donald L. Wass. 1974. "Management Time— Who's Got the Monkey?" *Harvard Business Review,* vol. 52, no. 6 (November/December): 75–80.

Oppenheim, Lynn. 1989. "Meeting as a Control System," Working Paper. Philadelphia, Pa.: Center for Applied Research.

Peters, Thomas J., and Robert H. Waterman. 1982. *In Search of Excellence: Lessons from America's Best-Run Companies.* Harper and Row.

Schön, Donald A. 1971. *Beyond the Stable State: Public and Private Learning in a Changing Society.* Random House.

Stein, Barry, and Rosabeth Moss Kanter. 1980. "Building the Parallel Organization: Creating Mechanisms for Permanent Quality of Work Life." *Journal of Applied Behavioral Science,* vol. 16, no. 3: 371–88.

Ware, James. 1977. *Managing a Task Force.* Harvard Business School Publishing.

Winnicott, D. W. 1971. *Playing and Reality.* Basic Books.

Vickers, Sir Geoffrey. 1965. *The Art of Judgement.* Basic Books.

CHAPTER FOURTEEN

Replication:
Adapt or Fail

Paul Berman and Beryl Nelson

IN OUR SCIENTIFIC and technological age, we dream of models and technologies that, once invented and proved successful in one place, can be replicated in many others. Over the past decades, particularly since World War II, governments, foundations, and international organizations have spent countless millions trying to make this dream come true.

The results, however, have often been disappointing. Efforts to replicate the use of technologies or land-use practices in developing countries has been discouraging.[1] Similarly disappointing is the history in the United States of many Great Society programs in housing, social services, and welfare.[2]

But disappointment has also come from another source: "imperfect replication"; that is, the failure of practices at an adopting site to be faithful to the design of the original model. The sponsors of an effort to reproduce an innovative program typically expect the replications to adhere to the original model. When the replicated program emerges looking different, many conclude that the undertaking has been a failure. Moreover, when a replication fails to perfectly copy the original program, it is not unusual for the sponsors and their evaluators to find fault with the implementors, not with their own concept of replication.

---

1. Merrill-Sands (1986); and Salomon (1993).
2. Pressman and Wildavsky (1979); and Rivlin (1971).

This problem is common in many policy areas. The uncertain spread of democracy and market economies to newly noncommunist countries shows not fidelity to the originating models, but something different— where positive change has taken place, the original models have been adapted to meet the realities of the situation.[3] Moreover, this widespread failure of replication is most pronounced in those areas where the models being implemented involve significant change of complex human organizations or patterns of behavior.[4]

Yet the evidence suggests an important hypothesis about the replication of innovation: no adaptation, no success. This adaptation hypothesis has important implications for both organizations promoting replications and those seeking to adopt successful models.

Models and Well-Implemented Programs

Some evidence supporting this hypothesis can be found in a study of California elementary schools that employed different models for educating students with limited English proficiency.[5] Fifteen schools that reportedly had exemplary programs for limited English proficient (LEP) students were intensively studied over a two-year period using qualitative and quantitative methods. A comprehensive selection process began with nearly 200 schools that were nominated as possible exemplars of one of five models for educating LEP students; this pool was winnowed down to fifteen case study sites with programs that the researchers concluded were well-implemented and competently delivered examples of the models. In addition to intensive interviews at the sites and the collection of data on student test results and program costs, the research team observed forty-five classrooms at different grade levels across the fifteen sites and five models. The study's methodology allowed for analysis of replication comparatively across the models and also in detail at the operational level. Examined were teacher-student and student-student interactions, practices within classrooms, school-level activities, and school-district procedures. This research thus provides some concrete evidence about replication and the adaptation hypothesis.

3. Berman (1974).
4. Berman and McLaughlin (1978); Pressman and Wildavsky (1979); and Timar and Kirp (1988).
5. Berman and others (1992).

The five models for educating LEP children—each based on research on second-language acquisition—had been approved for school district implementation by the California Department of Education. Three of these models rely on using students' native language to develop their use of language, teach content, and make the transition to classes taught only in English:

— Bilingual Late Exit, in which pupils are expected to achieve literacy in their native language as a means for accomplishing transition into mainstream classes taught in English;

— Bilingual Early Exit, in which pupils are not expected to become literate in their native language but have basic language development in their native language and make an early transition to mainstream classes taught in English; and

— Double Immersion (also called Dual Immersion or Two-Way Bilingual), in which English-speaking students and LEP students are instructed in both English and the language of the LEP students with the goal of bilingual literacy for both groups.[6]

The two other models do not utilize instruction in the students' native (non-English) language:

— English as a Second Language (ESL), or ESL Pull-Out, in which LEP students are taught to become proficient in English in pull-out classes but otherwise take content classes in English with English-speaking children; and

— Sheltered English, in which both content instruction and ESL instruction are provided in a self-contained classroom with only LEP students, and teachers use a simplified form of English and modify teaching techniques to make all-English instruction comprehensible.

Four of these five models have been implemented by a number of California school districts for many years. The fifth model—Sheltered English—is a relatively new one that schools began to implement only a few years before our study. The main elements and purposes of these models are summarized in table 14-1.

The California Department of Education allows schools throughout the state—including the fifteen sample schools—to select the model that best suits their LEP population, their resources, and their community. The department strongly recommends the use of the native language of LEP students when feasible, but it also allows districts to implement

6. English as a Second Language instruction is a feature of the three models that rely on the use of the student's native language. Typically, ESL instruction is part of instruction in the regular classroom.

Table 14-1. *Theoretical LEP Model Characteristics*

Feature	Bilingual Late Exit	Bilingual Early Exit	Double Immersion	ESL Pull–Out	Sheltered English
Use of native language	Yes	Yes	Yes	No	No
Goal of bilingualism	Yes	No	Yes	No	No
Special instruction in English as a subject	Yes	Yes	Yes	Yes	Yes
English taught in teaching other subjects	Yes	Yes	Yes	No	Yes
Nonlanguage subjects taught in native language	Yes	Yes	Yes and no	No	No

Note: LEP = limited English proficient; ESL = English as a second language.

other models when demographic or other conditions make implementing bilingual programs impractical.[7]

During the study's first year, we conducted an extensive search for exemplary programs for LEP students that could be categorized into the five models. This process involved discussions with knowledgeable people throughout California to gather nominations of schools with exemplary practices. These discussions were followed by phone interviews with staff at nominated schools and visits to some possible nominees to determine the extent to which they had implemented competently a particular program model for educating LEP students or had developed a well-executed model regardless of whether it fit our categories. Schools were sought that met the minimum criteria of program coherence and adequate resources necessary to competently implement a program for LEP students. Most schools in the initial pool of two hundred were eliminated on the basis of their failure to meet one or more of these criteria. For example, schools were eliminated in which the program's responsible individuals could not describe a coherent set of practices associated with a model; the program was in turmoil because of demographic, budgetary, personnel, or political circumstances; the program was not staffed by teachers holding an appropriate credential; or instruction was delivered solely by aides.[8]

7. California Department of Education (1990).

8. The California Department of Education requires that teachers for LEP students hold appropriate credentials or that the district obtain waivers based on the premise that teachers are participating in training. In the case of programs using the student's native language, teachers are required to hold a bilingual credential. For programs taught in English, the state has developed the Language Development Specialist credential.

That most programs nominated as exemplary were not being well implemented (as defined for the study) should not be surprising. The research literature on implementation consistently has found similar results: Most organizations fail to implement their programs competently, regardless of the model they adopt. Consequently, most replications of any model are likely to be stillborn because of factors that have little to do with the model itself.[9]

The implications for replication are profound. The purpose of replicating successful models is often to assist organizations, be they countries or schools, that are in need of change. However, those organizations that start out most capable are most likely to innovate successfully.[10] Capable organizations are likely to get better, whereas more needy, low-capacity organizations are, ironically, least able to implement models that might help them get better. Thus a prerequisite of effective replication is often the enhancement of the capacity of the potential replicators.

Design and Adaptation

For a school seeking to educate its LEP students, the choice of a model to replicate is the first decision that starts a design process. It is also the beginning of the adaptation of the model to the local reality of a district and school.

The design of programs for LEP students took on a life of its own, sometimes only distantly related to the adopted model. A wide variety of approaches were observed in the field sites even though the models being used could be roughly classified into the five categories. As part of the adaptation of a model, districts and schools had to define such programmatic characteristics as how the program integrated LEP students with English-only (EO) students or Fluent English Proficient (FEP) students; whether preschool was included; how the curriculum and instructional aspects of the program were to work; and how the students' native language, ESL, and classroom aides were used.

Schools that followed the same basic model often made different choices in the details of their program design. For example, the ESL Pull-Out model is based on the concept that students learn their content material in math, science, writing, and so on in English and have special

9. Murphy (1971); and Pressman and Wildavsky (1979).
10. Berman and McLaughlin (1978); and Furman, Clune, and Elmore (1991).

language instruction in content-free pull-out classes to learn English. However, one of the schools in the sample, the Maple School, added to its ESL Pull-Out programs multiple pull-out classes where the students' native languages were used to provide content instruction.[11] In some respects, this design modification violated a defining characteristic of the original model itself—that all content instruction be in English. Maple School not only operated differently from other ESL programs within the same school district, but it also, in effect, invented a new model.

Similarly, the Sheltered English model is designed to provide instruction in simplified English using specialized strategies and clarifications in the students' native language. Sheltered English is typically implemented in a self-contained classroom with only LEP students. At Ash School, with 54 percent LEP students, the Sheltered English program had been adapted to include ungraded ESL instruction, with students regrouped for social studies in their native language and grouped again for the remainder of their instruction in Sheltered English. Furthermore, Ash LEP students mix with English-only students for art, music, and physical education. As at Maple School, Ash School's program in some ways violated the Sheltered English model.

One might conjecture that these five education models were loose and ill-defined and, therefore, that schools had to flesh out the models to produce a real program. This explanation is partially valid, yet some of the models were specific. Nevertheless, even in these cases, the models were employed differently at different exemplary schools within the same district. For example, we visited schools that were implementing the Eastman model of Bilingual Late Exit; this approach had been developed over many years and had an extensive literature including training guides.[12] But the study found wide variations in the use of this model, even within the same district.

Adaptations from a basic model come not from the looseness of a model's concepts but from the willingness of local people to respond to local needs. Each school faces a different reality. It must mold a model to its own conditions. In designing its own program-in-practice, a school's choices are affected (as illustrated in figure 14-1) by two major conditions: sociopolitical circumstances (over which schools have little control) and organizational factors (which they can influence).

---

11. Schools in our sample were renamed to protect their anonymity.
12. Krashen (1985); and Los Angeles Unified School District (1987).

Figure 14-1. *Multiple Factors Affecting Replication*

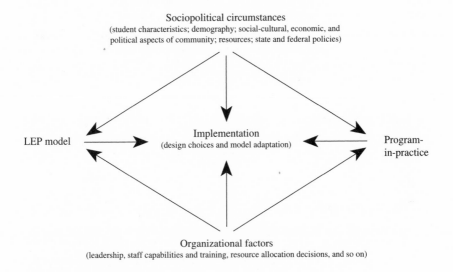

Note: LEP = limited English proficient.

The most relevant sociopolitical circumstances were demographic: the number of native languages; the proportion of LEP students in the district or school; and the stability of demographic conditions over time. In the Maple School's ESL Pull-Out program, its design alteration (using the students' native languages for content instruction) was a response to three demographic conditions: a relatively small percentage of LEP students, the many different native languages spoken at the school, and the continuous influx of immigrant students across the grade levels. These conditions influenced the local adaptation of the basic ESL Pull-Out design. Similarly, the Ash School implemented Sheltered English in response to a shift in the school's population from a single dominant non-English language to multiple languages without one language dominating. Resources, including both the availability of experienced teachers and money, also played a major role in how this and other schools designed their programs.

Thus exemplary schools started with a basic model and adapted it to create a program-in-practice that reflected local sociopolitical circumstances. They did not seek pure fidelity to the original models. Had they not adapted the models, these schools probably would have failed to develop effective programs.

Funders and evaluators thus beware. The sign of a healthy replication may be its departure from the original model. Therefore, evaluations that judge a program's success by its fidelity to a prescribed design may be creating mischief: The adopting site may think it must adhere to the prescription, even though to do so might be inappropriate. Evaluation should focus on results, not fidelity to a particular model. Three years are often needed for complex change to demonstrate improved outcomes. Therefore, evaluations should examine outcomes after initial adaptation and implementation has occurred, which is after about three years, and program funders should accept the need for programs-in-practice to adapt their design and work their own processes.

Mutual Adaptation

Design decisions are the first sources of adaptation, but they are only the beginning of an extended and continuous process. In the case of programs for LEP students, basic design decisions affecting the choice of the model and the parameters under which it would operate tended to be made by administrators at the district level or at the school level with district consent. Uncontrollable sociopolitical circumstances had a major impact on these decisions. After the basic design of the program had been set, however, staff at the school level made additional critical decisions when they put the model into practice. Moreover, teachers themselves made individual choices in their classrooms that also determined the reality of programs for LEP students. Thus, during implementation, exemplary programs evolved to meet changing conditions; they were shaped, crafted, revised, and renewed.

As suggested by the information in figure 14-1, after a model has been selected and designed, a cluster of organizational factors affect implementation. Regardless of the model selected, new programs must fit into overall organizational operations, and organizations accordingly must make choices about how the program should operate in their social and cultural context. Replication failures typically ignore the organizational context in one or more of three ways:

— They assume the context does not matter;

— They attempt to override organizational barriers by insisting on fidelity to the model; or

— They try to implement a program that runs parallel to the standard activities in the organization.

These efforts are unlikely to work or last, except if they are marginal activities that matter little to the core of the organization.

Replication activities that aim to change the host organization fundamentally, not marginally, must plan how the model can be adapted to the organization during implementation—and vice versa. That is, the organization itself must adapt to the demands of the model. This hypothesis about "mutual adaptation" emerges clearly whenever field research has closely examined the process of change.

During implementation of the exemplary LEP programs, faculty collaborated to ensure that students received coordinated lessons and a sequenced curriculum. Linking curriculum and instructional methods across classrooms and across grade levels was an important aspect of each of the programs-in-practice, though this collaboration took distinctly different forms. Some faculty developed team teaching, sharing lesson plans, assignments, and instruction; at other schools, faculty had regular and frequent coordination meetings but did not share assignments or instruction. Thus these schools had contrasting programs-in-practice—classes jointly conducted by a team of teachers or classes taught traditionally by a single teacher. As much variation was found in collaboration within models as among models. About a third of the fifteen schools employed team teaching, about third did not, and the other sites fell in between.

Why is it that some schools, when faced with the need to coordinate their curriculum, developed team teaching, regardless of model, and others did not? The answer is found not in the imperatives of the models but in organizational factors such as leadership, staff willingness to innovate, and so on. Those schools that developed team teaching adapted their practices to the needs of the program and vice versa.

Another example of schools displaying a pedagogical approach not implied by the model was the development of an preschool program. Each of the fifteen schools in the sample had an LEP program beginning at kindergarten. Some of the schools, however, had developed a preschool program that specifically targeted their LEP population. In each such case, the preschool program employed the instructional approach that had been adopted by the school. For elementary schools using models that relied on instruction in the students' native language, the preschool program also used the students' native language in similar ways. For example, if a kindergarten conducted 80 percent of its instruction in the student's native language, the preschool program would employ a similar ratio. (As with team teaching, the presence of a preschool did not correspond to models. Preschool programs were distributed across four of the five models.)

Significantly, the student outcomes for various exemplary schools appeared to depend less on the model adopted and more on the extent to which the schools practiced team teaching or created a preschool program. Similar conclusions can be reached about other crucial pedagogic dimensions of these exemplary programs-in-practice.

This suggests an important lesson about replication: If the outcomes of a replication depend more on adaptations during implementation than on the original model, evaluators should make exceedingly modest claims about the power of the model to cause positive results when applied to new sites. Much can be learned from studying replications that produce successful outcomes. Perhaps the most important lessons concern how adaptations occur and what organizational factors are likely to foster adaptations with effective outcomes.

Moreover, adaptation cannot stop with the full implementation of the program. In education, and in other policy areas, outside forces simply refuse to remain static. For example, California is in the midst of a profound demographic upheaval. During the 1980s, fueled by high birth rates and by immigration, the state's population grew 26 percent, faster than any other state in the nation. The 1990 Census counted six million foreign-born individuals residing in California. The public schools have been affected as these newcomers from every continent and from dozens of different cultural and language groups have joined an already diverse population. And the composition of LEP children in a school can change from year to year or even within a school year.

Most of the fifteen exemplary schools faced unpredictable change. Using one model and its own particular demographic circumstances, a school might design a LEP program, but then it would have to constantly adapt this design to new circumstances: unanticipated waves of students speaking languages not previously spoken at the schools; a desegregation order that altered the transportation patterns; or many other alterations in the fundamental conditions for which the original model had been selected and the program had been designed. Imagine what it must be like to have developed a bilingual program for Spanish-speaking students and then to have to use this model for a new crop of students who speak Armenian and Farsi.

Schools thus adapted their program over time. Five years after a model was selected, the program-in-practice often deviated remarkably from its progenitor.

Implications for Replication

The adoption of a model is a remarkably fluid process. The dream of easy and cost-saving replications of major public policy innovations remains just that—a dream. Instead of saving people from reinventing the wheel, the programs for LEP students illustrate that successful organizations invent their own adaptations, and the resulting programs-in-practice may be new creations. The argument is not that replication is not possible. In California, our analysis reveals, fifteen exemplary sites were able to successfully adapt and replicate models for teaching English to LEP students. Each of these sites identified a model that held promise for its situation; each was able to learn from the experience of other schools and districts that had previously implemented the model. Nevertheless, the exemplary sites found that the models as specified needed to be tailored to fit their sociopolitical circumstances and organizational factors. The California Department of Education's requirements were not interpreted at the local level to require that sites slavishly follow the models. Exemplary programs in our sample concluded that they could tailor the models in ways that made sense in their demographic, organizational, and political context.

The most important replications in the public sector are those that involve the need for a public organization to change to become more effective. A model that has produced desirable outcomes in some location by changing the organization is likely to require organizational change in another setting. The reasons that a model produces successful outcomes in its originating location inevitably includes factors beyond the characteristics of the model itself. Knowing that a model produces desirable outcomes in one location is not the same as knowing what makes that model work. Would-be replicators have stumbled in the past by not taking into account all of the sources for success in the originating site. In their attempts to export their model, many have ignored precisely the impact of those contextual and organizational elements that contribute to the model's effectiveness.

Many replications that require significant change fail to be effective because the replicating organizations lack the critical capability to adapt. These organizations need change the most; yet these are the organizations that are least able to implement models that require change. Unless they undergo the systemic, personnel, or structural change necessary to improve their capability, they are not ripe for attempting serious replication.

Moreover, nothing works well in all places at all times. Before initiating a replication, an organization needs to assess its own circumstances and capabilities. Then effective public organizations "redesign" models to adapt them to their sociopolitical circumstances and organizational factors. Therefore, replicators should carefully determine the conditions under which models seem best suited and consider what redesigns might be applicable to match their setting.

Successful implementation is a multilevel process that occurs over time with many different actors making decisions relevant to their own, particular context. The process is an iterative one with each decision creating new issues, new requirements, and new practices. A program-in-practice emerges from the implementation process, and the practices are distinct from the originating model. To produce the desired outcomes, funders must allow replicators the flexibility to adapt the model during implementation. Organizational factors determine what adaptations emerge and how effective they will be. The most help a sponsor of a replication can be for the continuing vitality and successful fruition of a change effort is to provide support and continuing assistance during the three-or-more-year period that it takes for a program to be adapted to the organization and for the organization to be adapted to the program.

The time has come to discard the technological notion of replication. Rather than a model being implemented with fidelity, replication in a public organization in need of change should be seen as a stimulus for a process of adaptation whose results, though unpredictable, are most likely to produce effective outcomes.

References

Berman, Paul. 1974. *Revolutionary Organization: Institution Building in the People's Liberation Armed Forces*. Lexington, Mass.: D. C. Heath.

Berman, Paul, and Milbrey Wallin McLaughlin. 1978. *Federal Programs Supporting Educational Change*, vol. 8: *Implementing and Sustaining Innovation*. Santa Monica, Calif.: Rand Corporation.

Berman, Paul, and others. 1992. *Meeting the Challenge of Language Diversity*, vol. 1: *Summary*, vol. 2: *Findings and Conclusions*, vol. 3: *Case Study Appendix*. Berkeley, Calif.: BW Associates.

California Department of Education, Bilingual Education Office. 1990. *Bilingual Education Handbook: Designing Instruction for LEP Stu-*

dents. Sacramento, Calif.: California Department of Education.

Furman, Susan, William Clune, and Richard Elmore. 1991. "Research on Education Reform: Lessons on the Implementation of Policy." In *Education Policy Implementation,* edited by Allan R. Odden. State University of New York Press.

Krashen, Stephen D. 1985. *The Input Hypothesis: Issues and Implications.* New York: Longman.

Los Angeles Unified School District. 1987. *Eastman Curriculum Project, Training Handbook.*

Merrill-Sands, Deborah. 1986. *The Technology Applications Gap: Overcoming Constraints to Small-Farm Development.* Rome: Food and Agriculture Organization of the United Nations.

Murphy, Jerome T. 1971. "Title I of ESEA: The Politics of Implementing Federal Educational Reform." *Harvard Educational Review,* vol. 41 (February).

Pressman, Jeffrey L., and Aaron Wildavsky. 1979. *Implementation: How Great Expectations in Washington Are Dashed in Oakland: Or, Why It's Amazing That Federal Programs Work at All, This Being a Saga of the Economic Development Administraton as Told by Two Sympathetic Observers Who Seek to Build Morals on a Foundation of Ruined Hopes,* 2d ed. University of California Press.

Rivlin, Alice M. 1971. *Systematic Thinking for Social Action.* Brookings.

Salomon, Jean Jacques. 1993. *Mirages of Development: Science and Technology for the Third Worlds.* Boulder, Colo.: L. Rienner.

Timar, Thomas B., and David L. Kirp. 1988. *Managing Educational Excellence.* New York: Falmer Press.

CHAPTER FIFTEEN

Public Sector Innovations and Their Diffusion:
Economic Tools and Managerial Tasks

Lee S. Friedman

THIS CHAPTER is about public sector effectiveness. The focus is on the management of innovations and their diffusion, and how this affects the value of public services delivered. Three major themes guide the analysis: (1) the importance of the details of operating procedures and organizational settings, (2) the economic tools available to link these detailed choices to their effectiveness consequences, and (3) the managerial challenge to maintain or improve the success of an innovation when adapting it to suit a particular locality. These themes are illustrated via an examination of the diffusion and effectiveness of pretrial release units in local criminal justice systems throughout the United States.

For at least the past half-century, critics of bail in the criminal justice system have argued that the bail process results in unnecessary pretrial detainment of the poor. In practice, it operates much like a market system for the buying and selling of pretrial freedom. An arrested individual will be detained unless he or she chooses to purchase pretrial release. The price of release is set by a judge or magistrate, who determines a bond amount to be posted with the court. Defendants may post bond with their own resources, or they may apply for a loan in specialized capital

A preliminary version of this paper was prepared for the Innovations Workshop, a conference held at the University of California at Berkeley, April 29–31, 1992. I would like to thank Eugene Bardach, John Ellwood, Mark Moore, Michael O'Hare, and Ronnie Weiner for their helpful comments on an earlier draft.

markets known as the bail bond industry. The bondsmen charge 10 percent of the bond amount as their fee, sometimes supplementing this with collateral requirements.

Two criticisms of this system are especially relevant to the formation of pretrial release agencies. First, the judge or magistrate, in determining the bond amount, does so primarily by the seriousness of the offense charged. William M. Landes presented empirical evidence that no relation exists between seriousness of offense and probability of appearance in court if released.[1] In other words, the information used by the judge is not appropriate to aid in achieving the appearance objective. Second, indigent defendants do not have the resources necessary to purchase their freedom and are, therefore, detained regardless of their probabilities of appearance.

One could imagine the possibility of altering the information that enters into the judicial calculus in such a way that decisionmaking would be improved on both scores: Release criteria could be better related to the probability of appearance, and the criteria might reduce dependence on the accused's own financial resources. In 1960 precisely such an innovation was attempted in New York City—the Manhattan Bail Project, undertaken by the Vera Institute of Justice. The idea behind the project was that individuals with "strong community ties" have a sufficiently high probability of appearing that they could be safely released on their own recognizance (ROR), without any financial incentives.[2]

The innovators designed a simple questionnaire (see figure 15-1), used it to conduct ten-minute interviews with indigent defendants before their bail hearing, and attempted to verify the answers over the telephone by checking with family or friends of the accused. Those with a certain number of verified community ties (for example, length of residence, presence of family, employment history) qualified to be recommended for ROR at the bail hearing. In the initial demonstration, those qualified for ROR recommendation were randomly assigned to an experimental or control group. The experimentals were recommended, while controls had the bail hearing in the ordinary way, with no court knowledge of their participation in the experiment. The court did grant ROR to 59 percent of the experimentals, while only to 16 percent of controls. Of all those RORd by the project's recommendation, only 1.6 percent failed to appear

1. Landes (1974).

2. The development of this innovation, its diffusion across the country, and its effectiveness over time in New York City are discussed in Friedman (1976).

Figure 15-1. *Manhattan Bail Project Point Scoring System*

To be recommended, defendant needs:
1. A New York area address where he can be reached, and
2. A total of 5 points from the following categories:

	Interview	*Verified*
Prior record		
No convictions	1	1
One misdemeanor conviction	0	0
Two misdemeanor or one felony conviction	-1	-1
Three or more misdemeanor or two or more felony convictions	-2	-2
Family ties (In New York area)		
Lives in established family home and visits other family members (immediate family only)	3	3
Lives in established family home (immediate family)	2	2
Employment or school		
Present job 1 year or more, steadily	3	3
Present job 4 months or present and prior 6 months	2	2
Has present job that is still available or unemployed 3 months or less and 9 months or more steady prior job or unemployment compensation or welfare	1	1
Presently in school, attending regularly	3	3
Out of school less than 6 months but employed or in training	2	2
Out of school 3 months or less, unemployed and not in training	1	1
Residence (in New York area steadily)		
1 year at present residence	3	3
1 year at present or last prior residence or 6 months at present residence	2	2
6 months at present and last prior residence or in New York City 5 years or more	1	1
Discretion		
Positive, over 65, attending hospital, appeared on some previous case	+1	+1
Negative—intoxicated—intention to leave jurisdiction	-1	0

TOTAL INTERVIEW POINTS
REC. NOT REC.
INTERVIEW VERIFIED
RECOMMENDED NOT RECOMMENDED

(FTA). The FTA rate for those bailed in New York City at the time was 4 percent, so the project was thought to be enormously successful.

The experiment was then institutionalized in New York City's Office of Probation, while other similar projects diffused to more than one hundred communities across the country, largely through the stimulus of a series of national conferences. Over time in New York, the effectiveness of the reform deteriorated. First, the failure-to-appear rate relative to bail rose dramatically. While the skip rate for those bailed remained at about 4 percent, those recommended and RORd had, by 1967, an FTA rate of more than 9 percent. Second, the rate of judicial acceptance for those recommended fell from a high of 70 percent to 32 percent—almost equal to the 28 percent RORd from those interviewed but not recommended. No evidence emerged of similar deterioration by 1970 in the Washington, D.C., bail reform operation, which started as a demonstration in 1963 and became institutionalized in an independent agency.[3]

Although the Manhattan Bail Project was widely taken as proving that those with sufficient community ties can be trusted to appear, the experiment demonstrated nothing of the kind. No investigation was made of the determinants of appearance. Possibly the questionnaire used does successfully discriminate among defendants by their tendencies to appear. Another (though not necessarily inconsistent) possibility is that the follow-up procedures, used by the project for those released on their recommendations, caused the low FTA rate. These procedures included a mailed notification, in the defendant's own language, of when and where to appear. They were required to report to the project office by 9 a.m. of the day of appearance. If they did not appear, telephone calls were made in an attempt to locate them, and field visits were made if necessary. Because all of these procedures were part of the original demonstration, it is not known is if any (or all) of them are unnecessary or inefficient.

Similarly, the experiment did not provide any evidence about the determinants of judicial acceptance of the project's recommendations. Perhaps it was the appearance by a Vera staffer at arraignment that precipitated the judicial acceptance, instead of anything substantive (that is, the results from the interview and verification process). Perhaps any randomly selected set of defendants who were all recommended for ROR by Vera staffers at arraignment and subject to the Vera follow-up procedures

3. Friedman (1976).

would achieve the same results. The experimental success reveals neither whether the interview and verification procedures had anything to do with it nor whether the released individuals were any more or less trustworthy than the average arrestee.

The Vera Institute of Justice created a successful innovation. Although its operating procedures may be simple to describe, the extent to which any particular aspect of these procedures may have contributed to (or retarded) the success of the innovation was unknown. Nevertheless, the reform (or various versions of it) did diffuse to many jurisdictions around the country. The effectiveness of the reform in these jurisdictions is not well understood. Studies were conducted of particular jurisdictions documenting, for example, deteriorating performance in New York City and the absence of deterioration in Washington, D.C., during comparable periods.

The Economic Tool: Understanding the Procedures That Determine Agency Effectiveness

A pretrial services agency operating a Vera-like reform has many choices about how to allocate and use whatever scarce budgetary resources are available. Choices must be made about the procedures and resources for interviewing, verifying types of recommendations possible, ensuring appearance, and trying to learn or study how to increase the agency's effectiveness. The manager of the agency has primary responsibility for making these choices. The manager does not usually have complete discretion; the court system in which the agency operates may choose to require or veto particular procedures. Thus the true extent of the manager's discretion depends on the latitude secured from the court, and this in turn may depend on the political skills of the manager.

To study the effects of these choices, I have taken advantage of two independent national surveys of pretrial release agencies: one by the Office of Economic Opportunity's Legal Institutions Division in the beginning of 1973; the other by the National Center for State Courts in the beginning of 1975. Both surveys gathered information about the budgets, operating procedures, and outputs (in terms of RORs and FTAs) of all agencies known to be operating. The appendix contains more detail about this data, its limitations, a description of the technical procedures used to analyze it, and the results.

Table 15-1. *Important Policy Choices for Pretrial Service Agencies*

Parental choice	Vera response
Interviewing	
1. Use point system?	Yes
2. If yes, allow subjective judgment?	No
3. Conduct interview when?	
(Before bail hearing, after, or both)	Before
4. Restrictive eligibility criteria?	Yes → No
Verification	
5. Try to verify defendant's responses?	Yes
6. If yes, field visits when necessary?	Yes
Type of recommendations made	
7. ROR only (or cash bail, ordinary bail, third party)?	Yes
ROR follow-up procedures	
8. Notify defendants of required appearances?	Yes
9. If yes, require acknowledgment?	No
10. Require defendants to call in regularly?	No
11. Day of appearance effort?	Yes
Learning	
12. Gather data and analyze it?	Yes
13. Invest in computerized information system?	No

Note: ROR = released on own recognizance.

In conducting interviews, virtually all agencies use standardized forms and questions at least somewhat similar to the original Vera form shown in figure 15-1 (see table 15-1). One important set of procedural choices is whether or not to use a point system to score a defendant's responses and to serve as the basis for making a recommendation decision. A second important procedural choice concerns the timing of the interview—whether it is conducted before the initial bail hearing, after it, or, in some cases, at both times. A third important choice concerns eligibility criteria: whether or not to exclude individuals accused of particular types of crimes (for example, felonies, violent crimes).

The intensity of an agency's effort to verify interview responses is another important choice an agency manager faces. Verification efforts can be restricted to telephone calls to family, friends, or employers or can include personal interviews. More resources allocated to verification will increase the accuracy with which community ties are assessed but presumably will reduce resources available both for interviewing and follow-up procedures.

The original Vera project only considered whether or not to recommend ROR. However, some agencies utilize other options in addition to ROR. Some may recommend that ordinary money bail be set for certain defendants. Some consider recommending release under the supervision of a third party. Other agencies may use the option of recommending a cash deposit (a low-cost alternative to ordinary bail). These options complicate the decision of what to recommend for any particular defendant, and the success of them depends both on whether such sorting can be meaningfully done and whether the agency attempting this is able to do so.

Follow-up procedures for ROR defendants may consist of four activities: systematically notifying defendants of their required court appearances, requiring acknowledgment by the defendant of the notification, requiring defendants to call in or report to the agency at regular intervals, and requiring defendants to contact or meet with agency personnel on the days of scheduled appearances. If an agency chooses none of these procedures—as many in the survey did—the implication is that normal court procedures will be relied upon to ensure a defendant's appearance. This choice is consistent with beliefs that the agency is identifying those who can be trusted to appear because of their strong community ties and that normal court notification procedures are adequate.

To learn or study about increasing the agency's effectiveness, managers could undertake a wide variety of efforts. Here, I focus on those that might require enough resources to reduce measurably (in the short run) the resources available for operations. The primary effort that I could identify from the questionnaires was in terms of data gathering.

To produce certain statistics, the agency has to systematically gather the necessary data. For example, many agencies gathered the data necessary to report the court dispositions of RORd defendants. Why would a manager divert scarce resources away from operations to do this? Understanding the effects of following the agency's recommendations could provide persuasive evidence to use in securing, maintaining, and increasing judicial cooperation and support. Similarly, agencies could choose to invest in computerized information systems (bearing in mind that personal computers did not exist during the 1970s) primarily for research purposes; these systems could be used as well for operations (such as the notification process), and the relevant case is when the system could not be cost-justified for operations alone.

Given all of these possibilities for use of the agency's scarce resources, what choices should a manager make? "Core choices" are those that increase or decrease the effectiveness of many different agencies, despite the variation in local environments. Although a project manager normally has to adapt the reform in some ways to suit the local environment, adaptation in terms of these core choices should be strenuously resisted. "Noncore choices" are those that are not associated with any general systematic effects, or the effects go in opposite directions (for example, more releases but higher FTA rates). The latter may pose important choices but involve difficult value judgments. The standard interpretation of the first type of noncore choice is that it has no significant impact on an agency's effectiveness. A second, less likely interpretation is that a particular noncore choice is effective in certain local environments, but its opposite is equally effective in other local environments. This also would imply that no "average" effect is detectable. In any event, the noncore choice is adaptable. It can be determined in terms of suitability for the local environment.

Certain choices may be necessary given the specific local environment in which the agency operates. For example, the court may give the agency permission to interview only after the initial bail hearing instead of before. My categorization of core and noncore choices is independent of local considerations; certain agencies may be forced to make poor core choices.

To determine which choices are core and noncore, the data from the two surveys were used to estimate the effect of each choice on the number of releases achieved per budgetary dollar and on a standardized failure-to-appear rate. The estimation procedures for this production analysis are somewhat complex, involving the pooling of cross-section and times series data to estimate and test the validity of a three-part technology structure. Although the full results are reported in the appendix, two core choices are concentrated on here.

The two core choices identified by the statistical analysis are (1) the use of point systems and (2) the follow-up requirement that defendants call in or report in regularly. Their positive effects are unambiguous. Furthermore, their implementation depends primarily on the manager's choice.

Other variables, such as the timing of the interview and ROR authority for the project, are also revealed to have a substantial impact on the agency's output. However, changes in these procedures require court permission at a minimum. Furthermore, the impact that is associated with them generally does not separate the simultaneous effect of changing the pool of clients and changing the procedure per se. For example, interviewing before the initial bail setting results in more releases (other things equal), but this does not mean the agency is truly more productive; it means it is working with a different and less risky client pool from the start. Whether or not this is appropriate for agencies to do involves a complicated question of values that is not addressed here.

Point systems and call-in requirements are used on the identical client pools. The use of a point system, compared with no point system, increases the number of interviews and the releases per interview as well as reduces the failure-to-appear rate. Substantial differences in effectiveness of a "representative" agency (one with characteristics at the sample means) are caused by this decision (see table 15-2). If the agency does not use a point system, its average cost per release will be $54.80. If it uses a strictly objective point system, this cost will drop in half to $27.53. Furthermore, the FTA rate will be reduced from 4.74 percent (no point system) to 2.19 percent. The cost per release can be reduced even further if a point system is used with some subjective judgment allowed, to $18.56, although the FTA rate is 2.64 percent—still much better than no point system, but slightly higher than the strictly objective system. Some value judgment is required to choose between the two types of uses of point systems (a noncore choice), but the use of a point system clearly greatly increases an agency's effectiveness.

Similarly, the call-in requirement also has advantages. The representative agency that does not require call-ins has a cost per release of $38.71. The same agency with a call-in requirement would reduce its cost per release by 31 percent to $26.65; furthermore, it would improve its FTA rate from 3.71 percent to 3.09 percent.

Changes in Industry Efficiency over Time

A key question to consider is the change over time in performance at the industry level. Although any single agency may improve while another may deteriorate, does the industry as a whole improve or deteriorate?

One way to examine the evolution is to count the number of agencies using the more efficient procedures and observe how this changes over time. To do this, the agencies are divided into three groups: survivors (those included in both surveys), missing (those only included in the first survey, probably because they did not survive), and new agencies (those only included in the second survey).

Table 15-2. *Point Systems and Call-In Requirements*

Policy choice	Interviews (number)	Releases (number)	Cost per release (dollars)	FTA (percent)
No point system	9,119	1,825	54.80	4.74
Points (objective)	12,519	3,632	27.53	2.19
Points (subjective)	10,119	5,389	18.56	2.64
Call-in	7,969	3,752	26.65	3.09
No call-in	12,469	2,584	38.71	3.71
Sample average	10,219	3,168	31.57	3.38

Note: Effects illustrated for average size agency. 1972 budget = $100,000. FTA = failure to appear.

Forty-seven observations on surviving agencies contain all the data necessary to estimate any changes in efficiency for this part of the industry.
The use of the two efficient procedures by agency is shown in tables 15-3
and 15-4. In terms of point systems, about an equal number of agencies
deteriorated as improved. The results on the call-in requirement are more
dramatic, however. While no deterioration was evident, fourteen of the
twenty-seven agencies not using this requirement at the time of the first
survey had begun to use it by the second. This is consistent with a strong
and rational evolutionary pattern of industry growth and development.

In addition, the data appear neutral with respect to rational selection
for those agencies that were missing by the second survey. The early data
on eight of these missing agencies are available. Of these eight, none was
using efficient follow-up procedures. But if the missing agencies were
simply chosen at random from those in the first survey, three with efficient follow-up would be expected. With respect to point systems, two
did not use them. If these agencies were selected at random, three agencies were expected not to use them. Thus these appear to be a group close
to the average efficiency level reported in the first survey.

Of the twenty-nine new agencies started since the first survey, eleven
did not use point systems. Based on the first survey distribution, this is
exactly the number of inefficient choices expected. Eleven did not use
the call-in requirement. But based on the first survey distribution, one
would expect eighteen not to use it. The new agencies are therefore more
efficient, on average, than the industry during the first survey. Compared
with surviving agencies during the second survey, however, they appear
about as efficient. (One would expect twelve not to use point systems,

Table 15-3. *Use of Point Systems*

		Second survey	
		Yes	No
First survey	Yes	24	5
	No	4	14

Table 15-4. *Use of Call-In Requirement*

		Second survey	
		Yes	No
First survey	Yes	20	0
	No	14	13

eight not to use follow-up.) Thus these data are also consistent with rational growth and development.

The method of examining the evolution by simply counting ignores the possibility that the changes are not randomly distributed with respect to budget size. If all the largest agencies were the inefficient ones and those whose effectiveness decreased, and all the improvements were concentrated in the smallest agencies, the overall picture of evolution might be different. Therefore, I checked this with a procedure that takes budget size into account.

The average cost per ROR was $32.57 in both surveys (this includes some observations not usable for the earlier statistical analysis). At the time of the first survey, the average cost was $36.07. By the time of the second survey, this had decreased to $31.10, a drop in average industry "output" cost of 14 percent. Thus, over this two-year period, the industry had achieved productivity gains at the level of almost 7 percent a year, a rate that most private industries would envy.

This "cost improvement" analysis must be qualified by the recognition that increased releases are not the only "output" of the agencies. A second important "output" is the level of pretrial misconduct of those released, here measured by the FTA rate. The efficient core procedures lead to better output levels in terms of both of these dimensions, but an attempt was not made to value the reductions in FTA achieved.

Taken together, these data are startling and important, for they suggest that public productivity does improve over time. Examining this in other areas and over longer time periods would be instructive.

The Mechanisms of Improvement

What might explain this evolution toward greater effectiveness? For those agencies that improved, the change could be initiated by their managers or staff or urged upon them by someone in their external environment. But what would cause these individuals to reach this conclusion? One possibility is vigorous managerial examination, perhaps motivated by some rough knowledge that other agencies achieve more releases and lower FTA rates. Do the managers of these agencies have incentives to improve their effectiveness? Perhaps the agency was formally evaluated, and the evaluatory process led to these conclusions. Still another possibility is the dissemination of social science studies (such as this one) urging that changes like these be made.

To a limited extent, I am able to explore some of these questions by making further use of the survey data. First, I ask whether any evidence exists that managers using the more effective techniques get rewarded with bigger budgets (appropriate for a young growth industry with agency budgets far below the level needed to serve the relevant pretrial populations). If the efficient agencies are expanded more rapidly than other agencies, this could create substantial imitation incentives in an industry with few barriers to the sharing of technical information. The answer appears to be yes, although it is not statistically significant. Average budget growth for these agencies over the two-year period was 49 percent. Inefficient agencies grew by 12 percent, agencies using one of the efficient core procedures grew on average by 48 percent, and agencies using both efficient core procedures grew by 86 percent.

To explore this further, I consider whether the type of agency overseeing the pretrial release unit makes a difference. For example, perhaps those units controlled directly by the courts experience rewards more closely connected to their effectiveness than do units controlled by probation departments. Again, the results of this analysis are suggestive but not statistically significant: Judicially controlled rewards are unrelated to effectiveness, while the positive relationship between effectiveness and budget growth is even larger for units overseen by nonjudicial agencies.

The above analysis considers whether rewards (budget levels for the second survey) depend on which agency is doing the rewarding. There is the other side of this relationship. Does agency behavior depend upon anticipated rewards? More generally, what explains agency choices of core procedures?

I consider two types of rewards: budget growth and stable source funding of the agency. I try to predict which agencies will improve and which will remain efficient. The predictor variables include indicators of the agency's goals from the first survey, research efforts noted in the first survey, the type of oversight agency, the manager's attendance at a national conference of pretrial release agencies in 1974, budget growth, and changes in funding stability between the two surveys. The two economic variables are the statistically significant predictors. Stable source funding by the second survey is positively associated with the agency's probability of improving effectiveness, and larger positive budget changes are associated with the probability of beginning and remaining efficient.

This analysis supports the conclusion that the behavior of public agencies is influenced by the rewards they expect to receive.

Evolution, Management, Incentives

The statistical analysis bounds understanding of this industry's evolution but, because of the limitations of the data available, cannot explain why individual managers made the choices they did. To supplement this analysis, I have interviewed several directors of pretrial release agencies to get a richer understanding of their behavior.

The statistical analysis reveals that practically all of the progress in the pretrial release industry came from the increased adoption of the call-in requirements; the use of point systems changed little over the time period studied. Furthermore, the manager of a pretrial release unit, if not directly accountable to a judge, judicial council, or chief court administrative officer, was most likely to be accountable to a probation department. Some evidence suggests that the probability of having a call-in requirement is higher under probation department supervision. What explains this?

Are probation department supervisors more alert to the benefits of a call-in requirement? Not according to the two managers I interviewed who are subject to this type of supervision. John Wallace from the New York Office of Probation and Susan Bookman of the Berkeley OR Project both report virtually no interest on the part of higher management from probation in the effectiveness of their units. Wallace, who took over the operation from Vera in the 1960s, explained that his primary concern was one of equity: to make the agency's services available to all New York criminal defendants. His requests for new budgets and the ensuing negotiations always had to do with how rapidly the agency could expand to achieve this equity goal, and nobody ever questioned the agency's effectiveness (which was deteriorating rapidly). Bookman also reports no interest from her probation department in the agency's effectiveness.

These interviews bring to mind the bureaucratic routine hypothesis.[4] That is, what could be more natural to a manager with close ties to a probation department than to have a call-in requirement? It is part of the standard routine of probation. A manager with roots in probation might do this whether it was efficient or inefficient. The increase in efficiency could result in part from the accidental coincidence of bureaucratic routines and what in this case happens to be efficient. This would not explain, however, why the rewards of budget growth and stable funding source are correlated with effectiveness.

Bookman described an ongoing research effort that she makes to inform those important in her external environment (judges, the board of supervisors) of the project's work: interviews conducted, releases, FTA rate. She also described an example of her internal use of the data gathered to improve performance. She found out that Sunday releasees had higher FTA rates than those released on other days and that the project provided no personal contact at the time of release on this day (as opposed to all other days). She responded by assigning a staff person to attend Sunday releases.

Bookman's example suggests that the correlation between rewards and efficiency could arise through indirect, but appropriate, means. "Better" managers—those who always want to improve their agencies' effectiveness, who take the time and effort to seek improvements, and who keep those in their external environment apprised of their efforts and results—may by these actions persuade funders that the agency is in

4. Allison (1971, pp. 67–100).

good hands and thereby increase the chances for securing better rewards. Even though this is indirect—funders do not know the true effectiveness of the agency, let alone what explains it—managerial efforts may pay off in terms of both improved effectiveness and better rewards.

Lessons for Improving Public Service through Innovations and Their Diffusion

Four major lessons can be derived from this analysis. First, the effectiveness of a diffused innovation cannot be assumed. Almost all public services are complex, and even when good judgment is used to identify a successful innovation—perhaps as with the Ford Foundation Program on Innovations in State and Local Government—more is needed to increase the odds of successful diffusion. The details matter. In responding to the demands of differing localities for adaptability, the baby must not be thrown out with the bath water. Effort is needed to make sure that the success is replicated and maintained over time.

Second, the economic tool of production analysis is valuable for helping to ensure this success. Production analysis has the potential for identifying the core choices, the parts of the innovation that are crucial to its success. In the case of the bail reform, the use of point systems and a call-in requirement can greatly increase the effectiveness of a pretrial services unit. Assuming one believes as I do in the value of analyses that examine questions like these, the organizational problem remains of who would call for it. The value is received by the industry as a whole, and no single agency has incentive enough to have one conducted. For most state and local services, appropriate national-level organizations for research and development of each do not exist.

Third, the study suggests that more thought be given to the external environments that determine the incentives operating agencies face. The pretrial release units were located, organizationally, in many different ways. Some evidence is available that those with nonjudicial overseers were more likely to improve, and to be rewarded for improvement, than those with direct judicial oversight. In this case, the more effective environment during the time studied may be so as a result of an accident of fit with the procedures that happened to be effective.

Finally, the study indicates that public managers do have incentives to improve their agencies' effectiveness. A link exists between effectiveness and the rewards an agency receives. This may seem trivially clear to public managers, but it is not to the general public and it remains to be examined further as a scholarly matter. Most would be surprised to learn that a public sector system had improved its productivity at all, let alone at a rate of 7 percent annually.

References

Allison, Graham T. 1971. *Essence of Decision: Explaining the Cuban Missile Crisis.* Little, Brown.

Friedman, Lee S. 1976. "The Evolution of a Bail Reform." *Policy Sciences,* vol. 7: 281–313.

Landes, William M. 1974. "Legality and Reality: Some Evidence on Criminal Procedure." *Journal of Legal Studies,* vol. 3 (June): 287–337.

Appendix

This appendix provides a summary of the statistical study underlying chapter 15. A full exposition including expectations of signs and relative magnitudes of variables and more discussion of the results is available from the author.

The Data

The Office of Economic Opportunity (OEO) survey covered 90 agencies; the National Center for State Courts survey, 111. Seventy-six agencies were common to both surveys. In each survey, a number of the agencies did not provide complete information, although the information provided was used whenever possible. The numbers of usable observations to estimate the three-part technology structure were ninety-three for interviews, seventy-two for releases, and seventy-eight for failure-to-appear (FTA) rates. Most of the incomplete information was concentrated in the second survey, but statistical tests found no structural differences between the usable observations of the two surveys. The included cases covered a broad spectrum of agencies with budgets ranging from $4,000 to $756,302 and averaging $104,821 (all in 1972 dollars). For the analysis of changes in agency procedures, between forty-five and fifty observations were usable from the potential set of seventy-six. While the results could be different if information was complete, to my knowledge no bias exists toward or away from any finding of this study.

The Technology Structure

Equations were estimated to explain each agency's number of interviews, releases, and failure-to-appear rates. The data from the two surveys were pooled under the statistical hypothesis of structural homogeneity, a hypothesis maintained as a result of the Chow test results reported in each table.

INTERVIEWS. The number of interviews (I) conducted by an agency is determined primarily by its resource allocation decisions. To the extent it devotes resources to activities other than interviewing, it should conduct fewer interviews. In the analysis, these other activities consist primarily of follow-up procedures (F) and research and development (R). Specific procedures are represented by dummy variables and distinguished by subscripts as described in table A-1 (six follow-up procedures, three types of research and development efforts). For example, $F_{12} = 1$ if an agency uses both a call-in requirement and systematic notification as part of its follow-up procedures, and $F_{12} = 0$ otherwise. Similarly, $R_1 = 1$ if an agency gathers data on the number of defendants excluded from project consideration (reflecting an interest of the agency in expanding its interviewing range), and $R_1 = 0$ otherwise.

In conducting interviews, virtually all agencies have standardized forms. The main procedural variables are whether or not a point system (P) is used to score the responses and to make recommendation decisions. Another factor that should affect the number of interviews completed is the timing (T) of the interview—whether it is conducted before the initial bail hearing, after it, or in some cases at both times (for example, when an agency serves more than one court, each court may have a strong and different preference about timing). The timing choice affects the nature of the population interviewed. For example, the "before" case presumably includes better risk defendants whose responses might be easier to verify. The intensity of verification effort is one variable for which no good measure existed, and its omission

Table A-1. *Definition of Variables*

Variable	Definition
A	1 if the agency has authority to release defendants
B	Annual budget of the agency, 1972 dollars[a]
C_1	1 if the agency may recommend defendants be released on condition of cash deposit
C_2	1 if the agency may recommend defendants be released on condition of money bail
E	1 if the agency is in a demonstration or developmental stage
F_1	1 if agency requires released defendants to report or call in regularly
F_2	1 if agency systematically notifies defendants of required court appearances
F_{20}	1 if systematic notification is the only followup procedure utilized by an agency
F_{123}	1 if an agency systematically notifies, requires acknowledgment of the notification, and requires defendants to report or call in regularly
F_{12}	1 if an agency requires defendants to report or call in regularly, and systematically notifies them of required appearances but does not require acknowledgment of the notification
F_{1w}	1 if an agency is not known to belong to categories F_{20}, F_{123}, F_{12}, but may have some followup procedures; these cases form a weak call-in category because most of them are known to utilize at least the call-in procedure
FTA	Failure-to-appear rate of defendants released on agency recommendation
I	Annual number of interviews completed by the agency
L	1 if the agency only serves lower courts (courts of special or limited jurisdiction)
P_1	1 if agency uses a point system when interviewing
P_{11}	1 if agency using a point system does not allow any subjective evaluation
R_1	1 if an agency gathers data on the number of defendants excluded from agency consideration
R_2	1 if an agency does not have tabulated data on the court dispositions of defendants released on their recommendations
R_3	1 if the agency uses a computerized information system
ROR	Number of defendants interviewed who were both recommended for release on their own recognizance and granted it
S	Population of the community served by the project
T_1	1 if the agency interviews defendants only before bail is set by a judicial officer
T_2	1 if the agency interviews defendants only after bail is set by a judicial officer
V	1 if the agency reported the use of volunteer staff
X_1	1 if the agency has two or three exclusion conditions
X_2	1 if the agency has more than three exclusion conditions

a. Budget data from the spring 1975 survey were deflated by 1.19 based on the state and local government price deflators for 1974 and 1972, as reported in *Economic Report of the President*, January 1976, table B-3, p. 175.

may be a source of bias if it is correlated with any of the included variables.

Two other nonresource variables should affect the number of interviews. One is that some agencies can release at least certain types of defendants on their own authority (A). The other is whether or not a project is in its initial experimental stage (E), when one might expect fewer interviews as procedures are being developed and community support sought.

All of the above variables interact with the program's budget (B) to produce interviews. In addition, some projects report the use of volunteers (V) as part of the staff, which should increase interviews, other things being equal. The vector form of the equation estimated is:

(1) $I = a_0 + a_1 B + a_2 V + a_3 [F+R+P+T+A+E]B + \varepsilon$

Table A-2 reports the estimation results. Column (1) contains ordinary least squares (OLS) results, and column (2) contains generalized least squares (GLS) results after correcting for heteroskedasticity by dividing all observations by the square root of the agency's budget. Column (3) is a simplified GLS specification of the model in columns (1) and (2), with broader distinctions among follow-up procedures and use of point systems by agencies.

The coefficient estimates vary little across the three equations estimated, lending some confidence to the stability of the estimates. The signs of the coefficients are virtually all as expected and their magnitudes plausible. The one exception is the positive coefficient in column (2) on F_{20} (systematic notification only, as compared with no notification), which was expected to be negative. This may result from interaction with the omitted variable for verification efforts because both depend on access to court records and calendars.

The most important findings from this analysis are that call-in procedures are costly in terms of interviews, while the notification procedures do not appear to be. The use of point systems results in more interviews per dollar.

RELEASES. The number of defendants recommended for release on their own recognizance (ROR) and released by the courts depends on the number of interviews conducted, the types of recommendations made, and the degree of judicial cooperation achieved. Judicial cooperation depends on the specific operating procedures used by the agencies. In addition to the procedural variables included in the interview equation,

Table A-2. *Interview Equation*

Independent variable[a]	(1) OLS coeff	(1) OLS |t|	(2) GLS coeff	(2) GLS |t|	(3) GLS coeff	(3) GLS |t|
F_1	-	n.a.	-	n.a.	−.045	(2.43)[b]
F_2	-	n.a.	-	n.a.	.054	(2.00)[b]
F_{20}	.048	(1.92)[c]	.058	(1.67)[c]	-	n.a.
F_{12}	.008	(.32)	.010	(.30)	-	n.a.
F_{12}	−.004	(.11)	−.002	(.04)	-	n.a.
F_{1w}	.003	(.09)	.006	(.14)	-	n.a.
P_1	.050	(2.85)[b]	.022	(.97)	-	n.a.
P_{11}	.024	(1.17)	.024	(.97)	.030	(1.62)
R_1	.003	(.10)	.028	(1.46)	.031	(1.72)[c]
R_2	.073	(5.39)[b]	.059	(2.99)[b]	.055	(2.88)[b]
R_3	−.029	(1.68)[c]	−.026	(1.05)	−.019	(.84)
T_1	−.045	(3.07)[b]	.023	(1.19)	.025	(1.35)
T_2	.088	(2.61)[b]	.071	(2.11)[b]	.073	(2.35)[b]
E	.045	(1.68)[c]	−.030	(1.03)	−.029	(1.06)
A	.075	(2.40)[b]	.054	(1.61)	.056	(1.78)[c]
V	−80.900	(.03)	2571.300	(1.93)[c]	2775.00	(2.17)[b]
B	.055	(2.18)[b]	.007	(.17)	.007	(.17)
$1/\sqrt{B}$	-	n.a.	461.300	(.32)	307.000	(.22)
Constant	−43.700	(.04)	−6.330	(.41)	−3.310	(.23)
n	93		93		93	
R^2	.86		.49		.49	
$\bar{R}^2$	.83		.35		.38	
Chow (d.f.)	-		1.09 (21,51)			-
k	20		21		18	

Note: OLS = ordinary least squares; GLS = generalized least squares; coeff = coefficient; |t| = absolute value of the t-statistic; n.a. = not applicable; $1/\sqrt{B}$ = reciprocal of the square root of B; constant = constant term to be estimated in each equation; n = number of observations; R^2 = the (unadjusted) proportion of variance explained by the estimated equation; $\bar{R}^2$ = proportion of variance explained by the estimated equation, adjusted for the degrees of freedom; Chow (d.f.) = the F-statistic for the Chow test for structural homogeneity, with degrees of freedom in parentheses; and k = number of parameters including the constant term and dummy variables constructed for missing data,

a. Estimates on the missing value variables are not reported here, as they have no meaning.
b. Significant at the .05 level.
c. Significant at the .10 level.

there are variables representing agencies that may recommend cash deposit or money bail (C) as an alternative to ROR, variables to represent agency conditions for excluding (X) certain defendants from consideration, and agencies that only serve lower courts (L). The vector form of the equation estimated is:

(2) $\quad ROR = b_0 + b_1 I + b_2 [F + R + P + T + E + L + X + C] I + \mu$

The results are reported in table A-3. As with the interview equation, the equation was first estimated by OLS and then reestimated by GLS to correct for heteroskedasticity. The estimated equations, shown in columns (1) and (2), have coefficients with signs generally as expected and magnitudes that are plausible. They are also stable across the equations, and the goodness of fit is relatively high.

Several important findings emerge from these estimations. First, the requirement for regular reporting or calling-in gains significant increases in judicial acceptance of release recommendations. While notification alone has some tendency toward increased releases, adding the call-in requirement substantially increases this (from .06I to .249I, a difference that is statistically significant at the .01 level with t = 2.43 using a one-tailed test based on the estimated variance-covariance matrix from the GLS estimation). Second, those agencies using objective point systems have some tendency toward increased releases compared with no point system (.031I, the difference between the two GLS point system coefficients), but the big gain in releases is for those with point systems that allow some subjective judgment (.212I).[1]

A third important finding is that those agencies that include the option of recommending money bail get significantly more RORs per interview. This is consistent with relatively little use of the option and with enhanced judicial beliefs in the appropriateness of the agency's ROR recommendations.

FAILURES TO APPEAR. Explaining measured FTA rates poses a few more estimation difficulties than the prior two parts of the technology structure. One problem is that great variation exists in the definition each agency uses to measure FTAs (for example, some count the number of appearances missed, while others count the number of people who

1. This may result more from politics than from better recommendations. In New York City's pretrial release agency, where no subjective judgments were made, the man accused of being the psychopathic "Son of Sam" murderer was found qualified for ROR. This created great embarrassment for the city, and occasions such as this can lead to judicial mistrust of agency recommendations. However, such judicial reasoning may be substantially erroneous. Employees of pretrial release agencies who conduct interviews should not be expected to be trained psychiatrists, and there is some evidence in the FTA equations that objective point systems lead to better appearance predictions than point systems that allow subjective judgments. It may be preferable to let pretrial release agencies be responsible for recommendations based on routinized information and to continue to leave the courts responsible for handling exceptional circumstances. The accused in this example was not released, and the only real shock would have been to find a judge, defense attorney, and prosecutor who would all agree to such a release

Table A-3. *Release Equation*

Independent variables[a]	(1) OLS		(2) GLS	
	coeff	$\lvert t \rvert$	*coeff*	$\lvert t \rvert$
F_{20}	.083	(1.46)	.060	(.85)
F_{123}	.001	(.03)	.043	(.66)
F_{12}	.224	$(3.30)^b$	.249	$(3.02)^b$
F_{1w}	.219	$(2.99)^b$	.209	$(2.56)^b$
P_1	.321	$(8.00)^b$	.212	$(4.12)^b$
P_{11}	−.240	$(7.30)^b$	−.181	$(3.65)^b$
R_1	.064	(1.52)	.002	(.04)
R_2	.034	(.70)	−.047	(.85)
R_3	−.024	(.43)	.043	(.66)
T_1	.126	$(2.82)^b$	.084	(1.64)
T_2	−.024	(.40)	.005	(.07)
E	−.162	$(2.73)^b$	−.085	(1.36)
X_1	.019	(.37)	.013	(.21)
X_2	−.090	$(2.41)^b$	−.097	$(1.96)^b$
C_1	−.196	$(3.90)^b$	−.183	$(3.13)^b$
C_2	.251	$(7.52)^b$	.188	$(3.81)^b$
L	.092	$(1.88)^c$	.068	(1.14)
I	.007	(.07)	.130	(1.24)
$1/\sqrt{I}$	-	n.a.	33.300	(.45)
Constant	−99.208	(1.03)	−2.400	(.54)
n	72		72	
R^2	.98		.81	
$\bar{R}^2$	.97		.72	
Chow (d.f.)	-		.69 (24,24)	
k		23		24

Note: OLS = ordinary least squares; GLS = generalized least squares; coeff = coefficient; $\lvert t \rvert$ = absolute value of the t-statistic; $1/\sqrt{I}$ = reciprocal of the square root of I; n.a. = not applicable; constant = constant term to be estimated in each equation; n = number of observations; R^2 = the (unadjusted) proportion of variance explained by the estimated equation; $\bar{R}^2$ = proportion of variance explained by the estimated equation, adjusted for the degrees of freedom; Chow (d.f.) = the F-statistic for the Chow test for structural homogeneity, with degrees of freedom in parentheses; and k = number of parameters including the constant term and dummy variables constructed for missing data,

a. Estimates on the missing value variables are not reported here, as they have no meaning.

b. Significant at the .05 level.

c. Significant at the .10 level.

miss appearances). Fortunately, both surveys included detailed questions about the calculation of this rate, and eight multiplicative dummy variables to control for these definitional differences were constructed and used as shown in table A-4.

A second problem in estimating the FTA rate is that it is bounded between zero and one. A functional form that meets this constraint and

Table A-4. *Failure-to-Appear Equation Measurement Variables*

Independent variables[a]	(1) OLS		(2) GLS		(3) GLS	
	coeff	|t|	*coeff*	|t|	*coeff*	|t|
M482	−.325	(1.16)	−.335	(1.21)	−.368	(1.29)
M491	.813	(2.45)[b]	.730	(2.34)[b]	.731	(2.26)[b]
M493	−.034	(.12)	−.016	(.06)	.041	(.15)
M494	.374	(1.07)	.384	(1.12)	.395	(1.12)
M502	.140	(.36)	.078	(.20)	.236	(.56)
M522	.986	(3.14)[b]	.927	(3.04)[b]	.852	(2.68)[b]
M523	.488	(1.49)	.470	(1.47)	.412	(1.25)
M525	.720	(1.92)[c]	.623	(1.76)[c]	.597	(1.64)

Note: OLS = ordinary least squares; coeff = coefficient; |t| = absolute value of the t-statistic; ROR = release on own recognizance; and FTA = failure to appear. Definitions of measurement variables are as follows: M482 = 1 if rate is for all people with required appearances (expected sign: −), with category of all people who obtained release omitted; M491 = 1 if rate is for all people granted ROR by court (expected sign: +); M493 = 1 if rate is for all people recommended by the agency (expected sign: +); M494 = 1 is rate is for all people both recommended and RORd (expected sign: +), with category of all interviewed by agency omitted; M502 = 1 if counted the number of appearances missed (expected sign: +), with category of counted the number of persons who missed appearances omitted; M522 = 1 if counted as FTA only if willful (expected sign: +); M523 = 1 if counted as FTA only if not remedied within _____ days (expected sign: +); and M525 = 1 if counted as FTA only when bench warrants issued (expected sign: +), with category of counted as FTA regardless of reasons or subsequent appearance omitted.

a. Estimates on the missing value variables are not reported here, as they have no meaning.

b. Significant at the .05 level.

c. Significant at the .10 level.

allows for the dummy variables as well as diminishing returns to agency efforts to reduce the rate is:

$$FTA = 1/(1 + e^{c_0 + c_1 Z + c_2 M})$$

where Z is a vector of substantive variables that affect the rate and M is a vector of variables to control for measurment error. This equation can be estimated with OLS through the following transformation:

$$\ln[(1/FTA)-1] = c_0 + c_1 Z + c_2 M$$

The specification of the Z variables is also more problematic than in the prior parts of the technology structure. In particular, the problem of omitted variables is potentially more significant here. The FTA rate is only partially determined by agency choices of procedures; other factors exogenous to the agency influence this rate. One set of exogenous influences might be thought of as characteristics of the community environment, and another set might be the responses of other criminal justice institutions to the environment. No data on these variables were collected in either survey. For the first set, a variable measuring the population of the jurisdictions served (S) by each agency was constructed. This variable is a crude proxy for the variety of community factors that lead one to expect higher FTA rates in more populated jurisdictions. The second set, however, remains omitted and is a source of potential bias if it is correlated with any of the included variables.

Agency procedural variables for follow-up (F), use of point systems (P), timing of interviews (T), and exclusion conditions (X) are all likely to influence the FTA rate. In addition, the agency's status as experimental (E), service to lower courts (L), budget (B), and efforts at research (R), all might represent important influences on the FTA rates. Thus the equation estimated has the vector form:

(3) $\ln[(1/FTA)-1] = c_0 + c_1[F+P+R+T+E+A+X+L+S+B] + c_2M + v$

The results are reported in tables A-4 and A-5. Because the dependent variable is a rate, heteroskedasticity is not a problem here and OLS is used. The three columns in each table represent minor variants in specification, and the coefficients are relatively stable across them. The signs are generally consistent with expectations (in these equations, positive signs are associated with lower FTA rates).

These equations highlight several important findings. First, the use of point systems shows a very strong and significant lowering of the FTA rate. The lower rate is with the objective, not subjective, point system, although the difference is not statistically significant. These results suggest the judicial response to objective point systems (in the release equation) is a substantial overreaction if not an incorrect one.

Second, none of the follow-up procedures achieves statistical significance. Nevertheless, the call-in requirement is associated with a tendency for lower FTA rates, as expected.

Finally, the impact of the budget is significant and as expected. Agencies with more resources given their potential workload have lower FTA rates, other things being equal.

Agency Rewards and Choices

A simple regression analysis was run on the forty-nine agencies with budget data for both surveys and in which the procedures during the time of the first survey were available. The second survey budget (B_2) was

Table A-5. *Failure-to-Appear Equation*

Independent variables[a]	(1) OLS coeff	$|t|$	(2) GLS coeff	$|t|$	(3) GLS coeff	$|t|$
F_1	-	n.a.	.201	(.88)	.188	(.73)
F_2	-	n.a.	-.438	(1.54)	-.371	(1.24)
F_{20}	-.502	(1.46)	-	n.a.	-	n.a.
F_{123}	-.185	(.55)	-	n.a.	-	n.a.
F_{12}	.072	(.17)	-	n.a.	-	n.a.
F_{1w}	.069	(.19)	-	n.a.	-	n.a.
P_1	.760	$(2.75)^b$	.714	$(2.61)^b$	.704	$(2.48)^b$
P_{11}	.088	(.30)	.168	(.59)	.192	(.65)
R_1	-	n.a.	-	n.a.	-.016	(.07)
R_2	-	n.a.	-	n.a.	.132	(.49)
R_3	-	n.a.	-	n.a.	-.301	(.88)
T_1	.340	(1.31)	.370	(1.43)	.365	(1.33)
T_2	-.377	(1.06)	-.309	(.91)	-.317	(.90)
E	.535	$(1.98)^b$	.595	$(2.29)^b$	.561	$(2.10)^b$
A	.723	$(2.44)^b$	.570	$(1.88)^c$	.638	$(1.99)^b$
X_1	-.312	(1.09)	-.313	(1.13)	-.405	(1.37)
X_2	.156	(.48)	.222	(.74)	.107	(.33)
L	-.322	(1.12)	-.332	(1.17)	-.378	(1.26)
S/100,000	-.023	$(2.57)^b$	-.022	$(2.46)^b$	-.023	$(2.51)^b$
B/10,000	.031	$(3.33)^b$	.029	$(3.16)^b$	.028	$(3.03)^b$
Constant	1.970	$(3.94)^b$	2.080	$(4.22)^b$	2.149	$(3.86)^b$
n	78		78		78	
R^2	.61		.60		.61	
$\bar{R}^2$	.38		.39		.37	
Chow (d.f.)	-		.78 (27,24)		-	
k	29		27		30	

Note: OLS = ordinary least squares; coeff = coefficient; $|t|$ = absolute value of the t-statistic; n.a. = not applicable; S/100,000 = S divided by 100,000; B/10,000 = B divided by 10,000; constant = constant term to be estimated in each equation; n = number of observations; R^2 = the (unadjusted) proportion of variance explained by the estimated equation; $\bar{R}^2$ = proportion of variance explained by the estimated equation, adjusted for the degrees of freedom; Chow (d.f.) = the F-statistic for the Chow test for structural homogeneity, with degrees of freedom in parentheses; and k = number of parameters including the constant term and dummy variables constructed for missing data,
   a. Estimates on the missing value variables are not reported here, as they have no meaning.
   b. Significant at the .05 level.
   c. Significant at the .10 level.

estimated as a function of the initial budget (B_1) and the presence or absence of each of the two efficient techniques (P_1, F_1); t-statistics are in parentheses.

$$(4a) \quad B_2 = 53,880 + .6211B_1 + .3738(F_1B_1) + .3590(P_1B_1)$$
$$(1.35) \quad (1.82)^* \quad (1.07) \quad (1.00)$$
$$R^2 = .32; n = 49$$

While the coefficients on the procedural variables are not statistically significant, they are both positive: Agencies using the efficient techniques do get somewhat better rewards than agencies not using them.

Unfortunately, the data do not permit detailed investigation of why this is so. For example, knowing if the role of formal evaluation of these agencies has been an important factor in explaining the observed rational selection would be informative. However, certain variations in organizational features can be examined. For example, the pretrial release agencies may be controlled by any one of a large number of other public agencies. Some are located in probation departments, some are run by the courts themselves (either by judicial council, chief judge, or court administrator), some are located in noncriminal justice public agencies such as community welfare departments and so on. Given the dynamics of court operations, one of these settings might be better able to encourage greater effectiveness than another. To test this, a regression equation similar to (4a) was specified, with two additional dummy variables to distinguish judicially controlled rewards (J) from all other selection agents:

$$(4b) \quad B_2 = \underset{(1.47)}{61{,}250} + \underset{(.40)}{.1909B_1} + \underset{(1.25)}{.7640(JB_1)} + \underset{(1.46)}{.6135(F_1B_1)}$$
$$+ \underset{(1.51)}{.6958(P_1B_1)} - \underset{(-.59)}{.5321(JF_1B_1)} - \underset{(-.73)}{.6748(JP_1B_1)}$$
$$R^2 = .35; \; n = 49$$

None of the coefficients in this equation is significant. Nonetheless, note that the positive coefficients on the variables indicating use of efficient procedures are almost completely offset by the negative coefficients on the same variables interacted with judicially controlled rewards. They suggest that judicial encouragement is unrelated to the efficiency of the agencies they control, while for other overseers a positive relation exists between efficiency and reward.

The rewards of overseers are important for two different reasons. First, relative expansion of efficient agencies makes the industry as a whole more productively efficient. Second, these rewards may be related to the decisions of agencies about which procedures to use.

The agency choice of procedures has been hypothesized to be a function of its goals, rewards, search activities, and information. Two logit equations concerning this choice are estimated: one looks at the probability of agency improvement (that is, a switch from some inefficient procedure to an efficient one, provided no deterioration has taken place elsewhere); the other looks at the joint probability of starting efficient and staying efficient.

The firm goals and internal search variables are represented by the three research activities used in the estimation of the technology structure. The use of computer information systems is a search in the wrong direction for the efficient procedures and may be negatively associated with both dependent variables. The interest in interviews, represented by gathering exclusion data, should be positively associated with point systems and negatively associated with the call-in requirement. For that reason, it has been omitted from this specification, which counts either improvement equally. Failure to gather disposition data could indicate a relative interest in interviews or failures to appear. Because both procedures improve the failure-to-appear rate, this variable is interpretable and included as a control.

Agency search is not limited to internal searching; it may also look externally for good procedures to imitate. In June 1974, a national conference on pretrial release and diversion was held in San Francisco, California. The scheduled talks and workshops at the conference did not suggest discussion, pro or con, of either of the procedures identified here as efficient (the primary focus was on legal issues, though the role of evaluation was discussed). However, informal communication during the conference might have some effect. I obtained a list of the attendees, and each agency in the sample with an attending representative was noted (CF).

Two types of rewards to firms are considered: budget rewards, which may be positive (PB) or negative (NB), and stable source funding, which was defined as local funding (single source) by the time of the second survey. For the latter, separate terms were entered to distinguish those agencies that were initially only single source (SS) and those that were initially multiple (MS), as well as those going from single to multiple (SM). (Thus those agencies that used two or more sources in both periods were the omitted category.) Finally, the governing agency was included as either the court (J), private agency (PR), or other public agencies (PU) with probation agencies the omitted variable. The equations are (with asymptotic t's in parentheses):

(5a) Prob [Improve] $= -1.3193 - .9516R2 - 2.3289R3 - .1270CF$
$$(-.79) \qquad (-.69) \qquad (-.79) \qquad (-.88)$$
$$+ 4.1503SS + 3.7078MS + 2.522SM + .0164PB$$
$$(1.88)^* \qquad (1.74)^* \qquad (1.36) \qquad (.13)$$
$$+ .0484NB - .8463J - 1.3806PR + .3709PU$$
$$(.35) \qquad (-.54) \qquad (-.61) \qquad (.26)$$

Likelihood ratio statistic = 14.25; n = 37; percentage correctly predicted = 75.68.

(5b) Prob [Always Efficient] = $-3.8693 + .3297R_2 - .0026R_3 + .8058CF$

$$(1.52) \quad (.21) \quad (.00) \quad (.45)$$
$$-.0031SS + 2.7835MS - .0536SM + .4139PB$$
$$(.00) \quad (1.41) \quad (-.03) \quad (1.85)*$$
$$+ .295NB - 4.4195J - .3841PR + 1.5887PU$$
$$(.65) \quad (-1.11) \quad (-.17) \quad (1.00)$$

Likelihood ratio statistic = 40.68; n = 46; percentage correctly predicted = 84.78.

The significant variables in these equations are the economic ones. Stable source funding by the second survey is positively associated with the probability of beginning and remaining efficient. Also as expected, the use of computer information systems has a large negative coefficient in the probability of improvement equation.

CHAPTER SIXTEEN

Notes from a Reflective Practitioner of Innovation

Ellen Schall

MANY OF THE QUESTIONS about innovation are posed from the outside looking in: How can society get more innovation? How can a good innovation be differentiated from a poor one? How important should innovation be as a public value?[1] This chapter is an attempt to answer a question posed by those on the inside looking out: What can managers do to foster innovation? How can they create organizational climates in which innovation can flourish? On this inside-out question, I offer the experiential perspective of the manager who has struggled to innovate and to create the conditions under which others could innovate.

Reflections

For years, before I knew it was a term of art, I was called a reflective practitioner.[2] To me, this meant that, in contrast to the practitioner who told war stories about his triumphs and defeats, I was someone who enjoyed thinking about my work at some distance and trying to abstract lessons for myself as well as for others. This tendency to reflect was clearly useful, but I have only recently come to try to artic-

---

1. Behn and Brough (1991).
2. Schön (1983); and Schön (1987).

ulate more precisely what it means so that I could develop the capacity in others.

Donald A. Schön, a consultant and Massachusetts Institute of Technology social scientist, has written definitively on the reflective practitioner. In *The Reflective Practitioner: How Professionals Think in Action,* Schön offers what he calls an "epistemology of practice" based on a close analysis of what practitioners do as they "reflect-in-action." In *Educating the Reflective Practitioner: Toward a New Design for Teaching and Learning in the Professions,* he offers guidance to those in the business of educating practitioners. Schön describes, in somewhat complex terms, his ideas about the "art" of professional practice and how and to what extent professionals think about what they know.

The concept of reflective practice has much to do with theories, developed over the years, on learning in general. James Coleman, a sociologist in the fields of learning and education, describes experiential learning as inductive, where one goes from the particular to the general. In inductive learning, the sequence would begin with "action in a particular situation and the observance of the effects of that action, move to the understanding of these effects in a particular instance, then to understanding the general principle, and finally to application through action in a new circumstance within the range of generalization."[3] Another learning theorist, David Kolb, has also described experiential learning as a four-stage process: (1) concrete experience, (2) observations and reflections, (3) formation of abstract concepts and generalizations, and (4) testing applications of concepts in new situations.[4]

These frameworks should help locate the contribution of practitioners and suggest goals toward which "reflective" practitioners might aim: generalizable observations grounded in the concrete that meet the test of applicability in new situations. The days are gone when any good story from a well-respected manager was considered useful (or when an academic could credibly spin theory not located in practice). Reflective practice can be understood as the ability to form abstract principles based on practioners' observations of their own concrete experiences and offer those observations for testing by others.

Thus I offer the reflections of one manager who attempted to innovate and to set the stage for the innovations of others. The organization

3. Auth (1991).
4. Auth (1991).

in which these observations are grounded is the New York City Department of Juvenile Justice (DJJ), where I served as commissioner from 1983 to 1990.

Department of Juvenile Justice: 1983–90

In 1983 DJJ was a city agency like many others. Its mission was not clear; it had responsibility for only a piece of the system of which it was a part; its staff was not working to its potential; its reputation was weak; and it had just lost a major political battle. In 1978 a mayoral task force had described Spofford Juvenile Detention Center, DJJ's major secure-detention facility, as a "case history in failure." Staff turnover was high, among both the line workers and top management: In twenty-nine years, Spofford had twenty-two directors.

In 1979 Mayor Edward I. Koch created DJJ as a separate agency, pulling its functions out of the Human Resources Administration, a much larger, superagency, created by John Lindsay when he was mayor. DJJ was charged with responsibility for pretrial detention and aftercare services for children under sixteen who had been arrested and were awaiting disposition of their cases.

In 1983 Mayor Koch appointed me commissioner of DJJ, and I embarked on an effort to transform the agency. To this task, I brought more commitment than experience. I had been a Legal Aid lawyer and had worked for the city in an oversight agency, the Office of the Deputy Mayor for Criminal Justice. Before moving to DJJ, I served for three years as deputy commissioner of the New York City Department of Correction, with responsibility for the implementation of programs and the oversight of compliance with federal court consent decrees on conditions in the city's jails. That job taught me the difference between announcing a policy and having line staff carry it out consistently. Mostly, however, it filled me with examples of the hazards of bureaucratic management. Other than three weeks at the John F. Kennedy School of Government's Program for Senior Executives in State and Local Government, I had little exposure to or understanding of what it took to transform a public agency.

My DJJ journey was a long but infinitely interesting one—with stops and starts, missteps and mistakes—as well as one graced with extraordinary help along the way. And I had the good fortune to attract a committed group of fellow-travelers, one of whom succeeded me and served for four years as commissioner.

Over a ten-year stretch, the agency reinvented itself. DJJ redefined its mission to encompass both custody and care, and then prevention. It created a case-management program for juveniles in detention.[5] It developed a community-based aftercare component to follow kids released from detention home. These two programs made DJJ a 1986 winner in the Ford Foundation and John F. Kennedy School of Government Awards Program for Innovations in State and Local Government. To New York City from Washington state, DJJ brought Homebuilders, a new way of serving families both intensively and preventively; adapted the program to work with families of children in the juvenile justice system; and seeded the effort to have that technology become part of New York state and New York City's systems of serving families.[6] DJJ reinvigorated existing staff and attracted talented new staff. It stanched the flow of staff leaving and turned around the pattern at the top; DJJ became distinguished for the number of people who stayed for the long term. Finally, the challenge that resulted in the demise of the agency's previous administration was met: In 1989 the last approval necessary was achieved for the physical replacement of Spofford; ground breaking began for two new smaller facilities in 1992, and occupancy is scheduled for 1998. In 1989 DJJ was featured in the Tom Peters's PBS documentary on *Excellence in the Public Sector.* And in 1992 it was selected by the Annie E. Casey Foundation as one of five sites for participation in a national juvenile detention initiative.

The reflective lessons from this journey are rich and varied. Those offered here concern the process of organizational transformation. In a study of organizational transition, consultants Richard Beckhard and Reuben Harris identify three stages: (1) articulating a vision for the future, (2) diagnosing the present, and (3) managing the transition from here to there.[7] At this last stage, the lessons of DJJ are most likely to be applicable to others.

From this DJJ experience, I can extract lessons that address three fundamental tasks facing any public manager, particularly one trying to be innovative:

— How to manage the work of the staff, which I call "Front Line";

5. Gilmore and Schall (1986).
6. Kinney, Haapala, and Booth (1991).
7. Beckhard and Harris (1987).

—How to structure the work of the organization, which I call "Main Line"; and

—How to deal with a more sophisticated and difficult set of dynamic issues, which I call "Over the Line."

Front Line

Very quickly, the executive staff at DJJ learned that the staff was a great untapped resource. When asked to tell their story, staff frequently explained that they were once "a kid in trouble," that some adult had helped them, and that they wanted to be that adult for another generation of kids in trouble. DJJ's line staff took their jobs because they cared about kids. My task and that of my executive staff was to reconfigure the organization so it could support, instead of block, the staff's work. In attempting to do that, we learned the following lessons:

SUPPORT YOUR STAFF. In any service agency, whether in the public or private sector, staff are likely to treat the clients or customers as they believe themselves to be treated. Staff who are treated harshly will, in all likelihood, turn around and impose that harshness on the people over whom they have some power—the clients or customers. Staff who believe that their basic needs are not being met are less likely to work hard to meet the needs of children in their care. We realized that, if we wanted staff to nurture the children in DJJ's care, we could not mandate it; the only way we were going to get there was to make the staff feel nurtured themselves. We looked for opportunities to acknowledge the difficulty of the work that staff was asked to do and sought to catch staff doing things right.

A sad illustration of the depth of our staff's neediness came early in my tenure at the holiday season. A famous local celebrity had a custom of giving children in institutions a goody bag with a scarf or mittens, an apple, and a box of raisins. When DJJ's staff was asked by the celebrity's organization how many children were in detention, they doubled the number so as to include themselves.

Managers whose goal is to change the way clients are dealt with have to work through staff on the line. The underappreciated tool here is the reverberations that flow almost inevitably from the way staff themselves are treated. Staff magnify and pass on what they receive from the people who manage them. This truism seems too often missed in public life as managers are quick to blame and punish staff and then wonder at the abuse staff devolve onto clients.

A caveat belongs here. My "pass-along theory"—if managers support and nurture staff, staff will be more likely to support and nurture kids— is premised on the notion that it is hard to give what you do not get, that staff will not be as likely to give nurturing if they do not get nurturing.[8] This seems true in my experience. Top management, however, may have to solve this problem for themselves. Leadership means, among other things, figuring out how to give to managers and staff the support and attention they need. Leadership means doing this even if leaders do not receive that same support and attention from their own superiors, be that the office of an elected official, such as the mayor, or an appointed executive, such as a cabinet secretary.

An illustration might help. DJJ was often ignored as an agency. In New York City terms, it was small. It dealt with issues that, in the absence of scandal, did not command attention. And it had no major outside constituency. Mayor Koch was known for a focus on himself ("How am I doing?"), and his memoirs boast of the times he reduced others to tears.[9] Even after DJJ won the Innovations award and received other significant national recognition, we received little attention or support from the mayor. We had to invent our own sources of support. Help here can come from peers in other agencies, from colleagues in similar roles, or from any other group the leader relies on. I had an understanding husband; a close group of friends, some of them in city government; and a set of colleagues both practitioner and academic I had developed through my Kennedy School connections (the executive programs and the Innovations network). I also had ongoing relationships with outside consultants who helped me keep perspective and served as safe sounding boards. Each of the executive staff coped differently, but we each relied on others for some sense of support.

Our general counsel, for example, who played a complex and important role at DJJ, created her own group of general counsels of small city agencies. They met monthly at each others' offices over a brown bag lunch and talked about the role dilemmas they shared.

Whether such support from the top exists, has to be supplemented or finessed, or the equivalent invented wholecloth, leaders need to keep in

8. Kahn (1993).
9. Koch (1990).

mind the critical importance of finding ways to attend to staff. This is particularly true in the public sector, where other incentives are less available.

CHUNK THE WORK. The expectations of public sector service agencies are enormous and potentially overwhelming. For example, telling staff that their responsibility is to eliminate juvenile delinquency, even for a limited group of clients, is to invite chaos or collapse. The task is just too overwhelming. Thus the manager has the responsibility to organize the work so that staff have clear, reachable milestones—specific objectives that can be identified and achieved.

In the Aftercare program, which provided services on a voluntary basis to children released home from detention, the needs of the families served were both deep and wide. So we narrowed the task and defined a clear goal: returning children to school. Work that helped achieve that aim was on target. Work that went beyond those boundaries was not encouraged. So, if a client was not going to school because he or she was kept home to babysit a younger sibling, getting day care for the younger child was within the scope of appropriate work. Without that specific connection, however, getting siblings into day care would have been nice but not useful. With clear objectives set by management, staff can more easily manage and organize the overwhelming demands from their clients.

By selecting a concrete and available goal and "chunking" the work into doable pieces, agency leaders make success both clearer and nearer. And they create opportunities for staff to get recognized for their work and accomplishments.

CELEBRATE SMALL WINS. Karl E. Weick of Cornell developed the notion of celebrating small wins in an article called "Small Wins: Redesigning the Scale of Social Problems."[10] Arguing that the "massive scale on which social problems are conceived" deters innovation, he suggested that reformulating broad social issues as "mere problems" allows for a series of "small wins" that can be built into a pattern of effective action.

Weick's article, which a consultant brought to our attention approximately a year into our effort, inspired the ideas of chunking the work and focusing constant attention on the need to recognize and celebrate small wins. To us, this meant everything from celebrating the day more children were enrolled in Aftercare than in detention (a long-held dream) to

10. Weick (1984).

taking the fiscal staff out to dessert when the bills were paid on time for three months in a row. We had a party (cookies in the shape of buses) when the new vans to transport children to court were delivered (staff had worked on the specs for those vans). We had another when we opened a separate intake facility as a first step in bringing case management to our network of group homes.

In general, we looked constantly to find people doing something right and then created opportunities to acknowledge their work.

CREATE APPROPRIATE FORUMS. In the public sector, satisfactory work is not generally a solitary experience. We learned early on that everyone needs a group at work: Everyone needs not only to feel part of some larger effort but also to have the opportunity to meet and talk regularly with others doing related work. We learned that creating groups that work in the organization's interest is critically important. Left on their own, staff will invent their own informal groups, which are much less likely to be working in the organization's interest. Some staff in one unit, for example, were unhappy with the decision to establish a group home for intake in the nonsecure detention program. They began to attract others to their informal group of disgruntled employees, and the unhappiness began to spread. When we included some of the original people who had opposed the decision in the work group to establish plans for the intake house, their complaints got aired in a setting where they could be directly addressed, and the energy previously directed to complaining shifted into more productive discussions of how to resolve real differences.

Leaders need to inventory what groups, both formal and informal, exist: standing meetings, task forces, special ad hoc committees. Much can be learned from seeing what is in place and where the gaps are.

Over time, and at least annually, we checked to see that, given the organization's current needs and state of development, the existing forums made sense. And we did not hesitate to end or redesign those that were no longer useful or to create new ones.

For example, we had an ongoing and useful weekly executive staff meeting that consisted of my five direct reports and myself. In addition, I led a monthly senior-management staff meeting with three levels of staff and about fifteen people; this meeting was deadly boring and generally ineffective. Little new thinking emerged, and few concrete issues got raised or resolved. When I removed myself from the senior-management staff meeting and turned leadership over to the remaining members of the executive staff, the meeting improved greatly and much more was accomplished. With this new arrangement, the staff who worked two levels down no longer had the urge or opportunity to bypass their boss and try out their ideas directly on me. Moreover, as the authority of the executive staff was reinforced, their stature grew.

Another example of rethinking our organizational structure was the creation of a wider management staff meeting. We wanted all those who had any supervisory role—even those who, because of civil service regulations or budget and personnel policies, did not have managerial titles—to think of themselves as managers and to identify with the agency as a whole. Our goal was to encourage the staff's identification with the agency's mission and goals and to maximize the potential of those already on board.

PUT ENERGY INTO HIRING. More discretion is available in the public sector for hiring and firing than executives use to advantage. Leaders need to view hiring—and selective firing—more strategically. These aspects of leadership are significant and too often overlooked.

We used the need to fill major vacancies as an opportunity to rethink where we were going. We were careful not to assume we needed to replace whoever had left. Instead, we thought hard about where we were organizationally and where we were going, so the person we hired would fit the future not the past.[11] We were lucky enough to have an executive search firm, then Isaacson Ford-Webb and Miller, now Isaacson and Miller, working on our behalf.[12] The early search for a new director of Spofford, the secure detention facility, offered the opportunity to learn what was for us a new approach to hiring.[13] We learned to scope the job, talking to internal and external stakeholders to develop a sense of the short- and long-term tasks of the job and then the qualities necessary to accomplish all this. Then we learned to think creatively about the kinds of places in which such people might be found. All this forced us to focus tightly on what we hoped to accomplish and how we intended to work together.

In interviewing candidates, we learned to solicit what could be called "work biographies." We learned to look backward—to peoples' experience—

---

11. Gilmore (1988).

12. The Edna McConnell Clark Foundation's Justice Program, led by Ken Schoen, was funding the search firm to help expand the pool of talented correction commissioners available for appointment by newly elected governors. The foundation was persuaded that this search, while not at the same level, was important and agreed to extend the services of the search firm and the organizational development consultant working in tandem with the search firm.

13. Isaacson (1983).

to find those who had risked, failed, learned, and gone on. We found that how people have dealt with challenges in their past was the best indicator of how they would handle the inevitable challenges and the inevitable failures at DJJ. Particularly when looking for managers, we looked for people with what executive search consultant John Isaacson calls hunger, speed, and weight:

—Hunger can be understood as drive, that internal connection between a person's self esteem and accomplishment at work, that self-regulated push to excel, to succeed, to prevail.

—Speed is the ability to juggle many things at once, to master large quantities of new material quickly, and to pick out the important from the trivial or irrelevant.

—Weight is the ability to handle authority fairly, with maturity, and to tell the truth up (to the boss), down (to subordinates), and sideways (to peers).

We took our hiring interviews seriously, often having someone go through multiple interviews. Just as we initially had carefully analyzed or scoped the job, we paid attention to reference checks, a task too often done so perfunctorily as to be meaningless. Learning something from reference checks involves going beyond the usual, two-minute conversation; it means developing a clear sense of what you think you know about the candidate and testing that out on the person with whom you are talking. It also means saying what you think you do not know and asking for specific examples that will help fill in the parts about which you are unclear. Good reference checking also involves going beyond a list and speaking to people "up, down, and sideways"—people to whom the candidate reported, people he or she managed, and peers. We made mistakes in hiring, as does everyone, but we were much less often surprised by what unravelled. Moreover, this process helped us find and attract people of great talent.

Main Line

Regrettably, no blueprints are available for organizational change. Like unhappy families, each managerial situation is different. And yet as in families, some structural decisions can add value and increase the chances of success. What follows is our contribution to the lore of effective organizational structure.

DEVELOP A LONG-TERM STRATEGY WHILE YOU MANAGE THE SHORT-TERM CRISES. The demands of the immediate crises can easily drive out any long-term thinking or planning. Consequently, any public manager who wishes to succeed and to effect significant innovation must develop the capacity to build a long-term strategic agenda while simultaneously managing the short-term crises. Do not wait until the short-term crises are resolved.

Public agencies crash on this shoal all too often. We public sector managers assume office with our eyes and our hopes on the future but tell ourselves we first need to attend to the present. A constant and unrelenting focus on the crises of the present will yield, at best, short-lived gains.

At DJJ, we found ourselves too easily falling into this trap. Thus we decided that the way for us to focus our own attention on the future was to create a group and then a schedule of meetings. We invented the "strategy group" whose task it was to decide where we were going with our mission of custody and care and then how we were doing getting there. In monthly meetings, over the space of a year, the strategy group developed the theme of case management. When the direction setting was sufficiently clear, the group disbanded and the responsibility for implementation was put with the line managers.[14]

When we waited until we had time to deal with the long-term, we did not get to it. When we created a mechanism to force ourselves to focus on the future, the effort was worth the pain. The success we saw in the seven years, and since, very much stands on the early, creative, and thematic work of that strategy group.

CHANGE THE CULTURE. Before a leader can attempt to change the organization's culture, she or he needs to understand the existing culture. What are the organization's basic assumptions? What behaviors do people assume, count on, and accept? What underlies why people act the way they do?[15] Only once the leadership understands the existing culture can it develop a vision of the new culture and create new artifacts to exemplify it.

For our central office, this meant everything from expecting excellence, to starting meetings on time, to having nice offices. Each of these shifts involved a struggle. Each began with an understanding of the role the original aspects of the culture played and an effort to devise a strat-

14. Gilmore and Schall (1986).
15. Schein (1985).

egy that would help move people in a new direction. Some things were reasonably straightforward. I was aggravated by meetings that started late—by the time wasted and the acting out displayed by people who arrived late knowing that nothing began until everyone was there. Convinced that it would work better for all involved, I began and ended all my meetings as scheduled even if everyone was not there to start. Soon, people started showing up on time.

Setting a standard of excellence included sending written work back until it was right. I remember an early bar chart that a staff person prepared for a city council hearing. The length of the bars bore no resemblance to the size of the corresponding numbers. I sent it back. I kept returning work until it was right.

At the most significant level of culture change, we had to act revitalized before we were. Early on, for instance, we had to act as if we were certain we could find a solution to the stalemate around the replacement of Spofford even when we had no clue whether that was so or what the eventual solution might be. Like much else asked of leaders who aspire to be innovative, this required a great leap of faith, fueled by arrogance perhaps, and best tempered by humility. We had to hold the future as real as we struggled to overcome the difficulties of the present. We needed to believe we could make a difference before we could do so. We had to convince others of our capacity before we were completely confident in it ourselves.

GET HELP WHEN YOU NEED IT. Good leadership means acknowledging what you know and what you do not—what you can do and what you cannot. Leaders need to hire people who are better at what they have to do than the leader would be. And they have to get the right kind of help from outside their organization.

We used this help early and often. We found the outside perspective that consultants brought very valuable, but we learned the hard way not to over-rely on consultants. We found out that we needed to manage the consultants' work, that the end product was only as good as the thinking we contributed up front. To improve the timeliness of the arrival of children in court, we asked one consultant to develop new schedules for DJJ buses. But the effort floundered at the first handoff to the consultant because we relied too much on what we thought was his generic expertise and failed to ground his work in the specifics of our needs and issues.

Learning the hard way about consultants meant once having a meeting in which more consultants were in the room than DJJ staff. It also meant

being disappointed at first when we realized we could not shift responsibility for developing the long-term agenda to a consultant (who was
smart enough not to be seduced into overfunctioning).

PLAN FROM BOTH THE TOP DOWN AND THE BOTTOM UP.
Once you sort out what work belongs to internal staff and where consultants can be helpful, the trick is to get decisions made at the right level.
Policy decisions that involve awareness of the whole organization and
the outside boundary generally need to be made at the top. Implementation decisions can often best be made by those involved in carrying out
the actions.

At DJJ, the executive staff was responsible for the major policy decisions; for example, the decision to implement case management or to
develop a family-based alternative to detention. We got input from
others. But we never suggested these policy decisions were democratic.
In fact, we had staff who made it clear that they disagreed with our
policy, and we made it equally clear that we were proceeding.

As we moved to implement any policy decision, however, we made
sure that the planning involved the line staff. For example, when we set
up the case-management system, the line staff involved in doing the case
conferences decided how often they were to be held, who was to be
included, and what information was to be gathered.

FACE MISTAKES AND FIX THEM. Facing and fixing mistakes is
tough in the public sector, where they are less easily tolerated.[16] We
managed by starting new efforts small. We believed that this approach
offered a more protected space in which to experiment and to learn from
our early efforts.

Small is a relative concept. You are looking for whatever size effort
allows for a "dynamic interaction between the innovation and the organization that maximizes the chance of learning as the new program unfolds
and of having learning influence the ongoing conceptual design. The scale
is small enough when [you] can hold the conceptual and the operational
close at hand and manage the interplay to the benefit of both."[17]

By working to get it right first, a manager can see gaps in the original
design and thinking. This approach offers the manager the opportunity to
get the program on a sound basis and document results before having to
argue for more resources or for expansion.

16. Behn (1991).
17. Schall and Feely (1992).

PICK FIGHTS CAREFULLY. We fought hard on selected issues and won. If you pick your early issues with care, you are likely to care more about them than the people on the other side and that will help you prevail. We were determined to get the city's Office of Management and Budget (OMB) to pick up funding for Aftercare, which began with a federal grant. Appeals to OMB's sense of what was right were getting us nowhere. Deputy Commissioner for Planning and Program Development Kathleen Feely invented a brilliant if far-fetched argument that Aftercare, by returning children to school, would allow the city to claim more state dollars in school funding because the city's claim was tied to school attendance. OMB was won over, perhaps as much by the lengths to which we were prepared to go as by the few dollars possibly gained. The point is we established ourselves as an agency always prepared, very determined, and incredibly insistent.

Once you win a few fights, people are less likely to take you on. This is particularly useful advice with oversight or support agencies in the public sector. Budget staff have many potential places to look for cuts. If they believe you are likely to appeal their decisions and win, they may think twice before they push hard.

CREATE OPPORTUNITIES. We did not wait to be asked to invent. We moved ahead and took risks. No one suggested that we find ways to work effectively with the families of children in our custody. It was our conclusion based on our work with clients, and we authorized ourselves to move ahead. We decided to bring the Homebuilders program to New York. And then we decided to do so in a way that encouraged the city agency with overall responsibility for funding preventive services programs to learn about Homebuilders and consider its usefulness citywide.

Much can be said for clear mandates or direct authorization of work, or for the notion that it is the citizens, or the elected officials who speak for them, who set the parameters of legitimate action. Certainly, much has been written about the legitimate sources of executive action.[18] It is not that we considered those theories and rejected them. Instead, we just moved ahead, being as careful as we knew how to keep our various overseers and involved publics informed. We moved ahead as we figured out where we wanted to go and how we might get there.

18. Moore (1995).

Over the Line

Over time, a leader and an organization can establish a sense of trust and teamwork and a willingness to take risks. This takes years, not weeks or months, and a commitment of self to work that goes beyond the ordinary. The payoff, though, also extends beyond the ordinary; the result is an organization that fosters both learning and achievement. When well done, that is an extraordinary combination. But even this achievement brings its own, more subtle challenges, which require more subtle strategies.

LEARN TO ACKNOWLEDGE WHAT IS HARD TO ACKNOWLEDGE: PEOPLE'S FEELINGS. The personal situations created by work are often painful. And group life is often irrational. But these problems can neither be dismissed or ignored. The leader must deal with them openly and explicitly.

Competition, for example, is ever-present in group life and drives some behavior, some to the good (more work gets accomplished) but some to the detriment of the task at hand. When competition was in the air, I could always tell because the "buzz" in my ear increased with a big jump in the frequency with which executive staff members would come in to report on their colleagues. At the next executive staff meeting, I would bring up this observation, and we would attempt to address whatever was making people feel particularly competitive.

Generally, the executive staff as a group found that our work was helped by creating opportunities to acknowledge and deal with our feelings. Irrational feelings are present at work and in group life everywhere. We found that allowing for their expression and working with these feelings, while difficult, made our work richer and more effective. Not facing the irrational does not make it disappear and eventually blocks effective work.

Resistance to change is often described as just such an irrational feeling and attributed to the other. Our executive staff approached this issue as we did all issues, by first trying to understand our own resistance to change. As we explored what we feared we had to lose, we began to understand the feeling in others. Resistance to change became discussable, not taboo. People in the organization could voice their own concerns and together solutions could be found, even to what was first expressed irrationally.

For example, people worried about the move of our central office staff from near Wall Street to less than a mile uptown, above City Hall. They worried about how they might "fit" in the new setting, but they would voice their concerns by raising questions as to whether they would be able to "fit" in the new chairs. So we distributed a map that showed where you could do errands, where you could get lunch, and people calmed down.

TALK OPENLY ABOUT DIFFERENCES OF RACE, GENDER, CLASS, AND AGE. Our work was complicated. No one person could work completely independently of others. It required both delegation and trust, actions difficult enough to begin with and often even more difficult across boundaries of difference—across boundaries in our case of race, gender, class, and age. Again, the executive staff worked these issues among ourselves first, both because they were there to be worked and as a message to the organization that these issues could be discussed. We talked about:

—What it was like to work for a woman executive;

—What it meant for an African American executive staff member to let down another African American on the executive staff;

—How women compete; and

—What it felt like to deal with issues of race in an organization whose clients were minority and in a city whose mayor was Caucasian and where racial tensions were rising.

None of this was easy. It took a long time working together to get to the point where we could talk these issues through. But the gains were definitely worth the struggle.

TIME YOUR STAY TO THE SIZE OF THE TASK. We took on a large task and thus needed to stay a long time. The core of the DJJ executive staff under my tenure remained intact for the seven years I was commissioner. The average tenure of less than two years for top-level agency staff may be as large an impediment to wholesale change as any other put forward by government-doubters. But this is one we can change.

Conclusion

These retrospective reflections on the process of creating a climate for innovation are offered to extend both some hope and some guidance. And, as is often the case, both hope and guidance come in the form of a story.[19]

19. Schank (1990).

Hope is needed by those charged with the seemingly impossible task of creating public agencies better able to serve citizens. Those entrusted with this task need new stories, stories that tell of real people who did not have a completely drawn map in front of them or years of success in similar efforts behind them. They need stories about people who somehow understood the importance of staying the course and were able to withstand the demands of the career fast track that beckoned. They need stories about people who can acknowledge all that went wrong while pointing out some of what worked.

Hope is also needed for others, whether citizen or academic, concerned about increasing the odds that government can work. People need stories of success to inspire them, to keep them going, and to motivate them to find ways to support those trying to change government.

Whatever guidance can be found here is offered primarily to those engaged in the work of changing government. It is my hope that our story will offer some guidance to help others invent their own stories of success.

References

Auth, Mary L. 1991. "Experiential Learning: Some Pedagogical Considerations for Public Administration Educational Programs." Paper prepared for the annual meeting of the National Teaching Public Administration Conference, Knoxville, Tennessee, February 20–23.

Beckhard, Richard, and Reuben T. Harris. 1987. *Organizational Transitions: Managing Complex Change.* Reading, Mass.: Addison-Wesley.

Behn, Robert D. 1991. "Innovations and Public Values: Mistakes, Flexibility, Purpose, Equity, Cost Control, and Trust." Paper prepared for the conference on the Fundamental Questions of Innovation, Duke University, May 4.

Behn, Robert D., and Regina K. Brough. 1991. "Research on Innovation." In *Research on Innovations in State and Local Government: The 1991 Conferences.* Duke University, Governors Center.

Gilmore, Thomas N. 1988. *Making a Leadership Change: How Organizations and Leaders Can Handle Leadership Transitions Successfully.* Jossey-Bass.

Gilmore, Thomas N., and Ellen Schall. 1986. "Use of Case Management as a Revitalizing Theme in a Juvenile Justice Agency." *Public Administration Review,* vol. 46, no. 3 (May/June): 267–74.

Isaacson, John. 1983. "Executive Search: A Manual for Commissioner Schall and Her Able and Willing Staff." Boston: Isaacson, Ford-Webb, and Miller.

Kahn, William A. 1993. "Facilitating and Undermining Organizational Change: A Case Study." *Journal of Applied Behavioral Science,* vol. 29, no. 1 (March): 32–55.

Kinney, Jill, David Haapala, and Charlotte Booth. 1991. *Keeping Families Together: The Homebuilder's Model.* New York: Aldine de Gruyter.

Koch, Edward I., with Leland T. Jones. 1990. *All the Best: Letters from a Feisty Mayor.* Simon and Schuster.

Moore, Mark H. 1995. *Creating Public Value: Strategic Management in Government.* Harvard University Press.

Schall, Ellen, and Kathleen Feely. 1992. "Guidelines to Grope By: Reflections from the Field." *Innovating,* vol. 2, no. 3 (Spring): 3–11.

Schank, Roger C. 1990. *Tell Me a Story: A New Look at Real and Artificial Memory.* Scribner.

Schein, Edgar H. 1985. *Organizational Culture and Leadership.* Jossey-Bass.

Schön, Donald A. 1983. *The Reflective Practitioner: How Professionals Think in Action.* Basic Books.

_____. 1987. *Educating the Reflective Practitioner: Toward a New Design for Teaching and Learning in the Professions.* Jossey-Bass.

Weick, Karl E. 1984. "Small Wins: Redefining the Scale of Social Problems." *American Psychologist,* vol. 39 (January): 40–49.

Contributors

Alan A. Altshuler is the Stanton Professor of Urban Policy and Planning at Harvard University, jointly appointed in the John F. Kennedy School of Government and the Graduate School of Design. He is also director of the Kennedy School's Taubman Center for State and Local Government and its Program on Innovations in American Government. A recent book, coauthored with José A. Gómez-Ibáñez, is *Regulation for Revenue* (Brookings).

Babak J. Armajani is chief executive officer of the Public Strategies Group and the Reinventing Government Network. He has combined twenty-two years of public management experience with stints in teaching and management consulting, pioneering the introduction of customer-oriented strategies in public, private, and nonprofit organizations. Armajani is a nationally recognized expert in management having recently collaborated with Michael Barzelay on a book entitled *Breaking through Bureaucracy: A New Vision for Managing in Government* (University of California Press).

Michael Barzelay is a lecturer in public administration at the London School of Economics, where he holds a joint appointment in the Department of Government and the Interdisciplinary Institute of Management. He also serves as senior adviser to the Office of Government Services of

Arthur Andersen and Co. in Washington, D.C. Barzelay is the author of three books, including, with Babak J. Armajani, *Breaking through Bureaucracy: A New Vision for Managing in Government* (University of California Press).

Robert D. Behn is a professor of public policy at Duke University and director of its Governors Center. For several years, he has coordinated a series of research seminars and conferences on "Creating Innovative Organizations" for the Ford Foundation. Behn is the management columnist for *Governing* magazine and the author of *Leadership Counts: Lessons for Public Managers* (Harvard University Press).

W. Lance Bennett is a professor of political science at the University of Washington. His research on press-government relations has appeared in the leading communications journals and in two recent books: *News: The Politics of Illusion* and *The Governing Crisis: Media, Money, and Marketing in American Elections.*

Paul Berman is president of RPP International, a policy research firm in Berkeley, California. Before founding BW Associates (the predecessor to RPP International), Berman was senior researcher at the Rand Corporation, where he was the senior author of the multiyear Change Agent study. Berman's pioneering research on school reform in California, Hawaii, Idaho, and Minnesota has led to major school restructuring efforts in each of these states.

Richard F. Elmore is a professor of education at the Graduate School of Education, Harvard University, and a senior research fellow of the Consortium for Policy Research in Education. His research focuses on state-local relations in education policy, school organization, and educational choice, and he teaches regularly in programs for public sector executives and holds several government advisory positions. He is coauthor of *Teaching, Learning, and School Organization* (Jossey-Bass, forthcoming).

Robert M. Entman is a professor of communication at North Carolina State University and an adjunct professor of public policy at the University of North Carolina at Chapel Hill. Author of *Democracy without Citizens* (Oxford University Press) and senior author of *Broad-*

cast Privatization in Transitional Democracies (Carter Center of Emory University and Aspen Institute), he is finishing two books, *Projections of Power: Media and the National Defense* and *Television, Race, and the Urban Community.* He holds workshops and consults frequently on public policy and communications for public and private sector clients.

Lee S. Friedman is a professor of public policy at the University of California at Berkeley. His work has focused on increasing the relevance of economic analysis in public policy settings. He has published studies in many areas including criminal justice, education, welfare, and regulatory policy and is the author of *Microeconomic Policy Analysis* (McGraw-Hill).

Thomas N. Gilmore is vice president of the Center for Applied Research and an adjunct associate professor in health care at the Wharton School, University of Pennsylvania. He is a former member of the Policy Council of the Association for Public Policy Analysis and Management and the author of *Making a Leadership Change* (Jossey-Bass). Gilmore's research and consulting concern the opportunities for substantial innovation in the wake of top leadership changes.

Olivia Golden is assistant secretary designate for Children and Families with the U.S. Department of Health and Human Services. Previously she served as commissioner of the Adminsistration on Children, Youth, and Families with Health and Human Services. Before her appointment as commissioner, she was director of programs and policy at the Children's Defense Fund in Washington, D.C., and lecturer in public policy at the John F. Kennedy School of Government at Harvard University. She is the author of *Poor Children and Welfare Reform* (Auburn House Press). The views expressed in her article do not necessarily represent those of Health and Human Services or the United States government.

James Krantz is a principal with the management consulting firm of TRIAD Consulting Group. His research and consulting focus on questions of strategy implementation and the dynamics of organizational innovation. Krantz is on the editorial board of the *Journal of Applied Behavioral Science.*

Laurence E. Lynn, Jr., is a professor in the School of Social Service Administration and the Harris Graduate School of Public Policy Studies at the University of Chicago. He directs the School of Social Service Administration's Management Institute and the Center for Urban Research and Policy Studies. He is a policy council member, past president of the Association for Public Policy Analysis and Management, and author of *Managing the Public's Business*; *Managing Public Policy*; and *Public Management as Art, Science, and Profession.*

Mark H. Moore is the Guggenheim Professor of Criminal Justice Policy and Management at Harvard University's John F. Kennedy School of Government. He is the author of *Creating Public Value: Strategic Management in Government* (Harvard University Press) and *Accounting for Change: Reconciling the Demands for Accountability and Innovation in the Public Sector* (Council for Excellence in Government).

Beryl Nelson is a senior analyst at RPP International, a policy research firm in Emeryville, California. In recent years, her research has focused on charter schools, innovative school programs for limited English proficient students and on the development of industry-based skill standards.

Ellen Schall is the Martin Cherkasky Professor of Health Policy and Management at New York University's Robert F. Wagner Graduate School of Public Service. She served as president of the Association for Public Policy Analysis and Management, and her presidential address "Learning to Love the Swamp: Reshaping Education for Public Service" was published in the spring 1995 issue of the *Journal of Policy Analysis and Management.* From 1990 to 1992, Schall served as the president of the National Center for Health Education and was, for seven years before that, the commissioner of the New York City Department of Juvenile Justice.

Malcolm Sparrow is a lecturer at the John F. Kennedy School of Government, Harvard University. He is the author of four books, including *Imposing Duties: Government's Changing Approach to Compliance* (Prager) and *License to Steal: Why Fraud Plagues America's Health Care System* (Westview Press, forthcoming).

William Spelman is an associate professor at the Lyndon B. Johnson School of Public Affairs, University of Texas at Austin. Before coming to Texas, he was a senior research associate at the Police Executive Research Forum, a national association of big-city police chiefs. Spelman is the author of several books on criminal justice innovations, including *Problem Solving* (with John E. Eck), *Repeat Offender Programs,* and *Criminal Incapacitation.*

Deborah A. Stone holds the David R. Pokross Chair in Law and Social Policy at Brandeis University. She received her Ph.D. in political science from the Massachusetts Institute of Technology. She is the author of three books—most recently, *Policy Paradox,* 2d ed. (W. W. Norton)—and numerous articles on health and social policy.

Marc D. Zegans is a doctoral student in public policy at Harvard University. He has served as executive director and research director of the Innovations in State and Local Government Program, a joint venture of the Ford Foundation and the John F. Kennedy School of Government. His dissertation, "Executive Energy in a Government of Laws: The Public Manager's Role in Democratic Decisionmaking," explores the problems for democratic theory raised by administrative reform.

Index